FOOD & PEOPLE

FOOD & PEOPLE

Third Edition

Miriam E. Lowenberg
Professor Emerita
The Pennsylvania State University

E. Neige Todhunter
Visiting Professor
Division of Nutrition, School of Medicine
Vanderbilt University

Eva D. Wilson
Professor Emerita
Ohio State University

Jane R. Savage
Professor of Nutrition
University of Tennessee, Knoxville

James L. Lubawski
Director of Marketing
Gambro, Inc.

JOHN WILEY & SONS

New York Chichester Brisbane Toronto

Library of Congress Cataloging in Publication Data
Main entry under title:

Food and people

Bibliography: p.
Includes index.
1. Food. 2. Nutrition. I. Lowenberg, Miriam
Elizabeth.
TX354.F66 1979 641.1 78-19172
ISBN 0-471-02690-5
Printed in the United States of America
10 9 8 7 6 5 4 3 2 1

To all who share our thoughtful concern
for the importance of nutrition,
be they students, fellow staffmembers,
or friends, here and abroad,
this book is dedicated.

Preface

General courses in foods and nutrition now are offered in many universities and colleges to meet the needs of students in home economics as well as in other areas of study. This general course may be the only one in foods and nutrition taken by students in various disciplines.

It is my opinion that the primary purpose of such courses should be to awaken the student's interest in the importance of food and human nutrition in his or her personal life as well as in the affairs of communities and nations. Once this interest is awakened, the student may then want to take courses in basic foods and nutrition. (This book makes no attempt to cover the basic principles of nutrition; Appendix 1 contains a list of books on basic foods and nutrition.) If this book stimulates the reader to begin to understand the vital importance of food and nutrition to everyone on earth, it will have fulfilled its purpose.

The topics covered were chosen because they relate to the following main concerns of this book:

1. Problems in nutrition such as chronic hunger and malnutrition.
2. Solutions currently being tried or projected. These include those of some national, international, and voluntary agencies whose primary purpose is to relieve hunger and malnutrition. In these programs nations and people can and are working together for mutual benefit.
3. The background of these problems. An understanding of this background can lead to more effective solutions. We need to understand food customs and the influence

of culture and religion, among other things, on food habits and foodways. The understanding of consumer behavior and problems is also necessary at present.

4. The history of how people have fed themselves, and the knowledge of their endeavor to understand the nutritive needs of their bodies and how food is used to satisfy these needs.

Because this book is intended to be used by the college student with no previous background in the physical or chemical sciences, the concepts are stated simply. This has been deliberate. A textbook such as this should have depth, but it should be interesting to read if a student is to be intrigued with this subject. The simplicity of a statement, I believe, has little relationship with how profound it is. I have been encouraged when teachers have reported that students like to read this book. It is, however, intended to be only a stimulus to further study; the creative teacher will help the serious student to pursue the subjects not covered here in depth. The concepts developed in this book are generously illustrated to bring the idea within the realm of the student's experiences.

This book has been used successfully for students at different levels in their educational preparation, including those who were doctoral candidates. Such use of materials is controlled by the way the teacher stimulates the thinking of students.

The entire book has been thoroughly rewritten and all chapters brought up to date with the inclusion of new material made available since 1974, when the second edition was published. The list of reference books for the use of students has been thoroughly revised and includes many new titles.

The authors wish to thank the staff at UNICEF, FAO, AID, WHO, PAHO, and other agencies for materials and criticisms so graciously furnished. Many other people have made helpful suggestions. I wish to thank especially the many teachers who used the other editions of this book for their helpful criticisms and suggestions. Special thanks are extended to my friends who have been especially helpful in the preparation of this manuscript. Mrs. Abbie Dale spent untold hours assisting me in library work and tracking down materials. Janell Douglas deserves special gratitude for her effective and interested typing of this manuscript.

The authors, however, assume full responsibility for the contents of this book.

Seattle, Washington

Miriam E. Lowenberg

Contents

FOOD & PEOPLE

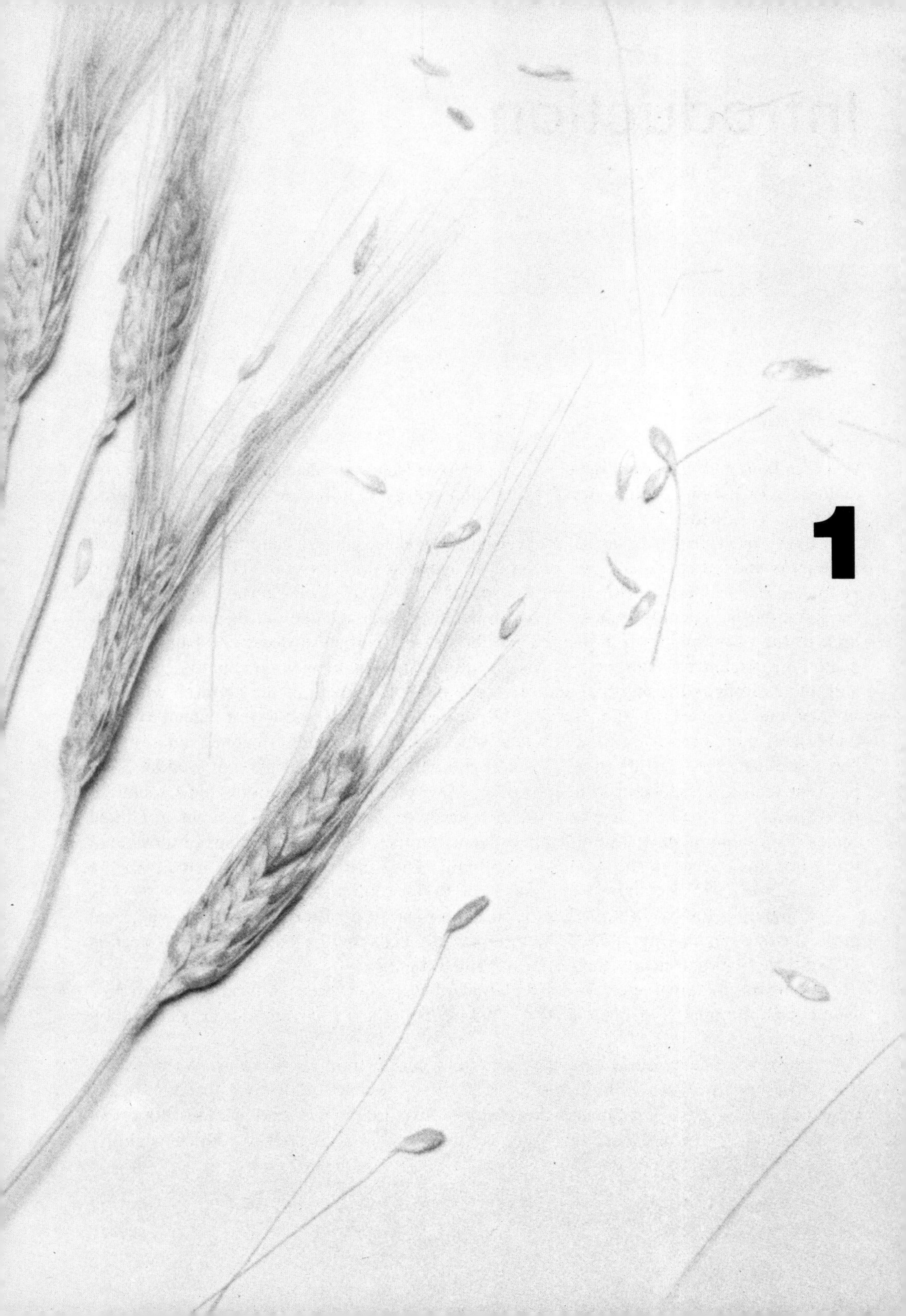
1

Introduction

Food for humanity has, over the centuries, been an important determinant of the rise and endurance of nations. Today, food, water, and energy supplies are vital and demanding problems worldwide.

Every individual is affected by the welfare of other people—and this includes food in quantity and with the quality which produces good health. Between 400 and 500 million people in our modern world suffer widespread and severe food shortages so that food consumption is generally below minimum health standards. One out of every five children in the developing world dies before the age of five and at least one-half of these deaths are related to malnutrition. Malnutrition of pregnant women, nursing mothers, and infants impairs the physical and often mental development of the children who survive beyond five years of age. Because of population growth, the recent annual average increase of three percent of food output is only a slight increase per capita. Inflation has had more disastrous results in areas where the annual per capita income is under $100 per year than in the developed countries. In some poverty areas families must spend 70 to 80 percent of their income on food in contrast to a mean of 16.8 percent of United States disposable income. (Some United States families must of course spend more than this.) For these areas of the world the doubling of the price of wheat and rice over the years 1973 to 1975 was almost the final blow to those on a meager diet.

Competing for North American food exports are the nations whose gross national product has risen sharply and who now reportedly consume two times as much beef as they did in 1940 and nearly three times as much poultry.

Some international agencies have claimed that the challenge of food for all (to provide even a minimally adequate diet) can not be met unless food supplies are doubled by the year 2000.

The peace of the world certainly rests on securing food for all. Kurt Waldheim in 1975 (*War on Hunger,* Vol. 9) said, "It is the experience of history that no society in which a few have wealth and the majority live in poverty and without hope can remain stable." He also said that "we cannot hope to have world political stability which is essential for human progress if we do not have a much greater degree of economic equity than we do at present.'' In March 1975 President Gerald Ford declared, "People throughout American realize that no structure of world peace can endure unless the poverty question is answered. There is no safety for any nation in a hungry, ill-educated and desperate world . . . Americans cannot adopt the view that we can no longer afford foreign assistance.'' He emphasized first, that, foreign assistance is a part of the price we must pay to achieve the kind of a world in which we want to live. Second, even with a recession we are the world's "most affluent country and the sharing of our resources is the right, the humane, and the decent thing to do.''

Congress declared its reasons why the U.S. must provide assistance in this struggle for food (AID Challenge to an Interdependent World): "The freedom, security, and prosperity of the United States are best sustained in a community of free, secure and prospering nations. Ignorance, want and despair breed the extremism and violence which lead to subversion.''

Daniel Parker, Administrator of the Agency for International Development (AID) until recently, said in 1976, "These past years have been of unimpaired change and uncertainty. But of one thing, we can be certain, today's world is smaller and the international community is more closely intertwined and interdependent than ever before in the history of man.'' He believed also that most people in our country know this.

Cold economic facts also support the need for considering the entire world. Only one-third of all the exports from the United States go to the developing world. By 1985, it has been estimated that the developing countries will require 100 million more tons of imported cereals than the present 17 billion they now use. Can these people pay for it? If not, who will, so that the producers are adequately recompensed?

Heady said in 1976 that between 1973 and 1975 "the grain exports of the United States accounted for 65 percent of the world's total grain exports.'' Shawcross commented in 1974 that the United States is now the world's largest exporter of rice. We produce two-thirds of the world's soybeans and we are also the greatest producer of wheat and field grains.

Brown believed in 1976 that this dependence on North America will continue and he said, "We must determine who will get the food.'' He warned in 1976, "If trends of the past several years continue, the collective import needs of 100+ importing countries will eventually greatly exceed the exportable excesses from North America particularly when the harvest is poor. This is creating a politics of food, a type of food diplomacy.'' Do North Americans have, as some from grain-hungry countries have claimed, a more powerful weapon than the atomic bomb in the protein food they produce? And is one-fifth of the U.S.-grown rice that in 1975 was shipped overseas under P.L. 480 (see page 317) truly a diplomatic crop?

When abundant harvests in many countries reduce the demand for United States exports and prices for the American products (crops) fall, who will subsidize farmers to make their operations profitable?

Cities dependent on food shipped from abroad have often been literally existing from "ship to mouth.'' Who can question what poor weather in the producing countries can do to those who live in this way, or what will happen when prices go up from Seattle to Singapore? What if American farmers consider cutting back their acreage because they haven't sold all of last year's crop?

In 1975 Brown predicted: "Food short nations will eventually have to feed themselves or the battle of malnutrition will be lost." He also observed that in the "past few years there has been an alarming increase in malnutrition." Along with many others he recognized that we really do not know how many people are malnourished and that any figure proposed is probably too low. But we must agree with Brown that only "a global strategy can reverse this increase in malnutrition and lead to the resumption of the slow though uneven and irregular improvement of the state of nutrition among the world's poor which has generally prevailed from 1950 to 1970 or so."

Mayer was more hopeful in 1975 than some people that "stopping famines before they begin" contrary to widespread belief "can be done" and "famines are not inevitable." He also said, "Today all of the necessary elements exist for a system to deal with one of mankind's oldest enemies. It is about time the world put this system into practice." Wortman said in 1975, "The world may have, for the first time in the world's history, the ability to deal effectively, with the interacting problems of food production, rapid population growth and poverty," and also that, "Clearly more is at stake than alleviation of world hunger, critical as it is. Improving production in developing countries can provide millions of people not only with food but also with housing, clothing, health care, education, and hope," and that "enhanced agricultural productivity is the best lever for economic development and social progress in the developing world."

In the long run the best solution to the problem of malnutrition in the world may well be the development of programs and policies to provide farmers in the developing countries with techniques and assistance to raise their levels of food production. This would also have given other people in those countries employment opportunities and increased their incomes to enable them to pay for the food so that they could become well-nourished. Brown (1974) stressed, "There is growing evidence which suggests that, where farmers have access to the needed inputs, credit and supporting services, they engage in labor-intensive cultivation and produce consistently higher yields of food per acre than farmers in larger estates."

The question of diverting cereal grains into animal flesh production is controversial. Knowledgeable scientists remind us that ruminants can use parts of plants that human beings do not digest and that some land can be used for forage but not for food crops.

Wharton, in 1977, cautioned that "the world is not only threatened with temporary food shortages but with chronically acute shortages." He cited the dangerously low food reserves and the fact that in 42 of 92 developing countries population grew faster than food production between 1961 and 1971. But how do these estimates apply to the present?

As incomes rise it has been shown that food preferences shift from the roots and tubers of cassava, manioc, yams, white and sweet potatoes to cereals. Many of us have watched the rice-eating residents of Hawaii and Japan increase their use of wheat flour products. It is well known that as incomes rise, the demand for meat, milk, and egg increases.

The developed countries should help the developing countries because their food production technology, modern food science, and food itself have much to contribute to those who desperately need it. Scientists, however, must find a way to choose parts of western technology that can be used or adopted without losing sight of the reality of the situation in underdeveloped countries. Those in the developing countries must be encouraged to examine their own local problems and to incorporate local technology. Such technology is often really efficient and even quite sophisticated and results from centuries of development. A greater component of cultural awareness must be injected into the education of students to make them more creative when they apply scientific knowledge to local problems.

Although the concern of governments about food supplies reaches back into Greek and Roman times, the interest in nutrition is much more recent as this relatively "new" science has developed.

Dr. Cicely D. Williams, a highly respected scientist and medical practitioner of many years, called herself a "grass roots pediatrician." She wrote in 1972: "No amount of science, biochemistry of the body or analysis of the food will achieve adequate nutrition of an individual or of a community until the application of nutrition *arts* and *crafts* (italics ours) receives more attention." She also said in 1971, "One of the most difficult things is to educate the educated," and in 1962, "Education of the experts is necessary as well as for the indigenes."

Serious students can no longer afford to ignore the importance of food and nutrition in the world today.

The following chapters present material that forms the backgrounds of why we eat as we do. First, it is necessary to understand how people have fed themselves through the ages. There are discussions of the many facets of foodways and food patterns, of the relationship of food and religion, and of the behavior of people as consumers. All these contribute to an understanding of the problems of malnutrition and of some current programs that attempt to deal with these world problems. Because the subjects covered are so broad, certain aspects are dealt with in detail so that the student may have a pattern to investigate in depth further subjects of special interest.

REFERENCES AND SUGGESTED READING

A.I.D. Growing Crises. *War on Hunger*. Vol. 9, No. 9, 1975, p. 1.

A.I.D. Challenge to an Interdependent World, p. 4, no date given.

Berg, Alan, *The Nutrition Factor*. Brookings Institute, Washington D.C., 1973.

Borgstrom, G. The Food and People Dilemma. *War on Hunger*. A.I.D. Vol. 10, No. 10, 1976, p. 12.

Brown, L. B. *By Bread Alone*. Praeger, New York. 1974.

———. Death at an Early Age. Fighting Child Malnutrition. Part I. *UNICEF News* 85, 1975, p. 3.

———. *War on Hunger*. A.I.D. Vol. 9, No. 9, September, 1976, p. 20.

Cassava Research. Fighting Child Malnutrition Part I. 85, 1975, p. 3.

Cook, R., and Yueh-Heng Young. The World Food Situation. *Cajanus,* April–May 1973, p. 77.
Darby, W. J. Nutrition, Food Needs and Technologic Priorities. *Nutr. Rev.,* 33:225, 1975.
Duncan, E. R. *Dimensions of World Food Problems.* Iowa State University Press, Ames, Iowa, 1977.
Economic Research Service, U.S.D.A. Foreign Agricultural Report No. 98. *The World Food Situation and Prospects to 1985.*
Food Politics, Economics, Nutrition and Research. A.A.A.S. P.H. Abelson No. 3 in a Special Service Compendia, 1975.
Ford, Gerald. Aid in an Interdependent World. *War on Hunger* A.I.D. Vol. 9, No. 6, June, 1975, p. 1.
Gamin, M. in Rechcigl M. *Man Food and Nutrition* C.R.C. Press, London, 1973.
Ghassemi, H. Nutrition Policy and Programme Planning. Chapter 13 in McLaren, D. S. (ed.). *Nutrition in the Community.* John Wiley & Sons, New York, 1976.
Jensen, L. B. *Man's Food.* Garrard Press, Champaign, Ill., 1953.
Johnson, B. F., and J. P. Greaves, Food and Nutrition Policy, F.A.O. Rome, 1969. *Nutrition Studies,* No. 22.
Mayer, Jean. Time for Appraisal, *J. Nutr. Ed.,* 7(1):8, 1975.
Mayer, Jean. Fighting Child Malnutrition Part I, 1975, p. 1.
Meeting Food Needs in the Developing World. Research Report No. 1. Feb. 1976. International Food Policy Research Inst. Washington, D.C.
National Research Council World Food and Nutrition Study Interim Report. *Nat. Acad. of Sciences,* 1975, p. 27.
Parker, Daniel. Aid and Agribusiness. *War on Hunger.* A.I.D., Vol. 9, No. 9, 1976, p. 1.
Saturday Review. Nov. 13, 1976. Our Newest Weapon—Food.
Science A.A.A.S. Vol. 188, No. 4188, 1975, Entire Issue.
Sengupta, P. N. Nutrition and National Development. *Cajanus,* Vol. 8, No. 2, 1975, p. 104.
Shawcross, W. Will the Politicians Let the World Starve? *Cajanus,* Vol. 7, No. 61, 1974, p. 235.
Time Magazine, November 11, 1974.
UNICEF News. Fighting Child Malnutrition Part II, 86/1975/4.
Waldheim, Kurt. *War on Hunger,* AID, Vol. 9, No. 9, Sept. 1975, p. 19.
Wharton, C. R. Jr. The Role of the Professional in Feeding Mankind. The Political Dimension. *War on Hunger,* AID, Vol. 11, No. 1, 1977, p. 8.
Williams, C. D. Malnutrition. *Lancet,* 2:342,1962.
———. What's the Use of Doctors? Frances Stern Memorial Lecture, *World Medicine,* Feb. 1971, p. 85.
———. Grass Roots Nutrition or Consumer Participation. Martha Trulson Memorial Lecture. *J. Amer. Diet. Assoc.* 63:125, 1973.
———. Nutrition in the Home. *Cajanus,* Vol. 8, No. 2, April 1974, p. 54.
Wortman, S. *War on Hunger.* AID, Vol. 10, No. 8, 1976.

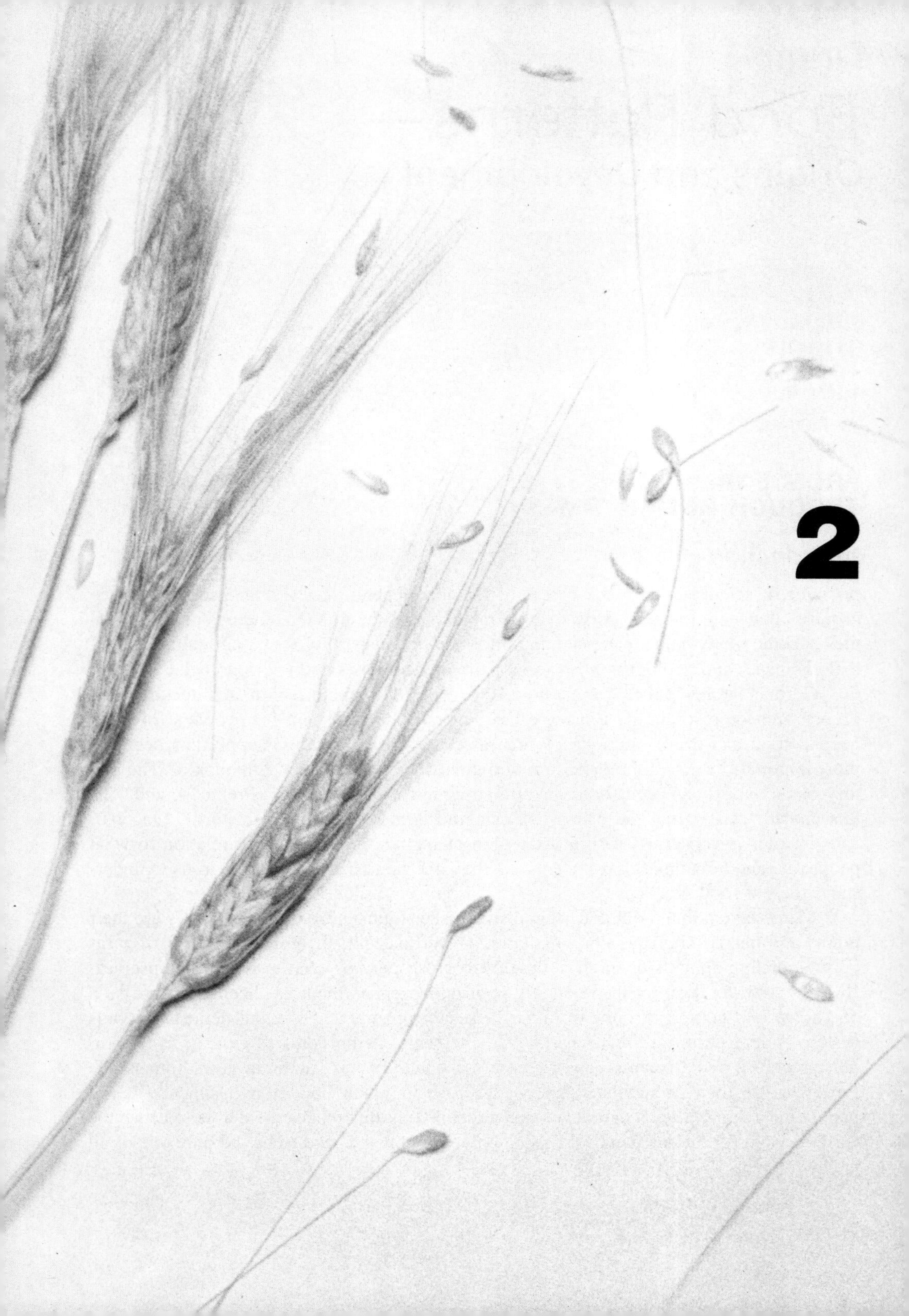
2

Food Patterns—
Origins and Development

FROM EARLY TIMES THROUGH ROMAN TIMES

Introduction

As modern scientists learn the extent of the interdependence among disciplines, they acquire knowledge of early peoples more rapidly, and their understandings of early peoples become more valid. Interested and informed botanists, biologists, agriculturists, cereal chemists, and geologists now accompany archeologists and anthropologists.

German archeologists were said to be especially interested in architecture, and French archeologists in art. But there has generally been disdain for people's foremost needs—food and drink—in spite of such assertions as "The food supply has been the most important factor in the evolution of human society" (Orr and Lubbock); "The history of the world has been the story of a struggle for daily bread" (Prentice); and "To this day few know that the history of mankind is also an agrarian history" (Jacobs). This chapter is concerned with a discussion of human development in relation to what people ate and how through past centuries they got their food. This can help us to understand present food practices.

Many have pointed out that what distinguishes humans from other animals are their brains and hands. Humans have no claws, powerful teeth, or hooves, no horns for fatally wounding animals or mighty muscles to grasp prey or even to defend themselves. "Man's compensation for his relatively poor bodily endowment has been his possession of a large and complex brain, forming the center of an extensive and delicate nervous system. These permit a great variety of movements, being adjusted exactly to the impulse received by the keen organs of sense" (Childe, 1951). The brain gives humans the power to use their accumulated knowledge to better their condition. Using the brain, people have devised tools and developed a technology that makes them able to cause the earth to yield for them a plentiful food supply. Humans are said to be the only one of all the animals who invites their own kind into their lair or home to share their food.

Some of the landmarks in human efforts to control environment as people progressed in their efforts to produce food abundantly and efficiently are discussed. Hoebel and Brace, as well as other anthropologists, give excellent charts of the geologic eras for the reader who wishes this information. Remington, in telling of the difficulty of studying the food patterns of ancient peoples, said that the study and evaluation of the social factors that have influenced the peoples' diet lead us back "to the very dawn of history, concerning which we must indulge in a certain amount of speculation which is more or less repugnant to the modern scientist."

Before people left their records in written language, we have only paintings on walls; most of these were in dwelling caves, so they were protected and have been fairly well preserved. Perhaps more important than the paintings are the more widely scattered and more abundant "kitchen middens"—the heaps of food refuse left by early humans. In Denmark, middens 100 yards long and 50 feet wide have been found. There are, of course, hazards from using these kitchen middens. First of all, only a few unbroken objects hard enough to stand the ravages of time are found. Wood, for instance, cannot long survive weather and time, and pieces large enough to identify the original object are not frequently found. Because not all of a person's possessions are ever found, one can only conjecture what part of the total was discovered. People probably only discarded the undesirable or inedible parts of their food. It therefore is easy to understand how uncertain these attempts are to learn what people ate more than 300,000 years ago. Kluckhohn said, "Not without justification has anthropology been termed 'the science of leftovers'."

From what animal did certain bones come, and how did the person who ate it treat it before eating it? Some of the important remnants are cereal pollens and bits of charred cereal grains; in later times in Egypt, yeast cells from the breadmaking process have been discovered. Or were the yeast cells ones that escaped when making fermented beverages?

Modern methods of dating now make possible fairly accurate estimates of the ages of these leavings. Pollen thrown out from a plant as early as 14,000 B.C. has been found (Flannery), as have remnants in caves in greater Mesopotamia of potentially domesticated sheep and goats from as early as 40,000 B.C. Many authorities, however, give later dates for what has been termed the preagricultural period. These differences of dates for periods in history only serve to illustrate that much is yet to be learned as new finds provide further evidence. In addition to studying records left in caves and kitchen middens, archeologists also have had for study the stomach contents of mummies, and bodies found in bogs as well as coprolites—the remnants of human feces.

There was no single type of food used by primitive people everywhere; the type of food consumed was related to climatic and geographic conditions. Scrimshaw said, "Man's need to obtain an adequate supply of essential nutrients through his diet not only is a part of his biological evolution but also has shaped his social evolution." He added, "It has been suggested that the migration of human groups to the northern regions of the earth was slowed by the limited amounts of ascorbic acid in the foods available in those areas during the long winter months." The story of how early voyages and exploration were hampered by scurvy is well known.

There are, and always were, more herbivorous people, the next most prevalent being the carnivore, followed by the omnivore (Davenport). People in the tropics are mostly herbivore. Carnivore are usually nomadic and often live in colder climates. Not all nomads, of course, were carnivore as is well told by Blainey in *Triumph of the Nomads,* a history of early successful food gathering by Australian aborigines. Omnivores in temperate zones have usually advanced technologically more rapidly. Loomis says, "The heavy emphasis on cereals reflects not only their food value but also their relative ease of culture, harvest, transport, and storage, and their wide range of climatic adaptation." This undoubtedly explains the preponderance of herbivorous people.

The Beginnings

Agricultural cultivation and domestication of animals may have taken place gradually from 40,000 to 10,000 B.C. (Flannery). The origin of agriculture probably was not due to a chance discovery, as the sprouting of seeds thrown away after a meal. People, it is thought, probably experimented and developed the raising of food over many thousand of years (White). Evidence refuting the "shock stimulus" has been produced during the past decades. Adolph suggests that these changes did not happen because of the survival of the fittest but that early people deserve credit for using their heads. One argument against blind choice is the widespread use of rice as a staple, with its high quality protein. Brown says that when people first turned to agriculture the earth supported no more than 10 million people or about as many as now live in one of the world's largest cities.

He also pointed out that since the beginnings of agriculture six technological innovations have enormously increased the earth's food-producing capacity. These are: "The use of irrigation, harnessing draft animals, the exchange of crops between the old world and the new, the development of chemical fertilizers and pesticides, advances in plant genetics, and the invention of the internal combustion engine."

Early Humans and Homo Sapiens

Hoebel placed the first appearances of what he chooses to call *Homo sapiens sapiens* (modern humans) at the time of the upper Paleolithic Age, or around 35,000 B.C. He also said that this age took shape quite suddenly in Iraq, Afghanistan, Israel, Cyrenaica, and North Africa. He lists *Homo sapiens neanderthalenis* and *Homo sapiens steinheimensis* as predecessors of *Homo sapiens sapiens*. Homo sapiens sapiens can interbreed freely, which sets them apart from the others. It is also said that early humans had the power of speech, so that they could tell others what they had learned to do. Shapiro places the date of the emergence of modern humans as around 30 to 40,000 years ago.

Humans do not seem to have inherited the instinctual abilities of other animals; from infancy, they must learn from experience. The human infant during the period of growth is nearly dependent on its parents. Because of their power of speech, parents can transmit to the child the results of efforts to control the environment, including how to get and use food. Human beings, speaking to each other, progress by pooling what they have learned individually.

Ages

The early stages of the culture of the past are divided into the Stone Ages (Old, Middle, and New, or Neo, Meso, and Paleo); the Bronze Age; and the Iron Age. After people learned to use metals their methods of food preparation, of course, changed drastically when they had the utensils in which to roast or boil their food. People of the Old Stone Age had to rely on hunting animals, fishing, gathering wild berries and shellfish, or digging roots and slugs. Some believe that the first human ate only plants, but this statement seems to need further authenticating.

How early peoples captured and caused huge animals to die would be a fascinating story if we could unravel all the details and therefore know with any degree of certainty. Did they wound the animal once they had tools and had learned to throw them, as modern Bushmen do? Did they, like some modern primitive Malaysians, build traps and pits into which the animal would fall and lie helpless? Or did they drive them off a cliff? These animals were so much larger than the people who sought them as food that killing them must have caused a great effort on the part of the hunter. These primitive people truly must have been ready to gorge themselves after this effort and probably previous starvation. When we watch television programs about animal preservation where people struggle with modern equipment to capture a live elephant or rhinoceros, we can admire even more the intelligence and skill of these early humans. The stories of how our American Plains Indians captured and manipulated the hugh bodies of the American bison in order to use them for food, clothing, and shelter can help us in these conjectures.

Use of Fire and Tools

According to Childe (1951), "The control of fire was presumably the first great step in man's emancipation from the bondage of his environment." Not only could people now cook their food, but the warmth of the embers made it possible for them to warm their caves and rock shelters so that they could move into cooler areas in deep caves and also into cooler climates, allowing them to search throughout a wider area for food. They may also have learned to use fire to drive large animals to places where they had a greater chance of mastering them.

Learning to use fire was undoubtedly one of the most important discoveries. Humans have been distinguished from other animals on the basis of their general preference for cooked rather than raw foods. William Howells (quoted by Brown, 1963) believes that there is less difference between Buckingham Palace and a cave where its occupants used fire than between a cave where fire was used and one where it was not.

Charles Lamb's essay "Dissertation upon a Roast Pig" is probably pure fancy, but it has charmed readers for generations.

People are thought to have fashioned rude tools of stone, bone, or wood. The latter was probably sharpened by flint-flakes of stone. There is even evidence that these tools were fashioned to fit their hands. Childe (1951)* reported, "In quite early Pleistocene times there were certainly men manufacturing unmistakable implements of stone and also controlling fire." Blainey describes in detail the use of fire by early Australians. He says, "Fire was central to their way of life, affecting nearly every activity."

At first, people probably discovered combustibles that had been ignited by lightning or by other natural means. These first were then kept constantly alive and alight. Later people learned to produce fire from the spark of a flintstone against iron pyrites or hematite or by friction of two pieces of wood as done by primitive peoples now. *People had truly created when they produced fire, and they were also asserting their power over nature.*

The Beginnings of Agriculture

We have seen how people changed from "food gatherers" to "food producers"; we now examine this development in greater detail.

At the close of the Ice Ages, during what has often been called the "Neolithic Revolution," people began to produce their food rather than rely on gathering it. Childe (1951) pointed out that climatic changes after the end of the last Ice Age were followed by changes in plant and wild animal life, thus altering human food patterns. For example, in the temperate zone of Europe, forests invaded the large tracts of tundra and steppes. Further south, the forests withered from drought, and prairies gradually turned into deserts. At about this time, some great rivers such as the Nile, the Tigris, the Euphrates, and the Indus began to overflow their banks in an established pattern. When people began to adjust to the new conditions, the Mesolithic cultures were created. They now appear to have "camped" more regularly than Ice Age people and they began the slow mastery of the environment. It has been said that when people changed from gatherers to producers they substituted the vicissitudes of the weather for the uncertainties of the hunt.

Harlan said that "some crops seem to have evolved over vast regions; there is no evidence of a center of origin." He believed "agriculture was not an invention and is not as revolutionary as we thought; furthermore, it was adopted slowly and with reluctance. . . . Current evidence indicates that agriculture evolved through an extension and intensification of what people had been doing for a long time."

Janick, et al., said that the wild progenitor of rice in Asia, sorghum in Africa, and beans in the Americas are widely distributed and were manipulated by various people over the entire range. They believe that "Each may have been repeatedly domesticated

*Dates for references are given only when more than one reference by the same author is listed.

at different times in different places or may have been brought into the domestic fold in several places simultaneously.'' They also point out that only in recent historical times did plants or animals spread very far so they think it is easy to trace their origins. They also add that plants and animals change drastically with domestication.

The last millennia of the preagricultural ages were, according to Vayda, a time of ''settling in'' to one's area; there was an interchange of resources among groups, causing a greater variety of foods to be used. About this time people probably removed certain key species of wild grasses from the niches where they were indigenous and put them in niches more convenient to them but foreign to the grasses. The term niche is used here to designate a habitat supplying factors necessary for the existence of the species.

When people used primitive devices to cut a grass they probably selected those stalks that held their seed heads most tightly. People may well have learned other things during these transition years. They may have learned that roasting the husk-encapsulated grains enabled them to remove the tough outer *glumes* more easily. This heating also killed the germ so that the grain could be stored without sprouting. Mutations and genetic changes undoubtedly took place to alter the character of both plants and animals during the development of agriculture and animal husbandry.

Just how this all happened has been the subject of various theories and conjectures. Some believe that wild grain stored in caves sprouted, and early peoples saw these growing plants. Others have thought that people observed the growth of wild cereal grasses where the alluvial soil waters had receded after spring flooding. One charming story written for young children tells of women throwing cereal seeds on the ground to thank the gods for food and then observing the growth of a patch of cereal grasses when they returned to this spot the next spring. This story may well have been originally true and subsequently preserved in the folk lore of the people. In the region of the Altamira Caves in Eastern Spain where plants and wild animals were abundant Wissler says people congregated.

The FAO Nutritional Study Number 23 (Aykroyd and Doughty) stated, ''Whatever uncertainties there are reasonable grounds for supposing that, in the so-called Fertile Crescent of Western Asia, the cultivation of wheat and other wild plants indigenous to the area began during the years 8000 to 6000 B.C. and perhaps earlier.'' The authors believe that ''the domestication of sheep and goats, common wild species of the area, took place simultaneously. How cultivation was initiated cannot be precisely known.'' The fact that nomads returned year after year to the places where wild food plants grew abundantly probably caused them to locate their permanent settlements there.

Emergence of Near Eastern civilizations is dated from such archeological sites as Jarmo, 6700 B.C. Africa is thought by some to be the site of the origin of agriculture. Others choose the Trans-Caspian Steppes, Iran in Anatolia (an ancient name for Asia Minor), as well as other Near Eastern places. Braidwood (1953) believes that following discoveries after World War II, it can be positively asserted that ''Civilization in its more useful sense of the word . . . had at least two independent beginnings. One of these was certainly centered in ancient Mesopotamia which thus took preference over

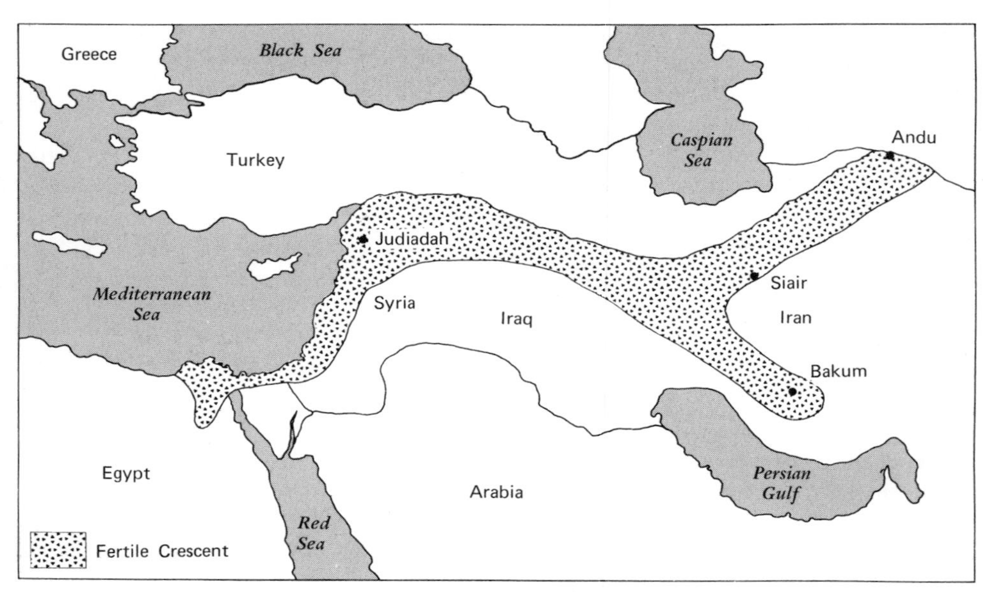

The Fertile Crescent

Egypt. One was certainly centered in the New World.'' He uses the word ''civilization'' to mean ''a culture with fully efficient food production, cities and urbanization, a formal political state, a new sense of moral order, formal projects and works, classes and hierarchies, writing, and momentuality in art.''

Mesopotamia in the *Fertile Crescent* is regarded by most authorities as one of the first if not *the* first center for the development of cultivation of plants and breeding of animals. This Crescent is usually defined as an area that begins in a small portion in Northern Egypt and extends through Palestine, Syria, and Mesopotamia and eastward across the oasis and mountain slopes to the Indus River and the Punjab of India. Flannery said that Mesopotamia was probably one of the few areas where agriculture and animal husbandry seemed to have originated autonomously.

Braidwood believed that the culture of Mesopotamia spread to Egypt, but he said that whether centers arose in Indo-Malaysia and China is ''still highly speculative.'' Jensen thinks that the transition from primitive to civilized life happened more than once.

Cereal pollens dating back to 14,000 B.C. have been found in caves of the preagricultural period and the remnants of ''potential animal domesticates'' (sheep and goats) have been found in cave debris dating back to 40,000 B.C. Flannery thinks that ''From 40,000 to 10,000 B.C. man worked out a pattern for exploiting the natural resources of this part of the world.''

Many archeologists agree that women were responsible for the first agriculture as they were responsible during the food gathering period for gathering plant food while the men hunted. Later when oxen and plows were used, the men of the family began to cultivate the fields and women stayed home to prepare food and perform the many household tasks.

When seeds were planted, primitive people regarded the earth as "the great mother." Around this idea and the prayers and religious rites for inducing fertility grew many practices. Women and fertility were, of course, associated then as they are associated today in the rites of many primitive peoples. It is also easily understood why, when the bodies of the dead were buried in the ground, prayers to ancestors were for good crops. "The cultivation of plants required no new facts or knowledge but was simply a new kind of relationship between man and the plants with which he was familiar."

It has been conjectured that Adam was a food gatherer before his fall in the Garden of Eden and that he became a food-producer after he fell because he tasted the fruit of the tree of knowledge. Genesis (iii-18:19) is quoted in support of this assumption: "Thou shalt eat the herb of thy field; in the sweat of thy face shalt thou eat bread." The term "herb" is often used in ancient literature to refer to wild plants and grasses. The strife between Cain and Abel has been said to symbolize the strife and jealousy between the food producers and the food gatherers.

This change in people's mode of getting their food was perhaps, *next to the use of fire in food getting and preparing, the most important occurrence in development of human food patterns.*

The ideas of agriculture were probably carried into Europe in two directions (Braidwood, 1948): (1) through Turkey and Greece into South Russia and up the Danube Valley, and (2) along North Africa or by the sea to Italy, Spain, France, and then on to Britain and north. Evidence of the early introduction of agriculture and animal husbandry into Europe is furnished in the artifacts of the culture of the Lake Dwellers of Switzerland, whose records date back to 6000 B.C. These peoples, among the best known of any early village assemblages, dwelt where they could throw their refuse into the water of the lake, and these water-logged remnants were better preserved than the middens on dry land. Stone tools set in wooden and antler hafts have been found along with pieces of cloth and remnants of grain, fruits, and vegetables. These peoples may not have been more clever than others (Braidwood 1953), but the remnants are better preserved.

A culture existed on the shores of the Baltic Sea (Jensen) when it was used as a fresh water lake where people lived on pine-log rafts moored to the shore. Their kitchen refuse, thrown into the water is revealed in layers of peat that have been exposed as the water receded. Fish, wild game, pigs, ducks, geese, and water fowl as well as seeds of the yellow water lily were used as food.

Wheat and Grain Culture

It has been pointed out by Loomis that throughout the ages "the heavy emphasis on cereals reflects not only their food value but their relative ease of culture."

Wheat always has had a central place among cereal grains; barley plays a secondary role followed by millet, rye, and rice. Wheat and barley offer the advantages of being highly nutritious and easily stored, and the return in usable food is relatively high in relation to the effort expended in raising them. In addition to the abundance of its yield, wheat has the greatest advantage in breadmaking of any cereal because of the proteins gliadin and glutenin that form gluten—the protein that because of its elasticity allows bread to rise and retain a light and porous texture. Rye has some of these proteins but other cereals lack enough of them to make an elastic dough.

Dinkels and *wild emmers,* grasses ancestral to wheat, are known to grow wild, the former in the Crimea and Asia Minor and the latter in Palestine and perhaps in Iran. It is thought that wheat and barley were grown in Mesopotamia as early as anywhere; probably wheat and barley seeds were taken into Egypt.

Wheat grows best in broad, well-watered valleys. In many places, the potential fields were former forests cleared by slashing and burning. The first cultivation was evidently done on small plots or gardens and was therefore termed garden culture by those who found evidences of it. The Egyptians (Wissler) put the seed in the soft alluvial mud and used animals to tramp it down. At that time, people probably did not know about the use of fertilizer or about allowing land to lie fallow; therefore, it was necessary for them to seek new plots every few years, and settlements were temporary. More permanent settlements were later apparently situated to take advantage of the alluvial soils produced by the intermittent torrents flowing from the hills to the plains and of the soils along rivers that regularly overflowed their banks. It has been pointed out that one reason why we know more of the details of the Egyptian use of grains is that their *mummified* grains have been better preserved than grains in other cultures. Helbalk told of the grain found in the galleries beneath the pyramids as well as in storage pits in the open desert. Grain was discovered that belongs to a species that has not been grown since Roman times and which is as fresh as when it was put there 5000 to 6000 years ago. The myth that some of it has sprouted and grown into a plant has been refuted.

Much of our other evidence about these grains grown in early times comes from carbonized seeds. Perhaps the people roasting them discarded them because they were burned, as we discard charred popcorn kernels.

Concomitant Innovations

Another innovation was necessitated when people began to cultivate food and breed animals. As they observed the close relationship of the growth of plants and the breeding of animals to the seasons, they made a calender. The early Egyptians devised a clever calendar that is really the forerunner of our own. About this time, they also developed astronomy and mathematics, which helped them in predicting seasons. This was, of course, of prime importance in countries that were dependent on seasonal rains like the monsoons or on the flooding of the Nile.

Planning for irrigation and water storage systems led to the development of the science of engineering. The planning for the storing of food brought into being the art of planning and administration.

In areas along streams and lakes where there were some primitive settlements, fishing was profitable and fresh as well as dried fish were probably used. Childe (1951) told of fishing nets weighted with perforated lumps of clay or "waisted" (weighted) stones.

Many have believed, as did Brogger, that the wealth of the sea was not well used by primitive people because they had not developed sufficient technology to make this use profitable.

Harlan pointed out that "cultivation refers to man's efforts to care for a plant" and that "domestication involves genetic changes."

Animal Husbandry Begins

Neolithic people around 10,000 B.C. were known to have had pets or sacred animals. We will probably never know, however, just when people first domesticated animals to raise them for food. As has been said, the taming and the domesticating of animals are very different processes. Domestication means continuous breeding.

Why did people seeking food want to domesticate animals? They probably did not at first realize what they were doing, but gradually domestication occurred as their association with their dogs and other young wild animals became stronger. People and the animals derived mutual benefits when they began to protect these animals from predators and to provide them with food. The animals that were tamed first were probably the ones most socially and psychologically adaptable to this association with people. Of course, it was necessary that reproductive ability was not interfered with. Undoubtedly men, women, and children made pets of young wild animals, which were probably penned up and watched as they developed before they were used as food. They were probably also used as decoys in hunting.

There is disagreement concerning whether the cultivation of plants or the domestication of animals took place first. Wissler wondered why it took man so long to undertake the raising of plants and the domestication of animals, when "instead of persistent killing of game animals, thus making them scarce and wild . . . he could have lived in friendly cooperation with them, protecting, conserving them and living in luxury on their increase by the simple device of saving the females and sacrificing the males. . . . Within a generation he could have come into control of his animal supplies."

How did people learn to domesticate animals? One theory is that pet dogs helped them corral servial animals at once, probably the younger and less powerful animals. North European people are known to have tamed the dog to help them in hunting and to have used it as a scavenger and as a companion as early as 6000 B.C. Jensen postulated that pigs, like dogs, were "attracted to man's communities by waste food."

Harlan says that jaws and teeth of domestic dogs have been found and identified and dated to about 12,000 B.C. in Iraq and 11,000 B.C. in Idaho. Otherwise he says there is little evidence before 9000 B.C.

Wild boars are known to have been adopted by villagers of prehistoric China and Egypt. Ames and Wyler credited the success and widespread use of the pig as a domestic animal to the fact that they have an appetite for all kinds of food and they raise large litters. Because the pig is not adapted to "pastoral nomadism," Vayda believed, it was not domesticated in certain places in the Near East rather than that religious or dietary laws forbade its use.

Harlan cautions that there is "respectable" data for domestication of plants and animals in the Near East but "no other parts of the world have been so well explored (except North America, where agriculture arrived comparatively late)."

There is evidence of the very early domestication of sheep in three parts of France as well as in the Near East. Sheep are known to have been domesticated and used by Neolithic and Mesolithic people in Southwestern Asia and Asia Minor. The Neolithic emigrants to Europe brought their sheep with them. Early Neolithic Egyptian sheep were of the hairy type, but around 1500 B.C. these were replaced in the Nile Delta and Upper Egypt with a fleecy sheep that had fat tails like the modern Afghan sheep.

Indications of the domestication of deer in Northern Europe have been found, as has evidence of domestication of horses in several great mountain ranges, particularly the steppes and mountains of Southern Russia. The Kassites, who invaded the Persian plateau in the middle of the eighteenth century B.C., are thought by some to have domesticated the horse. In many countries where early horses appeared, they were eaten as food, as is true in many countries today. Satisfactory evidence (Childe, 1951) of the use of horses for milking and riding is not available before 1000 B.C. There are, however, stories of earlier use of horses in different parts of the ancient world.

Cattle are the most important domestic animals in all history, according to Forde. Zeuner said, "It is no exaggeration that the domestication of cattle was the most important step ever taken by man in the exploration of the animal world after the domestication of the dog." The wild ox was widely distributed in Southwest Asia in the late glacial period, and it has survived in Eastern Europe until recent times. *Aurocks,* the ancestor of the domesticated European ox, were common in early Europe and in the Fertile Crescent and were widely distributed in both areas. The bulls of this species probably came out of the primeval forests and interbred with domestic cows. Egyptians in early dynastic times are known to have raised shorthorn and polled cattle as well as a type of longhorn cattle. Chickens were probably domesticated after cattle, sheep, goats, and pigs, and probably in India.

When people had to seek grasslands for grazing their animals, they began to prefer the plains rather than the forests where they had found it previously profitable to live when they survived by hunting alone. Large areas of grasslands were prerequisite for the domestication and breeding of animals. Domestication probably flourished during the time that grasses were spreading to their present area of growth over one-fifth of the earth's surface.

In the process of domestication of animals, people learned to exercise restraint not to kill the youngest and the tamest nor to frighten the beasts in which they were interested. Once they had inadvertently spared the shyest and most amenable bulls, they had begun selective breeding—they had now to learn to find out about their reproduction as well as their needs for food, salt, and water.

The domestication of animals is evidently a deliberate exploitation by people of their environment even though the practice is rooted deeply in man's natural contacts with the beasts. *As a deliberate exploitation of the environment, it is another important stage in the development of human food patterns.*

The Beginning of the Use of Milk and Other Uses of Animals

Once people began using animals for meat, they must have had herds and would have observed that they, along with young animals, could use the milk of these animals as food. They would also have found animal hides useful to keep them warm or to protect them from insects or other pests. They later learned to use animals as beasts of burden to help them with cultivation. They probably observed that where animal dung had lain and rotted, the young grass was greener, and so perhaps gained the first idea of the use of fertilizer to increase crop yields.

It is not known why some primitive peoples used milk whereas others did not. Marco Polo wrote of eating yogurt in China. Adolph pointed out that even in dim history the "bean" (soybean) was the "Milk of China." Coming down to recorded history, we find statements in the writings of Homer and others that milk was scorned as repulsive. We doubt, however, that this explains differences in the use of milk among primitive groups. Many old wives' tales and primitive practices that have survived the test of time have grains of truth in them. The Sumerians are known to have had a well-developed dairy industry over 5000 years ago.

In different parts of the world, people have milked cows, goats, mares, asses, reindeer, buffaloes, camels, and zebra. Early Persians used camel's milk; Asians and Africans used water and cape buffalo's milk; Europeans used the milk of the cow, ewe, goat, and ass; while the Tartars and Mongols used mare's milk. Northern European people used the milk of the reindeer. The milk of the yak has long been used in Pamirs (Tadzhikskaya, a U.S.S.R. province in Central Asia) and Tibet, whereas Peruvians have used the milk of the llama and vicuna for many centuries. In many of these areas, the same animals are used for milk today.

Other Inventions Useful in Food Getting

Pottery making, the use of the plow, the sickle, and the wheel, and metallurgy appeared in North Mesopotamia, Syria, Palestine, Iran, and Egypt after the early domestication of plants and animals.

The earliest generally established date for the domestication of animals is around 5000 B.C.; for metallurgy, 4000 B.C.; and for sailing ships, 4000 to 3000 B.C. The wheel probably appeared somewhat earlier than 3000 B.C., but more accurate dating must await more definitive evidence. It is thought that incipient agriculture began around 9000 B.C.

Possible Native Habitats of Different Plants

Rice was grown in North India 3000 years ago and probably in China 5000 years ago, according to Pirie. Because Southeast Asia is now the source of 95 percent of the world's rice, he thinks it originated there. He speculated that Africa may have been an independent center of its beginnings. Modern varieties of rice in Africa are different from those in Asia.

Pirie pointed out that, with the exception of rice, every plant now is grown more extensively in some countries to which it has been taken than in its native home. This is true certainly of maize in the U.S., which was brought from its native habitat of Mexico. Another example is the banana, which is thought to have originated in Southeast Asia; the peanut, in tropical America; the potato in Peru, Bolivia, and Chile; as well as the soybean, in Northeast Asia; and sugar, in India.

Most vegetables used today came to us before written records were kept. Prehistoric people took their vegetable and fruit seeds with them along with those of their cereals. Boswell thought that the best way to determine where a plant originated was to determine where it is still found growing wild. This is not always a reliable guide, however, as evidenced by the carrot, which is not native to North America but does grow wild here. Probably we need to seek the place where the greatest number of varieties grow wild. Boswell in his lengthy article gave a history of practically all commonly known vegetables. The reader is referred to this excellent article for further details on the origin of vegetables.

Table 1-1 Native Habitats of Plants (Vavilov)

County or area	Native plants
1. S.W. Asia: Asia Minor Persia Afghanistan Northwest India	Soft wheat, rye, flax, apple, pear, sweet cherry, grape, bean, pea, carrot
2. India: Valley of Ganges	Rice, "naked" oats, "naked" barley, millet, soya, sugar cane, tropical fruit
3. Great river valleys of East and Central China (These plants are supposed to have spread from here to Japan and Malaysia)	Radish, citrus fruit, peach, tea, mulberry
4. Mediterranean Basin: Iberia, Italy, Coast of Asia Minor, Syria, Palestine, Egypt, Tunisia, Algeria, Morocco	Olive, fig, oats, pea, barley, wheat
5. Mountains of East Africa and Abyssinia	Sorghum, coffee
6. Northern Mexico	Maize, cacao
7. Peru, Bolivia	Potato

In Southeast Asia, plants other than wheat and barley were available to the primitive cultivator. These were rye grass, wild flax, and large-seeded wild legumes like lentils, vetch, vetchlings, and chick peas. The lowland areas had dates; the foothills, acorns, and almonds; and the northern mountains, grapes, apples, and pears.

Development of Use of Metals Affects Farming Practices

The use of metals affected the production, storage, as well as food preparation as previously stated. Brew said, "Toward the end of the era of prehistory known as the Neolithic or New Stone Age, man became aware of special properties in some hard metals of the earth's surface." People "learned how to mine these metallic ores, and how to work the metals when they had been extracted.

Copper, the first metal used, was probably obtained from the rugged mountains of Iran around 4000 and 3500 B.C. (Brew believes that these dates need further authenticating.) Copper was also traded with people living as far away as the Assyrian Steppes. Later, people learned to smelt it with tin to make the harder and more useful bronze. But apparently several centuries passed before copper came into general use. In order to make bronze tools, according to Childe (1951), a "community must produce a surplus of foodstuffs to support bodies of specialists—miners, smelters, and smiths." Some people had to withdraw from direct food production to become workers in metals. The making of bronze possibly began in the mountainous regions of Asia Minor and Armenia around 3000 B.C. Experimental alloys of it appeared in Egypt around 3000 B.C. This metal (Brew) was probably used 500 years later in India, 1000 years later in Northern Europe, and possibly 1500 years later in China. The use of bronze may have been taken north and west as peoples moved out of Mesopotamia, and it has been conjectured that the Neolithic peoples of Europe traded their valuables, such as Danish amber for bronze knives, swords, and pots and pans. The first Bronze Age people in Britain came from Spain.

Although gold and silver were known to have been used in Neolithic times, they were too soft to be used in food getting or preparation, and people had to wait for copper and bronze to make a great difference in their daily lives. Iron came into use later because of its advantages as a material for tools and weapons, as well as the fact that it could be found almost anywhere. The time of the introduction if iron is not known; according to Brew, it is said to have been "invented" in Asia Minor at "an unknown date." It was apparently known in the Near East as early as bronze (about 3000 B.C.) but many centuries passed before it was in general use. Iron was used, according to Linton, in the Near East in 4500 B.C. and reached Britain by 2500 B.C. although he thought that there is evidence of its use in the western plateau of Turkey by 1800 to 1600 B.C.

This discussion of the use of metals is presented here because it affected farming practices, food getting, food storage, and food preparation.

People Make Tools and Devise New Methods with their Needs

Once people began to cultivate plants, they had new needs for tools—to sharpen the digging stick, to make a hoe, and later to make a sickle and a plow. People also had need for vessels for storage of grains. The archeologist finds only a part of a tool when excavating a site, making it difficult to know what the original tool was really like. Keeley recently devised a method to identify the use made of some ancient flint tools by examining them under a powerful microscope.

Early Digging Tools and the Plow

In the development of agriculture, the plow was a comparatively late invention. The digging stick, weighted with a stone, was the first digging tool; from this stick, the spade and garden fork were developed. The plow and the horse were both used in the Bronze Age in Europe (Linton); according to Wissler, the Spanish took the plow to Mexico.

As soon as the wheel was made, people found many uses for it. After its invention, oxen were drafted to help do the heavy work of cultivating plots.

Early Cooking Utensils

It is thought that people first roasted their grains on hot stones heated by the sun or near the fire they had lighted. Later these grains may have been ground on a kind of mortar and pestle. Possibly the earliest method of grinding was the use of clubs of wood against stones. In 1959 Senegalese women were still using hugh stone containers for grinding cereal grains and dried roots. Against these stone surfaces they used large wooden pestles with handles long enough to allow them to stand upright.

Different kinds of mortars and pestles have been found in the remnants of successive cultures. In the early twentieth century, children in California were still digging up mortars and pestles with which early Indian women had ground their acorns.

Ground-up grains were probably first used for porridge. It is possible that early people used leather vessels by placing hot stones in them for some of their cooking. Northwest American Indians are known to have used tightly woven baskets for this type of cooking.

Pottery making was another innovation. One story says that women first put wet clay inside baskets woven of reeds to make them hold water. As these were used on fires, the clay was hardened by the heat into a form of pottery. Harrison says that when people invented pottery, for the first time, instead of using natural materials, they altered natural materials for their own use.

Pottery may have been used for boiling as well as for roasting meats. Roasting over an open fire was undoubtedly the first form of cooking meat. In modern times the terms roasting and baking are sometimes used less accurately than they probably were originally. Were the Polynesians the first to use pits filled with hot stones to roast an entire pig? This is not known.

Other Advances

Between 6000 and 3000 B.C., people learned to use oxen, and they invented and learned to use the plow, the wheeled cart, and the sailboat to fish from. They also devised and used the solar calendar to help them in producing food.

The creation of canals for irrigation called for disciplined group work; some claim that this was the time when people became self-disciplined. The large-scale canal irrigation in Mesopotamia around 3600 B.C. has been credited for the spectacular rise in population and the creation of cities in Mesopotamia.

Jensen said that, whereas the discovery of agriculture gave people earthroom to spare for hundreds of years, "climatic changes and growth of towns ushered in man's everlasting productivity and warfare." He also believed "that a cycle of interplay of planned labor, which increased food supply, with increasing population of workers, resulted in increased complexity of organization, until we now have our industrial and social-political wheels creaking and rolling at great speed—no man knows whither."

Childe (1951) gives 3000 B.C. as the approximate time that merchandise was carried on donkeys back and forth between Babylonia and Asia Minor. The donkey, a native of Northeast Africa, had probably been domesticated there long before 3000 B.C.

Migrations in Europe

Montague (1969) told of the 1965 announcement of the discovery of the earliest known site in Europe in the Macedonian Plain of Northern Greece. The probable date for existence of this village was 6220 B.C. There farmer-herders raised wheat, barley, and lentils and tended sheep, goats, and almost certainly cattle and pigs—this was the earliest dated occurrence of cattle anywhere in the world. These people also are thought to have hunted birds and wild animals and fished.

The first farmers probably migrated into Greece and Anatolia (Waterbalk). They slashed and burned the forests after the change from nondeciduous species of trees. The seacoast peoples who had lived in that area by hunting and fishing were receptive to new ideas of food production so that, when the migrating farmers arrived, they probably followed the ideas of their new neighbors.

The Swiss Lake Dwellers

The lake dwellers of Switzerland and elsewhere—the first peoples of Western Neolithic culture for which there are reliable records—lived together in rectangular wooden houses raised on wooden piles and strung out along the lake shore. Their houses, first probably built along the shore, later, when flooding occurred, were surrounded entirely by water. They cultivated emmer wheat, barley, linseed, caraway, poppy seeds, beans, lentils, carrots, plums, and apples, and they are thought to have brewed cider. They raised pigs, sheep, goats, and horned cattle, "stalled" their cattle, and used cow manure as a fertilizer. They also speared and netted fish. Leather and pottery cooking and storage vessels were used.

The remnants of their bread show that the dough was not fermented, but they knew about fermentation because they made wine from raspberries, cherries, and mulberries. They used wheat, barley, and rye and apparently emphasized the growing of cereals. Cattle, pigs, sheep, game, fish, and shellfish were used as food, as were seasonal fruits and nuts. They also used ox-drawn plows.

About 3000 B.C. the plains south of the Scandinavian Mountains were inhabited by peoples who lived in more or less permanent villages. They cut deciduous forests with stone axes, cultivated a variety of crops, and raised cattle, sheep, goats, and pigs; hunting was of little importance.

Remnants of pottery of varied shapes and with various ornamentation have been found everywhere in this region.

As peoples migrated, they went into a broad zone between the Alps and the west coast of the North Sea, as well as across the European continent to the Danube (Waterbalk). The diffusion of culture, however, was slow during the Neolithic ages in Northern Britain, Northern Norway, and Sweden due to isolation.

Present-Day Primitive People

Even today there are many groups on earth who are using methods credited to early peoples. Anthropologists often conjecture about early people by studying modern primitive people, although this approach is undoubtedly misleading because the influences of highly developed peoples do touch these primitive peoples. One of the best illustrations is a drawing in an anthropology textbook of Australian aborigines tearing down a telephone line in order to obtain the materials they need for hunting and other primitive pursuits. There are, however, many remnants of primitive food patterns. Reports of the symbolic uses of food come from nutritionists working among some of the most primitive tribes in Central Australia. Women of the Bushmen group of Africa gather roots, fruits, and seeds while the men hunt. Some Tanzanian tribes still use digging sticks in planting. The Hunzas, a fascinating group of North India, are hardy physically, possessed of superior strength and physical endurance and apparently enjoy buoyant health. These people have interested nutritionists since 1921, when McCarrison first found that their diet consisted of cereal grains, vegetables, fruits (especially apricots), milk and butter daily, and goat's meat on feast days only. They eat the same diet today and still eat sparingly. Their agricultural practices are traditional; they terrace and irrigate their fields and renew the soil by bringing "glacial milk" from the nearby mountains. They also return to the soil all human, animal, and vegetable refuse.

Only a few of the food patterns of ancient peoples are discussed here.

EGYPT

The early Egyptians left us better records of what they ate than some ancient peoples because they believed that food must be placed in tombs for the use of the dead in the afterlife. The Pharoahs were especially well supplied with food for their afterlife. The poor, however, who could afford only a coarse cloth for a coffin and had to be buried in communal graves were provided with only a few scraps of food. The dead who had been wealthy were offered food daily, whereas those of moderate means were offered food only on festivals.

The Egyptians believed in "eat, drink, and be merry" in this life because they were perhaps not really sure of an afterlife. Even the poor were said to have been gay and to have loved life.

Foods Used

The Nile left fertile silt along its banks after the seasonal floods. In these lush bottom lands were grown vast fields of grain, mostly wheat. After the Egyptians learned to make leavened bread, the use of barley decreased.

Beans, parsley, radishes, and especially onions, leeks, and garlic were grown and used. Some say that the Greek historian Herodotus was the first to report that onions and garlic were the main foods of builders of the great pyramid of Cheops at Gizeh, 2900 B.C. This assertion is probably not true, although the early Egyptians liked onions and garlic and Egyptians still grow them for export. Melons and grapes flourished in the Nile Delta, and olive oil was probably used as early as 3000 B.C. The Egyptians developed a less bitter table olive. Fish was preserved both by salting and by drying; grapes were dried for raisins.

Hunting was a favorite pastime of the wealthy, and wild fowl were prized. As many as 1000 geese were said to have been consumed in one day at opulent public feasts. Some fish were considered sacred and there was a proscription against their use, but the poor paid little attention to such regulations.

Egyptian priests who were able to predict the flooding of the Nile gained power, thereby becoming some of the first rulers to demand food as tribute. Thus, some of the farmers' harvest had to be used as payment for taxes. Much grain was stored and saved for use in years of famine.

Grain was reaped with a sickle, carried in rope baskets, and threshed by oxen treading on the grain; finally it was winnowed by allowing the wind to blow out the chaff. These processes are well depicted in murals; in one of these, four scribes are recording yields. Records of yield per acre have been found.

Ancient Egypt is best known of all ancient cultures for developing the art of breadmaking. Grain was crushed between heavy grindstones; water was added to make dough. At first, flat cakes of bread were baked in clay-lined ovens hollowed out of the ground; and heated by burning coals. Some people placed outside their houses earthen jars that were heated by hot coals much as hearth ovens have been heated throughout the centuries since the Egyptians first used them.

Meals and Banquets

The first course at an Egyptian banquet often consisted of appetizers such as green cabbage (supposed to delay drunkenness), pickled onions, and sesame, anise, and cumin seeds. The main course usually consisted of roast goose, legs of small calves and gazelles, wild duck or quail, fish served raw or grilled, or a combination of these. Such vegetables as lettuce, endive, dried peas, cardoons (forerunners of artichokes), onions, leeks, beans, parsley, and radishes might also be served with this course. Beer was usually served but wine was sometimes used. Sweets such as fruits, cakes, and melons were served as dessert.

GREECE

The Grecian food patterns after the rise of Athens and Sparta and those of their colonies are especially interesting. In early Greece many of the poor were on the very edge of starvation so that they demanded land and power from the rich.

The city, or polis, was a political and geographical center. A rich civic life emerged in the polis to distinguish the Greeks from their neighbors. The Greek farmers were never able to feed all the population. They did, however, produce olive oil, wine, and wool, which could be used in addition to their pottery and jewelry to trade with the peoples around the Mediterranean and the Baltic Seas for foods that they needed. They evidently journeyed as far as the Crimea in the East and to France and even to Ireland in the West, so they knew what foods other peoples produced. There are records of their journeys to Sicily and southern Italy as early as 750 B.C., and they traveled up the coast of Italy as far as the Bay of Naples. These travelers are said to have brought back cheese and pork from Sicily.

When these cities became overpopulated, colonists were sent north to the Aegean littoral, to the Sea of Marmara, and finally to the Crimea. These colonies provided new sources of foods that were scarce at home.

In science as in medicine, the Greeks were good observers. In contrast to the modern scientist, "The Greek philosopher began with little data, developed his theories by the application of logic, and then stopped. . . . The influence of this attitude was reflected in Greek technology. Until well into the Hellenistic period, it was characterized by an increasing perfection of manual dexterity and an almost complete lack of new basic inventions or even of borrowings which might have fundamentally altered the existing technical patterns" (Linton). He was speaking here especially of architecture, but this influence was no doubt also relevant to agricultural practices.

The early Greeks apparently knew nothing about crop rotation (they used little fertilizer), but they probably, by necessity, allowed their fields to lie fallow one season.

They reaped their grains with a sickle and had no scythes. They threshed grain by driving cattle over the stalks, as was done by others in ancient times and can still be observed as a practice among some primitive peoples today. They, however, drained the swamps and terraced their hillsides to use all available land efficiently. It is said that, during the fourth century B.C., agricultural experts began to study crop rotation and means of soil improvement; they also began to use manure as a fertilizer. Their first attempts toward improvement in the production of food concerned arbor culture of olives, grapes, and figs.

One of the Greek inventions that greatly facilitated foreign trade was their production of coins, which were much more convenient for barter than food and wine. It is said that the earliest merchants traded their barley, but it often went moldy before they could use it for barter. Some of the earliest Greek coins were stamped with an ear of wheat, a reminder that one of the world's first forms of money was food. Greek civilization arose because Greek farmers could produce more of certain foods (primarily olives and olive oil and wine) than they needed, so they could trade these for other foods that they did need (Orr).

The ancient Greek farmer's life was one of hard labor and want. They had, except for some water power, no mechanical source of power to supplement their own labors; animals were probably infrequently used. One author mentions a farmer using mules to draw a plow but finishing by hand with a hoe. "The civilization which hand labor supports is a simple civilization. This is the secret of the 2300 years of what seems to us a stagnation, if so we may call it, which lasted from early history to the beginning of the nineteenth century" (Prentice).

The Grecian supply of a variety of foods was influenced by their love of travel; their invention of coinage, which enabled them to buy foods from other lands; their overcoming the difficulties of an inhospitable land; and their using readily available seafood.

Boetia (cow land), from Homer's time to the classical period, had pasture lands lush enough to graze cattle. Boetians also bred cattle and pigs, and mules and donkeys were used for farm labor. The fact that the lushness of Boetia is mentioned often in discussing agriculture and food in Greece leads us to the supposition that other portions of Greece, except perhaps Thessaly, did not grow lush grass. It is said that the Boetians were gluttons who made their probably hungry, frugal neighbors jealous. Some Athenians are said to have called them "pigs."

At best, the Greek diet was not lavish. But the Greeks apparently enjoyed living frugally; their ability to do physical exercise regularly is well known, as is their excellence in physical pursuits. "It is interesting to note that the Greeks said they must never forget the body in training the mind" (Jensen). They believed that they must train the whole man by gymnasia and diet. Jensen believed that their good diets and frugality influenced greatly the success of the Greek civilization. He also said that the decline of Athens after 350 B.C. was "closely connected with shortage of foodstuffs" and that the reduction of their marketable goods resulted in their not being able to import the needed foods.

Foods Used

The simple Greek diet consisted mostly of olive oil, fish, goat's milk, cheese, wine, and bread. Occasionally, probably mostly at festivals, they had goats and sheep for meat, but these animals usually served as a source of milk to make cheese. Honey from the mountains of Hymeltus near Athens was said to be famous throughout Ancient Greece. This area was also famous for its olives.

Greek pigs were allowed to forage for "mast" which consisted of nuts, such as acorns or beechnuts, found on the forest floor. The pork was not eaten fresh but rather as salted meat. Beef was a rarity because the land was not suitable for grazing cattle.

They had a variety of fish during the seasons when fishing was possible. In fact, the Greeks came to know the sea well. They caught and used tunny, mullet, anchovies, and sardines and dried fish was imported from the Bosporus. They also caught fresh water fish. There was alarm among the people when the price of sardines and anchovies increased. Shellfish, mollusks, squid, and octopus were available. Often fish was smoked or preserved in brine and used in winter. In Homer's time, however, fish was despised as a "poor man's food." Was this the same attitude that made a New England Puritan family hide the shad (then costing less than 10¢ a pound) when during a meal an unexpected knock was heard on the door? Three hundred years later, however, fish was considered a gourmet food in Greece yet Homer considered roasted or boiled meat the only fare for a gentleman's meals and thought that it should be served with bread, cheese, and salad, which was a food for the gods. Milk was drunk only in the rural areas sometimes as soured milk, but it was used for making the cheese eaten by all ancient Greeks. Cheese was also imported from Bithynia. It is said that garlic with cheese was eaten in large quantities.

In Homer's day the people were called "grain eaters," and porridge made from wheat and barley was called *sitos*. This term was probably used for their yeastless bread, which was baked in thin cakes. The porridge, made from grain ground in a mortar, was served with salt and honey.

Wheat was difficult to grow on the Greek barren soil without summer rains. Barley grew better on these soils, but the yield of all grains was low and a farmer could expect to get only 9 to 10 bushels per acre from 2 bushels of seed (Prentice). Yet porridge kept the early world alive. No wonder the Greeks looked to the full granaries of their neighbors and early became good traders, importing wheat and barley from Sicily, Thrace, Egypt, Cyprus, and Southern Russia.

Bread was sometimes made from wheat but more from barley. Because their barley cakes were "stodgy and rather flavorless" (Perl), they were often dipped in honey and vinegar to make them taste better. These cakes or scones were said to have been served on straw or clean leaves. Barley was also made into flat griddle cakes, or *maza*, which was a staple in the diet of many people. One of Solon's ordinances decreed that "wheaten bread proper (*artos*) baked in round loaves should be served only on feast days." Bread and cakes were inspected for weight and contents by market police. In Pericles' time, both maza and artos were obtainable from bakers daily. Xenophon mentions leavened bread, but it is not known when it was first made. Olive oil and wine were used to supplement the porridge diet, but butter was not used.

Vegetables were mostly eaten fresh, but they were also pickled in brine. The Greeks grew grapes and olive trees in the narrow fertile valleys between the mountains. Here they could also grow some grain. Within the walls of a great villa, the family might grow apricots, peaches, plums, figs, and almonds. One author called oranges "golden apples of Hesperides," while another said the Greeks had no citrus fruit. Lemons, which are now much used in Greek cookery, were brought from India after the invasion of Alexander the Great in 326 B.C.; rice was also acquired at this time. Apples, pears, and quince were grown at home, but plums and currants were imported. Nuts were imported from Babylonia, prunes from Damascus, and raisins from Bertytus. The importation of much of their foodstuffs kept Greeks well fed in the frugal way they apparently enjoyed.

The old Greeks were fond of a little roll of spicy chopped meats wrapped in grape leaves resembling the dish now called dolmas. The recipe for fava, a thick stew of dried split peas seasoned with onion, garlic, parsley, and oregano (the favorite Greek herb), has changed little over 2500 years.

Beverages

A popular beverage of the Spartans was a famous black broth, which was a thick stew made of pork, blood, and vinegar. Another cross between liquid and solid food popular with the Greek peasants was made with barley meal and water. The most popular drink was water, but country people also drank milk. Sometimes for drinking, honey was mixed with water.

Wine was not aged, so it had to be preserved with salt to keep it and was usually drunk mixed with water. Hippocrates is said to have drunk wine made from honey and herbs, probably later known as *mead,* a favorite drink of medieval Europeans. Hundreds of years later, mead, made from almost the same ingredients, can be purchased in the United States today.

Seasonings

The Greeks used the word *aroma* for all spices that they used judiciously and with respect. In addition to adding flavor, parsley was supposed to improve brain power and was believed to be a cure for intoxication, so men wore garlands of parsley when embarking on a drinking bout. Dill seeds were chewed because the Greeks believed this kept them awake and was also a brain stimulant.

The Markets

In ancient Athens, life centered around the marketplace, or *aroga*. Portable booths, probably one for each kind of food, were set up each morning in a long, covered promenade supported by a row of columns. These markets were conveniently located near the government buildings and meeting places. There were no fixed prices so purchasers bargained for wares. The poor carried their coins in their mouths and used baskets for their purchases; the rich, however, had purses and servants to carry their goods. Some middlemen also sold to the public.

People came to the market from single-story homes along narrow, crowded, and refuse-strewn lanes because they had no sewer system as the later Romans did. Even wealthy Greeks had no water supply in their homes.

Poor Athenians ate their porridge of wheat and barley (flavored with salt and honey), barley cakes, beans, peas, lentils, cabbage, onions, figs, and other fruits, and olives. Beans and lentils, the cheapest food they had, were usually eaten in stews. People were fond of sausages and black pudding, which probably was like modern European blood pudding. Even for those of moderate means, the diet was largely vegetarian; however, they had mutton, pork, dog, and dairy foods. Fish and eels, served mostly at festivals, were popular. The well-to-do ate more than the poor of eels, fowl, lamb, pork, wheat bread, fruits, and vegetables.

In the country, the farm people had a regular diet of mutton, goat meat, and fowl. Vegetables were dressed heavily with olive oil, vinegar, sauces, and honey. It took, however, 14 years to mature an olive tree, and one had to be wealthy to wait for his or her own trees to mature. Imported vegetables were considered a luxury but were highly appreciated, as were the home-grown Attican vegetables—cabbage, lentils, peas, onions, and garlic. Mushrooms, lettuce, asparagus, cabbage, beans, radishes, and varieties of leek, onions, turnips, and lentils were eaten in large quantities by all Greeks. Walnuts and almonds came from Persia and Mesopotamia, and beets, citrons, melon, apricots, sesame, geese, and pickled pork were introduced from the East.

Sauces for fish, meat, and game were made from vinegar and wine, seasoned with salt, mustard, garlic and onions, pennyroyal, and marjoram. No pepper was available, and their only sweetener was honey.

A family might have a stew simmered in a pot put over the fire on a tripod and the cauldron containing the stew would be brought to the table like modern cook-and-serve ware. The author is also reminded of seeing, 20 years ago, cooks for a school lunch in Accra, Ghana, cooking in a kettle over a very simple clay stove made of three clay legs under which a small fire was built on the ground. Even now Africans such as the Zulus successfully use such primitive stoves out-of-doors.

Meals

Spartans and Athenians ate lightly; the warm weather and scanty supplies were probably partial explanations for this frugality. Breakfasts were composed mostly of bread dipped in wine with a few olives and figs. The Athenian businessman came home and ate a light lunch, often of fresh or salted fish, ham, or sausage. He usually spent his evenings at home, sometimes with guests coming to dinner around sunset. The Athenian dinner is said to have been for social enjoyment to be eaten without gluttony; to eat alone was "feeding" and not "dining." Greeks wanted only a little of all good foods; it is said that in Homer's day all meals in aristocratic homes were served daintily. But such was Greek hospitality that even male strangers off the street were invited in to dine.

Foods were eaten with the fingers and gravies and sauces were sopped with bread and spoons were used only for soups or purees. No forks or knives were used at first, but later knives were used to cut meat. Wooden bowls and flat scones of maza mostly served as plates, but they did have some terra cotta and metal platters and wooden or metal goblets.

Place of Women

Some have said that women, especially slave-women in wealthy homes, did the cooking. In early ancient Grecian times, women baked their own bread; but later it was baked in bakeries, as were fancy cakes and pastries. Women ground the cereal in a mortar and probably baked bread and made porridge and soups, but men did the "serious" cooking (Jensen).

Women lived and ate by themselves even in a villa, where there were often as many as 50 women including slave girls. Men ate alone in the dining room. Grecian women were expected to run their households and to stay out of sight, enjoying their husband's company only when there were no guests (Bowra). There seems to be disagreement, however, among some writers about whether the women were present at family meals and banquets. Some reports state that women had their own banquets separate from the men. During the Periclean Age, however, women were said to be present only at the male banquets to amuse the men with music, dancing, and seductive charms.

Cooks and Chefs

When pastry cooks began to appear in the fourth century, all professional cooks were highly respected as artisans and were paid higher wages. Some were educated, and a cook was often invited to drink with the guests when he had produced a masterpiece because Greeks considered a new dish as important as a new poem. In Sybaris, cooks were said to be respected more than in Attica, and there the cook who served the best dish at a banquet was crowned on a dias before the crowd.

Tracts on the culinary arts were produced beginning in the fourth century, and twenty cookbooks are said to have been produced in the time of Pericles. Archestratus produced his masterpiece, *Gastrology,* in 350 B.C. after he had traveled widely to gather the recipes, many of which are still in use. Others besides epicurean aristocrats collected recipes, and historians tell us that a law was passed by which a cook could copyright an outstanding recipe so that he got all the profits from its sale for a year during which no one could copy it. In how many modern plays do cooks give out recipes over the footlights, as they did in the old Greek plays?

Banquets

Banquets, which were popular with all Greeks except the Spartans, were given by those who could afford them and were lavish even though other home meals of the same people were simple. A Greek is supposed to have said, "Tomorrow I go back to barley meal and cheese" as we might say "I'll go back to bread and water."

Men ate in reclining positions propped on cushions on couches. It was customary to offer guests basins of water to wash their hands before eating. They had no napkins and guests wiped their hands on pieces of bread which was then thrown on the floor for the dogs.

One cup of herbally infused wine was often served as an apertif. The main course usually contained meat. After this meat course, there might be a course at which hare, kid, doves, partridge, and every imaginable kind of bird might be served. The dessert course was fresh fruit and salted nuts, often almond and sweet meats. Salted cheese might also be served at this course. They used sweet meats and cheese cakes, which were deep-fried pastries holding a soft cheese mixture; other pastries, molded and chilled in snow, might be served in a box. Some so-called cheese cakes had no cheese in them but were made of nuts, fruits, oil, and honey; some were made with sour wine blended with soft cheese, or with a mixture of grated or sieved cheese and mead.

One historian said that, at a wedding feast for 20 guests, a hugh platter was presented to each guest. Each platter contained a roast boar stuffed with thrushes and garnished with egg yolks and oysters or periwinkles. Hippocluchus told of an Athenian friend who presented each guest with a platter containing a whole roast kid.

It is said that a wedding feast might last for days. At a Macedonian wedding feast in 310 B.C., each guest brought a servant to carry home the gifts. The first course of wine was served in silver drinking bowls, which were given as a gift to each guest. The brass Corinthian platters on which were served poultry, ducks, pigeon, or goose were also given to the guests. No one was expected to eat everything, so servants wrapped up the leftovers and carried them home along with the gifts of silverware.

Drinking was controversial in Greece and Plato, whom some called a prig, was not the only one to plead for temperance. In Sparta, a fine was exacted from anyone found drunk even at festivals for Bacchus; drunkenness was forbidden by law, and the Greeks were proud of their fashion of sobriety.

Epicurus, an idol of Athenians, said that boys should not taste wine until they were 18 years of age. After 40 they should relax and enjoy themselves invoking the gods especially Bacchus. He is also quoted as saying "The fountain and root of every good is the pleasure of the stomach."

At the end of a meal, wine was drunk. Then a chairman of the symposium was elected. The word symposium originally meant a drinking party session. This chairman decided how much water would be added to the wine; he probably also decided how much the guests should drink, and he always chose the topic of conversation.

In one elegant picnic in which each guest contributed his share of food and wine (Wason), the food was carried to the picnic in baskets like food for a modern pot-luck dinner. The Greek picnic guests ate more elegantly than modern picnickers do, however, using alabaster dishes and silver bowls. For dessert, they nibbled cheese cakes served in gaily decorated boxes.

After the Golden Age

The downfall of Athens and other Greek cities probably occurred at a time when exports fell off so that money was no longer available for imported food.

Wechsberg says, "The Greeks had more than a word for the art of cooking" and "The Greeks were the first Europeans to have a literature of gastronomy. . . ." He remarked, however, that modern French critics doubt that "the Athenians ever knew great cooking in the French term of the word."

ROME

What the Romans ate was influenced by previous discoveries and the stage of agriculture and animal husbandry.

About 1500 B.C. invaders, who are thought to have come from Central Europe probably through Hungary, knew and used bronze before they established themselves in the Po Valley. This theory is supported by reports that they almost certainly spoke an Indo-European language. They were able to establish villages, and to dominate and absorb the older Neolithic peoples. Archeology was in its infancy in the 1880s when these villages were unearthed and the sites were not dug with the care employed today (Linton). However, Middle-European-type bronze objects and pottery from early Italian cultures of traders and farmers were found.

By 750 B.C. there was a fortified marketplace settlement made up of traders and farmers on the left bank of the Tiber River about 15 miles from its mouth. By 338 B.C. Romans had made themselves masters of the area of Latinum and by 270 B.C. they had conquered the Greek cities in Italy and Sicily and welded the whole southern peninsula into a single confederacy. One group of invaders, the Etruscans, were able to stay, leaving their influence on Roman culture. It is believed that the Etruscans came from Asia Minor around 900 to 800 B.C., probably in search of copper and tin to make their bronze, bringing a civilization with them. The Etruscans, who lived north of the Tiber and copied the artistic forms of the Syrians, Egyptians, and Greek with whom they traded, had a society with marked upper and lower classes. Each city was ruled by priest-kings.

Food Patterns

During the Republic, which lasted almost through the second century B.C., the Romans are said to have cared little for the pleasures of the table. They ate frugally; many were vegetarians and ate their food cold. "So long as the Romans were a race fighting for independence, or to win the mastery over neighbors as poor as themselves, good cheer was unknown among them; their very generals were plough men and lived on vegetables, etc.'' (Brillat-Savarin, 1960).

At this time, food was served and eaten in common crockery and iron, but a silver salt cellar was a prized possession. To be seated above the salt at the table was to be honored, as it was in later times. Table knives and forks were not known, but spoons like those of today were used.

There was little distinction among different classes in what foods were eaten. In the last two centuries of the Republic, these simple ways yielded to luxurious living for the rich, but the poor still lived frugally. This luxury followed successful wars in which fertile lands were conquered and acquired; thus, more food was furnished for all. After imported foods came from Mesopotamia and North Africa, meat became more common; among the upper classes a vegetarian diet came to be despised.

There are better records of what the wealthy ate in the luxury-loving periods than what the poor ate. We do, however, have some records for the diet of the poor. It is said that the principal food of the poor Roman was a thick soup; undoubtedly the thickness varied with the availability of food. With this soup the common person had coarse bread and water. Yet it is claimed that even the poorest had common wine at least to flavor their drinking water but often this wine was diluted eight to one. These people might also have had turnips, olives, beans, figs, and cheese, which were evidently cheap and abundant. During these times, pork was supposedly the only meat and one author said a suckling pig was made to last three days. The people who lived close to the sea also had fish. An ordinary dinner of the poor may have been a meal of salt fish or goat's milk, bread, olive oil, and wine mixed with water (Perl). The more prosperous in Rome had eel and pike from the Tiber and fish brought the 17 miles from the sea by runners. The bread of the poor people, called common, army, or dark, contained much of the husks of the grains and sometimes was probably made entirely of husks. It differed greatly from the fine white bread or even the second grade white bread of the wealthy.

The Roman fondness for food is an historical fact. Balsdon (1969) said, ''Fortunes were squandered on food by men who lived for their palates whom Seneca regarded as the most deplorable spendthrifts.'' In extreme cases, eating led to bankruptcy. It is said that the Romans tried to ape the Greeks, whom they met in travels and wars, but the rich in the Roman Empire became gluttons rather than gourmets, as the Greeks were.

The ostentatious waste of food in a world of want apparently resulted when, with the abolition of the old Roman Republic and the establishment of the Empire, citizens found their sphere of activity very much restricted (Prentice). It was no longer wise to spend money on the ''pleasures of properties,'' and other outlets were denied them. So there was practically nothing on which they could spend their money except costly dwellings and expensive food.

There were probably not more than 200 great houses that could afford the luxurious diet (Root). The inhabitants were not the patricians but the newly rich, who won attention because their feasting was astonishing, extraordinary, and excessive.

During the Empire, Vulgarians (as Seneca called them) were fascinated mostly by gourmadism and boasted about the expense and origins of the dishes they served guests. Some of the emperors, such as Tiberius Caesar, who wrote a cookbook in which he discussed 17 ways to cook suckling pig, were evidently gourmets; some even called Tiberius a "wealthy glutton." He reportedly committed suicide after spending 100 million sesterces on food and having only 10 million left. One wealthy Roman spent 10 million sesterces for one dinner party. Historians say, however, that the cost of a dinner party also included gifts for the guests. One sad note about the dinner parties was that the guests sometimes fought over their gifts, thus frightening the women—often the gifts were *the women*. Atticus, who spent only 3000 sesterces per month on household expense, is reported to have spent 200,000 on one meal at which Pompey and Cicero were entertained. Rare and very expensive fish, one of which Cato said cost as much as a cow, were used at these feasts in the second century A.D. Peacocks costing as much as $10 apiece and wild boars were some of the rare foods served. The peacocks were often garnished with their own feathers after they had been cooked.

The men in power were alarmed by the excesses in food, and from time to time laws intended to curb these excesses were passed. These laws included how much could be spent on food; in one law, the number of guests was limited to five at a dinner party and three for a family meal. Such laws were difficult to enforce; however, soldiers are said to have had the right to enter private houses while a meal was in progress.

Food of Special Groups

What the Roman soldiers ate is difficult to learn in detail. The modern cereal advertisement that the Roman soldiers lived and marched on grain probably has some basis in fact. Caesar remarked during the Gallic campaigns that Roman soldiers regretted it when they had to eat meat instead of grain. Perhaps the meat was often tainted and putrid by the time it could be distributed to the units engaged in warfare (Jensen). Therefore, cattle on the hoof were often taken along by Roman armies.

On the Roman farm, the main meal of the day was eaten at noon, and an early light supper of food left over from noon was served with some raw vegetables or fruits raised on the farm. This may sound familiar to American farm folk.

MEALS

Most historians say that almost all Romans ate a modest breakfast, sometimes only water, or bread dipped in wine, or bread and honey, and these sometimes with cheese and a few olives and raisins. Lunch, called *prandium,* was a light meal of cold meats or eggs, cheese, and fruit with or without wine. The workers as well as the rich ate the meal around noon; the latter then took a siesta and the workers went back to work. The poor are said to have bought their lunch at cookshops where cauldrons of stew, lentils, peas, or beans steamed over the charcoal fires. This food, dipped into little cups by the seller, was eaten on the spot by the workers standing up.

There were servants to do the cooking, serving, and all household duties. During the second century A.D., it was a pauper's household in which the same person had to do the cooking, dusting, and bedmaking. Wealthy households had large kitchen staffs. Cooking was considered an art, and good cooks were ranked with artists. The chefs were said to be one of a wealthy family's prized possessions; a chef cost as much as a horse or, as one author says, even three horses.

Banquets and Dinner Parties

Baldon (1963) said that a dinner party often consisted of three courses: the appetizers, the main course, and the dessert course. Some writers also tell of a fish course separate from the meat course and of another course of savories served after the dessert, as is often done today in Great Britain.

The appetizer course, called *gustus* or *gustatio,* was made up of vegetables and herbs such as lettuce, leek, and mint. With these might be served sliced cooked eggs, snails, or shellfish such as sea urchins or oysters.

The second course was called *cena* and might have three parts, *cena firstus, cena secunda,* and *cena tertia.* Some called this *mensol.* For this course, young kid, fowl (chickens, ducks, pheasant, geese, or pigeons) were popular. Guinea fowls were expensive but valued. Ham cutlets, hare, or fish might be served if the latter was not used as a separate course. Sow's udders and wild boar were sometimes served. Fresh fish, some rare and very expensive, was used, as were oysters, which were as popular then as now. A cheaper salt fish was used also perhaps more by the poor. Elaborate and rich sauces covered the dishes; some say that the Romans had counterparts of many of our modern sauces. For dessert, called *secunda mensa,* apples, pears, grapes, nuts, and figs might be served followed by savories. It is told that many guests had a hard time making a choice among the foods offered and that not everyone tasted everything. A dinner menu of 100 A.D. was said to go from "eggs to apples" as we now say from "soup to nuts."

There are stories of people eating to excess at banquets and then going out to vomit so they could eat more; we read of vomitoria and Seneca wrote "men eat to vomit and vomit to eat." He said that, even though foods were brought from every corner of the earth, guests did not "deign to digest them." Doctors prescribed emetics and abstentious people also took them. Gross overeating and vomiting is not reported to have been typical in daily life of the common people but was indulged in by wealthy dilettantes.

The dining room was an important room in wealthy homes, since the dinner party was the main event in Roman social life. Guests half reclined on couches beside the table. Position on the couches denoted the rank and importance of a guest. When the guests were ushered into the dining room (Johnston), the gods were invoked, a custom much like our saying grace. After the guest had been seated, an attendant removed his shoes; then water and a towel was passed around for the guests to wash their hands. Johnston also wrote that each guest brought his own napkin, which seems strange to us. Trays were used to carry in each course and also to remove dishes. Between courses, the table was wiped with a cloth or sponge after it had been cleared, so tablecloths must not have been used. Guests threw shells of sea food, cherry stones, and apple cores on the floor, and servants cleaned them up.

Wine was used sparingly during meals for guests, but drinks were served afterwards to accompany the entertainment of poetry, music, or conversation. Some guests had drunk heavily before they arrived. It is said that toasts were offered after the banquet, rather than before, as was true in later times. Romans were interested in good wines, and the art of wine making is said to have developed rapidly once it became of serious interest; 121 B.C. during the last century of the Republic was the first vintage year of which we have a record.

Cereals and Breads

In addition to wheat, the Romans had barley, oats, and rye. Probably they found the latter growing on the farms of the middle or northern European barbarians, whom they met in their efforts to extend their Empire. Rye and barley, however, were not much used. Romans also learned from these barbarians to cultivate new kinds of wheat and oats.

In earliest times, the cereals were pounded in a mortar with a pestle, with the resulting meal mixed with water and cooked into a porridge called *puls*. This dish was long remembered as a national dish, as is the oatmeal porridge of Scotland. Later the wheat and water mixture was made into flat loaves of bread baked in front of a fire.

Mills for grinding the grain gradually developed. An excavated Pompeian bakery shows several hand-turned mills, probably used by the baker to prepare his own flour. Much of the grain came from Egypt and North Africa. Nearly 1.5 million bushels were said to have been imported from Africa in one year. The exact date of the first use of ovens, either in the home or in a bakery, is not known, but in 171 B.C. there were professional bakers who were organized into a guild with a president. Before 164 B.C. the mother baked the family's bread at home. Only the very wealthy families who had servants used their own ovens, but the farm housewife was said to have baked her own bread.

Bread was so basic in the Roman diet that the word became synonymous with the word food, as it is in the Bible. It is reported that at one time as many as 62 kinds of bread were baked by the Romans. In the "latter days of the Empire, Rome was weaker and the supply of grain could no longer be depended upon" (Prentice), but it was still true that grain was the staff of life.

There are records of bread instead of grain being doled out to the poor as early as the latter part of the first century and during the early part of the second century A.D.

The fine wheat flour for the best bread was produced by the use of fine sieves in the milling process. "People preferred fine white bread though then as now they considered whole wheat bread more nutritious" (Johnston). Some say that it was not, however, the fine-grained white bread as we know it.

Cakes, pastry, cookies, and confectionery also were made and sold by the bakers.

Specimens of buns with crosses on them as well as charred loaves of bread of a variety probably dating back to 1800 B.C. have been found in the ruins of Pompeii.

Use of Other Foods

The Romans used dairy products such as milk, cream, curds, whey, and cheese freely. They drank and made cheese from the milk of the cow, sheep, and goat. They occasionally used butter as salve, but olive oil was their chief edible fat; later they learned to use butter as food from the Northern Europeans, who salted their butter to keep it fresh.

It is said that the Roman meat shops, which closely resembled many in Europe today, were sanitary and that police patrolled to watch over the sale of meat, exacting fines and ordering the spoiled meat thrown into the Tiber. They had mastered the technique of boning beef, lamb, veal, and pork. They sold retail and wholesale cuts of meat similar to those of today.

These butchers and meat chefs (Jensen) prepared and used cracklings, bacon, tenderloins, oxtails, pigs feet, salt pork bellies, loins, kidneys, shoulders, liver, and lungs. They had fig-fed hogs from which they made many varieties of pork sausages as well as meat balls. They used steaks, chops, and roasts. Because the meat dealers lacked refrigeration, poultry was easier to sell than beef or pork.

Johnston and others have said that honey as well as sweet fruits such as dates were used as sweetening and that sugar was unknown. However, this point has been disputed by some writers. Jensen claimed the Romans did get sugar from India and that their word "saccharum" refers to sugar. Aykroyd said that there are some vague references to sugar in the literature of classical Greece and Rome. He also said that "Pliny, the Elder, had heard of 'honey from reeds' which is not surprising since Rome was in contact with India and Indian sugar had reached markets on the coast of the Red Sea as an article of commerce." However, he considered Pliny "not well informed" about sugar because he said it was used only in medicine. Galen commented that "it" was not as sweet as honey so he must have tasted sugar. Apparently not until the sixth century A.D. did much sugar move westward from India into the Mediterranean area and Rome.

The Romans had many of our common vegetables; among them were lettuce, cucumbers, beets, cabbage, turnips, and radishes; asparagus is said to have been a favorite. Apples, pears, peaches, grapes, mulberries, and raspberries were used.

Roman beverages consisted of water, milk, cider, and wine; the latter was drunk by all classes. It was considered by some peole as uncivilized to drink wine and only the most dissipated were reputed to do so. Often it was diluted 8 to 1 with water. Ordinary wine sold for a few cents a quart, but choice wines were expensive.

Wine was made primarily from grapes. A drink called mulsum was made of four parts of wine and one of honey. When fermented, it was called mulsa. Cider was made from apples. Tea, coffee, and cocoa were unknown.

Salt was obtained first by evaporating sea water but later it was mined. The government maintained a monopoly on this industry, so the price was kept low. When more was made than was needed, it was exported, and some fortunes are said to have been founded on this trade. Our word *salt* comes from the Latin word for salary, *salarium,* because Roman soldiers for a time were paid in salt.

Sources of Foods

Fine wheat is said to have come from Etruria as well as from Egypt; milk and cheese, from Tuscany; wine, from Campania; game, from the Laurentine forests; olive oil, rabbits, pickles, and more wine, from Spain; apricots, from Armenia. Peaches and apples came from Persia; pears and dates, from Chios; pomegranates, from Libya; plums, from Damascus; quince, from Sidon; cherries, from Pontius. Pheasants were brought in from Greece; guinea fowl, from Africa; and from Gaul came pork sausage and venison. Scotland, China, India, Africa, the Near East, and Arabia also traded and furnished the Romans with food.

The Roman Kitchen and Equipment

Liversidge, writing in Rosenbaum's 1958 revision of the Apicius Cookbook, said that we know more of the kitchens of Pompeii than about other Roman kitchens. Several of them have been unearthed from under the lava thrown out by the 70 A.D. eruption of Mount Vesuvius. She described the hearth as the most recognizable feature; the raised masonry platform was faced on top with tiles. Much of the cooking in one Pompeian home that has been excavated and studied was evidently done in the hearth on small iron tripods and gridirons over burning charcoal. In the hearth of that kitchen the cooking pots were found still standing on the tripods. Ovens, constructed of rubble and tile, shaped like low beehives and provided with a flue in front furnishing a draught, have been found. As in hearth ovens of later times, the stony interior was heated with an active fire that was scraped out before the food was put in to be baked. Charred loaves of bread almost 1900 years old were preserved in the volcanic ash and only relatively recently excavated. A stove was discovered also in which a low iron frame with a cement hearth could have been used for either wood or charcoal.

Possibly wood was burned on the raised hearth, with the smoke escaping through a vent in the kitchen wall. Sausages or suckling pig were hung on a well-placed hook over the fire to smoke, according to Apicius.

Collections of kitchen equipment from various military sites as well as in Pompeii include gridirons and cooking vessels of various shapes and sizes; all these show evidence of hard usage and of having been burned (Liversidge).

Roman utensils were amazingly modern in appearance (Wason). For mincing herbs, meat, or vegetables they had a crescent shape blade attached to a wooden handle. The Romans also had strainers and colanders of many sizes and shapes, a device to deshell shrimps, and a small spoon to remove snails from their shells. When the food was dished up, it was put on a circular plate or dish. Large platters and shallow bowls of silver, bronze, and pottery have been found, but it is also thought that some fine pottery was used in the Roman dining rooms.

Cookbooks

Apicius, who is sometimes called the Fannie Farmer of Rome and was referred to by his countrymen as the uncrowned king of the culinary world, wrote what has remained probably the most famous Roman cookbook. It is called *Romanae Artis Coquinariae Leber* (The Roman Cookery Book); it was translated into English and printed again in London in 1958 by two authors who meant it to be a real cookbook and not just another history of Roman foods. They tested the recipes and tried to write them for modern usage. Apicius was a rich merchant who gathered information about food wherever he traveled. He is credited with inventing new ways to handle food, such as spraying his lettuce with mead the night before he picked it, so he thought it tasted like "green cheese cakes." He is also credited with having devised a way to store oysters in pitch or in vinegar to keep them fresh. He knew how to keep certain fresh vegetables green by cooking them in copper pans with soda added. He sweetened salt meat or fish by boiling it in milk and even used sour vinegar dressing to keep vegetable foods "safe" from causing food poisoning.

Restaurants and Inns

"There were no public dining places in Rome that came anywhere near meeting the lavish standards of the aristocracy," according to Perl. She said that the better restaurants did, however, send vendors to the public baths with trays of sausages, eggs, and sweet cakes for sale "to the people who frequented the special rooms for recreation and relaxation." She also said that "the inns and restaurants were crude and dirty."

Was Food a Cause of the Decline of the Empire?

Jensen attributed the failure of the great cities and their trade after 250 A.D. to the poverty that descended on city dwellers and country people alike. He believed, as some others also have written, that decline in fecundity due to the lack of proper food was not the main cause of the failure of the Roman economy. Rather, the Germanic and Gothic hordes, when they invaded the classical world, precipitated the Dark Ages because of the breakup of political unity.

It has been said that the food supply of Ancient Rome was often critically low. Because people were crowded at the foot of the capital, feeding them was often one of the most critical problems faced by the magistrates. As frequently seen in modern poverty areas in great cities, the maintenance of order was closely connected with the food supply. Hordes of poverty-stricken freedmen, former farmers, were in trouble because imported foods sold below the prices they could match when they raised these foods—which sounds very similar to a modern problem.

Because many of the references for this chapter have also been cited in Chapter 3, a general bibliography for Chapters 2 and 3 is found on page 94.

STUDY QUESTIONS

1. How different are the findings from archeological expeditions when botanists, cereal chemists, and geologists accompany the French or German-oriented archeologists?
2. What conditions were necessary for the beginnings of agriculture?
3. What events led people to have time or desire to develop the arts that included more attention to their choice among foods?
4. How did the Greek and Roman diets differ in general? What were the underlying reasons for this?
5. What are the principal foods in the United States that came from Mesopotamia? India? China?

TOPICS FOR INDIVIDUAL INVESTIGATION

1. Compare the diets of the peasant in Egypt and in Greece.
2. Trace the development of the culture of modern United States wheat and show how important changes took place.
3. Investigate the growth of the cultivation of rice as a major world's cereal.
4. The efforts of people to assure a safe food supply were crucial to their survival. How did people guard their food supply in pre-Christian times?
5. Compare the productivity of early gardens and fields with modern United States yields. Give proof of the efficacy of people's efforts in this area to control their environment.

For references, see page 94 after Chapter 3.

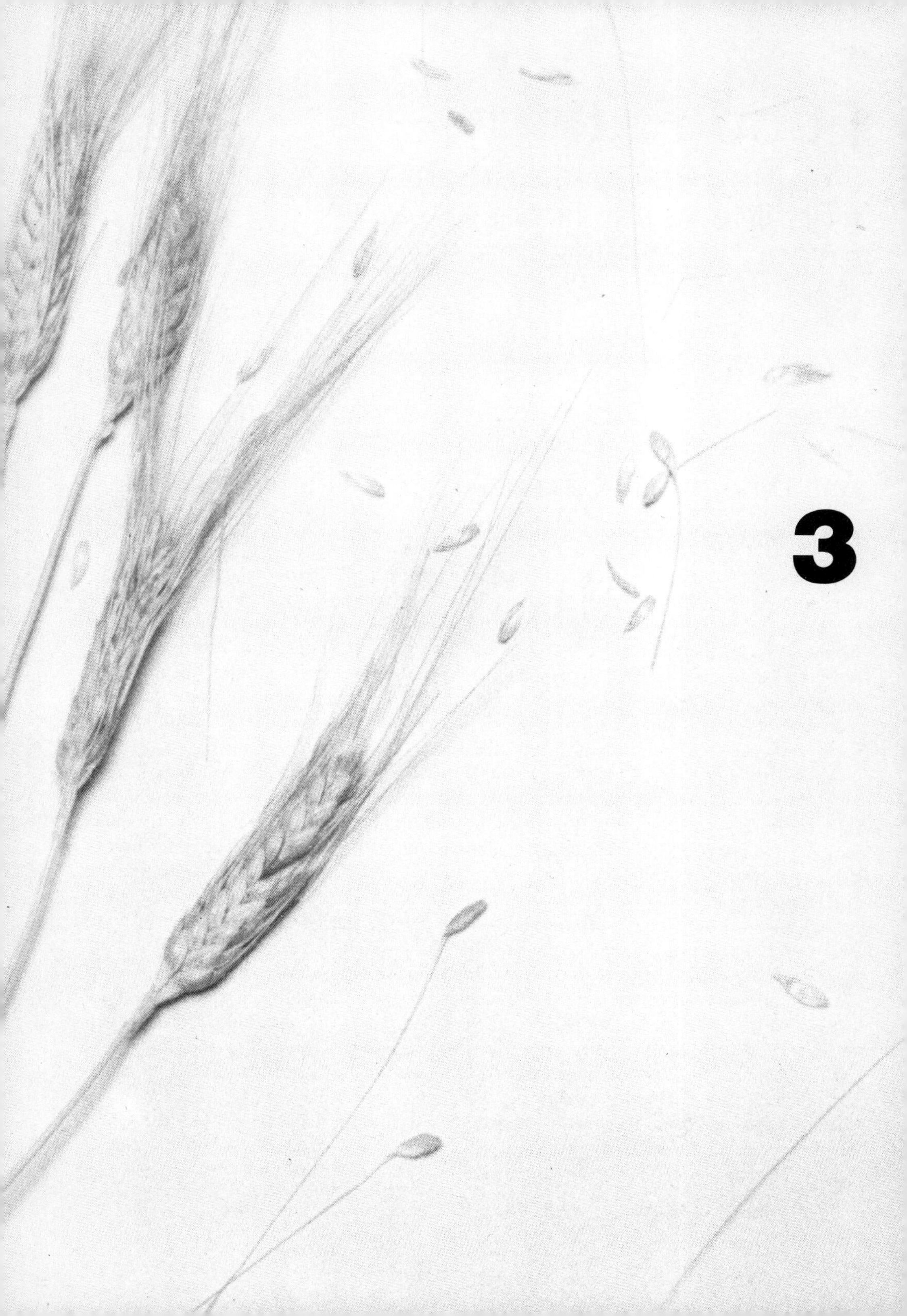

3

Food Patterns—
Origins and Development from Medieval Times through the 19th Century

MEDIEVAL TIMES IN EUROPE

Early Middle Ages

After the last western Roman emperor left his throne in 476 A.D., many northern peoples came south and took control, bringing in an immense new vitality. The entire Mediterranean world underwent a profound transformation at this time. Once vigorous Roman-controlled cities became ghost cities from which the population had fled. As the powerful landowners resisted the nomadic Germanic hordes, they withdrew behind high walls where, with their newly assembled armies and attendants, they resisted tax collectors. For about 300 years, the invading hordes lived their nomadic life while a self-sufficiency necessarily developed within the walled fortresses.

Charlemagne became the King of the Franks and the Lombards in 774 A.D. The new creative upsurge that had been at work during previous centuries was apparent also in agricultural technology. Food production increased beyond the levels of the Romans and was the result of some important inventions and new technology. The Slavs used a new plow with wheels, a colter, a plowshare, and a mold board that cut deeply into the soil, turning it into ridges and furrows. This plow was a great improvement over the old scratch plow of the Romans. Because few individual farmers could afford one of these plows and the oxen to pull one, villagers shared their equipment.

Between 476 and the eleventh century A.D., the peasants throughout Europe became firmly attached to the soil, even though they had infinitely diverse agrarian practices. Councils were necessary to make their systems work. At this time, from a dozen to several hundred families, later each with separate farms, clustered together in villages for their mutual benefit. There were only a few separate farms outside of these villages. In twentieth-century Germany, there still exist many such villages.

At about this time, the three-field system, one for autumn planting, one for spring planting, and one for fallow, replaced the Roman two-field system, which had included only one for planting and one for fallow. With increased productions of food, new prosperity came. The new technology, however, was more adapted to use in Northern fields than it was in the Mediterranean food-producing areas.

Along with these innovations came greater use of water-driven mills to grind grains. The pagan Nordic peoples who worshipped Odin credited poor farm production to supernatural forces and resisted man's use of water power in milling grains. The Christian priests persisted at length in their efforts to Christianize these peoples and to persuade them that "The mill makes your bread and bread is Christ." In due time, the lords of the manors succeeded in making a regulation that all grain must be ground at the mill and not at home, thus claiming one-third of the flour as their due. This practice was one cause of the peasants' wars.

Around 1000 A.D. the horse shoe and the horse collar, invented in Siberia and Central Asia, came to Europe; the more energetic horse replaced the slower ox as the draft animal.

In the twelfth century, the Dutch windmill provided additional energy for the farmer. During the High Middle Ages, 1050–1300 A.D. (a classification devised to aid historians), the economies in many places were improving, and human labor was augmented by mechanical devices and animal power. Of course, many peasants still remained on the subsistence level; one year of bad weather could ruin a farmer.

During the previous ninth and tenth centuries, when the Vikings were invading Europe, feudalism began in France as the loyal warriors clustered about their kings, counts, bishops, or abbots. Here as elsewhere in Europe, the manors became political, legal, and economic units; one lord might rule from his manor over one or several villages. Some villagers were bound as slaves to the lord of the manor.

At first, the fields were open and unfenced and farmed in common. Each peasant, however, usually had his own garden, orchard, and a place for fowls as well as a field for pasturing work animals; wooded areas were also kept as a source of fuel and building materials. One stream for fishing, a water mill for grinding grain, and a bakery to bake bread were used in common by all the villagers.

By the eleventh century, most village communities were organized as parishes with a village church and a priest from the peasant class. This village community formed a closed system which did not provide much contact with the outside world, nor did it promote the development of a vigorous commercial life or lay the foundation for a significant urban population. The only markets were those which handled the surplus grain of the farmers. At this time, peasants were also beginning to have fields of their own.

High Middle Ages

During the High Middle Ages with the expanding markets, improved agriculture, and therefore an increase in surplus grain, the village system eroded; the uneventful, tradition-bound, circumscribed, and narrow horizons gave way to a different kind of life. The holdings of the lords known as *demesne* comprised one-fourth to one-third of the available land. The rest belonged to peasants whose holdings, really intermixed with those of the lord, were known as *tenements*. The lords by strong custom were prevented from exploiting the peasants; the latter were not chattel slaves. Expansion of arable land occurred when primeval forests were reduced to isolated patches. Swamps and marshes were drained, and many new areas were opened for cultivation.

A new age dawned rather gradually and unevenly, with a great cultural awakening and new creative energy, during the eleventh, twelfth, and thirteenth centuries. Innovations of this time—the three-field system, the new plow, the use of the horse alone and in tandem, and the water mills and windmills—caused increased production of food and a great commercial revival. With these changes, there was a general awakening of urban life; towns became the foci of this reinvigorated culture. Commerce also thrived along some seacoasts. The population, however, as far as numbers were concerned, remained mainly agrarian because the surplus grain was still the wealth to be traded for foreign goods.

The tillers of the land were chiefly freemen, and even the serfs, though legally under the lords, were not slaves. The lords on the continent, who now did not have enough dependent laborers, leased their lands.

By 1050, England and Germany were well organized into comparatively stable kingdoms. The French monarchy, still weak, took another century to dominate France. Normandy, Flanders, and Anjou were moving toward coherence. Hungary, Poland, and the Scandinavian world had become Christianized. In 1095, Pope Urban II summoned the European nobility to take up the cross and rescue the Holy Land from the Moslems. So the Crusades, prompted by religious fervor and also probably by greed and stubborn wills, were launched. Their cause was greatly promoted in the summer of 1099 by the successful siege of Jerusalem under the knights of the First Crusade. No further crusade enjoyed such success, and in 1157 Jerusalem again fell to the Moslems. The impact of the returning crusaders on the people's food patterns is described later.

Late Middle Ages

About the year 1300, at the end of the High Middle Ages, Europe suffered a depression resulting from debilitating wars that had brought about a decline in population among the rebellious peasants. These following few centuries are known as the Late Middle Ages. The economic boom had ended. The Black Death (the Plague), 1348–1349, which caused a death toll of one-fourth to one-third of the people of Europe during the mid-fourteenth century, certainly accounted for much of the decline in the population, which in turn caused contracting markets, economic slump, and deepening social antagonisms. Northern Italy suffered less than other parts of Europe, thus accounting for the agricultural period of prosperity in Lombardy and Tuscany. Some people remained wealthy and some nobles were able to hold their land, but serfdom had almost disappeared. Fields were abandoned; landless people wandered about. Eastern European peasants suffered even more than those in the West. Western monarchies began to curb the powers of the landed aristocracy. The Tudor monarchy of England initiated the giving of favor to the mercantile class. By 1789, France had not yet passed beyond the stage of tenth-century agriculture. It had had eight famines and a short crop in 1788, which was one cause of the revolution. Heavy taxation in France also contributed to the misery of the common people.

Food Patterns

In Italy, which remained more affluent than most European countries, Italian cooks had gained fame; Catherine de Medici took her Italian cook to France with her when she left Italy. Splendid banquets and gargantuan feasts staggered the imagination (Wason).

During the thirteenth century, cloth tablecloths came into use; it was then acceptable to wipe one's fingers on the edges. The tablecloth had to be changed several times during a feast. At the time of Louis VII of France and as late as the fifteenth century, rushes were strewn thickly on the floor to absorb grease.

It became fashionable for knights and ladies to eat together; previously they had been seated on separate sides of the room. They now drank from the same cup and ate from the same trencher, which was sometimes a piece of hollowed-out bread. Some pewter trenchers, however, were used. There were no forks or spoons at the time. A knight wishing to place a piece of meat in his lady's mouth might pick it up with his fingers, his pocket knife, or a short dagger.

During the late fifteenth century, there was a general economic upsurge following the long depression, during which technical progress had not ceased. Advances in ship design and navigation made possible longer Atlantic sea voyages. In 1500, Europe experienced the full impact of the introduction of printing. It was then possible to publish the maps needed for exploring new regions. Cookbooks and Bibles were the first books printed. Ideas about food subsequently spread.

Because commerce again thrived, the population of Europe grew, although somewhat slowly. England, France, and Spain now had stabilized governments. European ships had reached America and India. There were probably no great increases in population in Europe over the long period of the Middle Ages until around 1650. Famines and the great pandemic bubonic plague, as well as wars of conquest and intertribal wars, kept the population in check. Death rates were high, and infanticide and abortion were probably common in some groups. Low birth rates probably were also now a basic cause of the stabilization of the population.

Later, advances in medicine and sanitation came into being, along with systems of law and order. Per capita income increased; and as production increased, there was greater interdependence; one family no longer had to sustain itself alone. All of these were basic reasons for the later increasing rate of population growth.

In 1000 A.D. when the population was widely scattered, transportation was underdeveloped, difficult, and expensive. People ate only what was produced in their immediate neighborhood. At this time, diets probably differed from region to region. In eleventh-century London, there was said to be little food on the table which was not produced in England, most of it coming from a few miles away. At this time, 90 percent of the food was consumed by the family that produced it.

Age of Explorations

No other age in history has seen such an increase in knowledge as the age of explorations. This knowledge greatly affected the food patterns of peoples over the period from 1420–1620. Europeans, interested for various reasons, now learned that all seas were one, a fact fundamental to undertaking long sea voyages. They also gained confidence in sailing the oceans when they realized that seamen, given adequate ships and stores, skill, and outstanding courage, could reach any country in the world that had a seacoast and that at least some of the sailors could return home. On some of these voyages, the return of 50 percent of the seamen was counted as a successful voyage. With all this unprecedented increase in knowledge of the planet, much was yet to be learned about how to deal with and conquer illness and malnutrition (often scurvy on the long voyages), tempests, unmarked shoals in unmarked seas, cannibals, and constant uncertainties. Travel was not new to the world, but the systematic organization of the knowledge of it and the rapid improvement of maritime techniques were.

Why did people undertake these voyages? First of all, there was the desire for wealth and a desire to acquire rich new lands. In addition, life at home was hard and uncertain; life expectancy was only 30 years. In some cases, more farmers died of plague than sailors died of scurvy. The pay for the seaman on the government-financed voyages was frequently higher than pay at home. The captains often had a great crusading zeal and a desire for glory. They did not, however, become rich. Great profits were realized only by administrators and the later conquistadores. These captains endured many hazards, one of which was mutiny.

Why did Europeans become explorers? There were probably a number of reasons. First, there were available ambitious captains and skilled, adventuresome crewmen, both of whom felt the pressure of material needs. Europe possessed the needed technology; the people were psychologically distinguished by an individualism that promoted action. European living standards were higher now than in much of the then-known world, and Europeans aspired to become rich. "Institutionally, Europe was a densely packed mosaic of thriving, thrusting, independent states, jealous of one another and determined not to be left behind in any race for power and wealth. Where Portugal led, Spain was bound to follow, France to envy, England to intervene" (Hale). In addition, European Christians had "a militant and expansionist religion that in practice allowed as much scope for profit as for the prophets."

Two distinct traditions of European shipbuilding gave these explorers a distinct advantage. The stout, broad, square-sailed trader of the North Sea and Atlantic Coast was combined with the oared galleys and lanteen-rigged, coast-going vessels of the Mediterranean. Increased trade by the Europeans led them to know about both kinds of ships and use them to advantage. These ships were more adapted to long strenuous voyages than, for instance, the open boats of the Norsemen or the Polynesian boats that depended on wind and currents. In addition, European ships were armed with guns firing fore and aft and some of which could fire from the portholes cut in the side of their ships.

At this time, Southern Europe was in need of metal to make coins, since their own sources were insufficient to keep up with the demands. Furthermore, the unappetizing

European food was another strong motivation for these people to risk so much and for governments to put forth finances for the explorations to find spices to cover the flavor of the food. The meat available during the long winter months was spoiled and generally unpalatable. Spices were the only substances that could cover the foul flavor. Some people, as for instance the English, used onions, garlic, and native herbs, but pepper covered the flavor more effectively. After Constantinople fell to the Turks in 1453, the Turks, Moors, and Arabs were exacting impossible tribute from the overland caravans that had been bringing spices from India and Southeast Asia. So the finding of a sea route as short as possible was necessary.

The less advanced tribes of the West Indies and of Brazil offered the least resistance to European domination. Even though the Iroquois Indians in North America were good hunters and strong in their political organization, they could not cope with the quick-thinking and clever invaders. The weapons of the Yucatan and Guatemalan Mayan were far inferior to their advanced agriculture, their organization, and urbanization; the people of these countries had also been weakened by civil wars. The Aztecs and Incas also proved vulnerable to the invading Spaniards. So what the Europeans decided to do, they were able to accomplish.

Scurvy on the long voyages was one of the greatest deterrents to success in these early explorations. This is discussed on pages 151–154. Various nations have throughout history learned to use different foods to prevent scurvy. Citrus fruits were used in England and other countries. The Saracens taught the crusaders to use a brew of the leaf of a tree, Norwegians used sauerkraut, Eskimos used a brew of the newly emerged leaves of trees, especially the willow, which has been and is now used by other groups. A brew of pine needles has been used for centuries by Laplanders.

The explorations had a marked effect on agriculture all over the world because of the exchange of plants from one country to another. Thus, more crops were made available to be raised in a give locality.

Aftermath of the Explorations

Several factors caused a great upsurge in the world's population after the explorations (Bennett). They were:

1. Dispersion of plants and animals.
2. Inventions and innovations in every line of economic effort.
3. Savings and investment of capital.
4. Division of labor or economic specialization.
5. Growth of exchange that accompanied this division of labor and specialization.
6. Expansion of facilities for transport more efficient than the backs of people and animals and crude carts.
7. Widening use of crop rotation.

This economic advancement was most readily apparent after 1750, although more than one aspect of it emerged earlier.

European Foods

Lester Brown said that "Christopher Columbus is not customarily credited with a major role in expanding the earth's food producing capacity, but his contribution was profoundly important. He joined like systems of agriculture of the old and new world which had evolved separately."

When the Moslems from Arabia, Asia Minor, Persia, Syria, and Egypt invaded the Iberian peninsula during the seventh and eighth centuries, they brought in many new foods. Also, a diffusion into Europe of foods from China, India, and Western Asia resulted from the emigration of these people to other countries. Sugar cane and rice were two of the principal foods, but the invaders also brought figs, dates, almonds, mulberries, pomegranates, lemons, citron, and bitter oranges. The sweet oranges came from China in the late 1400s. When the Phoenicians had sailed to Spain in the twelfth century B.C., they brought garbanzo beans, which became a staple of the Spanish diet. The Spanish conquistadores brought these beans to Florida and New Mexico. Olives and olive oil also were taken from the Mediterranean. From the Greek colonists and the Roman conquerors, the Spanish had learned to make wine; from the Germanic tribes, they learned to keep this wine in wooden kegs.

The Moslems had green thumbs; they knew about irrigation, crop rotation, and fertilizing the soil. They had skill in grafting fruit trees, and they loved gardens and orchards.

Columbus brought chocolate, vanilla, tomatoes, pimentos, pineapples, white and sweet potatoes, maize, varieties of squash, turkey, and tobacco back with him from America. The Spanish in turn took sheep, pigs, chickens, wheat, sugar cane, citrus fruits, apricots, peaches, grapes, olives, and other fruits and vegetables to America.

Many foods have come to us in the United States from Europe, some dating from medieval times and some from more ancient times. Young children may when they are older be surprised that the idea of hamburgers and frankfurters came from overseas. Even baked beans, now considered such a real part of the foods of New England, came to us from a probable origin in North Africa when Jews there baked a pot of beans in the ground for Saturday's food, a day when strict Jews do not cook. Of course we have made our own variations of the original recipes.

As we look at the loaded shelves of many kinds of yogurt in a modern supermarket we may remember its origin. In the warm Near Eastern countries this form of milk had a real reason for being soured.

The modern barbecuing meat on a stick can be traced to cooking *shish kebabs* in Turkey or meat marinated in a soy sauce called *satay* in Indonesia.

Did the smorgasbord of Scandinavia with many foods served in one meal affect the "covering the table cloth" by the Pennsylvania Dutch who of course brought their food patterns from their native Germany?

The serious student will be interested in tracing the reason for the popular rijsttafel (rice table) among restaurants in the Netherlands and why one finds Algerian restaurants in France.

Also interesting are the variations of the so-called Oriental foods in Thailand, Indonesia, Philippines, Korea, and Japan as well as from the different regions of China.

Thin breads such as crepes in France, tortillas in Mexico, chaputis in India, blintzes in Jewish communities, and thin pancakes in Scandinavia may have had a common origin of fuel scarcity.

Because the limitations of this book prevent us from discussing in depth the foods of many countries, we have chosen to discuss in some detail the foods of Britain through its history, cultural, social, economic, and technological development.

Eating Utensils

In 1662, when Catherine Braganzo became the bride of Charles Stuart, King of England, bowls and trenchers were still used to hold mounds of food, and thick liquids were drunk from mugs or tankards. These utensils used by the common people were made from porous earthenware. Burlwood or stitched leather, pewter, silver, or very rarely fragile china was used by the wealthy. Forks were still scarce and a curiosity in England so that guests had to bring their own when they came to dine.

Sweets

Honey was the basic sweetening for centuries in Europe, as it had been in Egyptian, Grecian, and Roman times. Until the sixteenth century, sugar was a luxury in France as well as in England. Although sugar had been imported, possibly from India, into the Middle East around 300 B.C., it reached Europe much later. It is said that colonists took the European honeybee to America in the seventeenth century.

Spices and Herbs

Undoubtedly the search for strong flavorings to make spoiled meat palatable sent people searching for wild herbs and led to the domesticaton of herbs. Angelica, basil, bay, chervil, chives, dill, fennel, juniper berries, marjoram, and mint were known to have been used. Black and white mustard seeds, pennyroyal, winter and summer savory, sorrel, tansy, tarragon, parsley, sage, rosemary, and thyme extended the list of medieval herbs. The spices of the East had been found to be better than native herbs for covering the flavor of spoiled meat. As has been said, pepper was especially effective for this purpose, but cloves, ginger root, nutmeg, mace, cinnamon, turmeric, cardamom, and coriander also were used. So the Eastern spices became desirable and were often more precious than gold or gemstones.

As is well known, Columbus was looking for the Spice Islands when he landed in the New World. Perhaps less well known is the fact that Vasco da Gama's spice cargo on his return around the Cape of Good Hope from his second trip to the lands of spices was worth 60 times what it cost to outfit his 13 vessels.

Of course Columbus could not know that the American food, maize, would be worth more as a crop someday than the gold and spices he sought.

Marco Polo had, over a period of 20 years, told of fortunes that could be had in Java by obtaining their peppercorns, nutmegs, and cloves. Ever since the Crusades, Europe had received only a trickle of spices from the Orient. By the time it got to Europe, pepper reached 40 times its original purchase price, and one pound of cloves was worth as much as one cow.

The contrast of the medieval search for and use of spices is interesting in comparison with what we now use. In 1968, according to statistics from the International Trade Center in Geneva, Switzerland, 178,560 metric tons of spices were imported by the U.S., Canada, West Germany, France, Italy, Netherlands, Belgium, Great Britain, Switzerland, and Japan—nations that import more spices than other countries.

The United States spice industry alone has in 1977 become a $500 million business. This included 300 million pounds imported of the 450 million pounds consumed annually.

When it is remembered that the unpopular "spoiled" flavor of meat was basic to the desire for spices, it becomes interesting to note that the American Spice Association reported in 1977 that the largest single customer of spices was the meat industry. Even with adequate methods of preservation of meat modern people apparently like their meat spicy, especially their sausages.

The Rich and the Poor

There was always a vast difference between what the poor and the wealthy people ate. Mush, flat cakes, or leavened bread for the poor were always made from coarse grains, often with additions of the ubiquitous peas and beans. The grain for the rich was always whiter and finer. The poor thus probably profited by having bread from which less nutrients had been removed. Great contrasts between the monotonous and meager diet of the poor and the unbelievable extravagances in food and drink of the wealthy may be traced through all times, probably even more so before modern times.

Famines

A famine differs from a period of scarcity of food in several ways. A famine is usually agreed to be a general, acute, and extreme shortage of food within a region, which is not relieved by supplies of food being sent in because of inadequate distribution. Famines cause deaths from starvation and diseases that follow the extreme shortage of food, calories, and nutrients. Infections readily take their toll under these circumstances.

Bennett said that famines, which were always localized, usually lasted a year; only occasionally were they longer. They were most frequently caused by the vagaries of weather, by insects such as locusts, or by plant diseases such as the fungus that caused the 1845 potato famine in Ireland. Devastating wars were also contributing causes of famines.

The European famine of 1315 stretched over an unusually wide geographic range from the British Isles to the North Pyrenees and the Alps and eastward to the Russian border. In upper Flanders, burials rose by 33 percent in one month and 60 percent in three months, falling by 85 percent during the first week after the new crop was harvested. During the eleventh and twelfth centuries in England, a famine was recorded on the average every 14 years.

Such famines should not and do not usually occur now because the seas, open to traffic, permit food to be shipped; most governments now permit the passage of food. We cannot, however, forget the relatively recent Biafra and Sahel disasters. The network of other means of transportation also is another way in which the medieval type of famine has, in recent years, been prevented. Western Europe is no longer dependent on local food products; heavy industrialization, economic reserves, and credits are now also deterrents to medieval-type famines.

Medieval attempts to prevent famines were inadequate, but they must have warded off some hunger. For example, farmers planted rye and wheat in the same field because wheat grows better than rye in wet weather and rye grows better than wheat in dry weather. Also, monasteries kept stores of food and fed the people in the area as much as they could and as long as their food lasted.

The Potato Famine (1845) in Ireland

In 1845 and 1846, Ireland had a universal failure of its potato crop. The potato disease attacked the growing and thriving green plants without warning and before the tubers could be harvested, they had begun to rot. Even the potatoes gathered previously, rotted before use. The consequences are well known and cannot be detailed here; for those seeking more information, Salaman (1970) gives a detailed description of this famine. Also well known is the fact that the Irish came to America in large numbers as a result of this disaster, and by 1850 Ireland had replaced England as the chief source of settlers. The Irish represented 44 percent of the foreign-born in the United States between 1820 and 1920, when 4.25 million people left Ireland to come to the United States.

Britain: Backgrounds for Food Patterns

In medieval times, there were two kinds of cultivated lands in England. One included the lands belonging to the great manors. These lands were the first to be cultivated by the serfs who then farmed their own plots, although they lived in villages under a primitive communal system. A century later, the villagers had common fields, which proved disadvantageous because the individual farmers had less incentive to farm efficiently than when the land belonged solely to them.

The manors had their own gardens, orchards, and vineyards, and considerable numbers of draft animals, cows, sheep, pigs, and poultry were kept. The villagers usually had an ox, a cow, pigs, a few sheep, and poultry of their own.

Britain is even now a young country compared with many others. Osborne said, "4000 years before Britain's inhabitants emerged from tribal chaos, the Egyptians had reared an empire along the Nile." He also reminds us that "When Christ died for a world already surfeited with vanished civilizations, head hunting was still a practice among the island's [England's] tribesmen," and "Fifteen centuries of the Christian era had passed before England fully acquired the qualities of a nation and began to reach for world power." Yet the British character began to take shape long before Britain as a nation existed.

The first Stone Age tribesmen who had come from Europe were adept at farming and animal husbandry and knew how to use copper and bronze. Later, the Celts who came from east of the Rhine River brought fine metal crafts as well as their proclivity to war with other tribes. Imperial Rome as ruler of Britain for three and one-half centuries left little except the site of London and fine roads. The invading Norsemen and Normans in turn gave names and essential characteristics to the people. The Angles, Saxons, who are usually grouped together as Anglo-Saxons, and the less numerous Jutes from Germany and Denmark, gave England its name. They had, before they came, been noted for their farming, their loyalties to rural life, and their tender regard for women while the men were still savage warriors. These later people who had first raided the coast of England came in to settle after Rome collapsed around 450 B.C.

During the sixteenth century, a depression occurred (Drummond). There were several causes: Many farmers had taken up raising sheep for wool at the expense of raising food crops; coinage was debased, raising the price of food and resulting in unemployment; and the government was unstable. Progressive Tudor landowners began paying more attention to manuring for the main crops of wheat, barley, rye, beans, and vetch. In the gardens, the greatest change occurred when the 1568–1572 terror drove the Flemish to England to resettle. These excellent gardeners brought their knowledge and skill with them. The productivity of modern English gardens for vegetables and flowers is said to have dated from this time. Also about this time, with the dispersal of the monasteries, the vineyards disappeared. Now the lords drank ale, cider, and every kind of mead. Some had the wines of France and the Rhineland. Both the villagers and those in the manors brewed beer and ale from barley, wheat, and oats.

The government began protecting the consumer as early as 1319, when the mayors and their officers visited meat shops to watch for abuses. When prices of grain (called corn in England) rose about 1390, the civil authorities bought quantities of grain for the poor and held large reserves in granaries. Rules were also made to assure equitable distribution and to prevent waste. The famous Corn Laws of 1815 were passed to placate the farmers who protested that cheap corn (grain) would ruin them. This of course made the price rise and caused severe hardship among the poor, whose condition went from bad to worse until the repeal of these laws in 1846.

Famines are known to have occurred in Britain in 1371, 1383, 1437, and 1439. The Plague sometimes followed hunger.

During the seventeenth century, great country estates were founded by those who had made fortunes from trading ventures; the rural areas in some instances came under the control of these landlords, who were receptive to new ideas and had the money to indulge them. The big landowners are said to have lived extravagantly in gluttony and overeating. French and Italian cooking became popular in their homes. There was now a steady increase in the acreage of wheat. Many new books on agriculture and gardening were published due to the influence of the Flemish and the Dutch. The improved vegetables became more popular as articles of the diet. Also, a new growth of market gardening occurred following the influence of the Dutch and Flemish immigrants.

Only a few farmers, the progressive ones, paid attention to the quality of their farm animals and tried to improve them by better breeding practices. The approach of winter still meant little food for the animals until the late seventeenth century, when turnips came to be used as stock food. Their use increased during the eighteenth century. Lord (Turnip) Townsend discovered what was an almost obvious fact—crop rotation preserved the nutritive elements in the soil. He rotated turnips and clover with wheat and used the turnips as forage for livestock. Another discovery Dutch farmers made was that cattle would eat and thrive on the mealy residues after the crushing of the rape seed for rape seed oil, which was used then in Holland for lighting.

During the nineteenth century, scientific agriculture came to England largely due to Liebig, whose work helped the farmers begin to understand what nutrients were needed by plants. John Lawes, who had considerable estates, decided to use his fields to test the manuring process. This laid the foundations for the Rothamsted Experiment Station. Progress was also made in winter feeding of livestock by the use of the by-products of the crushing of cottonseed and linseed for oil.

English Fairs: To Buy and Sell Food and Other Things

The English fairs, of which there were two or three dozen by 1400, each lasting one to seven days, provided a place for the selling of some foods as well as a place to buy other needed products. In the fourteenth century, the St. Giles Fair at Winchester, and in the fifteenth century St. Lukes at Huntingdon, the Stourbridge Fair at Cambridge, and St. Bartholomew at Smithfield in London were the most important. The fairs were suited to the period, because there were not enough goods available for permanent shops to be open all of the time.

Retailers

During the time of Elizabeth I, retail merchandising came into being. *Corn chandlers* or *meal men* were retail dealers who found their customers multiplying as London grew because the poor and those who lived in small rented appartments needed to buy small quantities of grain. The chandlers broke the old laws that would have prevented their trade, and despite persecution, they flourished. Middlemen were needed; during the 100 years between the ascension of Elizabeth I and the restoration of the Stuarts, the middlemen came to be important in the business of the sale of food. They were fruiterers, butchers, poulterers, fishmongers, cheese, and dairy-produce sellers. So in the seventeenth century, London was able to turn its back on the local markets and fairs as the chief places to buy foods. Thus, food buying became, during the eighteenth century, shopping and not marketing.

Food Patterns in Particular

According to Drummond in *The Englishman's Food,* there were at different times in English history four classes of meals: (1) those of the village laborer, (2) those of the lords of the country manors, (3) those of artisans, and (4) those of the wealthy merchants and nobles of the towns. In general, the English were better fed than the equivalent classes on the continent; during the good years, even the English peasant was better nourished than his or her equal on the continent.

During times of a depressed economy, the peasant might eat only coarse black bread made from maslam (wheat and rye) or from barley, rye, and bean flour, as well as cheese and eggs; sometimes milk and occasionally fowl and bacon were added to this fare.

The general character of the peasants' diet improved during the greater part of the fifteenth century, but there was a sharp turn for the worse following a later period of deep depression when food prices rose rapidly. During these latter times, soups were popular. After the people began using potatoes, they were used in hearty stews. Gruels and pease and bean potages were also used, with fennel often added as flavor. When peasants could get bacon, they had bacon and eggs—eggs were cheap. Drummond thought that the traditional bacon and eggs probably came from this time. Prosperous yeomen ate beef and mutton, which gave rise to the story that the British were a meat-eating people. The beef, beer, and bread diet of England became famous at that time.

During the Early Middle Ages, the pattern of eating mostly what one grows was the same in England as elsewhere. The vast majority of the people were peasants, although some peasants were richer than others. Churchmen and nobility were very powerful but few in number. Peasants had to use money for taxes and anything they wanted to buy.

The extravagance of the wealthy was illustrated by the fact that they might be served three different meats and three different kinds of fish at each meal. After each of these six courses, they might have some kind of pastry, sweetmeat, or a jelly of gooseberries or cherries. The gargantuan meals were largely for special occasions, but the ordinary meals were always extravagant both at the tables of the lords of the church and of the state.

The size of towns and markets grew as the economy prospered. Markets were usually held once a week; some small markets were held outside churches on Sunday for country folk to buy and sell. We have better records of the legal and administrative matters than of those concerning food—that is, lacking are the homely details of what the vast numbers of the poor ate, but their diets were no doubt monotonous. Probably they bought food infrequently and in as large amounts as they could afford. The wealthy bought foods in large quantities.

Town people bought bread, meat, and ale as well as cooked foods, firewood, candles, articles of leather, wood, or metals, and linens and cloth. Some merchants tried to buy for later retail selling, but at first this was frowned on and rules were set up against such selling. At one time, a London fishmonger could sell only a fish already exposed for three days by the person who caught it.

There were always quarrels over weights and measures. One of the problems in English markets was that England has no small coins, and small French and Scottish coins had to be used. Prices varied, and one of the early attempts to stabilize and control prices and weights was an ordinance called the Assize of Bread of 1266.

Bread

Bread was considered the staff of life, and its quality and sale early became the concern of governmental authorities. The laws, Assizes of Bread, were passed and in effect until 1822, when the first so-called Bread Act replaced them.

Breads of three kinds were used: white or wheaten, labeled with a *W* by the baker; brown or whole wheat; and black rye; the latter two were labeled with an *H* for household bread. The bakery also used an identifying initial for the two bakery companies, so bread could be traced to its source, if necessary, when it was inspected. Whole wheat bread was thought to be more nutritious, but white bread was preferred. Hot, unleavened coarse breads were considered indigestible. Alum was used as an adulterant when whiteness of bread became prized.

The poor still took their dough to the bakery for baking. In summer before the grains had been harvested, poor people used horse bread, a bread made of peas and beans ordinarily used to feed horses when hay was scarce.

Davis said in *Fairs, Shops and Markets—A History of English Shopping,* "Nothing can recall for us the taste and texture of seventh century bread; one deeply suspects that it was pretty poor stuff."

Bread had been made at home for a long time except when it was baked in manorial bakeries. The baker baked the owner's bread, meat, meat pies, and pease pudding. It was common for the baker to stay open on Sunday even when by law other businesses were forced to close because many people depended on the baker to cook their Sunday dinner—they did not have their own cooking facilities.

Drummond says that it has been impossible to trace any ergotism in England, except for one eighteenth century outbreak in Suffolk, where rye was mixed with other grains. He believes that this was because at no time were the English wholly dependent on rye.

Meat, Fish, and Dairy Products

The peasants ate little meat, except what they poached or were given by their lords. Most animals used for meat were raised at home, but even so quite a lot of meat was sold by the butchers. These butchers sold the fat for candles and the hide for leather; the by-products were almost as valuable as the meat. The rules said that the meat must be fit to eat (Davis) and that the animal must not have died by itself. A rule was made that meat could not be sold by candlelight; all leftover meat not sold within a specified time had to be salted. There were also recipes in the cookbooks of that period recommending the use of garlic, as well as hot spices, to make tainted meat palatable. Large amounts of onions for flavoring meat were imported from Flanders. Because of the demand for imported pepper, the ''Peppers'' who sold it were first organized in the eleventh century. These Peppers became known as Grossari (from which the word *grocer* came) because they were allowed to use the great beam that had 15 ounces in one pound. This was the origin of our avoirdupois system which now uses 16 ounces to a pound.

Under Henry VI, the Freemen of Mistry of Grocers sifted spices; they were empowered to confiscate poor and adulterated spices. It was said that Edward I spent 1600 pounds on spices in one year. Sugar was also sold by these grocers, although at first it was used mostly for medicines. Later, it was used for marzipan and other sweetmeats.

Next to bread, meat was the most important food. The very poor often had only tripe, offal, trotters, and ''hoggs'' pudding made by country women. The more affluent ate beef, mutton, pork, veal, and hens, the latter raised in some Londoner's backyard. Choice poultry and wild fowl were a luxury enjoyed only by the rich.

Slaughtering took place in any convenient shed or backyard in certain areas of London. Much of the meat was tough and stringy flesh from runts or oxen too old to work. In order to get good meat at a reasonable price, a housewife had to go to market early. Fat flesh sold at a premium. Butchers were said by some to be deceitful who often did not take out as much blood from an animal as they should have. They also cheated on weights.

Fish was a good substitute for meat; shipbuilding and the training of mariners was encouraged; and everyone was urged to eat fish on Friday and on Lenten fast days. Fish, however, except salt herring, was expensive, so anyone who could caught his or her own fish. Salt herring was a staple of European diet by the twelfth century (Brown). Two of the fatty herring giving 200 calories and two and one-half ounces of protein per serving could contribute much to a limited diet.

Scandinavians had trouble salting fish; the water from their ''sweet'' Baltic seas and their sunless west shores made obtaining salt from evaporation of sea water difficult. The Germans thus found it profitable to export salt to Scandinavia, bringing about the Hanseatic League. In England, oysters and mussels were popular; the latter inexpensive, as was salmon. In the fifteenth and sixteenth centuries, apprentices protested too frequent servings of these seafoods.

Eggs were plentiful and cheap all during the Middle Ages and were used liberally, as was butter, cheese, and sometimes milk, although milk and cheese were often scarce in the spring and summer, and milk could not be kept fresh. Butter was salted to keep it fresh.

In the fifteenth and sixteenth centuries, the price of milk was low during most of the year. Dairy products, known for a long time as white meat, were eaten mostly by peasants. The milk production of a cow was low; sometimes it took one week's milk from a cow to produce one pound of butter. Butter was also used to oil cartwheels because other oils were almost unknown. During early Tudor times, however, the wealthy used olive oil, imported from Spain, for cooking.

Pigeons poached from the landowner's own stock by the less fortunate were used often. Pigeon lofts were found on all the lands of the rich.

Meals

The English usually ate three meals a day, the heaviest at midday. A working man might take a meal of roast meat or meat pies at the tavern. Stews or soups might also be bought at the cookshop and taken home to be eaten with bread, cheese, and ale or beer. The 5 P.M. supper usually consisted of cold meats, cheese, bread, and ale or wine. Vegetables apparently fell into disuse in the thirteenth and fourteenth centuries. There is

Early Victorian milk shop in Golden Lane London (*Courtesy British Museum*).

much more written about Middle Medieval gardens on the continent than about those of England. The earliest work, published in 1440, on English plants, lists 78 as suitable for cultivation, but many of these were savory herbs; the only ones mentioned in this list used as vegetables are radishes, spinach, cabbage, lettuce, onions, garlic, and leeks. Apples, plums, and cherries were said to be plentiful. Only the wealthy in town could have their own gardens inside their own walls; however, some less wealthy people in the suburbs did have gardens and orchards.

During the seventeenth century, the Jerusalem artichoke, sometimes later called the Canadian potato, and the sweet potato, called the Spanish potato, came into use. White potatoes, which had been rare until this time, were now used as a substitute for grain products even in making of bread and cakes. Around the middle of the sixteenth century, the sale of fruit increased, but it was sold in the public markets because hawking fruit on the street was prohibited. Improved quality of apples, cherries, strawberries, and gooseberries now appeared. New strains of raspberries and walnuts came from America, and later currants and apples were available from there. Oranges, lemons, plums, apricots, peaches, and quince were more plentiful, but supplies were erratic and prices were high and the price of fruit was still beyond the purse of most people. The only vegetables commonly eaten before the Flemish gardeners brought better methods for home gardening to England during the late sixteenth century were onions and cabbage, which were used to cook with meats and in soups. Vegetables were considered "windy" and unfit for use as food except in soups, in broths, or occasionally with oil in salads, which were made largely of onions and herbs.

Beverages and Their Service

Coffee houses became popular in seventeenth-century England when many of them were opened. In 1688, there were said to be 100 coffee houses in London; in Queen Anne's time in the early eighteenth century, there were 500.

The use of tea, made in the Chinese manner as a weak infusion, by all classes expanded enormously after 1700 and replaced coffee as national beverage because it was cheaper and because one pound of tea made more cups than a pound of coffee. In Victoria's reign, all tea came from China. For the poor, tea was a warm drink in a cold climate, and the boiled water was safe to drink. It was then drunk without milk, but later it became popular to put milk in it. After sugar became cheaper, it was also used more commonly in tea. At that time sugar was one of the most important imported items, although the first sugar that came from India and Arabia was expensive. After it was imported from the Caribbean Islands, the price fell. Around 1680, the use of sugar also made fruit a more popular item in the English diet.

The passion for fine china grew along with that for tea, and the quality of English-made china improved very rapidly to meet the demand. Chelsea, Worchester, and Derby china appeared along with the more common and cheaper Staffordshire ware, with which Josiah Wedgwood made his fortune. He was a clever salesman who sold china and tea together.

Other Foods

In the nineteenth century when the English people bought most of their food, the diet of the rural areas, towns, and cities became more uniform. The building and rapid increase in the use of railroads promoted the distribution of food.

Milk was first pasteurized in 1890. The first powdered or dried milk came after an 1855 patent. Borden's patent for condensing milk in 1856 also brought that form of milk into use. After 1850, the conditions under which animals were slaughtered and meat was produced improved. Food preservation both by canning and drying improved. Captain Cook is said to have taken, in 1772, portable soups (dried) for his round-the-world voyage. The staple food was still bread, but more vegetables and meat were eaten even by laborers, the latter always at least for Sunday.

After 1722, the west end of London was known for its good class of butcher and fruiterer shops that catered to the well-to-do. Food generally was cheaper, more plentiful, and of better quality than it had been. Fresh fruits and vegetables, however, still often needed to be bought from farmers if one wanted them fresh. Butter and cheese were cheap, but the former often was not good. There was plenty of milk, but methods of distribution were not adequate. It is said that "milchasses" were driven from door to door to furnish fresh milk for infants and invalids who needed it.

One hundred years ago, 50 percent of the shops in England were food shops. Peddlers with their packs of food as well as other items on their backs were common in the fourteenth century, but only after 1872, when Thomas Lipton opened his first grocery store in Glasgow, did one-man grocery stores come into being. Twenty-six years later, he had 245 grocery stores all over England.

AMERICA

The food patterns of early North Americans were greatly influenced by East Coast and Florida Indians. Later, American Indians in the Southwest shared some foods they had adopted from the Mexicans. Both the food patterns of the American Indians and of the colonists who came from Europe during the early seventeenth century were dependent on a staple food not previously known to Europe and Asia. This food, called *corn* in America, is more properly named *maize*.

Many of the foods American Indians used came from wild plants and grasses known and used by the Incas of Peru, the Mayas of Central America, and the Aztecs of Mexico. Hays and Hays believe that the Incas "have never been surpassed in agriculture." These authors defended this position by citing the Incas' hybridization of fields with vast systems, their terracing to conserve soil, and their rotating of crops as well as allowing fields to lie fallow to restore fertility.

The question of how corn—which is now known to have originated in Mexico—traveled north and south is interesting. It is thought that other Indians did visit the great Inca cities and that Inca merchants sent caravans to distant cities. Llamas were very effective beasts of burden as they served the Incas. Sea trade with the Mayas and Aztecs probably also promoted the exchange of seeds. Modern archeological diggings show that American Indians traveled great distances in spring, summer, and fall to attend social gatherings. Hays and Hays cite the fact that artifacts uncovered in Cape Cod proved that the tribes from the midwest and northwest gathered for clam, oyster, and corn feasts. Such proof is also found as far south as Florida where feasts were of shrimp and fish from southern waters. It can probably be safely conjectured that seeds for plants that would grow in a new locality were exchanged at such gatherings.

It was indeed fortunate for the settlers of Jamestown and Plymouth that the seeds of corn, beans, and squash had reached the local Indians before these settlers arrived.

Food Patterns of Early North American Natives

Although most authorities agree that some Asian people driven by hunger probably came across the Bering land bridge, what other groups came in prehistoric times is still not entirely clear, and detailed discussion of their food patterns is not attempted here.

Apparently the first North American natives hunted only easy-to-kill game. They led furtive lives, were afraid of large animals, and probably only rarely were able to obtain animal flesh for food. Instead they gathered wild fruits, nuts, and roots. Around 12,000 years ago, a dramatic change took place—these early people learned to make tools for killing. Beautifully made spear heads dating to 10,000 B.C. have been found at Clovis, New Mexico. These artifacts were discovered among the bones of mammoths, American camels, and hairy elephants. Hunters may have stalked a mammoth, wounded it with a spear, and then followed and harassed it until it was weak enough to kill with the same spear by stabbing at a vital organ. Modern day Bushmen do this. The early Americans may have driven these animals into bogs or ponds or over cliffs. It is thought that they ate the flesh of smaller animals as well as vegetable food. About 7000 B.C. the glaciers retreated and the climate of what is now the Western United States became hot and arid; the large animals therefore disappeared.

Food of Indians of the Later Periods

After the end of the Ice Age, the southwest Indians developed into seed-eating agricultural people and began to live communally in villages. The remnants of domesticated red and yellow beans have been found. Around 2500 B.C., a variety of maize with a tiny ear made its appearance; by 2000 B.C., maize was a well-established crop.

It is understandably difficult to compare the food eaten by peoples living under such different geographic and climatic districts as all the American Indians. Most American Indians were and still are, however, semi-agriculturists. They also are clever and industrious in gathering the bounty of forest, field, rivers, and sea: wild huckleberries and cranberries; wild plums and cherries; and lobster, salmon, and other fish. They gathered wild rice in Minnesota, acorns in California, and the bulb of the camus and of the sego lily in the meadows of the Rocky Mountains. They killed and used the bison of the Great Plains. They learned to dry fruits and meats and taught the white people how to make jerky and pemmican. They extracted and used the oil of chestnuts and walnuts and learned to boil down, in birch-bark vessels, the sap of the maple tree to use in sweetening food.

Hays and Hays say that 80 percent of our present food plants were unknown in Europe before 1492. Today much of the world's peoples eat our native Indian foods corn, potatoes (both white and sweet), beans, squash, cocoa, tapioca, and native Indian (from the western hemisphere) fruits.

Many of the foods we have on our tables today were known and used by the Indians when the white settlers first came to our shores. Indians had pumpkins, squash, melons, various kinds of beans including lima beans, wild turkey, walnuts, hickory, and butternuts. Most important of all, however, was that almost all the Indians grew corn and used it in many ways. They roasted the unripe ears, soaked the dry corn in the lye of wood ashes to make hominy and grits, soaked and ground it into meal for kinds of bread that the white people came to call cornpone, hoe cakes, and Johnny cake. The Indians also had a kind of popcorn. An Indian is said to have produced a bushel of popped corn as a surprise after-meal treat at the first Thanksgiving feast in Plymouth in 1621. From the beans the Indians planted among the rows of corn, they made and taught the white settlers how to make succotash.

These Indians have been called rudimentary, sedentary cultivators by Bennett, who suggested that they were in a "transitional position emphasizing cultivation of the soil but not excluding hunting and gathering." Had they not known and taught the Pilgrims how to fertilize each hill of corn with a dead fish, the rocky barren soil around New England would probably not have supported life for those early colonists who were neither agriculturists, hunters, or fishermen but were ex-tradespeople and craftsmen. The Indians taught them to plant four seeds of corn in a circle in a hill and to form a row of these hills, and they shared with them the ingenious method of planting beans, peas, pumpkins, squash, and melons between the rows of corn, which allowed these plants to form a symbiotic relationship.

The Indians in Central America are said to have made beer from corn, but North American Indians did not make or use fermented drinks from corn or wild grapes. The first alcoholic drinks apparently came to these Indians from the white settlers.

The Indians dried wild berries, plums, cherries, beans, peas, pumpkins, squash, meat, and fish.

Some of the now classic dishes the Indians gave us are roast turkey, barbecued meats, steamed lobsters, spoon bread, and cranberry sauce. Verrill said that, when we gather for a Thanksgiving feast, we enjoy an almost all-American meal: pumpkin pies, cranberry sauce, turkey, white and sweet potatoes, the vanilla in the cake and ice cream are from North, South, and Central America. The tomatoes in the salad and some of the nuts of the last course also originated in the Americas.

For further discussion, it will be necessary to divide the food of American Indians into regional patterns. Kimball said that there are five distinct areas represented by typical tribes, as follows:

1. Southwest: Pueblos, Papago, and Hopi (Navajos might also be added here)
2. Northwest Coast: Tlingit, Kwakiutl, Salish
3. Vast Plains: Nomadic Dakotas, Cheyennes
4. Warm South: Powhatan, Cherokees, Creeks
5. New England: Narragansett, Penobscot, Iroquois, and other woodsmen

Southwest Indians

As has already been mentioned, after the Glacial Age, the inhabitants of our Southwest were forced by the different climate to change from hunters to semi-agriculturists. Corn became their primary crop. From Mexican Indians, the Southwest Indians learned to soak the corn kernels in lye and to make a paste which they later baked in flat cakes on hot stones, as present-day Mexicans and Indians make tortillas.

Beans were also one of their important foods; some of these were used as Mexicans use frijoles. Prickly pears and the fruit of other cacti were eaten. Mesquite furnished a yellow starchy substance between the seeds that the Indians used to make a cake that Newberry said has a little of the appearance taste of yellow cornmeal. Buffalo berries were much used and esteemed by Indians in Montana, Colorado, and New Mexico. The California Indians used acorns in their somewhat different diet. They made a meal from these which, when mixed into a paste with water, was baked or steamed. During this process, the bitterness of the acorn was lost and the bread was reputed to be well flavored and wholesome. As much as 100 bushels of acorns were reported by archeologists to have been found in one wigwam.

The Northwest Coast Indians

Salmon, giant clams, crab, mussels, barnacles, cod,, whale, halibut, flounder, herring, sturgeon, smelt, seal, and sea otter were the principal foods of these people, who lived richly from the sea. In some of the Pacific Northwest Indian languages, the word for salmon is the same as the word for fish, which suggests their high regard for salmon. These fish are even now treated with great respect by these Indians. They early believed that salmon were "spirit people," and there was a ceremony for the first salmon caught. Waterfowl, ducks, geese, and gulls were also used, as were kelp and seaweed; sea water furnished the salt in soups and stews. Small cranberries were found in the bogs of Oregon, although they were not as abundant as they were in Maine. Service and salmon berries, huckleberries, blackberries, raspberries, and salalberries were used fresh and in dried pastes. The Klamath Indians also used the seeds of the yellow water lily. For Indians in Utah, the bulbous root of the sego lily was an important food, as was the bulb of the blue-flowered (not the poisonous white-flowered), onion-like camas for the Nez

Perce of Idaho. The latter Indians fought wars with the white settlers over the preservation of their camas meadows. The land also furnished deer, elk, bear, and wild goats as well as small game birds, acorns, hazelnuts, and wild carrots.

Feasting occurred frequently. One of the most colossal of their feasts was the *potlatch,* to which a chief invited both friends and enemies to show how powerful he and his tribe were. The practice became very competitive because each guest strove to provide a bigger and better potlatch.

Food was easy to get; therefore, there was much leisure time, and the civilizations were able to develop to a high degree. The arts of basket and rug weaving and wood carving were advanced or even more advanced than similar arts of other American Indian tribes.

The Great Plains and Other Western Indians

The Plains Indians were great hunters of bison, antelope, deer, and some small game. Those who have tried to study the habits of these meat-eating Indians have had to look at the bones outside the remains of a camp. Apparently the large dead animals could not be brought home intact, so the women brought home small parts or stripped off the meat to carry home either to eat fresh or to dry for later meals. The small limbs of antelope and deer, however, have been found in the remains of an old campsite in the Angostura Basin, once occupied by South Dakota Indians.

In arid regions of the West where pine trees grew, pine nuts were gathered regularly and were a principal food. Farther East, water chinquapins (filbert-like nuts), found in a few places around Lake Erie, were a prized food.

The diet of the Indians of the Midwest, especially in Minnesota, was different because they had thousands of acres of wild rice, found in the shallows of their chain of lakes. Women working in boats beat off the seeds with sticks.

Indians in Florida and the Warm South

The Creeks and Seminoles taught the Spanish colonists of Florida how to make a sweet milk to use in enriching soups by pounding the hickory nut (Kimball and Anderson). These Indians also taught their new neighbors how to wrap a fish in grape leaves and steam it. The Spanish brought the orange to these Indians, who then used it to cook with fish as well as with honey for dessert.

Venison was used with corn cakes; it was either barbecued or stewed with bear's oil. Cherokee women used green beans from the field in making delicate stews from venison, squirrel, or rabbit; they also prepared puddings of wild persimmons and a bread of dried beans and corn meal. They used many kinds of wild berries and fruits. Contributions of these cooks were recipes for succotash, Brunswick stew, corn pone, hominy and hominy grits, roasted peanuts, fried green tomatoes, and a stew of fresh shrimp and okra.

New England and North Eastern Indians

The Iroquois are said to have known about and used 40 methods of cooking corn, including soups and broths from ripe and unripe corn, succotash, and different kinds of unleavened breads that were boiled or baked in ashes; they also used hominy made from corn by soaking it in lye.

A visitor to a feast of the Iroquois in 1743 described the meal as consisting of an Indian corn soup in which eels were boiled, a dish of squash and its flowers, and Indian dumplings made of new soft corn scraped from the ear, mixed with boiled beans and wrapped for cooking in corn leaves.

Feasts and ceremonies around planting and harvesting time were common among the woodsmen Indians of the East. They were mostly "solemn religious affairs" and "seasonal thanksgiving"; the land was good to them, and they appreciated it. These Indians gave us what now are considered New England classics, such as codfish balls, clam chowder, Boston brown bread (probably sweetened with boiled-down maple syrup), cranberry puddings, satin-smooth pumpkin soups, and wild beach plum jam.

Cornfields were limited to eastern Connecticut, Rhode Island, central and eastern Massachusetts, and a fringe not more than 50 to 75 miles inland from the coasts of New Hampshire and Maine (Bennett). Evidence indicates that corn raising was risky in the Northeast because of the climate. All of the seacoast Indians relied heavily on fish and sea foods and wild game from their forests and probably did not use nearly as much corn as did Indians living farther south.

The Northeast Indians cooked in pits dug in the ground and heated with hot stones as well as in kettles; they also broiled or roasted meat over open fires and baked it over hot ashes. Food was sometimes rolled in a cover of fresh leaves or ingeniously baked on hot stones under an inverted kettle covered with coals. They also stored their supplies in pits dug for that purpose.

It seems probable that these Indians used maple sap boiled down as a sweetener until later, when wild honey became available to them. It is thought that the tame European honeybees brought by the white settlers escaped and became wild, therefore making wild honey available to the Indians.

These Indians knew and used the Jerusalem artichoke, which grew wild; it may possibly have been cultivated by them. Bennett summarized his extensive article by saying that "Indians—even the Christianized ones—took to domesticated animals and European crops only in a small way, continuing to prefer their traditional hoe-culture of corn, beans, squash, and pumpkins, and their activities in hunting and fishing."

Corn—Beginnings and Widespread Use

The word "corn" outside America means "grain," especially wheat and barley. Columbus and his men, landing on the shores of North America, expected to find rice because they had known for years that rice was grown on the Spice Islands. Instead they found a grain they had never seen before, and it was very different from rice. Jacobs quoted from the diary of Columbus, dated November 5, 1492: "It (corn) is good tasting and all of the people of this land live on it." The seeds of this "tall grass," which they found American Indians growing and using, were new to them. The American Indians called it *zea mays*, from which we get the word "maize," a more precise term for world use. Maize came from a plant larger than other known grains; the grains grew on huge ears that were protected by husks, and the plant had large green leaves.

One year's crop of corn in the United States today is worth much more than all the gold and silver gathered by all the galleons of the fleets of those who sought gold and silver in the new world.

The Spaniards must have been astonished when the Indians said corn grew in 90 days, wondering probably whether one could see it grow. (In the latter part of the twentieth century, the sounds of corn growing rapidly have been recorded by scientists! Walden told of seven scientists who went with wire recorders, microphones, and wind gauges deep into a 100-acre Wisconsin cornfield "to hear corn grow." If some were skeptical when they went in, they later believed that "occasional cracklings were identified as the sound of corn growing.") Hariot, after a 1588 voyage from England to Roanoke, Virginia, wrote about maize, which he called "West Indies guinney wheate." He noted in his journal that it increased greatly, yielding 2000 grains for every grain planted.

All American Indians have surrounded corn with mysticism, legends, and religious ceremonies. They knew it did not grow wild. Even the Incas of Peru had lost or forgotten all history of corn. Because they did not know where corn came from, all tribes had fanciful tales about it. Verrill said that the Indian tribes living in other parts of the Americas who had never heard of the Incas or even those who dwelled in Mexico, where corn probably originated, never dreamed that it had made its way step by step, mile by mile, from hand to hand, thousands of miles from lands unknown to them. American Indian fables credit the crow with bringing them corn. They believed that corn was always a gift of the gods.

Scientists have puzzled over where corn really came from, and though they believe that it was a native of the Americas, the wild corn ancestor was not found for years. Corn in its present form or even in the earliest known form cannot seed itself, which is of course necessary for any plant to grow in the wild. The husk of corn completely covers the grain, preventing autonomous reproduction.

The first important contribution to the archeological solution of this problem was the finding of prehistoric vegetable material in Bat Cave in New Mexico in excavations by Herbert Dick in 1950 and 1968. Cobs and other parts of corn were found here in the layers of accumulated trash, garbage, and excrement. The cobs of this corn showed a distinct evolutionary sequence from the lower to the upper levels; the lowest ones (both pop corn and pod corn), dated at 3600 B.C., were approximately one inch in length.

Mangelsdorf later was able to produce a genetic reconstruction of the ancestral form of corn by crossing pod corn and pop corn. This ancestral form had seeds borne on the fragile branches of the tassel, as well as seeds on the ears, which were not entirely enclosed by husks. After these discoveries, the scientists knew what to look for in wild corn. In 1949, MacNeish found corn in similar evolutionary sequence in some caves in northeast Mexico; others found similar remains near Mexico City. The cobs found in these places are the oldest (from 5200 to 3400 B.C.) available for botanical analysis and are thought to be those of wild maize. It has been conjectured that perhaps only a small amount of wild maize grew in a sheltered and favored spot, and that as soon as it was cultivated, the wild corn was crossed by natural forces with the cultivated and thus the wild grain was lost. Walden said that pollen grains found by Sears and Clisby 200 feet below Mexico City were assigned to the last interglacial period and thus were 80,000 years old. Mangelsdorf believes that there may be two or more geographical races of wild corn.

The pollen grains buried for 80,000 years are now accepted as evidence that corn is a native American plant. Some of it may have been taken from Brazil to Africa, which would account for the reports of maize having been grown in Africa from the beginning of the sixteenth century or perhaps even earlier on the Guinea Coast. There are also stories of maize having been used as payment of tribute in South China in 1575. It is thought that perhaps the Portugese took it to India and it spread overland to the north. Flint maizes, which have harder kernels and contain a higher percentage of hard or flinty starch than flour corn, were grown in Europe soon after Columbus returned. These are said to have spread to Egypt within a few years.

The Inca civilization was founded on corn; without their stores of corn, the armies of the Incas could never have traversed the Andes Mountains or the deserts and subjugated distant tribes to extend their domains and develop one of the most advanced civilizations in their world.

The later developments of scientific breeding, hybridization, and introduction of modern machinery have written the later history of corn in North America.

Food of the Colonists

When the Pilgrims landed at Plymouth Rock in 1620, they were hungry and tired of what had been their fare—hardtack, salt horse (salted beef), dried fish, cheese, and beer. They came ashore ravenous; after prowling along the shore looking for shellfish, they found soft-shelled clams, young quahogs, and large fat mussels. The latter are said to have made them sick.

It is said that the Pilgrims landed at the wrong time of year, December 23, 1620, at the wrong place, and with the wrong amount of food. They were expecting to land on the James River, where they hoped they would be fed by their countrymen who had preceded them. For the 63-day sea journey, they carried 15,000 brown biscuits, 5000 white hard bread (crackers) and were rationed to only three pieces of bread and biscuits per person per day. With this bread stuff they had smoked or half-cooked bacon, salted and dried codfish, and smoked herring. They also had parsnips, turnips, onions, and cabbage for boiled dinners with their pease pudding, boiled mush, and beer. But instead of fertile and warm Virginia, they landed on the rocky, forbidding Northeast coast.

In the Pilgrims' first searching for food, it is reported that they found buried in the ground a large number of Indian baskets filled with corn. This was a welcome sight; although they had never seen corn before, they used it. One wonders how they cooked it. This corn was the winter's food supply and seed for spring of a group of local Pamet Indians. The Pilgrims did replace the corn as they promised their consciences they would, but meantime the Pamets starved. Because they did not have proper gear or technical skills, the Pilgrims were not at first successful in fishing.

The Indians in the immediate vicinity mostly had been wiped out by a smallpox epidemic. Squanto, who was said to be the sole survivor, taught the Pilgrims how to plant corn and other crops. He probably also furnished directions for cooking these foods. A peace treaty with Chief Massasoit and his strong confederacy of followers allowed the Indians and Pilgrims to live in peace for half a century.

The celebration of the first Thanksgiving feast, to which Massasoit brought 90 brightly painted braves, was symbolic of the good relationship. The Indians also provided wild game and taught their newfound friends how to hunt for game and wild foods. This Thanksgiving holiday, first proclaimed as a national holiday in 1863 by President Lincoln, had for years been celebrated religiously in New England.

Colonists in the South

On June 2, 1607, nine ships carrying 800 passengers and a crew set sail from England for Virginia. To last them for the journey and until the first harvest, they carried cheese; dried salted fish; cured beef, pork, and bacon; oatmeal; biscuits; and bread and butter, the butter probably spoiled before the journey was one-fourth over. They also carried pease, onions, raisins, prunes, and dates, barrels of cider, beer, and sack (a dry white wine), as well as drinking water. For future planting, they had seeds of mustard, cabbage, turnips, lettuce, onions, and garlic. When they landed, the 650 survivors joined the 80 people already in the James River settlement. They scooped up oysters, which were plentiful, and learned how to hunt deer and wild fowl, how to fish, and how to use the corn meal which the Indians gave them. They also found wild turkey nests with eggs in them, wild grapes, strawberries, raspberries, and mulberries. There was plenty of fish, especially sturgeon, and there were large meadows for pasturing the animals which they had brought with them.

These British settlers were not accustomed to agricultural work, and the expected supplies from England failed to arrive on time. Of necessity, they made friends with local Indians and from them learned how to steep maize for two hours, to pound the softened corn in a mortar, and finally to form it into molded balls or cakes. These were then baked in ashes, which were washed off while the bread was hot. Sometimes the bread was boiled in water. The Indians taught them how to make *suppawn,* a kind of porridge, and *samp,* a porridge from parched corn; they also learned how to make succotash with beans, how to roast green corn ears, and how to pop corn. The Indians also shared their knowledge of how to prepare and use acorn flour for making bread. They helped the British find walnuts, chestnuts, wild plums, cherries, and crab apples. They also instructed them in ways of hunting and fishing. In the areas where food supplies did not last until the next crop of corn was harvested, the tender young shoots of wild plants—what we probably would call weeds—were used as food.

In 1608, Captain John Smith asked two Indians to show him how to plant corn, and the 40 acres he planted yielded a good crop. At first, the fields were communal, but when the results of this arrangement proved disastrous, each farmer took his own lands, where his incentive to grow a good crop was greater.

Corn is said to have been taken for taxes once a governing body was set up. It was legal tender along with the scarce gold and silver coins. Corn was used even in balloting; a grain of corn signified a positive vote and a bean signified a negative vote.

Native pumpkins, squash, beans, and sweet potatoes were used; the latter probably came from farther south after the Spanish had brought them to Florida.

Food Patterns of Colonists

It will be easier to discuss the food patterns by separating those of the North from those of the South. The topography, the weather, the kind of settlers, and the potentials for future crops made a great difference in the kinds of foods grown and used. The Southern colonists soon began raising crops for money, which led to a need for cheap labor; consequently slavery came into being. Tobacco proved to be a valuable crop for exporting to England; the owners of large tracts of tobacco lands became wealthy. Living was easier and for the rich became luxurious. In contrast, the puritanical, religious Pilgrims of the North had a forbidding soil and climate, and their general motivation was fundamentally different. However, some who built fishing ships and others who undertook to build commerce with England and Europe became wealthy. These differences should not be oversimplified, because other peoples—Dutch, Germans, Swedes, and Irish—soon came to America, bringing their own motivations, ideals, skills, native abilities, and foods. They intermingled and became a part of the total Northeast coastal settlement. Any divisions are, therefore, artificial ones used here only to clarify points in this brief discussion.

Food Patterns of the Northern Colonists

Once the colonists learned what food was available and how to get and cook it, the supply was plentiful. Deer were so numerous in the forests that by 1695 they were frequently killed only for their hides. Wild turkeys weighing 30 to 40 pounds apiece came in flocks of 100 and could be captured by placing corn in pens. Pigeons, pheasants, partridge, woodcocks, and quail were abundant, as were water birds—plovers, snipe, and curlew—in the swamps.

There were said to be as many as 100 kinds of fish available. Lobsters were plentiful; some caught around Salem weighed up to 25 pounds. Patriarchial lobsters caught in New York Bay were five to six feet long. Governor William Bradford is reported to have been ashamed that, when 67 new colonists arrived, he had only lobster to serve to them. By the mid-nineteenth century, this lack of respect for lobster had been overcome. When we now pay a very high price for lobster, we should remember its early history.

Codfish of the first grade was exported to Europe and sold to Roman Catholic Europeans and to the English for their high church fasts. The second class codfish was used at home, and the third class was sent to the West Indies as ballast on ships sent for molasses and rum. Salt codfish even today is a main article of diet in Puerto Rico and the Virgin Islands, which surprises some people visiting the Caribbean area for the first time.

Woodward said that, during the seventeenth century in Boston, money was scarce, two shillings a day being a wage for a skilled worker. A 12-pound fresh codfish sold for two pence (pennies to us), and a quarter of venison, enough for a large family, was only nine pence. Beer was one penny a quart. Everyone had a garden in which to grow their own vegetables. Candles were often too expensive to use, so splinters of pine and rushes soaked in oil were used for lights.

Salmon was then held in low regard and sold for one penny per pound. Shad was profoundly despised; it was thought to be disreputable to eat it. There is a now familiar story of the family, when a knock was heard at their door during a meal, who first hid the platter of shad before opening the door. As has been described elsewhere, corn was used in many ways. It was mixed also with huckleberries and sweetened to make a fruit cake called Indian pudding. This was evidently very different from what is now called Indian pudding in New England. Potatoes were brought from Ireland to New Hampshire in 1719 by a man named Derry.

Wheat did not ripen well in New England, so white bread was rarely eaten. If a family had any white bread, it was saved for the minister's visit, because brown bread was supposed to give him heartburn and inhibit his preaching. Rye-and-Injun bread was made of one-half rye and one-half corn meal. Later even bakeries made this bread, but it was so dry that those eating it were forced to drink water to get it down. Later, milk was drunk when available, and breakfasts and suppers of bread and milk became common. In Salem in 1630, milk cost one penny per quart. In 1836, milk was delivered in cities by wagons carrying it in wooden barrels; housewives and serving girls came out and dipped their pitchers into the barrels.

The Indians did not have wheat and oats until the white settlers brought them. A small bag of rice is said to have been brought from Madagascar in 1671 by Henry Woodward, a sea captain, but it did not become a staple food until the 1800s, when it was first raised in South Carolina.

The settlers had wild grapes. Cider was diluted with water; bread and Johnny cake were soaked in diluted cider much as the Greeks and Romans soaked their breakfast bread in wine. Bread was said to be buttered only by the wealthy because butter was three to six pence a pound. Cheese was plentiful and good, especially on the East Coast after the Dutch and Germans introduced their excellent cheeses. Scrambled eggs, called battered eggs, were used.

There was no way of preserving meat by refrigeration, so as in medieval Europe, spices were used to cover off-flavors. Even perfumes are said by Earle to have been used with meats in Colonial America.

The colonial housewife made pickles, spiced fruits, preserves, and candied fruits and marmalades, putting the very sweet, nonspoiling food in large, unsealed jars. These people knew and used herbs to improve the flavor of food. Most families had only maple sugar or maple syrup as sweetening until the importation of the honeybee. Honey had become an important sweetening agent by 1638 to 1648. Housewives of dignity and elegance, said Earle, had loaf sugar—great loaves or cones weighting nine to ten pounds, which had to last a thrifty family for one year. Later, around 1650, ships began to bring sugar in from the West Indies; but not much came until the 1700s and even then it was expensive. Molasses and tropical dried fruits were also brought back from the merchants' voyages to the West Indies. Spices, a luxury to English housewives, now became more common in North America. Spice trees grew well after they were introduced into those islands by early explorers. Spices were obtained whole and ground in the home with a mortar and pestle or in mills similar to modern pepper mills.

Nutmeg graters had been known in Europe before colonial days so they were also used. Did colonial dames wear lockets that contained a nutmeg and a grater to cope with offensive odors as ladies of those days in London did?

For drinking, perry was made from pears, cider from apples, and peachy from peaches; all were very popular drinks during the seventeenth and eighteenth centuries. Mead and methegalin, drinks from the days of the Druids, were made from honey, yeast, and water, with locust beans added to make methegalin. Mead (honey wine), discussed previously, is the oldest of alcoholic beverages. In olden times, it was called the nectar of the gods and was used as a festive drink, a drink of courage, and a love potion. The Druids, Greeks, Romans, Hindus, and Norsemen all drank it. The word honeymoon, some say, comes from the practice of Viking newlyweds drinking mead for the first 30 (a lunar month or the full cycle of moon) days of marriage, probably to encourage fertility.

Light drinks were made from persimmons, elderberries, juniper berries, pumpkins, cornstalks (for their sugar), hickory nuts (a form of milk also used by the American Indians), sassafrass bark, and birch bark. The leaves and roots from other plants were also used. Chocolate and coffee were used later as drinks. In 1670, a Boston woman who was licensed to sell coffee and chocolate opened the first coffee house in New England. Two dealers who were probably apothecaries were licensed to sell tea in 1712 in Boston. An almost unbelievable story is told that at first the colonists boiled their tea in water a long time, threw the water away, and ate the leaves. In Salem, this tea was considered unappetizing, and butter and salt were added. When Bostonians learned to brew tea correctly, it became as popular there as in England. For those who could not have tea or coffee, substitutes were used, such as dried raspberry leaves for tea and caramelized grain for coffee. The afternoon snack called "Tea" probably originated on the American Continent in New York City where, in wealthy homes, coffee and chocolate and later tea were served with small meat pies, cheese, delicate sugar cakes, and confections.

Carson said, "Perhaps only a sturdy race of fishermen, farmers, and freeholders could have subdued the glaciated, rock-strewn Yankee land and flourished in the robust climate. Yet they formed there a pattern of civilization which has been dominant in the social development of the northern parts of the United States, determining not only how we think and feel but also what we eat."

Agricultural Practices and Equipment

In 1797, Newbold invented an all-iron plow, cast in one piece, which could be operated by one person driving a yoke of oxen attached to it. The farmers at first would have nothing to do with this plow, saying that iron poisoned the soil. Jethro Wood, a New York farmer, improved Newbold's plow by using several parts of iron attached to each other, so when the plow hit a rock and broke, only a part of it needed to be replaced. His plow was accepted because by this time the farmers began to think iron was good for the soil. Newbold's plow was ahead of its time, but Wood's was invented at the right time. The Puritans then plowed a furrow for their corn, an improvement over the Indian way of digging holes.

Meals and Utensils

The early New England housewife had no servants, so she probably was forced to use the slow methods of cooking meats and fish stews and baking beans in open fireplaces, because these needed little constant attention while cooking. She used a Dutch oven to bake bread or potatoes but was too busy to fry much food. It is said that kidney beans and salt venison was one standard dish in simple meals; pumpkin was often served for dessert. The seeds were taken out of the opened pumpkin, which was then cooked; afterwards milk was poured into it so it could be eaten as a pudding. Mince meat for pies was made of bear's meat, dried fruits, with cider or wine added. Hasty pudding was made of cornmeal mush, maple sugar, and cream.

The housewife made apple butter; dried corn, fruits, and vegetables; made cheese and butter, soap and candles; and brewed wine and beer. To make cheese, she obtained the rennet to curd the milk by soaking dried stomachs of unweaned calves.

Colonial women brought their cooking vessels and recipes with them from the old country. The ancestral saltbox for storing cooking salt hung beside the fireplace. It was often made of black cherry wood and was the colonial symbol of good cooking and provident domestic management.

Families ate from wooden plates, called trenchers—one for every two people. From this the word "trencherman" is derived. These plates might be carved out of a plank of wood in rows and the board containing the trenchers set on trestles for a table. Thus, the trencher could be removed and washed. Sometimes one side of a plate-like trencher was used for the main course and the other side for pie. When a maid and man ate from the same trencher, they were known to be engaged to marry. During the seventeenth and early eighteenth century, wooden, pewter, and silverware spoons were used. Knives and forks came later. The first fork, which had white steel tines, reportedly belonged to Governor Winthrop of Boston; it was imported from England in 1633 encased in a leather pitkin.

Midway down the length of the family table a polished silver bowl standing on three legs held the precious salt. This so-called standing salt cellar was a prized family possession. It was coated with a lining of gold to prevent corrosion by the salt. As in Roman times, there was a rigid custom of who should sit above and below the salt. Servants and children were always below it, but the chief of an Indian tribe who was a dinner guest would always be seated above it. Anyone who sat below the salt was not supposed to start conversation, only to follow.

The Puritans carved and whittled many thousands of household items. One of these special tools was used to crack and pound the cones of sugar for use. Copper kettles were used for making apple butter because iron turned the butter black. Jacks were used to turn meat on the spit on the fireplace. Dutch ovens were later used for cooking fowl and meat.

Pewter made in Holland and England was expensive. After 1750, when pewter was made in America by Paul Revere and others, it became cheaper. Before this time, tankards were made of wood and stitched leather.

In 1770, Baron von Stiegel brought expert glassmakers to America, and glass was made for the first time in the New World. A little imported Chinese pottery and porcelain was used.

Wedding feasts included a great variety of dishes and prodigious quantities of food. At even a simple ceremony, roast venison, roast turkey, fricasse of chicken, beef hash, boiled fish, stuffed cod, pigeons, boiled eels, roast goose stuffed with chestnuts, succotash, many kinds of other vegetables, pumpkin pies, and apple tarts might be served. All the food was put on the table as a single course, so each person could eat any food at anytime according to his or her own fancy. Beer, cider, claret flip, syllabub, brandy, ale, and a heavy sherry called sack might also be served.

Most New England colonists were thrifty. In 1787, one colonist is said to have spent only $10 for nails and salt in one year; these were probably most of the supplies he found it necessary to buy.

During 1789–1840, there was no lack of food, but travelers complained about the quality and the monotony. They claimed that they had salted meat three times a day, although the lack of other methods of preservation, particularly in certain seasons of the year, should have made the reason obvious. Brillat-Savarin, in *Physiology of Taste* (1960), praised a dinner he said he enjoyed at a Connecticut farmhouse. The colonists probably had more meat than they had enjoyed in Europe. But perhaps the women who gathered wild greens like dandelion, pigweed, and cowslip were discouraged when their men called green vegetables "fodder."

Food Patterns of the Southern Colonists

The foods of the Southern colonies differed from those of the Northern ones. Yams and sweet potatoes, the latter known as Spanish potatoes, pecans, and wheat did not grow well in the North but were important foods in the South. Opposum, turtle, and terrapin for stew and green turtle for soup were favored foods. Negro cooks whose main job was preparing food had much more time for cooking than did the Northern housewife, so they made such time-consuming foods as beaten biscuits. Rice cultivated after 1694 became a favorite food. It is believed that oranges for marmalade were used as early as 1770 in South Carolina.

In the waters off the Virginia Coast, lobster and huge crabs (the latter said to be a foot in length and six inches broad) were often caught. These crabs, described as having ''many a long tail and many legs,'' were each said by Earle to have been sufficient for one meal for four men. In these waters, oysters which measured 13 inches in length were found. The fish were so abundant in the brooks that they could be killed by hitting them with a stick.

Blacks lived on grits, black-eyed peas, sweet potatoes, and pork; on prosperous plantations, they also had molasses. In winter, they ate salt fish and sometimes even fresh beef. One white woman noticed that black children were healthier than her children. She accredited this to the ''pot liquor'' from vegetables which she observed the black children drank, so she gave it to her children and thought that their health improved as a result.

Large plantation-manor houses had detached kitchens. They also had their own mills for pounding grain. Other buildings were used for grading and polishing rice and other grains.

Farther west, the Southern settlers were influenced by Mexican food and copied their chili con carne and out-of-door barbecues. They learned from these neighbors to grow avocados, olives, citrus fruits, white walnuts, almonds, and grapes. Because they had food fresh all year around, they did less preserving than settlers in colder climates. Lye hominy was used as in New England, but here the water was often thrown on the lye-soaked corn so that it could be mashed, forming a *masa,* a paste from which the Spanish tortillas were made.

As more money became available to spend on food, meal service became more elaborate. French influence, beginning in the mid-seventeenth century, probably stemmed both from the French in New Orleans and from Thomas Jefferson's influence when he returned from France after the French Alliance of 1778. George Washington had a French steward during his stay in the White House and Jefferson had a French cook during his life there.

In Williamsburg, Virginia, in 1742, William Parks published a cookbook written by E. Smith called the *Compleat Housewife,* the first work on the art of cookery adapted to American needs. He had published an earlier edition of this book in 1727 in England.

Food Patterns of Other Colonies

New Orleans. After French explorers came to Louisiana and Florida, the French influence was added to the Spanish, especially in New Orleans. This Creole cooking combined the delicate foods of the French with the highly flavored Spanish foods. The black cooks also contributed their skills in cooking, and the Indian contributed herbs and wild game. The French use of onions and the *roux* combined well with the hot piquant foods introduced by travelers returning from Mexico.

Cacao beans were used sometimes as a medium of exchange. The tribute paid to one great Indian chief is listed as maize, cacao beans, and 2000 pounds of fine salt. Taxes and church contributions sometimes were paid in agricultural products.

In Florida, fruit was the principal crop from the beginning. Guavas, peaches, grapes, pineapple, figs, limes, oranges, and lemons, along with sugar cane and molasses, were grown and used. Both corn and rice were grown and eaten.

The Settlers in New York. In 1623, thirteen families of *Walloons*—Celts from Southern and Southeastern Belgium and France—set up a trading post on Manhattan Island. They had brought with them farm equipment and livestock, which they cared for well. The patroons were the owners of manorial estates along the Hudson given to them in the orginal Dutch grants. Other settlers rented land from them. On these estates good rye, wheat, and corn were grown. These patroons also meticulously planted and tended their orchards. Food supplies were carefully stored. Fish and game were carefully and well used.

The Dutch also settled in New York. Dutch housewives contributed doughnuts, pancakes, crullers, and waffles to the American diet, as well as cakes using honey and ginger. From their meats, they made beef and pork sausages and pasties, or meat-filled pastries. Early writers called the Dutch settlers milk-and-cheese people because of their abundant use of dairy products. Dark breads were among their principal foods. The father drank beer, the mother tea, and the children milk. Their hearty meals lacked green vegetables, however, and had too much pastry by modern nutritional standards. Extensive baking was a part of the celebration of Christmas, Easter, May Day, and St. Valentine's Day. As previously mentioned, they were the first to make a social occasion of tea drinking. The early records of the use of tea are few, but one report tells that when tea was first imported from Java it cost as much as $100 per pound, so it must have been used carefully.

The Dutch had come to America better prepared than other ethnic groups. Instead of wooden trenchers they had brought Delft pottery ware, silverware, good china, kitchen crockery, and glazed earthenware.

The Settlers of Delaware. The Swedish settlers came well supplied with domestic animals and settled mostly on small farms, where they had fruit orchards and garden plots. They started the fruit and garden vegetable truck industry in New Jersey and Delaware. They also also cured and salted meat and fish, but most of their food except for rye crisp was different from that of their native Sweden. When food was scarce, they lived on oysters and cornbread. Wine and beer were approved beverages. They did not have forks, but they did use wooden spoons and metal knives.

The English and Scottish Peoples of New Jersey and Pennsylvania. The Quaker settlers, many of whom had been well-to-do in England but who had lost their possessions, built wooden houses at first. Later they learned how to glaze bricks and use them to build houses with glass windows. Most of the landed gentry lived along the rivers, but there was really little social distinction among the economic classes of the Quakers. They were not hunters, but they did fish and gather native blueberries and cranberries, which they later cultivated. They took up grazing of sheep in the hills, whereas most other colonists did not raise sheep.

Some of the early Dutch and Swedish settlers had slaves, but the Quakers were opposed to slavery and did not own slaves.

The Pennsylvania Germans. During the seventeenth century and the early and mid-eighteenth century, German settlers from the Palatinate came seeking religious freedom and were welcomed into Pennsylvania by William Penn. The first of these settlers came in 1683, two years after Philadelphia was founded and they formed the sturdy backbone of a prosperous state after they chose and cultivated their fertile farmlands. They built big red barns and plain homes and were noted for ample meals of home-produced foods. They also gathered wild foods, such as berries. They were heavy users of milk and other dairy products and were good millers, became known for their excellent baked goods, and they contributed the idea of the round pie. Muskmelons, watermelons, asparagus, and cauliflower were introduced by them. They used little tea and coffee.

In contrast to the Netherlands Dutch, these Pennsylvania Dutch (from *Deutsch,* or Germans) used large amounts of many vegetables, quantities of which were stored during the winter. Sauerbraten, "Philadelphia scrapple," "schnitz and knepp," and Lebanese sausage were some of their contributions to the American cuisine.

Thomas credited the mixture of Pennsylvania Germans, English, Swedes, Finns, Scottish, Welsh, French, and Irish settlers with making Philadelphia a culinary capital. She says that even the simplicity-loving Quakers prized good food and extended hospitality graciously.

Pennsylvania had several sects of "Plain People" to whom food became a religious symbol. The Dunkers held love feasts after church workshop services, suppers in which the main dish was a lamb stew symbolizing the "Paschal Lamb." The Moravians, who lived largely in Bethlehem, Pennsylvania, held love feasts in their churches, especially on Christmas Eve; they served warm, fragrant buns and steaming hot coffee. The House Amish, probably to keep members from backsliding, held (and still hold) church services in their homes. The custom of following the service with a sumptuous meal persists to the present day.

Cookies baked at Christmas times were symbols of the season even before the Christmas tree was used. Original cookie cutters are now prized possessions of antique collectors. The eating of animal cookies was probably a remnant of pre-Christian and early Christian religious sacrifice of animals.

The modern Amish farm differs less from the old ones than do farms of other cultural groups. It was and even now is a food factory, where the surplus food brings a good price when sold to "the fancy" (non-Amish) at a farmer's market.

Diets of Frontier People. Early explorers and travelers found deer and wild birds plentiful in forest, fields, and swamps. French woodsmen and mountainmen pushed west for various reasons; some wanted to live as the Indians did. On their journeys, most of them carried hard biscuits and depended on the land for the rest of their food. Because they had to travel light, they usually carried a kettle and sometimes a skillet as their only cooking equipment. Flavorful stews were their mainstay. It is said that travelers on the Old Northwest Trail carried salt-cured pork for making stews with dried peas, so on the "fur frontier" they were known as "pork eaters."

Frontier people considered beaver tail a great delicacy. They were prodigious eaters, especially of buffalo meat; it is said that thirsty travelers even drank the contents of the buffalo paunch. They learned from the Indians how to make and use jerky and pemmican, although they preferred fresh meat. Cannibalism was not unknown among them when they were driven to it. Mountain men are said to have bled their horses and drunk the blood when they were starving.

Some of these men were not fortunate enough to have meat on the new lands they explored, but many of them caught and cooked fish. Bread was mixed from the eggs of wild birds, flour, and water and baked before the fire on a frying pan. They used lumps of dough saved from each bread-making to make their sourdough bread, as did the explorers in the Alaskan Klondike.

Prices for such beverages as alcohol, often used raw and unmixed, and coffee were high when these items were bought at trading posts. Flour is said to have cost the gold-seeking California 49'ers, $40 a barrel.

From the tales of prodigious appetites and the lusty traveling frontier people grew the tales of Paul Bunyan told all the way from Minnesota to the Far West.

John Chapman, known as Johnny Appleseed, planted his way west from the Alleghenies to the Mississippi River. An old apple tree in Vancouver, Washington, is said to be the product of British seeds: a young woman, a guest at a farewell London dinner party for a departing seafarer, put seed from the apples served as dessert into the traveler's pocket to wish him luck. Seeds of grape, pear, peach, and plum were also put in the pockets of some of these adventurers. An old diary and the letters of the first white woman who went overland to Fort Vancouver verify the origin of this apple tree, which was discovered and reported by Lucille Palmer. This woman is said to have been surprised to be served apple pie and other unusual foods at Dr. John McLoughlin's Fort Vancouver.

Corn was still the most important food in newly settled areas because it could be planted even before all the stumps were out of a field. But salt was almost more important than food to the frontier people. It was essential for farm animals as well as for meat preservation; in the beginning, salt cost four times as much as beef. (The term "packer" refers to packing meat in barrels of salt.) Daniel Boone was noted for his ability to find salt licks where his animals could find their needed salt; his last land grant on the Missouri River is known as Boone's Lick.

The coming of railroads made it possible to ship fresh produce, meat, eggs, and milk into cities like New York and Boston. The preference for white eggs in New York City and for brown eggs in Boston has been accounted for because the chickens raised around each city produced that color of eggs. When eggs of the other color were seen, it was known that they had been shipped in and would not be as fresh as local eggs.

Gustavus Franklin Swift, a Yankee from Cape Cod, went to Chicago in the 1870s to set up a packing plant. He is credited with true Yankee thrift because he used all parts of the animal and with being the first one to use and promote the use of refrigerator cars in which to ship meat. He had the vision to see that excellent dressed and well-fattened beef could bring a high price in the Eastern cities. The large meat-packing firm he founded is testimony that he was right. P. D. Armour founded his meat packing firm in the same year—1875.

In 1890, cattle drives of 60–90 days' duration brought over 10 million cattle from San Antonio, Texas, to Kansas. The blue stem grass around Abilene and Manhattan had a reputation as excellent cattle feed.

The process of making artificial ice was patented in 1846 by John Dutton, who lived in Pennsylvania; four years later, Alexander Twining patented an ice-making machine, which was a great boon to the meat distribution industry and furnished cleaner and more sanitary ice to be used around food. It also made possible the shipment of tropical fruits for long distances.

After Nicolas Appert showed the way to can foods in 1819, William Underwood and Thomas Kensett landed in New York City and founded a firm to preserve foods by canning. The need for canned foods to feed the armies during the Civil War gave a great stimulus to this industry.

Few inventions for the home have ever affected life as much as the invention in Europe by Massachusetts-born Benjamin Thompson, later called Count Rumford. During the late eighteenth century, in a workhouse in Munich, he invented and built the cooking range. He worked assiduously for a long time on different models and pans to use on this range. In 1840–1850, old fireplaces were beginning to be boarded up, but even in Eliza Leslie's *Cook Book,* published in 1870, it was taken for granted that cooking was still being done in the fireplace. Marian Harland, in 1872, noted that some housekeepers still used a spit. Some thought that the food cooked on a range did not taste as good as that cooked in a fireplace, an attitude with which modern barbecue fans would probably concur. But the task of cooking was certainly made easier as gas and electric ranges later replaced wood- and coal-burning rnages.

Transporting and Selling Food

The rivers were the highways before the days of roads, and goods were transported on rafts. A "raft of pins" meant just that. After roads were opened, the Conestoga wagon, usually 16 feet long by 4–5 feet wide and 6–7 feet high, afforded a cargo space of 500–600 cubic feet; a raft 60–100 feet long could easily carry ten times what the wagon could.

Peddlers with packs on their back could walk through fields and unopened brush-lands. It was more efficient and less tiring, however, to use a horse or mule and a wagon as soon as paths or roads were opened up and made this possible. Sometimes a peddler, tired of traveling, settled down in a likely place, usually at a crossroads, and opened a general store. These merchants carried food, household items, and farm supplies and equipment. The first specialty stores in America and England were bakeries. Some of these stores used barter, exchanging feathers for molasses, potatoes for salt, cherry boards for tropical dyes, or hemlock bark for tea and coffee.

In 1789, when George Washington was on a tour, he stayed at a tavern in Milford, Pennsylvania. He criticized the tavern for the poor food and the fact that they had no silver spoons. Not much relishing his supper of meat and potatoes, he called for a bowl of bread and milk. When a pewter spoon with a proper handle was served with this and he complained, he was told the house could afford no silver spoons. He gave the serving maid a two shilling piece and told her to go and borrow a silver spoon, which she acquired from the minister.

In 1825, John Delmonico, a Swiss captain of a trading ship going to the West Indies, wished to sell European wines; he opened near a bakery in New York City what has often been and still is called "a hole in the wall." This was the small beginning of Delmonico's Restaurant.

G. H. Hartford and his partner, G. Gilman, watched tea being unloaded from ships and decided to devise ways to sell it more cheaply. They bought tea wholesale and brought the cost down to $.30 per pound. Thus, they founded the great American Tea Company, which later was called the Great Atlantic and Pacific Tea Company. The day book of a midwestern grocer in 1862 is said to have shown the entire list of imported articles of food to be coffee, tea, figs, mustard, pepper, cloves, allspice, nutmeg, ginger, cinnamon, lemons, oranges, sago, prunes, raisins, and almonds.

Farm Machinery

The plows used by early settlers were discussed on page 73. John Deere, a blacksmith in Vermont, peddled the first 3 plows, which he had invented, in 1837. They were designed so that they would slide smoothly over the sticky prairie earth and come out clean. In 1839, he made and sold 10 plows; in 1842, he sold 100. Cyrus McCormick invented the reaper in 1832. Later a binder and the J. J. Case threshing machine were developed. Modern mechanized farming followed.

Food preparation on the nineteenth- and twentieth-century farm was influenced

"Shake hands?" Kitchen of mid-nineteenth century (*Courtesy Library of Congress*).

Electric Stove. First patented in 1895 in United States (*Courtesy Seattle City Light*).

when more men were needed to run the huge machines. The farm wife then had to cook in a much larger quantity. The large threshers dinners became neighborhood affairs. The farm wife and her helpful neighbor housewives prepared the big dinner. Often the woman of the house and her daughters worked for days in advance preparing the food.

Large-Scale Farming Begins

Oliver Dalrymple of the Northern Pacific Railroad began what was then called "bonanza" farming on the 75,000 acre holdings of that railroad in the Eastern North Dakota Red River Valley. In 1880, Dr. Hugh Glenn harvested a crop of one million bushels of wheat on his Sacramento Valley, California, ranch; this was one of the largest wheat farms of the times. These were the forerunners of the large-scale farm food production of today.

Improving the Quality of Food

An expert on the household, Lillian W. Betts, complained in the late nineteenth century that cookbooks were not scientific; "they not only contradicted each other, they contradicted themselves." She encouraged a young woman, Fannie Farmer, who was interested in preparing good food, to write a scientific book. By the time Miss Farmer was 39 years old and had suffered two paralytic strokes, she had distinguished herself as a teacher of cooking. She had attended the Boston Cooking School and graduated when she was 32. After graduation, she was asked to be assistant director of the school; two years later, she became its director. Fannie Farmer's *Boston Cooking School Cookbook,* said to be the first scientific cookbook, was first published at her own expense in 1896. The page of copyrights in new editions of this book gives an interesting history. In

1965, the eleventh edition, called *Fannie Farmer Cookbook,* came out. At that time, over three million copies had been printed. Miss Farmer saw this book through 2 revisions and 18 reprintings herself before others took over. In these first 18 printings, 291,000 copies were produced. Because the Preface to the first edition (1896) is historic in itself, it is quoted here:

With progress of knowledge the needs of the human body have not been forgotten. During the last decade much time has been given by scientists to the study of foods and their dietetic value, and it is a subject which rightfully should demand much consideration from all.

It is my wish that it may not only be looked upon as a compilation of tried and tested recipes, but that it may awaken an interest through its condensed scientific knowledge which will lead to deeper thought and broader study of what to eat.

So nutrition and food preparation were jointly promoted. The work of Ellen H. Richards and Mary Hinman Abel in the New England Kitchen in Boston forms another interesting chapter that can be found in other books.

Legal attempts to improve food are illustrated by Massachusetts' passing of a law

Gas range 1930 (*Courtesy Brooklyn Union Gas Company and Washington Natural Gas Company*).

An electric kitchen of the 1970s (*Courtesy Seattle City Light*).

in 1850 prohibiting the adulteration of milk. Milk was sold in bottles in the late 1850s in Brooklyn; bottling and the concept of certified milk, for which the medical milk commission set up standards, were further efforts to produce and sell safe milk. Dr. Harvey Wiley, who was the prime mover in the enactment of federal pure food and drug legislation, became chief of the Chemical Division of the Department of Agriculture in 1883.

These are only a few of the early efforts that have developed into the present system of safeguarding our food supply. Others can be found in other source books.

The Land Grant College Movement

In 1862, President Lincoln signed the famous Morrill Act which granted the proceeds from federally owned lands for perpetual endowment of what would be colleges for the sons and daughters of the industrial and working classes. These colleges were directed to offer instruction in agriculture and the mechanical arts; the latter included home economics. These colleges, most of which later became universities, were directed to teach, to do research, and to take knowledge to the people. The Iowa legislature had passed a bill in 1858 to establish an agricultural college, so they promptly took advantage of the proferred aid, becoming the first state to accept the provisions and responsibilities of the

Land Grant College Act. Other states used the money which came to them in different ways, making it difficult to state which was the first Land Grant college.

The Iowa Agricultural Experiment station, established in 1888, has a long history of research designed to help farmers. Many people credit the bounty of our food supply to the increase in production made possible by the Agricultural Research Stations and Land Grant Universities in every state in the union.

America is said to have given the world 11 botanical beverage plants, 5 cereal grains, 145 fruits, 24 nuts, 34 root plants, and 27 miscellaneous plants.

Important Foods

Space does not permit extensive discussion of the many foods especially important in our diet; therefore, we have chosen to tell in depth only a few of these stories. Potatoes and bread as widely used staple foods around the world are discussed separately here.

The White Potato: Number One Vegetable of the World. *Papata, Murphy, mickey, spud, and Irish potato* all refer to the vegetable we commonly call the white potato. Yet the uncles, aunts, cousins, and grandparents of this potato have skins of white, pink, red, yellow, brown, green, purple, orange, black and spots of many colors. Their meat may be yellow, lavender, pink, or white. No one quite knows how many varieties of this useful vegetable grow in its native home, the Andes Mountains of Peru, Bolivia, and Chile.

When the potato was first found in Peru, it was observed that the natives in the high country—10,000 feet altitude or more—had a method of freeze-drying their potatoes in the sun. They used the frozen potato cooked whole or pounded into a flour, which they dried in the sun. Frozen potatoes could be kept from one season to another. Prehistoric stories of dried potatoes have been found, showing that potatoes were as much in demand in the days of the Incas as they are today. The skins of the frozen dried potatoes were rubbed off by walking over them with bare feet, which must have been a hard task. These potatoes turned black and were as hard as stones, so they had to be soaked three to four days before they could be cooked.

Salaman said that the natives of Peru and Bolivia, having been frightened by the terrors of the jungle that spread over the plateau to the coast, migrated out to the eastern slopes of the mountains. They found secluded valleys and fertile portions of the high tablelands around the great inland sea of Lake Titicaca, where the altitudes vary from 12,500 to 15,000 feet above sea level. Because their usual plants, such as manioc and maize, would not grow at such altitudes, they had to look for hardier plants. They also had to protect their food supply by using a vegetable that would be edible after it was frozen. Salaman commented on this: "Perhaps one of the most remarkable of man's conquests of nature gave him the key to success." It is for this reason that the potato is discussed separately. On the Andean highlands from Columbia on the north to Chile on the south, these early people found the different species of the tuber of the parent stock of our domestic potato, the species named *Solanum*. It is thought that the hybrids were not produced by these people but were found as wild varieties. On these highlands, the use of the potato made life possible, giving the people a way to survive in this environment.

The frost-resistant varieties now grown around the highest levels are said to be tasteless and insipid and are reserved to make *chuno* (the sun-dried potato). Other varieties were probably grown by the Incas to use fresh, as they are today. A recent observer says that she counted 89 varieties of these potatoes at the Potato Fair in La Paz, Bolivia.

History has recorded that the potato has made more trans-Atlantic voyages between Europe and America during the past 300 years than any other vegetable. During the latter half of the nineteenth century, research by the eminent Russian scientist, Vavilov, proved that the European potato had come from Peru. Others believe these primitive potatoes also grew in Chile and Bolivia. From available records, it has been concluded that the potato reached Spain between 1564 and 1576, where for a time its cultivation was local and insignificant. It probably left South America around 1569 and arrived in Seville in 1570. It is said to have been brought to New England in 1719 by Irish immigrants from Londonderry.

Some credit Sir Walter Raleigh with first growing potatoes in England in 1585, and others say Sir John Hawkins introduced them into Ireland in 1565. Others believe that Hawkins' potato was the *batatas,* or Caribbean sweet potato. In some of the early records, the Jerusalem artichoke and the sweet potato have been confused with the white potato. Salaman, who has studied extensively the history of the potato, supports the belief that Sir Walter Raleigh introduced it into Ireland. Salaman also says that it possibly may have reached there accidently when, at the dispersion of the Armada, some ships were wrecked on the west coast of Ireland, the hulks were plundered, and potatoes were found in the cook's stores. These may have been planted on the coast of Kerry and Cork; Whichever way they came, Salaman fixes their date of entry into Ireland at between 1586 and 1588. He says of the potato that "One can only suppose that it won the confidence of the people because it fitted readily into the economic structure of their life. . . ."

The people in the rich, semi-industralized western part of Europe took 100 years to begin to appreciate the merits of the potato. It took 250 years for the potato to gain acceptance in England and only 50 years for the Irish to adopt it as their own because the latter appear not to have developed prejudices against it originally.

There are numerous stories, not all of which can be recounted here; the reader is referred to Salaman for a fuller description. The stories detail the difference between the autocratic methods of the Prussians trying to force people to grow potatoes and the clever method of the French, carefully guarding potato plots during the daytime and purposefully leaving them unguarded at night so people could steal the plants. Louis XVI is said to have worn a potato blossom in his buttonhole and Marie Antoinette to have worn one in her hair. The nobility also planted potatoes in their gardens and were careful to be observed by the peasants as they ate the potatoes. Parmentier, a French military pharmacist, is credited with having learned to eat potatoes as a prisoner of war in Germany, and in 1780 he encouraged the French people to grow and eat potatoes.

By the middle of the nineteenth century, the potato was a staple of the British Isles, Northern Europe, and North America. Although the potato has been known in Japan for 200 years, according to Boswell, the Oriental people have never cared for it. Even after World War II, the state of culture of the potato in Japan was below that of other foods.

Brogger said that the potato, introduced into Norway about 1750, contributed slowly to the transformation of agriculture there. He describes the resistance it encountered during the generation which was required to introduce it. The Presbyterian clergy in Scotland also are said to have opposed the use of potatoes as food, because they were not mentioned in the Bible and therefore were not safe to eat. At one time, Europeans believed that potatoes caused leprosy, fevers, and other maladies. As late as 1771, the French government asked the medical faculty of Paris about the ill-reputed potato, and they replied that the potato was a good food of great use and not injurious to health.

The potato produces more food per acre than most other crops and can be raised in a variety of climates. It grows farther north and at higher altitudes than cereals. It is easy to cultivate and pleasant to eat. It furnishes great protection against hunger in times of want and has spread extensively over widely scattered populations and territories. The Irish found the potato easy to grow; it was not necessary to plow before planting—all they needed to do was to spade and to dig trenches. The word *spud* is said to have come from the word *spade*.

Although potatoes are credited with having saved people from famine after the 30 Years War, the one-crop potato economy brought about disaster in Ireland in 1845–1847. See page 53.

The Sweet Potato. The word potato really comes from the Inca word for the sweet potato—batata. The Inca word for the white potato was papa but the Spanish called both the white and sweet potato batata, which the British called potato. The sweet potato requiring a moist, warm climate, a longer growing season than the white potato, as well as sandy soil, was early found to be best adapted to our southern states when it was first planted in Jamestown, Virginia. Boswell says that Columbus and his associates probably found the sweet potato on various islands of the West Indies. He says that it was taken to Spain about 1508 and early Spanish explorers are believed to have taken it to the Philippines and the East Indies from whence it was carried to India, China and Malaya by the Portuguese voyagers.

The soft, rich, moist varieties are as Boswell said, erroneously called "yams." True yams are seldom seen in the United States.

Bread. Our word *cereal* comes from *Ceres*, the Roman goddess of agriculture and the harvest. When people first began to cultivate grains or used wild grains as food, they first parched them to make them edible. To be able to remove the tough glume (outer husk covering the grain), they had to parch the emmer wheats. They then learned to grind the grains to make a porridge. The next step was to make a flat loaf of bread from the heavy cereal paste and to bake this in front of the fire, as did the marching Roman soldiers even after ovens were in use back home.

The earliest records of the use of wheat are said to come from the ''finds'' of the archeologists at Jarmo, 6700 B.C. It is said that the seeds of wheat are the seeds of civilization. During the thousands of years that followed its domestication, wheat was grown in ever-increasing amounts in the Fertile Crescent.

Wheat is the only cereal grain that contains sufficient gliadin and glutenin, two proteins that, when mixed with water, form the elastic protein gluten, making possible the rising and elasticity needed for bread. Rye contains some gliadin and glutenin and can be used to make bread, but for a more highly risen bread, some wheat flour is mixed with the rye flour. Barley, the other cereal used by early humans, does not have the proteins to form gluten and therefore makes heavy loaves. Barley was, through the centuries, the cereal of the poor. It is said that as soon as wheat became plentiful the Egyptians abandoned the use of barley. Naked wheats became important during the Middle Ages. These wheats have glumes less coarse and less difficult to remove than the earlier varieties of wheat, hence their threshing is easier. Rye grows more easily and abundantly on the soils of Northern Europe, which probably explains why the people of this region have for centuries used much rye bread.

The next development in bread making was fermentation. There are various theories of how people discovered that this process could be used to make heavy cakes lighter and more palatable. Perhaps they forgot to bake some cakes, the dough fermented, and they discovered the air bubbles in the cakes. The Egyptians were probably the first people to use fermentation in their bread, although the peoples of Mesopotamia may have done so; the former often are called the ''fathers of bread'' and the ''bread eaters.'' The Greeks and the Romans both recognized the hard and soft wheats and the use of the former in breadmaking. The Egyptians undoubtedly advanced breadmaking more rapidly than any other ancient peoples. Dough found in a 4500-year-old Egyptian tomb showed, when examined microscopically, 100 million yeast cells per grain of dough. When did the art of cultivating yeast begin? This is not certain, but we do know that the Egyptians brewed beer and probably would not have used a piece of dough as the source of that yeast; so they must have cultivated yeast. It should be pointed out that each stage in the use of cereals and in breadmaking can be found today, beginning with porridge, flat cakes and other flat breads, and sour dough starters.

The whiteness of bread has been prized from Egyptian times through Grecian, Roman, and Medieval times, as it is today. The Romans recognized the higher nutritive value of whole wheat (brown) bread. See page 37. The theater-going public, if they could afford it, as well as other wealthy people in Athens, are said to have demanded and eaten white bread. The Greeks, however, called the whole-wheat cakes ''health cakes,'' probably because they considered the bulkier stools produced when whole wheat bread was eaten as healthier. White bread is said to have been given by the Greeks when an individual had diarrhea.

Throughout history, there are records of the adulteration of flour; in Medieval England, for instance, flour was adulterated with alum and ammonium carbonate to make the bread whiter. Barley meal and cooked potatoes were used also for this purpose. The

Kitchen bakery thought to be from Wayfarers Lodge in 1890s
(Courtesy Library of Congress—photo by C. H. Currier).

weight of the loaf of bread and the adulteration of flour have been the subject of laws since Grecian and Roman times. Market police watched the weight closely. The description of these ordinances is discussed on pages 28 and 57.

It is easy to understand how the development of a civilization is often a story of breadmaking. First of all, people had to settle in a permanent village before they could grow grain efficiently and make bread. The kind of ovens that people learned to use rather early in the process were not portable. In order to improve methods of grinding and milling, the wheat demanded man's best efforts; baking of large numbers of varieties of bread was considered worthy of praise and reward. The Egyptians are said to have prepared and baked 50 kinds of bread and cakes, muffin-shaped long rolls, spiced breads, and breads sprinkled with seeds, like today's caraway rolls.

Improved agricultural methods made more abundant crops of wheat available, giving a nation such as Egypt money and power. So it was said in Roman times "who controls Egypt will be Emperor of Rome." Under Augustus, at the beginning of the Imperial Period, 144,345,000 bushels of wheat, enough to feed two million people for one year, were imported into Rome from Egypt and Africa.

Grain cutting progressed from the sickle to a scythe to the great modern combines. Threshing was first done by men stomping on the grain and later by the use of animals to tromp on it. The Romans are said to have had a water mill in 100 B.C. From the use of the first primitive mortars and pestles to modern rolling mills is a story of people's

In Tunisia bread is precious (*Courtesy* CARE).

struggle to produce food with less human effort. Aykroyd and Doughty said that, today in North America, it takes 3 man hours of work to harvest an acre of wheat, whereas it took 50 hours 100 years ago.

The prestige of the miller and the baker was great during Egyptian, Grecian, and Roman times but fell drastically when the barbarians took over Europe. However, Christians considered bread holy because of Christ's prayer "give us this day our daily bread" and because he said "This is My Body"; and as Christianization took place, the barbarians' respect for bread changed. Early Christians put three crosses on each loaf of bread. The word bread occurs 264 times in the Bible, and it probably always refers to wheaten bread. Israelites are thought to have learned to make bread from the Egyptians.

In 100 A.D., Roman miller-bakers were well organized into a college (guild), the members of which were represented in the Senate and were forbidden to associate with comedians and gladiators. They were classed as artisans along with tailors. Every year, these bakers' guilds celebrated a festival on June 9, when baking tools and ovens were wreathed in flowers.

Around 1000 A.D., the situation of bread bakers worsened. The hatred of millers and bakers by the populace arose probably because some millers stole grain when they were hard pressed. These millers were, however, the only knowledgeable engineers among the technically ignorant people of the Middle Ages, so they did acquire some power, even police powers—rights of local jurisdiction. They began to interfere in peasant's affairs, which was one cause of some of the peasants' wars.

The bread of the Middle Ages is said to have been of lower quality than that of Classical times. When grain became moldy or cultivation was interrupted because of war, the terrible famines of the twelfth and thirteenth centuries resulted.

During the days of the luxury-loving kings and queens of France, poor people were starving for lack of bread or other food while the tables of the court had heaping baskets of bread on them. Trenchers were made of bread and were usually 6 inches wide and about 3 inches high. The table cloth was also often made of bread. Paupers waited at the doors in the courtyards to get this food-soaked bread after the royal meal.

In these terrible times, tenderness toward bread was especially evident. In the Medieval German provinces, all bakers always faced and avoided turning their backs on ovens to show respect to bread.

In early societies, the housewife baked the bread, but as populations became more concentrated and artisans came to be specialists, bread was made in bakeries. In Jerusalem, the bakers took their bread to a bakery-factory for baking. Aykroyd and Doughty

Kurdish woman baking bread (*Courtesy Food and Agriculture Organization—photo by Jamal Hammad*).

said that commercial bakeries have existed in towns and cities for 4000–5000 years.

In ancient Egypt, bread was the coinage of the realm; for hundreds of years, workers were paid in bread; for the servant, the daily average wage was three loaves of bread and two jugs of beer. Old Anglo-Saxon landowners, called halfords, believed that in order to do good work a person must be well fed. The title lord came from this old word and it came to mean "Man who gives out bread." In the middle of the eighteenth century, alms bread was made of five parts of wheat, four of rye, and three of peas (Ashley).

It is said that, if the Egyptians had not developed the art of breadmaking, the French would have because they are alike in their worship of bread. Bread has been held to be precious by many peoples throughout all history. In modern Romania, if a person drops a piece of bread, he or she kisses it after picking it up. Every Greek who had any part of the souring or making of bread was held to be performing a priestly service as a religious apprentice to Mother Earth (Jacobs).

Hot-cross buns, which Christians use on Good Fridays, actually originated in pagan times (Spicer). The early Egyptians offered to their moon goddess cakes marked with horns said to have been symbolic of their horned ox, used as a sacrifice. Early Greeks presented horn-imprinted cakes to Astarte and other deities. Later, the horn became a cross. This cross was supposed to have represented the quarters of the moon. The Romans ate hot-cross buns at sacrificial feasts. The Saxons inscribed loaves with crosses in honor of Eostre, the Teutonic Goddess of the Dawn, who was associated with the vernal equinox. Our word Easter came from Eostre. The early Christian fathers adopted making crosses on bread, and the eucharistic wafers were imprinted with the Greek cross as an emblem of the Host. The English have made hot-cross buns for centuries: the original Royal Bun House in Chelsea made buns that became famous. Everywhere pastry cooks and bakers competed. Hawkers peddled buns on the streets from 6 A.M. to 6 P.M. One cry of the sellers went like this:

Hot cross buns
If you have no daughters,
Given them to your sons;
But if you have none of these merry little elves,
Then you may keep them all for yourselves.

In 943 A.D. a plague struck the Franks around Limoges. They ate a bread that was wet and had a black, sticky substance inside. Today this illness is known as ergotism, caused by a fungus that grows on rye. Insects visited the "sweat drops" on the blackened grain and spread the spores in wet weather. No Roman farmer would have used this grain, nor would a Roman miller have milled it or a baker have baked it; Columella had instructed the Roman farmers how to fight the disease. Romans also knew that cleanliness was necessary in breadmaking. This tenth-century plague in France was the only mass disaster from ergotism (occurring because knowledge of technical procedures in the art of milling and baking had declined). The church had banned medical research as magic, so not until the late Renaissance did two physicians, one in 1582 and one in 1600, discover the cause of ergotism.

Bread for the poor has been made throughout the ages from many foods other than our common cereals. Prentice told of the use of acorns, fine sawdust and bark of young pear or cherry trees, or the twigs of young chestnut or oak trees. He also recounted the use of a number of vegetables and their roots, as well as beechnuts and chestnuts.

In Auvergne, France, loaves of bread weighing 20 to 30 pounds were kept for a month in winter. In an Austrian country home museum in the Tyrol, huge doughnut-shaped loaves of bread can still be seen strung on the original wires. Because it was scarce, this bread was used dry as crumbs on soups and stews so less would be eaten.

STUDY QUESTIONS

1. Why do we have more information about the eating habits of some early Europeans than about similar habits of other groups?
2. How did early food production and distribution in England lay the foundations for our great modern food industry?
3. In what ways are we in debt to the entire world from medieval times until the nineteenth century for our abundant food supply?
4. Describe how the foods and food preparation of a seventeenth- or eighteenth-century American Thanksgiving dinner compares with such a meal in the late twentieth century?
5. How is the potato connected with American politics of this century?

TOPICS FOR INDIVIDUAL DISCUSSION

1. Trace the development of agriculture and animal husbandry for one of the following cultures: China; one section of Africa; the Mayan or Aztec; one group in Northern Europe.
2. Trace Medieval agriculture through its major stages with illustrations of the following:
   a. Development of efficiency of tools
   b. Attempts to deal with weather conditions
   c. Interchange of foods with groups who lived great distances away
3. Show how the European backgrounds of early colonists affect our modern-day foods.

4. Discuss in detail the contributions of one group of American Indians to our modern-day food.

5. Trace one major food industry through its development during the last 150 years.

REFERENCES AND SUGGESTED READING
Early Peoples

Adolph, William H. What Early Man Discovered about Food. *Harper's Magazine,* 212:67–70, May, 1956.

Brace, C. J. *The Stage of Human Evolution.* Prentice-Hall, Englewood Cliffs, N.J., 1967 Braidwood, R. J. *Prehistoric Men.* Chicago Natural History Museum Press, Chicago, Ill., 1948.

Braidwood, R. J. Did Man Once Live by Beer Alone? *Amer. Anthropology,* 55:515–516, 1953.

Brew, J. A. The Metal Ages. Copper, Bronze and Iron. Chapter V, pp. 111–138. *Man, Culture, and Society,* Ed. H. L. Shapiro. Oxford University Press, New York, 1960.

Brogger, A. W. From the Stone Age to the Motor Age. *Antiquity,* 14:163–181, 1940.

Brown, Lester R. *By Bread Alone.* Praeger, New York, 1975.

Caldwell, J. R. *New Roads to Yesterday.* Basic Books, New York, 1966.

Childe, V. Gordon. *Man Makes Himself.* Mentor Books, New American Library, New York, 1951.

Childe, V. Gordon. *New Light on the Most Ancient East. The Oriental Prelude to European Prehistory.* Appleton-Century-Crofts, Inc., New York, 1934.

Childe, V. Gordon. *What Happened in History.* Penguin Books, London, 1946.

Curwen, E. Cecil. *Plow and Pasture (Present and Past Studies in History of Civilization).* Cattell Press, London, 1946.

Davenport, C. B. The Dietaries of Primitive People. *Amer. Antiquity,* 47:60–82, 1945.

Flannery, Kent V. The Ecology of Early Food Production in Mesopotamia. *Science,* 147:1247–1256, 1965.

Harlan, J. R. The Plants and Animals that Nourish Man. *Scientific American,* 235:89, 1976.

Harris, David R. The Origins of Agriculture in the Tropics. *Science,* 60:180–193, March/April, 1972.

Helback, Hans. Studying the Diet of Ancient Man. *Archeólogy,* 14:95–101, 1961.

Hoebel, E. A. *Anthropology. The Study of Man.* 3rd Edition. McGraw-Hill Co., New York, 1966.

Keeley, L. N. The Functions of Paleolithic Flint Tools. *Scientific American,* 237:108, 1977.

Keesing, R. M. and F. M. Keesing. *New Perspectives in Cultural Anthropology.* Holt, Rinehart and Winston, New York, 1971.

Kluckhohn, Clyde. *Mirror for Man.* McGraw-Hill Co., New York, 1964.

Kroeber, A. L. *The Nature of Culture.* University of Chicago Press, Chicago, Ill., 1952.

Lamb, Charles. *The Essays of Elia.* Malcolm Elwin, Ed., MacDonald and Co., London, 1952.

Linton, Ralph. *The Tree of Culture.* Vintage Books, Random House, New York, 1955.

Loomis, R. S. Agricultural Systems. *Scientific American,* 235(No.3) 105:98–105, 1976.

Montagu, Ashley. *Man: His First Two Million Years—A Brief Introduction to Anthropology.* Dell Publishing, New York, 1969.

Moore, Alma Chestnut. *The Grasses. Earth's Green Wealth.* The Macmillan Company, New York, 1960.

Orr, John Boyd. *The Wonderful World of Food.* The Substance of Life. Garden City Books, Garden City, N.Y., 1958.

Quennell, M. and C. H. B. Quennell. *Everyday Life—Early Iron Ages.* G. P. Putnam and Sons, New York, 1955.

Quennell, M. and C. H. B. Quennell. *Everyday Life in Prehistoric Times.* G. P. Putnam and Sons, New York, 1959.

Reed, Charles. Animal Domestication. *Science,* 130:1629–1638, 1959.

Scrimshaw, N. S. and V. R. Young. The Requirements of Human Nutrition. *Scientific American.* 235:51, 1976.

Waterbalk, H. T. Food Production in Prehistoric Europe. *Science,* 162:1093–1101, Dec. 1968.

White, Leslie. *The Evolution of Culture.* McGraw-Hill, New York, 1959.

General

Ames, G. and R. Wyler. *Food and Life.* Creative Education Society, Inc., Mankato, Minn., 1966.

Aykroyd, W. R. and Joyce Doughty. *Wheat in Human Nutrition.* FAO Nutritional Studies #23, FAO, Rome, Italy, 1970.

Bennett, M. K. *The World's Food.* Harper & Row, New York. 1954.

Bitting, A. W. *Appertizing or the Art of Canning. Its History and Development.* The Trade Pressroom. San Francisco, Calif., 1937.

Boswell, V. R. Our Vegetable Travelers. *National Geographic Magazine,* 46 No. 2:145–217, August, 1949.

Brillat-Savarin, J. A. *The Physiology of Taste.* Dover Publications, New York, 1960.

Brogger, A. W. From the Stone Age to the Motor Age. A Sketch of Norwegian Cultural History. *Antiquities,* 13:163–181, 1940.

Brothwell, Don and Patricia Brothwell. *Food in Antiquity.* Frederick A. Praeger, New York, 1969.

Brown, Ina Corrine. *Understanding Other Cultures.* Prentice-Hall Inc., Englewood Cliffs, N.J., 1963.

Brown, Lester R. and G. W. Finisterbusch. *Man and His Environment-Food.* Harper & Row, New York, 1972.

Butzer, Karl W. *Environment and Archeology.* 2nd Ed. Aldine and Atherton, Chicago, 1971.

Cottrell, Leonard. *The Anvils of Civilization.* A Mentor Book, New American Library, New York, 1957.

Crissey, Forrest. *The Story of Foods.* Rand McNally and Co., Chicago, Ill., 1971.

Cuppy, Will. *The Decline and Fall of Practically Everybody—Some Royal Stomachs.* Ed. by F. Feldkamp. Holt Publishing Co., New York, 1950.

de Kruif, Paul. *Hunger Fighters.* Harcourt Brace Jovanovich, New York, 1928.

Harlan, Jack R. The Plants and Animal that Nourish Man. *Scientific American,* 235 (No 3):88–97, 1976.

Harrison, Molly. *The Kitchen in History.* Charles Scribner's Sons, New York, 1972.

Hazlett, W. Carew. *Old Cookery Books and Ancient Cuisine,* Elliottstock, London, England, 1902.

Howell, William, *Mankind in the Making*. Doubleday and Co., Garden City, New York, 1967.

Jacobs, H. E. *Six Thousand Years of Bread—Its Holy and Unholy History*. Doubleday and Co., Garden City, New York, 1944.

Janick, Jules, C. H. Noller and C. L. Rhykerd. The Cycles of Plants and Animal Nutrition. *Scientific American*, 235 (No 3):74–86, 1976.

Jensen, Lloyd B. *Man's Food*. Garrard Press, Champaign, Ill., 1953.

League for International Food Education Newsletter. February 1972.

Lee, Norman E. *Harvests and Harvesting*. Cambridge University Press, London, England, 1960.

Lehner, E. J. *Folklore and Odysseys of Food and Medicinal Plants*. Tudor Publishing Co. New York, 1962.

McCarrison, R. *Studies in Deficiency Diseases*. Oxford University Press, New York, 1921.

Milikian, C. and L. K. Rudd. *The Wonder of Food*. Appleton-Century-Crofts, Inc., New York, 1961.

Orr, John Boyd. *The Wonderful World of Food. The Substance of Life*. Garden City Books, Garden City, New York, 1958.

Orr, John Boyd and David Lubbock. *The White Man's Dilemma*. Barnes and Noble Inc., New York, 1964.

Peacock, J. L. and A. T. Kirsch. *The Human Direction*. Appleton-Century-Crofts, New York, 1970.

Perl, Lila. *Rice, Spice and Bitter Oranges. Mediterranean Foods and Festivals*. World Publishing Co., New York, 1967.

Pirie, N. W. *Food Resources. Conventional and Novel*. Penguin Books, Baltimore, Md., 1969.

Prentice, E. Parmalee. *Hunger and History*. Caxton Printers, Caldwell, Idaho, 1951.

Remington, Roe E. The Social Origins of Dietary Habits. *Science Monthly* 43:193–204, 1936.

Ritchie, Jean A. S. *Learning Better Nutrition*. FAO Nutritional Studies #20, FAO, Rome, Italy, 1967.

Sauer, Carl O. *Agricultural Origins and Dispersal*. M.I.T. Press, Cambridge, Md., 1969.

Shapiro, Harry L. (Ed.). *Man, Culture, and Society*. A Galaxy Book, Oxford University Press, New York, 1956.

Smallzried, Kathleen Ann. *The Everlasting Pleasure*. Appleton-Century-Crofts, New York, 1956.

Tannahill, Reay, *Food in History*. Stein and Day, New York, 1973.

Tartan, Beth. *The Good Old Days Cookbook*. Westover Publishing Co., Richmond, Va., 1971.

Traeger, James. *Foodbook*. Grossman, New York, 1970.

Vayda, A. P. *Environment and Cultural Behavior*. American Museum of Natural History, The Natural History Press, Garden City, N.Y., 1969.

Wason, Betty. *Cooks, Gluttons and Gourmets. A History of Cooking*. Doubleday and Co., Inc., Garden City, N.Y., 1962.

Wecksberg, Joseph. *The Best Things in Life*. Little, Brown and Co., Boston, Mass., 1965.

Wissler, Clark. Wheat and Civilization. *Natural History*, 52:172, 1951.

Zeuner, Frederick E. *A History of Domesticated Animals*. Harper & Row, New York, 1963.

Medieval

Bailey, Adrian. *The Cooking of British Isles*. Time-Life Foods of World Series, Time-Life Books, New York, 1969.

Brown, Dale. *The Cooking of Scandinavia*. Time-Life Foods of World Series, Time-Life Books, New York, 1968.

Davis, Dorothy. *Fairs, Shops, and Supermarkets*. University of Toronto Press, Toronto, Canada, 1966.

Drummond, J. C. and Anne Wilbraham. *The Englishman's Diet. Five Centuries of English Diet*. Jonathan Cape, London, England, 1969.

Erlanger, Philippe. *The Age of Courts and Kings. Manners and Morals 1558–1715*. Harper-Row, New York, 1967.

Hale, John R. *Age of Exploration. Great Ages of Man*. Time-Life Inc., New York, 1966.

Hazlitt, W. Carew. *Old Cookery Books and Ancient Cuisines*. Elliott, London, 1902.

Hollister, C. Warren. *Medieval Europe—A Short History*. 2nd Edition, John Wiley and Sons, New York, 1968.

International Trade Center, UNCTAD/GATT, Geneva, Switzerland. Markets for Spices in North America, Western Europe and Japan, 1970.

LaFay, H. *The Vikings*. National Geographic Society, Washington, D.C., 1972.

Merrill, E. D. *The Botany of Cook's Voyages and Its Unexpected Significance in Relation to Anthropology, Biogeography and History*. Chronica Botanica Company, Waltham, Mass., 1954.

Osborne, John. *Britain-Life World Library*. Time, Inc., New York, 1967.

Penrose, Boies. *Travel and Discovery in the Renaissance 1420–1620*. Harvard University Press, Cambridge, Mass., 1960.

Perl, Lila. *Rice, Spice and Bitter Oranges—Mediterranean Foods and Festivals*. World Publishing Co., New York, 1967.

Prentice, E. Parmalee. *Hunger and History*. Caxton Printers, Inc., Caldwell, Idaho, 1951.

Quennell, Marjorie and C. H. B. Quennell. *A History of Everyday Things in England 1815–1914*. G. P. Putnam and Sons, New York, 1965.

Stewart, C. P. (Ed.) and D. Gutherie. *Lind's The Treatise of Scurvy*. University Press, Edinburgh, Scotland, 1953.

Tannebaum, Edward R. *European Civilization Since the Middle Ages*, 2nd Edition. John Wiley and Sons, New York, 1971.

Thomas, G. Z. *Richer than Spices*. Alfred A. Knopf, New York, 1965.

Trevelan, G. M. *Illustrated English Social History*. 4 volumes. Penguin Books, London, 1964.

America

American Heritage Editors, *American Heritage Cook Book*. Simon and Schuster, Inc., New York, 1964.

Bennett, M. K. Good Economy of the New England Indians, 1605–75. *Journal Political Economy* 43:369–397, 1955.

Carson, Gerald. *The Yankee Kitchen from American Heritage Cookbook*. American Heritage Publishing Co., Simon and Schuster, New York, 1964, Chapter 3.

Crawford, Mary Caroline. *Among Old New England Inns*. L. C. Page and Co., Boston, Mass., 1907.

Crawford, Mary Caroline. *Romantic Days in Old Boston*. Little, Brown and Co., Boston, Mass., 1910.

Cummings, R. O. The American and His Food, Revised Ed. Arno Press, New York, 1970.

Dolan, J. R. *The Yankee Peddler of Early America*. Brownhall House, New York, 1964.

Drucker, Philip. *Cultures of the North Pacific Coast*. Chandler Publishing Co., San Francisco, Calif., 1965.

Earle, Alice Morse, Abridged and edited by Shirley Glubok. *Home and Child Life in Colonial Days*. The Macmillan Company, New York, 1969.

Farb, Peter. *Man's Rise to Civilization—As Shown by the Indians of North America from Primeval Times to the Coming of the Industrial Stage*. E. P. Dutton and Co., New York, 1968.

Farmer, Fannie M. (Ed. by Wilma Lord Perkins). *The Boston Cooking School Cook Book*. Little, Brown and Co., Boston, Mass., 1965.

Hays, Wilma and R. Vernon Hays. *Foods the Indians Gave Us*. Ives Washburn, Inc. 1976.

Kennedy, John F. *A Nation of Immigrants*. Harper and Row, New York, 1964.

Kimball, Yeffe and Jean Anderson. *The Art of American Indian Cookery*. Doubleday and Co., Garden City, N.Y. 1965.

Kluckholm, Clyde and D. Leighton. *The Navaho*. Harvard University Press, Cambridge, Mass., 1956.

Langdon, William Chauncey. *Everyday Things in American Life 1607–1776*. Charles Scribner's Sons, New York, 1937.

Langdon, William Chauncey. *Everyday Things in American Life 1776–1876*. Charles Scribner's Sons, New York, 1941.

Leonard, Jonathan N. *Ancient America. Great Ages of Man*. Time Inc., New York, 1967.

Lowenberg, M. E. and B. L. Lucas, Feeding Families and Children 1776–1976. *Jour. Amer. Diet Assoc*. 68:207–215, 1976.

McMillen, Wheeler. *Land of Plenty. The American Farm Story*. Holt, Rinehart, Winston, New York, 1961.

Newberry, J. S. Food and Fiber. Plants of the North American Indians. *Popular Science Monthly*, 32:31–46, 1887.

O'Meara, Walter. *The Last Portage*. Houghton-Mifflin Co., Boston, Mass., 1962.

Palmer, Lucille. The Pacific Northwest's Oldest Apple Tree. Magazine Section, *Seattle Times*, March 19, 1972.

Renaud, E. B. Influence of Food on Indian Culture. University of Denver *Social Forces*, 10:97–101, 1931–32.

Scully, Virginia. *A Treasury of American Indian Herbs. Their Lore and Their Use for Food, Drugs, and Medicine*. Crown Publishers, Inc., New York, 1970.

Thomas, Gertrude I. *Foods of Our Forefathers*. F. A. Davis and Co. Philadelphia, Pa., 1941.

Verrill, A. Hyatt. *Foods America Gave the World*. L. C. Page and Co., Boston, Mass., 1937.

White, Theodore E. Observations of Butchering Technics of Some Aboriginal Peoples. *Amer. Antiquities*, 17:357–8, 1952.

A Winnebago Family Dries Food. *Christian Science Monitor*, April 19, 1962.

Woodward, William. *The Way Our People Lived*. Washington Square Press, New York, 1965.

Yearbook of Agriculture, 1962. *After a Hundred Years*. Superintendent of Documents, Washington, D.C.

Bread

Ashley, William. *The Bread of Our Forefathers*. Oxford at Clarendon Press, Oxford, England, 1928.

Aykroyd, W. R. and Joyce Doughty. *Wheat in Human Nutrition*. FAO Nutritional Studies #23, FAO, Rome, Italy, 1970.

Furnass, C. A. and S. M. Furnass. *Man, Bread and Destiny*. Williams and Wilkins, New York, 1937.

Graubard, Mark. *Man's Food—Its Rhyme or Reason.* The Macmillan Company, New York, 1943.
Jacobs, H. E. *Six Thousand Years of Bread.* Doubleday-Doran, Garden City, New York, 1944.
McCance, R. A. and E. M. Widdowson. *Breads, White and Brown.* J. B. Lippincott and Co., Philadelphia, Pa., no date given (about 1956).
Moore, Alma Chesnut. *The Grasses—Earth's Green Wealth.* The Macmillan Company, New York, 1960.
Spicer, Dorothy Gladys. *Feast-Day Cakes'.* Holt, Rinehart and Winston, New York, 1960.

Potato

Salaman, Redcliffe. *The History and Social Influence of the Potato.* Cambridge University Press, Cambridge, England, 1949, reprinted in 1970.
See *General.*

Egyptian

Casson, Lionel, *Ancient Egypt. Great Ages of Man.* Time-Life Books, Time Inc., New York, 1965, 1957.
See *General.*

Greek

Bowra, C. M. *Classical Greece. Great Ages of Man.* Time-Life Books, Time, Inc., New York, 1965.
Flacliere, Robert. *Daily Life in Greece at the Time of Pericles.* The Macmillan Company, New York, 1965.
See *General.*

Roman

Aykroyd, W. R. *Sweet Malefactor, Sugar, Slavery and Human Society.* Heinemann, London, England, 1967.
Balsdon, J. P. V. D. *Roman Women—Their History and Habits.* John Day and Co., New York, 1969.
Hadas, Moses. *Imperial Rome. Great Ages of Man.* Time-Life Books, Time Inc., New York, 1965.
Johnston, Mary. *Roman Life.* Scott, Foresman and Company, Chicago, Ill., 1957.
Root, Waverly. *The Cooking of Italy.* Time-Life Books, Time, Inc., 1968.
Rosenbaum, Elizabeth and Barbara Flower, Translators. *Apicius, The Roman Cookery Book.* Peter Nevill Limited, London and New York, 1958.

Corn

Mangelsdorf, Paul C., Richard S. MacNeish and Walton C. Galinut. Domestication of Corn. *Science,* 143:538–545, 1964.

Mason, Gregory. Native American Food. *Natural History,* 37:309–318, 1936.
Reports Arizona's Oldest Cornfield. *Science,* 132:33, 1960.
Walden, Howard T. *Native Inheritance. The Story of Corn in America.* 2nd Edition. Harper-Row, New York, 1966.
Willett, Frank. The Introduction of Maize into West Africa—An Assessment of Recent Evidence. *Africa,* 32 (No. 1):1–13, Jan. 1962.

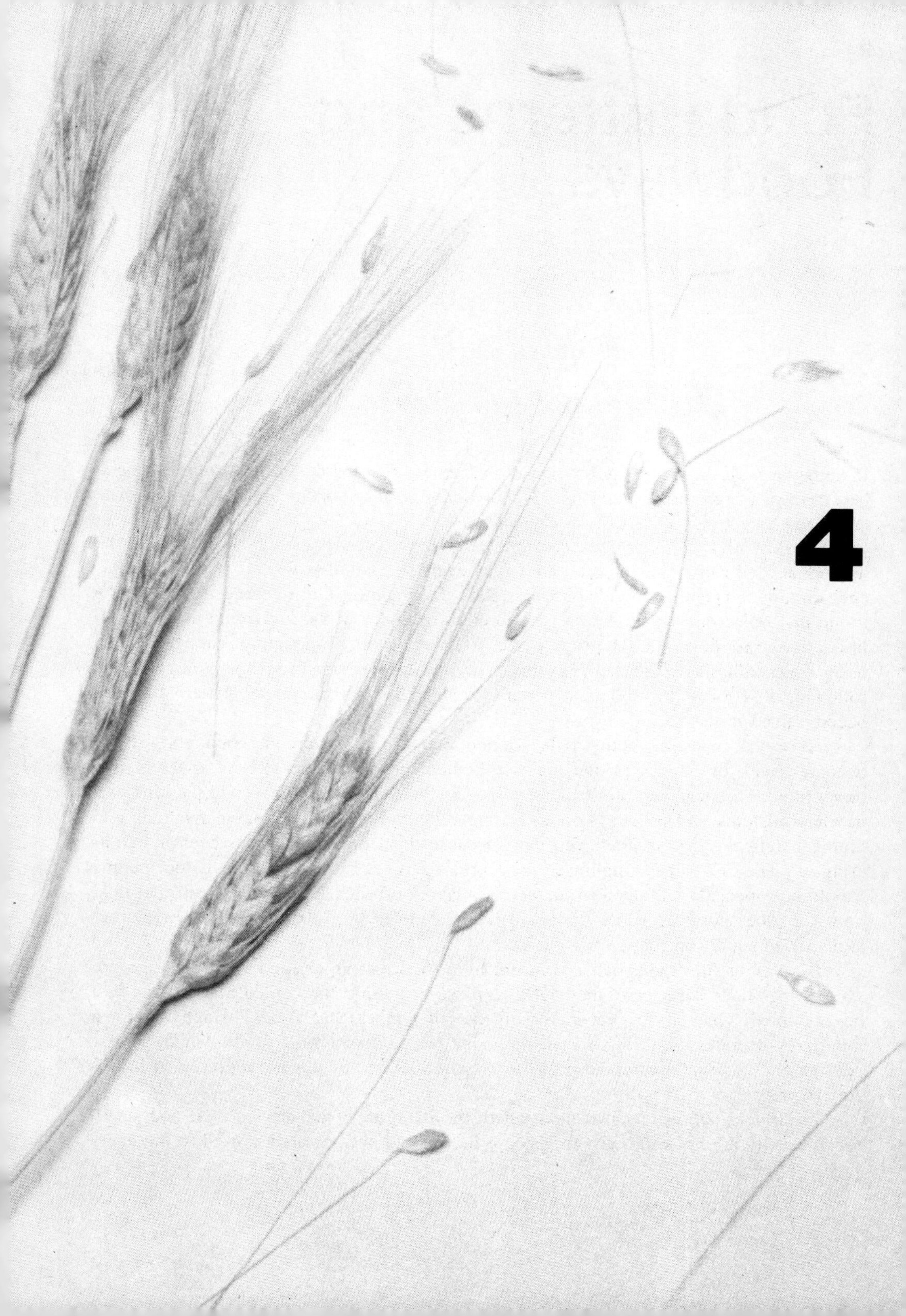
4

Food Patterns and Foodways

In some parts of the world, grasshoppers and grubs are food delicacies; in others, aged beef brings a high price. Food habits and foodways differ from group to group. The term *food habits* may have different meanings.

Cussler and DeGive pointed out that "*in general,* foodways do determine what the individual food habits are and often they may exert a negative as well as a positive influence on him." The term food habits is used by these authors "in reference to habits of a group that reflect the way a culture standardizes behavior of the individual in the group in relation to food, so that the group comes to have a common pattern of eating." When used to describe the eating behavior of an individual the term foodways is used in the following discussion to refer to a pattern of behavior with a general pattern that has become fixed in nature.

As travel increases both in the United States and in foreign countries, people become aware of likenesses and are less bothered by differences. It is apparent that many more Americans are now appreciating, as Perl has said, "The vivid patterns of a nation's customs and folkways, holiday and religious festivals, cooking methods and dining habits. . . ." She believed that, because the United States has been a "gathering-in place of a wide sampling of the world's peoples in modern times," our people should be especially "attuned to the diverse flavors of other lands." She said that this, however, does not keep some Americans from shuddering at the mention of boiled octopus, fried squid, or goat's milk cheese.

By way of illustrating what is meant by a food pattern or food habits of a group, some things that characterize the pattern and use of food in the United States today will be examined. One is the ever-increasing use of convenience foods, which require a minimum of preparation; the other is the value placed on gourmet foods, which are expensive and take great care and effort to prepare. Two extremes are represented in this American pattern.

In affluent nations such as ours where the majority of people are well nourished, foods usually are not eaten just to appease hunger but because they appeal to the appetite. For the upward socially mobile parts of the population, status is attained by the foods purchased, served, or eaten at the restaurants at which these people entertain. Once individuals in this group are secure in their social position, they may go "slumming" for their food, seeking the alien and exotic.

Adults in America, in general, prize variety in their food and consider a monotonous diet undesirable. Nursery school children usually prefer familiar foods and do not react against a sameness in the way adults do (Lowenberg). Dorothy Lee pointed out that, in contrast to our preferences, some cultures value sameness of diet and monotony is "good and sought."

In American supermarkets, the display of foods is elaborate, giving evidence of great abundance—seven thousand or more separate items is not unusual. The display of exotic foods shipped from distant places varies with the affluence of the district in which the supermarket is located.

It has been said that, in addition to the foods people have available, food habits depend on a combination of psychological and biochemical factors. Within limits, people eat what they like and what they think is good for them. Food patterns are based on food lore and in part (at least in a modern, highly technically developed country) on commercial advertising and sound knowledge of nutritional needs.

The term *food patterns* has a connotation of less rigidity than the term *food habits* and it is used in this discussion in that way.

Jacques May said, "The factors governing human diets can be listed as follows: (1) men eat what they can get from the environment, (2) given a choice they eat what their ancestors have eaten before them." It must be pointed out, however, that what is eaten must be related to the physiological needs of the body or the group of individuals do not survive. Choices among foods are made only when food is plentiful enough to permit choices. It is common knowledge that food taboos and restrictions are relaxed during starvation. In fact, hidden in the annals of our own history are examples of startling changes—cannibalism among starving pioneer migrants. When there is sufficient food so that choices can be made, a set of food habits and foodways develops with their attendant taboos and prejudices.

Cultural Backgrounds

Every individual belongs to a number of groups. The companions in one's own group form an "in-group." Dodd and Starr point out that group conflicts and rivalries of groups may affect social behavior. Food patterns must be considered a part of this social behavior. Every community has networks of such social relationships (Dodd and Starr) as kinship, patron-client, ethnicity, fictive "(establishment of ties with persons not related by blood ties), voluntary association and friendship." They also believe that channels of influence can be used to block change as well as to facilitate innovations. Food patterns vary from one cultural group to another because each group, in its own evolution, sets up a complex pattern of standardized behaviors. Individuals within a culture respond to the approved behavioral pressures by selecting, consuming, and using those foods that are available. Food habits of a group are quite evidently the product of the group's present environment and past history. Those food patterns and customs that have become meaningful to a group are carefully held and not quickly changed. It follows, therefore, that anyone who would change a food pattern must first understand the deep meanings of the particular pattern to the people. Those patterns that do not have deep meaning may be changed rather easily. Stacy found that working with an isolated group of Australian aborigines, it was very difficult for government health workers to understand the meanings of food to the group and the aborigines in turn felt that, they could not make the health worker understand the peculiar meanings of food to their group.

Superstitions relating to food can pose serious problems for those who are attempting to improve diets as for instance the belief of some of the indigenous peoples that the vitamin C-rich West Indian cherry causes appendicitis.

Except for people who live apart from other groups, as do the aborigines of Australia and the Bushmen of Africa, it must be expected that outside influences affect the environment, resulting in changes in food patterns as well as in other patterns of living. Such changes have been seen when white flour and white sugar have been shipped into developing countries. When a group is subjected to outside influences, it has often been observed that the older people in the group change less quickly than the younger.

Two excellent examples of the initial retention of native food patterns by several cultural groups living within a confined area and the consequent blending of these patterns into a new cuisine are seen in Viennese and in Hawaiian foods. Poles, Bohemians, Hungarians, Yugoslavians, and Moravians kept their native food patterns when they first migrated to Vienna and for many generations thereafter. Finally, all of their foods were blended into a new cuisine, the now famous Viennese food. Hawaiian food shows the same blending; the sweet potato, the pit-roasted pig, and the many products from the coconut came from the Polynesians; vegetable and meat cookery, from the Chinese; soups, raw fish dishes, and rice and seaweed combinations, from the Japanese; curries, from India; pickled vegetables, from Korea; and sweets and pastries, soft drinks, hot breads, hot dogs, and expensive steaks, from United States Mainlanders. Thus, Hawaii has become a paradise for those who are interested in intercultural foods. The food markets, especially the ones with many stalls, are fascinating for a Mainlander to poke around in to see unusual fish, vegetables, and fruits.

The mark of the immigrant is left on the food patterns in every one of the fifty United States states. Kolachies from Bohemia are found in parts of Iowa; limpa, lutefish, and lefse, as well as lingonberries (especially at Christmas-time) from Scandinavia are common in Minnesota; chili con carne from Mexico is found in Texas; and German sausages are served in Pennsylvania. Some of these foods now are considered almost native to these regions.

Campbell says that in Jamaica the African heritage of the people there remains strong even today. In her excellent article she discusses 31 food fads and superstitions that tradition has kept alive.

Stability of Patterns

Each ethnic group carefully passes on its foodways through the training of children so that each child knows what is considered to be food and what is not. The primitive African child learns early to prize grasshoppers and grubs as food, as the American child learns to drink milk. Children also are taught socially acceptable behavior in relation to food. Thus, they come to know what the limits for food refusals are, so the original impulses of children toward the satisfaction of hunger are transformed into socially acceptable appetites.

The parents' direct control exerts an important influence on the eating habits of their children. They may pass on their own dislikes or force themselves to eat disliked foods in order to set a good example. Usually they attempt to have their children eat what they believe is good for them—by buying the food they truly *control* most of the food that comes into the home.

Not everyone in a cultural or ethnic group eats exactly alike. Small and large subgroups form. Differences in food habits arise because of differences in environment such as climate or growing conditions or differences in religious beliefs. One of the best examples of this division into subgroups is shown in the variety of food patterns in Italy, in part due to differences in growing conditions from north to south.

Changing Food Habits

The profound and complex effects of culture on human behavior must not be underestimated; nor is there an easy way to circumvent culture. At the same time, however, it is not wise to stereotype all the people in a cultural group as being exactly alike. Human behavior is always multiply motivated, and every human being is endowed, from birth, with physical, intellectual, and emotional characteristics, all of which have the capacity for change. We also know that, when individuals are confronted with a need for change in their food habits, especially for health reasons or during periods of privation, they react differently.

Dodd and Starr cogently pointed out that "although prosperous communities may have the power to change their situations, poor communities usually have little control over the conditions which govern their lives."

It has been said that humans are distinguished by the very wide range of foods they can eat because of their teeth; their incisors are similar to the ones of a rodent, their molars resemble those of plant eaters, and their canines are like those of carnivore.

There are many blocks to the changing of food habits, some of which may represent inertia or even resistance to change. People have been categorized as: (1) those who seek to lead groups to change; (2) those who accept change easily; and (3) those who resist change.

Certain factors that relate to the reaction to change in food patterns must be understood and considered by those who wish to make a change. The primary deterrent to this change may be fear of the loss of a familiar food that has been basic to the individual's security. Here there is a conflict of choice between the old and the new. Lack of understanding of what is needed and why may also block a change. E. E. Patrice Jelliffe pointed out that "many nutrition education programs flounder on the rocks of sophistication, as mothers from humble home circumstances cannot translate what they have seen at demonstrations at the clinic or home economics center into practical reality in their own environment."

Rebellion against authority and the insult of being deprived of personal choice likewise can be basic deterrents. Resistance to change also may be traced to treating the *effect* of a food habit, such as obesity, instead of recognizing, understanding, and effectively treating *underlying* or *accompanying* psychological factors.

Graubard, in his discussion of food taboos, said:

A taboo may become established because the animal is a totem, or because it resembles some other animal already in ill repute, or because its name may inspire some evil association, or it may symbolize an undesirable quality. Often animals become tabooed simply because they are not eaten.

He speaks of shellfish not being eaten in places far from the source of supply. Margaret Mead, in *Cultural Pattern and Technical Change,* said that changes that concern a program aimed at control of the social processes are more effective than changes directed to individuals.

The Committee on Food Habits, in Bulletin III, pointed to some basic reasons why some foods are eaten:

Whenever food becomes a part of the celebration of a holiday, the observance of a religious feast, the mark of some life crisis such as a funeral feast, the setting for some business transaction or for the maintenance of social position, a great many reinforcing factors enter in to make certain foods valued and others disapproved or reserved for special occasions.

It is also true that resistance to a series of suggested dietary changes may be traced to fear of losing the food in its "culturally oriented significance." Jelliffe calls some foods "cultural superfoods" such as wheat in some groups and rice in others. He says that these foods "often have semi-divine status, being interwoven with the local religion, mythology, and history." The visitor in Bali will perhaps recognize the significance of rice to those people when observing that it is always among the offering to the gods in the family temples.

So even the inclusion of one favorite dish into a menu for mass feeding may weaken the resistance to change. This has been experienced often by nutritionists and dietitians in school and hospital feeding. Burgess and Dean, in *Malnutrition and Food Habits,* pointed out that in self-sufficient, peasant-type cultures, where even a meager diet has proven adequate for survival, planting, harvesting, storage, and consumption are closely interwoven. Survival in such a situation demands transmitting the whole pattern to each succeeding generation; a single change in this pattern may bring disaster. Margaret Mead, contrary to some other writers, warned that food habits are not always harder to change than other personal habits. She believed that the resistance to changing food habits may be related to patterns of rearing children. Thus, she postulated that where children "are fed lovingly and food is a great source of pleasure and delight" there is resistance to change. She also said that the difference in how immigrants change their food patterns is related to whether they like the foods of their native lands. It is known that immigrants first change the kind or manner of wearing clothes and their language because they do not wish to be conspicuous. But eating is a private affair; therefore, food habits are changed last. Others have postulated that immigrants to a new country, especially if they eat out at their place of work, change their weekday meals but cling to the Sunday dinners of their native land.

Some believe that food habits are resistant to change because they are a form of self-expression, but it is hard to understand why this is more true of food than of clothing.

Many studies have shown that it is easier to change food habits in the young than in the old; therefore, a delay in attempting to make a change is unwarranted.

The mere possession of knowledge does not guarantee a change, though probably too often professional people whose business it is to give out knowledge behave as if this were true. Charlotte Young's studies have shown that nutritional knowledge is greatest in the younger, better-educated homemakers from the upper-income brackets. When she studied what the homemaker knows about nutrition she found that the number of years of formal education—even when nutrition *per se* was not studied—was highly related to the knowledge of nutrition. Many of us also agree with her that studying what to eat does change food patterns, at least in some people.

Frederick C. Fliegel, in a study of food habits and national backgrounds, also found that educational level was a potent factor in the adequacy of the diet served in the families he studied. He pointed out that occupation reflects income as well as status and also believed that such factors as the Italian background of liking fresh fruit and vegetables in their homelands also may have affected his findings.

In a study of changing food habits of rural children in Dakota County, Minnesota, it was reported that the children improved their food practices when they discovered what changes they needed to make and were "strongly motivated to learn about foods and to apply what they learned to their own diets—that is, if they had access to these foods in needed amounts." These investigators point to the fact that the best teaching is done where the teachers are well informed and highly motivated to teach the subject and where the facts are put into practice within the environment, as in the school lunchroom. Projects under the poverty program, such as Head Start, also makes food available to children for the purpose of trying to improve their food habits. Therefore, these programs require that parents be educated simultaneously with their children.

Martha Hollinger and Lydia J. Roberts, in their 1929 study of "Overcoming Food Dislikes: A Study with Evaporated Milk," pointed out that favorable attitudes are contagious, that repetition itself is not enough, but that "repeated tastings together with the right mental attitude are essential to learning to like a new or disliked food.'' Many studies during the last 50 years have reinforced these ideas. Increased income and improved standards of living bring a simultaneous change in food patterns especially in the use of more expensive animal foods.

The philosophy of community development programs around the world emphasizes that the first prerequisite, especially where outside food aid is given, is to find out what the people themselves want. Roberts and her co-workers, in their reports of the Puerto Rican Dona Elena Project, said that changes in nutrition must first be preceded by general changes in ways of living that follow the desires of the people. Burgess and Dean confirmed that this first step may have little to do with nutrition, but it must be founded on what the people want and can take part in accomplishing. Thus, successful achievement, hope, and confidence are engendered, and horizons of needs and motivations are widened.

It also has been recognized that the majority of the peoples of the world, especially those in the developing countries, now live in societies that are in a state of rapid change and where old patterns are being replaced quickly by new ones. Masuoka said, concerning the change of food habits of Japanese living in Hawaii, ''The introduction of a new mode of eating and production of food, as well as an impact of commercialized foodstuff and new modes of cultural life, all function to modify man's pre-established food habits.'' He cites ''external and impersonal forces as trade, rise in income, and the availability of different kinds of food and such subjective and personal forces as changes in food tastes and in conceptions of social status'' as causal factors. He also says that ''disorganization of traditional institutions is probably the most important force to be reckoned with. This unfastens the traditional and customary control over what man eats and how he eats.'' In most of these groups, there are desires to improve the standard of living and to give the children a better chance for survival. Often, however, it must be demonstrated to these people that there is a connection between health and food. Those who work in international programs believe that the task of changing food habits in many places is one in which the nutritionist, the agriculturist, the economist, and the anthropologist must work together to change present nutritional patterns to more desirable ones. Jean A. S. Ritchie warned that:

> With the rapid spread of modern civilization during the present century, many peoples are in a transitional stage between old and new cultures. Too rapid an advance can create grave difficulties.

She also said that to teach people to drink milk and eat raw salads may be disastrous when the available supply of these foods may carry organisms of dangerous diseases. The UNESCO book on *Cultural Patterns and Technical Change* gave reasons why ''the introduction of change, however limited and harmless, can be very disruptive.''

To introduce adequate nutrition, it is most important to bring about changes that are in keeping with the established food habits of the people, and are acceptable within the framework of their value system.

It is known that it is better to improve than to change a food habit because every diet has its good as well as bad points. Often increasing the use of a highly nutritious food, such as certain varieties of beans in Latin American countries, is wiser than upsetting a familiar, trusted, food pattern. Roberts, for instance, in Puerto Rico, promoted the use of calabaza, an already acceptable yellow squash.

National influences are described by Todhunter in a talk which she gave at the Plenary Session of the Third International Congress of Dietetics in London (1961). She summed up changes in the American dietary history during the last 350 years by dividing this history into three periods. The first was the colonial period (1600–1800); the second was the period of westward exploration, development, and industrialization (1800–1900). In describing the third period, the twentieth century, she discussed the new influences that have been brought to bear on the food pattern:

> . . . [the] twentieth century, brought new influences to bear on the basic food pattern. The young science of nutrition grew rapidly, food values received attention and the knowledge was spread throughout the land by the schools of home economics, the experiment stations, and the extension service home agents who worked with rural families in every state. Tomatoes ceased to be regarded as a luxury and were recognized as sources of vitamin C as were citrus fruits; fruits, vegetables, and salads received new dietary emphasis. Regional food patterns, such as the fried chicken, corn bread, grits, and greens of the South; chile beans and barbecued beef and corn cakes of the Southwest; and German-type foods of Pennsylvania, which had been maintained in early isolation continued to be used and still are but they were quickly shared by others as highways and automobiles linked every hamlet of the country.
>
> Today is the age of technology with new means of preservation and packaging and endless new products, such as packaged mixes, cooked frozen meals, minute preparation foods, and fast transportation. These make all food products available the year around to everyone. More food is purchased at the supermarkets and more people eat away from home. Three meals a day is the pattern with a coffee break, mid-morning and afternoon.
>
> Today's food pattern retains a dominance of the early foods of the new land but these have been modified and have blended with the patterns of scores of nationalities that came as immigrants. There have been shifts in the amounts of various foods used, as nutrition science spread and all this has given rise to a more universal pattern accepted because of advertising and the mass media and because of the remnants of the pioneer spirit which leaves people still willing to try something new, especially in food and recipes.
>
> The country that has been called the melting pot of all nationalities also has become the melting pot of all nations' food patterns.
>
> Over the last fifty years there has been little change in the consumption

of meat, fish and poultry; an increase in the use of diary products especially over the last twenty years; slight increase in fats and oils,* increase in sugars and syrups; a steady decrease in grains and potatoes; and a marked increase in the use of citrus and tomatoes and also in green and yellow vegetables.

This excerpt describes a national pattern made by many individuals and forming the background for the individual food patterns of millions of Americans. Perhaps this, best of all, illustrates what Margaret Mead and Jean Ritchie mean—that to change fundamental food habits, a whole culture must change.

We have numerous other proofs of the changes of food habits from countries all over the world and throughout all history. It is said that humans probably gave up the use of acorns as one of their staple foods after a devastating blight of oak trees, when they found other foods they preferred. Wheat bread is said to have been first prepared in Egypt when the use of barley declined. Oats have been either stoutly defended or rejected as food, and the idea of rejection probably spread from predynastic Mesopotamia into Greece and Rome. It is said that the Scythians scorned the Gauls for using a cattle feed for human food, as the English later scorned the Scots. At the present time, the Japanese are reported to drink 20 times more milk than they did 20 years ago. Kluckholm pointed out that, under present-day conditions of communication, only a small percentage of the material objects used by any people represent its own inventions. As an example, he cited a menu for a week in an American home, which, may include "chicken, which was domesticated in Southeast Asia; olives, which originated in the Mediterranean region; cornbread, from the meal of an American Indian plant, baked in an aboriginal fashion; rice and tea from the Far East." Coffee "was probably domesticated in Ethiopia"; and "citrus fruit, which were first cultivated in Southeast Asia . . . reached Europe by way of the Middle East. . . ." Four steps have been shown to be desirable in a deliberate attempt to bring about a change.

1. Those who possess the knowledge must want to bring about a change.
2. The group whose practices need changing must be helped to know that they need to change.
3. This group must be motivated to make the change.
4. It must be possible for the group to make the change; in other words, in the case of changing food habits, the food must be available.

Discussion-Decision Method

Ben Willerman, working under Kurt Lewin in 1942 in Iowa City, investigated the relative effectiveness of two methods of changing food habits. He used the so-called *group*

*Data to 1961. Beginning in 1957 use of fats and oils has shown a decrease.

decision method, in which the group decided for itself whether it wanted to change and to what degree it wished to change. The second method, with which the first was compared, was the *request method,* in which a group was asked to make a change, and the goals were set by others outside the group. Willerman's 1942 experiment concerned the increase in consumption of whole-wheat bread as compared with white bread. It must be remembered that white bread, which was not then enriched, contained less of the needed nutrients than did whole-wheat bread.

Men from eight cooperative dormitories at the University of Iowa were used. The eight groups containing from 20 to 44 men each, were arranged in four pairs of groups, matched on similar consumption of whole-wheat bread. One of each of these group pairs was to make a group decision, and the other was presented with a request.

For the week before and during the experiment, no breadstuff except white and whole-wheat bread was served. Waiters counted the slices of bread eaten during both periods and made certain that as much bread as was wanted was available. The student proctor in each dormitory read a letter by an authority to the decision group, urging the students to eat whole-wheat bread. Then he called for a discussion. At that time, if the group agreed to cooperate, they set their own goals of how much they would increase the consumption of a whole-wheat bread. In the request groups, the proctor merely read the request letter and asked for comments. The amount of change for the *request group* was set at the same level as the amount which had been chosen voluntarily by the *decision group* with which it was paired. The results were obtained from a questionnaire filled in by each student at the end of the experiment.

From their previous levels of 50 percent consumption of whole-wheat bread, one group voted to go to 66 percent, another to 90 percent, and two to 100 percent—the group designated as the D group being one of the latter. In the *request group,* 48 percent reacted favorably, whereas 78 percent in the *decision groups* were favorable to the proposal as read. Although the majority (80 percent for *request groups* and 86 percent for *decision groups*) considered the request reasonable, only 22 percent of Group D considered it so. It must be pointed out that, in Group D, a *decision group,* the 100 percent level of change was arrived at after a bitter fight in which a small vocal minority swayed the decision.

The results showed that with the *group decision* method:

1. A more favorable attitude was created.
2. Individuals were more eager to succeed.
3. The wish to cooperate was more independent of personal likes and dislikes.
4. There was a "kickback" in the groups where the decision was based on too small a majority. This made the outcome less favorable than with the *request method.*

Others later working under Lewin (homemakers who were asked to consider changing their food habits for the war effort) obtained similar results in trying to introduce a new vegetable, escarole, and organ meats such as kidney, brains, and heart.

Marian Radke and Dorothy Klurisch, in 1947, used the methods described by Willerman in trying to change infant-feeding practices and later in increasing milk consumption in families of low socioeconomic status. They say, "The group decision method was significantly more effective in leading mothers and housewives to action than were either individual instruction or lectures." Lewin's explanation of why the group decision method works better is worth reviewing here. He states that he believes the effectiveness of the method is due to:

1. The higher degree of individual involvement required in the discussion method.
2. The existence of resistance to change, perhaps due to a disinclination to deviate from a social norm or from standard group values. The discussion method offered the individuals the chance to see how others felt on the question, thus making their own decisions easier.
3. The group decision method placing full weight behind one of the two conflicting alternatives so that one choice completely displaces the other.

He also says that, when change is facilitated, resistance is lowered and vacillation ceases. He says, further, that the process of social change is a three-step procedure: (1) unfreezing the old level, (2) moving to the new level, and then (3) freezing at the new level of performance. Marian Radke and Elizabeth Caso, in 1948, tried a similar method, which they called the lecture and discussion-decision method, with junior high school students in Newton, Massachusetts. They used the improvement of poor lunch habits as their goal. The discussion-decision method proved superior, and improvement proved more lasting with this method.

Perhaps some of our ineffectiveness to bring about changes in food habits should lead us to pay more attention to these theories and researches of Dr. Lewin and others.

Public Health Needs for Change

D. B. Jelliffe and F. J. Bennett, working in Uganda, pointed out that it is helpful to divide the food practices in a cultural group into categories based on public health needs for change. They suggest that, before any attempt is made to change practices, they be divided into:

1. Beneficial practices such as breast feeding. These should be supported and promoted in local health teaching.
2. Neutral practices such as massaging the limbs with oil to make the bones strong. These seem to have no significant value nor to be harmful and should be let alone.
3. Unclassifiable practices such as the mother's pre-chewing of foods for her infant. These need further observation and consideration in special groups.

4. Harmful practices such as failure to give young children fish in Malaya where it is the main source of protein but is said by the people to produce worms. This fourth category should be the basis for "friendly persuasion and convincing demonstration."

Whether the food habits be those of a group in Uganda or a group in the United States, it would probably be wise to make a decision, after careful study, of what particular habits are most in need of change.

The Philadelphia Child Health Society prepared some years ago, for use by public health workers, an exceptionally useful chart, which could be copied for modern use. For each of the major cultural groups in the city, they listed typical daily meals with food preferences. They also listed good points about the diet as well as points to emphasize or discuss and to consider in need of changing.

Making Food Available

Many examples of changes in dietary patterns because a food becomes available in a convenient form have already been cited in the quotation from Todhunter on page 109. The extensive use of frozen orange juice today is one illustration. Many of the older generation no doubt still remember the one orange a year in their Christmas stocking. The frozen-food industry has made locally produced foods available all over the United States and, in fact, in many other countries of the world. When production costs, as with frozen foods, decrease so that the average consumer can afford the item, the use of that food often increases.

The story of the Aarey Dairy Project, located some twenty miles from Bombay, India, is worth telling here. Once one of the startling sights to a stranger in this part of the world was the filthy open sheds for water buffalo that were then used in dairies in this region. It was not difficult for the observer to understand why these animals gave a low yield of milk. Nor was it difficult to understand why, in 1916, Dr. Lamuel Joshi, who was then the municipal analyst for the city of Bombay, found that samples of Bombay milk contained more bacteria than the sewage water of London. He found many causes, including adulteration, antiquated methods, bad sanitation, ignorance, and greed. So the name "dirty milk" lingered for some decades. For years apparently little was done to clean up this deplorable situation. In 1940, however, a special campaign to feature the "dirty milk" of Bombay was undertaken when D. N. Khurody reproduced the 1916 statistics in his report on "Marketing Milk in Bombay."

In 1941, World War II conditions further increased the troubles encountered in the milk industry of India. The price of milk also increased sharply. With the bombing of Calcutta, evacuation from the large cities, including Bombay, took place. Food rationing included food for cattle, and the ban on exporting animals from other provinces to consuming centers such as Bombay made the milk problem more than a municipal one.

The Civil Supplies Department of the Bombay state government took a great step forward on August 17, 1944, when they introduced the Bombay Subsidized Milk Distribution Scheme. Near the village of Aarey this group acquired 1100 acres of land and built a dairy plant on it. Milk from the surrounding area was brought into the new diary. A bold plan was made for having all of the milk-producing water buffalo of local farmers in one colony on the 1100 acres. Very soon the number of animals increased to 15,000 which were then housed and milked in clean sheds.

It was also decided that the pasteurization, bottling, and distribution should be done by modern methods. "Toned" milk was made of the 7.5 percent fat buffalo milk, powdered nonfat milk, and water, and this milk was then sold for one half the price of the whole fat milk. In 1962 the imported nonfat milk powder for making this was 5500 tons.

The project combined the efforts of the municipality of Bombay and the state of Bombay with the efforts of international organizations such as UNICEF, which in 1958 put a large sum of money into the equipment and building for the pasteurization and processing plant. The nonfat powdered milk was being donated by the U.S. and New Zealand. For what UNICEF contributed, the government of Bombay agreed to distribute one and one-half times the original investment in free milk to mothers and children.

Technical assistance was partly supplied by outside agencies such as U.S. AID (Agency for International Development). The farmers care for their own buffalo and sell the milk to the city of Bombay after it is pasteurized.

Within a relatively few years after the organization of this Aarey Project Diary, it had supplied at least some milk daily to approximately one half the people of Bombay. Another plant (Worli) located just outside the city of Bombay was opened in 1961; during its first year of operation it processed 53 million quarts of milk, and in 1963 had doubled that quantity.

The entire district around the Aarey Dairy became more prosperous and in the surrounding villages all sanitation improved. The food of the people was better and even more and better schools were built. Many families came to the clean park-like dairy grounds for a day's outing and while there were shown how the diary produced clean milk. Samples of milk and ice cream were served free of charge.

The 1976 meeting for the World Food Program received reports of the remarkable expansion of the milk schemes now all over India at present under the Indian Dairy Corporation. UNICEF also reported in 1976 that it had helped to equip 220 milk plants in 45 countries.

Milk production in the greater Bombay area had increased approximately 800 percent in 14 years. In the city of Bombay, recently the average household consumption of milk was 1.31 liter per day. This varied from 0.68 liter for households having an average of $20 income per month or less to 2.01 liters per day where incomes were $133 or more per month. The India Dairy Corporation is still striving to improve the quality, price, and hygienic conditions of the milk as well as the distribution. Coin operated vending machines are reported as being successful.

Programs for free distribution of milk in supplementary feeding programs reach some children where the daily milk supplies 400 extra calories and 15 grams of needed protein. Nutritional surveys by the Indian Medical Council have shown insufficient intake of energy and that the intake of protein, of iron, or vitamins A and C, also calcium intake was frequently low; extra milk can make a significant contribution to relieving these dietary deficiencies. It should be pointed out here also that even extra milk does not represent all the answers. It has been estimated that buffalo milk in India costs on an average of 30 cents per 1000 K Calorie whereas controlled-price wheat costs only 4 cents. Now government planners in India are advising that the average milk consumption per household be kept at its present level. Their efforts are to increase the milk consumption of low income households and to have milk production only keep pace with population increase. It would not be fair to leave this discussion of making a good food available without pointing out that the institutions of these dairy projects, called *Operation Flood,* has had a marked effect on rural development in general. The 1976 report calls them "an important instrument of development and social change by building up in villagers' self-confidence in self-help and in the value of participation in public affairs." At the present time this milk project is managed by Indian Nationals and has reached the stage where it can continue without outside aid. In this, modern science and technology have provided for "socially well-balanced improvement of the quality of life for a large number of people."

The report by UNICEF, *Children of the Developing Countries,* said:

> The rapid growth of dairying and industrial milk processing in Europe, North America, Australia, and New Zealand in the first third of the present century probably did more to improve the nutritional status of children and mothers in these countries than any other single development in the field of food and nutrition.

Group Influences

Sociologists and anthropologists have pointed out that in primitive cultures, with the exception of the most simple societies, the raising and harvesting of foods are often group activities. Rice harvesting in Bali, where the small fields of rice are full of people working, would remind tourists of this point.

Pride and satisfaction in food production become forces that cement the group together. Individuals cooperate and yield to mutual preferences that are culturally acceptable; in many of these groups, eating together is also intimately associated with the family group. The cooperative efforts and this eating together come to imply a kind of kinship even outside the family of true blood relatives. Cussler and DeGive pointed out that "securing food and eating together entails an intensifying of communication and an increase of the rate of interaction to a degree found in no other act repeated so constantly."

Some types of food production basic to the group's economy, such as the production of grapes for wine, are long-lasting, whereas others may be temporary in formation.

The tendency of a society to have pockets of culture with groups of individuals who keep their own food habits is greater perhaps in societies where communication across a country is not highly developed. In larger cities, groups that move in from totally different cultures may exert potent influences for change and, therefore, cause a change in food patterns. Wherever travel to outside places becomes common, suspicion of strange foods breaks down. The more secure individuals in any group dare to try new foods; in this type of people, there is less rigid demarcation in what is considered a proper food.

In many cultures, eating is considered a private affair to be enjoyed within the confines of a family group. There are reports of places where individuals eat away from all others, even family members. For instance, in some parts of Melanesia and Polynesia, men and their wives lead separate lives; they have separate lodgings, meals, work, and property. There the rule is that men and women should never see each other eat. Among the old Semites, it was not the custom for a man to eat with his wife and children. Sumner in *Folkways* (1960) reported that, in northern Arabia, ''no woman will eat before men'' and ''there is a widespread notion that one should not be seen to eat by

A child eating in India (*Courtesy Rockefeller Foundation*).

A nutritious school lunch in Bulgaria (*Courtesy World Health Organization*).

anybody.'' In the Sudan, it is said that the practices of eating and drinking in private and covering the mouth when eating and drinking were to prevent the evil eye from affecting the individual. It is thought that this belief originated from the watching of others eating by hungry people who might be envious. Others believe that the homeless evil spirit could wander into their open mouths and cause trouble. In some countries, workers as well as schoolchildren are given long noon hours so that they may go home to eat with their families. In the United States, family members make great efforts to be together for dinner on Thanksgiving or Christmas. There is the now oft-told tale of the Greeks, after the World War II occupation of their country, who preferred to take hot soup given to them by the Red Cross to their cold homes to eat with their families rather than eat it in the warm Red Cross canteens. It is said that in the early middle ages in Germany, after the formal marriage ceremony, the spouses ate together as a part of the total procedure of marrying. So the origin of the American custom of the bride feeding her new husband the first piece of wedding cake she has just cut may be very old.

Jensen said that with primal man the ``sharing of food and drink between man and woman universally defines the legal relationship between the two.'' He also says that ''The offering of cooked food and sometimes ale (bride-ale of the Vikings hence 'bridal') figures largely in early day marital ties.''

Ethnic Influences

In the UNESCO book, *Cultural Patterns and Technical Change,* it is pointed out that ''where food practices reflect cultural structuring and values, any change introduced into the society may produce imbalance.'' For instance, knowing the structuring and meaning of meals among the working classes in Japan following World War II, their nutritionists, also knowing the importance of miso soup for the first meal of the day, introduced the idea of adding the extra fat needed in their diet to that food.

Families also tend to develop their own food habits. The attitudes toward food vary in different families, from indifference to excessive preoccupation with food. One of the best illustrations of differences in food practices among families in the United States of America is the bread stuffing with which the family thinks it is proper to stuff the Thanksgiving turkey. Some of us know of women who put one kind of dressing in the front part of the bird and another in the back part to satisfy the firmly held opinions of her husband and herself. In fact, our feasts often become unnecessarily elaborate because each partner wants a special kind of food that was used in his childhood home, such as mashed white potatoes for northerners and sweet potatoes for southerners.

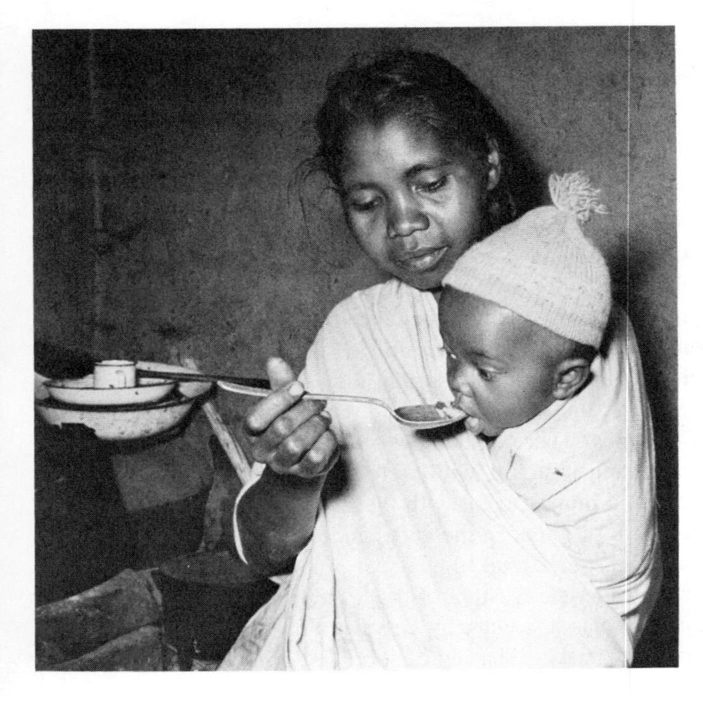

Feeding an infant in Madagascar (*Courtesy Food and Agriculture Organization*).

Methods of eating differ—these children live in India (*Courtesy Food and Agriculture Organization*).

In diverse ethnic groups, food has different prestige and emotionally satisfying properties. The French, for instance, hold food in high regard and are justly famous for their cuisine; the Italians take great pleasure in eating and in family meals. In some cultural groups and families, eating is a matter of duty and is lacking in emotional satisfaction.

In other groups, thrift may be uppermost in the minds of people, even going beyond the requirements of income restrictions. For some people, the nutritive value or even supposed value may dictate food patterns. One is reminded of the old story of the daughter whose mother was trained in nutrition. When asked what she wanted to eat, she surprised her hostess in a restaurant by replying "Anything but healthful food. I get so much of that at home."

In some ethnic groups more than others, the women are said to be kitchen-bound or neighborhood-bound. When migrating to a new home, these people tend to settle in neighborhoods where they find former emigrants of like ethnic backgrounds. They spend their lives near where they live and even shop in grocery stores carrying only foods of their nationality. In some of these groups, of course, change comes about as children go to school and bring home new ideas. Often, though, the group-imposed ideas of marrying one of like nationality tends to preserve the group patterns.

It has been said that cooking reveals the culture of a country and that a country's soul is reflected in its food. For instance, Felix Martin-Ibanez suggests (though some others disagree) that the tendency of the Spaniard for violence and his love of bright

Facilities help determine the kinds of food eaten—food ways are affected by technological and economic factors (*Courtesy the Upjohn Company*).

color are reflected in the sharp-flavored polychrome *paellas,* that the food of the Japanese reflects their love of order and cleanliness as shown by the array of beautifully cleaned and cut foods for *sukiyaki.* He also believes that the national foods of Britian reflect their aseptic robustness and reserve, while the Gaelic subtlety of expression is shown in their delicate sauces. And the earthiness of the Italians is demonstrated in their *pastas.*

Cussler and DeGive, from a study they did in the southern United States, believe that of all group influences on food patterns, the family exerts the greatest effect. With Renner, they wonder why any food habits change since, as he says, "there is a circle. What one eats when young, that one likes and hands on to one's offspring which should rotate forever."

The Committee on Food Habits of the National Research Council, in their 1945 Bulletin III, summed up the subject when they said,

> Another aspect of the way in which edible materials are classified as inedible, edible by animals, edible by human beings, but not my kind of human being, edible by human beings such as self, and finally edible by self. These classifications are further reinforced by various sorts of attitudes—that materials which are not eaten are defiling, wicked to eat, coarsening, would alter one's status, etc.

We are at once reminded of the derision of Samuel Johnson that the Scotsman eats oats which should really be fed only to horses. We remember that the Irish rejected corn (maize) as inedible by human beings during the mid-nineteenth-century potato famine, as did the hungry Germans in the mid-nineteen forties, when they said it was only feed for chickens. Pirie said that "irrational food prejudice is extraordinarily widespread." He points out that "in Britain a chicken would be rejected long before it has putrified to the extent considered proper with pheasant, raw oysters are eaten but snails are not eaten even when cooked, and the pig is accepted but not the horse."

What food is considered edible by a group is an important consideration, as was illustrated when a new kind of hybrid corn was introduced into a Spanish-American group. Although this corn gave a yield three times that of the one commonly used, within half a decade these people ceased to grow the new corn because the wives objected to the texture in the tortillas and no one liked the flavor. Edibility or acceptability was foremost when the hungry rice-eating people in India rejected wheat because it was not white like their rice. In the United States, many complaints were registered about the gray color of the bread made from the more nutritious and economical high extractions of wheat flour used during wartime conservation of wheat. Large numbers of people the world over feel that the lighter the color of a food, the more desirable it is.

It should be pointed out that individual food dislikes and reactions fall between the classes of edible by individuals like myself and edible by self. One person may eat liver, but another finds it inedible. This may be partly because two people as individuals taste its flavor differently and react differently to its texture.

Pirie pointed out that some people have rational reasons for rejecting foods, but these rejections are regarded as prejudices by those who do not understand them. He cited rejection by mountain dwellers of cereals and beans, which require an intolerable amount of time to boil at the lower boiling temperatures at 10,000 foot altitudes.

Meal Patterns

Cultural and group influences determine not only what foods are eaten, but they also determine the meal patterns, the number of meals in a day, and the methods of eating and utensils used. Travelers in Europe perhaps have watched an American order bacon and eggs and pay a price many times the cost of the European's continental breakfast of rolls and a hot beverage. The habit of having tea even at a business conference in Iran and in India surprises many Americans and sometimes is a bit trying to them when, in true American style of rushing about, a busy morning calls for several conferences. The meal hours for dinner at nine o'clock or later in some tropical countries often tries the patience of American tourists, who may find themselves the only diners if they eat earlier. The National Dairy Council once had a poster showing different kinds of breakfasts in a number of countries around the world and the time of eating in relation to Central Standard Time in the United States. Miso soup may be a commonplace breakfast in Japan, but when a well-known United States soup company gave a "Soup Breakfast" at a national meeting, many people were surprised. Although some of us in the United States believe that the continental use of the knife and fork is perhaps more efficient and even more graceful, we stubbornly cling to what we learned as children.

The history of manners for eating and etiquette is an interesting study in itself. Sumner, in *Folkways,* said: "The conquest of the art of eating with propriety was accomplished by the introduction of forks. Before that, the bread was a tool with which to eat, and it required cultivated skill to handle it properly." The dainty use of fingers for eating in Moslem cultures is often amazing to Americans.

There are also fashions in food and fashions in meal patterns. These may be based on the intellectual approach of the low-calorie breakfast or lunch. In the calorie-conscious food culture in the United States, it is now fashionable to omit bread and desserts for dinner.

After the urbanization of many Americans made it impossible for the breadwinner to eat at home at noon, the heavy meal of the day naturally came to be served at night. Although, quite logically, it could then be called dinner, many considered this an affectation; the name of this meal was often confused with that for light supper.

The usual seems natural to us, and the unusual seems unnatural or suspect. Yet habit rather than logic must be given credit for many of the group customs of foods eaten, manner of eating, or even times of eating. Ritchie Calder pointed out that abalone steak is an expensive item enjoyed by gourmets in California, but he doubted that they would enjoy the up to three-quarters of a pound of meat of the large African black snail, which has the texture and other qualities of abalone. In Coastal West Africa, however, this snail is a festival food as is our Christmas turkey. In some areas no one can be found at home when weather conditions make a large harvest of these snails available.

The staple food of a country usually enjoys high prestige. This is true in Uganda, where steamed plantains, called *matoke,* are a staple food, as is cassava in Ghana and bread in Greece. Poi, made from taro, once was a staple food of Polynesian Hawaiians. Now that it has become expensive and scarce, it is not commonly eaten in Honolulu but is still highly prized.

In addition to cultural, ethnic, and family influences on food habits, individuals differ, as we all know, from the moment of birth. Good and poor digestion, food allergies and idiosyncracies, the rate of the body's use of food for energy, the ease of adjusting to the environment, the degree of intelligence, the difference in imagination, the effect of education in making the individual aware of the body's needs, and drives such as the desire to attain status all combine to give an individual his or her own peculiar eating pattern. Mothers who try to feed a family made up of strong-minded individuals are well aware of these differences, as are those whose business involves serving food to the public. Reactions to coffee, good or bad, served by different restaurants point to the fact that the descriptions are colored by more than the coffee brew itself. It has been found experimentally that some individuals rate the same brew of coffee as weaker when it is served in thin cups than when served in heavy pottery mugs.

Probably everyone has a unique pattern of food behavior that is shared with only a few others. Individual differences in some cases may obscure the common food habits and attitudes of a shared culture that are brought about in a group by similar physiological makeup and environment.

To summarize group and individual differences in food patterns, we quote from the FAO Bulletin Basic Study number six, "Education and Training in Nutrition":

What people are willing to eat is determined by a complex system of attitudes, ideas, and assumptions that form the local cultural patterns. These include religious restrictions, taboos, ideas pertaining to the merits or demerits of a food, and other attitudes which are as yet little understood.

Geography

In addition to the other factors discussed, it is well known that geography exerts a fundamental influence on food habits. Although the inhabitants of Puerto Rico and Hawaii come from entirely different ethnic backgrounds, there is a great similarity in the tropical fruits used in each of these countries. In Southeast Asia, where rice and not wheat flourishes due to the water soaking of the lands (by the monsoon rains) and high temperatures, the people are rice eaters. The introduction from the New World of maize into sections of Africa and of the potato into Europe where the climate favored their production brought about fundamental changes in the diets of the people. Sugar cane, now cultivated in many tropical countries, was said to have been brought by early travelers from India. The liberal use of pineapple, even in iced tea, and other tropical fruits in Hawaii at once suggests the influence of climate and geographic conditions on food habits. Where else will wild huckleberries be so commonly eaten as in the mountainous areas where they grow abundantly, or salmon be such a favorite food as in the water-surrounded Pacific Northwest and Alaskan coastal area?

Methods of cooking are influenced by the fuel available. In areas where fuel is scarce quickly cooked breads become a staple food. See page 51.

Climate and seasonal production also affect food habits, especially when methods of preservation and storage are not highly developed. In many places, foods can be eaten only in season. In parts of the Near East, grapes and fresh figs, although abundant in season, can be eaten only during two months of the year.

Technological Development

Technological development exerts a pronounced influence on food habits and is one of the strongest forces causing change. The introduction of the freezing process for perishable foodstuffs profoundly affected our use of canned and fresh vegetables, fruits, and meats. The development of refrigerator cars also meant that fresh fruits and other foods from faraway places could be sold cheaper. The American homemaker with a freezer ample for storage can reduce the number of her shopping trips and total time of the preparation of family meals when she prepares several meal-size portions of food at one time and freezes these for future use. Now that adequate refrigeration has come within the reach of a majority of families, frozen foods have become popular. This food preservation method makes it possible, as an example, for a well-known United States brand of frozen chicken to be served at a Sunday dinner in the hills of Accra, Ghana. Perhaps it should be pointed out that the introduction of these necessarily more expensive convenience foods into a developing country only widens the gap in foods used by high- and low-income families. Air transportation has also changed food patterns, as evidenced by the foods now available in Alaskan markets as well as by papayas from Hawaii and Granny Smith apples and kiwi fruits from New Zealand in mainland United States markets.

Technological developments are, of course, basic to the production of enough food for all the people in a country. The reclamation or better use of the arable land, the use of fertilizers and insecticides, the making available of needed water, the supplying of good seed, the improvement of the methods of sowing, the use of improved cultivating and harvesting equipment, the provision of adequate marketing facilities with money for seeds and machinery, and the development of facilities to distribute the food produced all profoundly influence the foods available to a people.

The kind of transportation also markedly affects food habits. The Egyptian who never travels may never taste citrus fruits even though he or she lives only a short distance from where they are grown. In India, the millet, wheat, and rice grown in different regions of the country are not available in other parts, even though the people from different sections might use the other grains and be better nourished by varying their diet.

For the fortunate people who live in technically developed countries, a worldwide diffusion of foods is taking place due to the increased ease of traveling and the possibilities of air transport of foods from one country to another, as well as purposeful transportation of seeds, plants, and food animals. The members of the armed forces who have known the foods of Korea, Vietnam, and other places in Europe and Asia often come to like them and want them when they come home, so restaurants serving widely varied cuisines have become popular. Food patterns are also affected when traditional methods of preservation are no longer used. The once familiar sun-dried corn of the farm belt in the U.S. is eagerly purchased when available by some people who remember it from their childhood.

Uses of Food

The primary use of food is always first to satisfy hunger and then to satisfy the needs of the body for growth, maintenance, and energy. These we choose to call the nutritive uses of food because nutrition of the body is involved here. Dorothy Lee said:

> Culture may present food mainly as a means of the stilling of hunger, or of getting nutrition, or as a way to psychosomatic health; it may regard eating

as a duty or a virtue, or as a gustatory pleasure, or as a social or a religious communion.

There are, however, many other uses of food; only a few of these are discussed here.

Food is used to promote friendliness and social warmth or, as it has been called, the ritual of hospitality. Food is also used in many ways to promote interpersonal acceptance. This becomes so strong a motive that most of us offer food or drink quickly when friends call. A relationship develops between the giver of the food and the recipient. In fact, we all accept food more readily from our friends than we do from strangers because it is easier to develop a relationship with friends.

The common use of food as a gift varies from a neighborly present of homemade bread to the elaborate and expensive packages, often of strange and unusual foods, given at Christmastime. These foods, the purpose of which is to signify friendliness, are usually choice or especially attractive or perhaps rare, exotic, or fraught with nostalgic memories. At Christmastime, the advertising pages of gourmet magazines are filled with pictures and descriptions of expensive macadamia nuts from Hawaii, of genuine aged Smithfield hams from Virginia, of live lobsters from Maine, or of Black Sea caviar. On the other hand, the home magazines display and explain in detail how the homemaker can make attractive gifts of inexpensive foods in her own kitchen. Whether the food gift is expensive or homemade depends on how and by whom it is used.

In some societies, homemade food products are considered inferior; to these people, processed and packaged foods are considered items worth giving. To others, homemade foods are considered especially desirable. Gifts of foods, however, are always considered delicacies by the giver and are not staple items of diet; the filling of a need even seems to negate the spirit of the gift. Christmas baskets for needy families are usually better received if some unusual foods for a treat are included.

The prominent part food plays at funerals and during the days preceding the funeral is well known. As a visible offering of sympathy, often our first thought is to give the grief-stricken family some food.

The importance of inviting newly made acquaintances to eat in our homes is recognized. It has been said that to eat with a person is to say, "I am your equal." The tension felt by many a young wife when she first invites her husband's boss and his wife to dinner and the extent of her efforts to provide the best meal she can are mute evidence of this. Will they accept? Will they like our kind of food? What shall I prepare? Am I equal to making a satisfactory menu? Will I be able to make the food good enough? What will he talk about? Will he be a friendly guest? I wonder what she's like?

All the restrictions of the hierarchy of dining rooms in a business, government firm, or hospital have some of this philosophy of equals eating with equals. Who can eat in the executive dining room? Perhaps guarded secrets are kept by this closed system, but it must be admitted that there is still the philosophy that only equals eat together.

It is well known that the barring of blacks from some restaurants has caused some of the worst race riots. As Harry Golden said, it is only when people sit down together in a restaurant, at a family table, or in a schoolroom that they must do so as equals; standing together usually has not caused trouble. In some societies, social class is a greater barrier to eating together than race.

Many people working in different aid programs, such as the Peace Corps, have found that the local people are especially sensitive to the behavior of the outsiders when they are invited to eat in local homes. It is said that the American refusing to eat the prized sheep's eye at a Near East meal can undo much former work to cement friendship.

Many hostesses enjoy giving outstanding dinner parties as a means of creative expression. On the other hand, some extremely wealthy people give great parties to keep their names in the public press. This is not new, for when the Roman Lucullus (for whom Lucullian feasts were named) realized that his wealth was nearly dissipated and that he could no longer continue to give his splendid parties, he splurged one last time and then committed suicide.

It is equally true that we accept foods from our friends most easily and suspect and reject food offered by enemies. The latter was especially true in early times when royalty, threatened by their enemies, had tasters whose job it was to test food for poison. The closing of many German restaurants during World War II was necessitated by these strong feelings.

In some U.S. groups today, foods are being used as a protest against "The Establishment." The rise in popularity and the use of so-called organic or health foods is a protest against the use of chemical fertilizers and added preservatives. Another example of protest is the macrobiotic diet that some young people follow without understanding the deficiency of needed nutrients in it.

At the present in the United States food fads flourish. The use of high fiber in the diet is a dominant theme in TV advertisements; high protein diets are promoted and followed sometimes with the fatal results as reported in 1977. The controversy over massive doses of vitamin C rages and the results of well-done research are not heeded. Those who take large doses of vitamin E for heart trouble follow the advice of untrained authorities more avidly than they follow the advice of their medical heart specialist. Shops selling organic foods, at three times their price in supermarkets, flourish in every large shopping center. Yet even some well-informed people do not question the meaning of the term "organic foods."

Attaining Status

Food is often used to promote an individual's or group's welfare. It is said that in Ruanda the Urundi keep cattle not for meat or milk but as a bank account, a symbol of family wealth. The improvement of status rather than friendship may even be involved in gifts of food or invitations to meals. Those who strive to climb the social ladder, advancing also their economic status, shun the foods of the poor. Nothing less than the best steak is offered. Some people try to build a reputation as gourmets by serving exotic foods. These may be even infrequently liked, expensive, and difficult to prepare; excellence of flavor may be sacrificed for the visible signs of the unusual. In some groups, there is nothing to indicate that this is unacceptable social behavior.

Achieving Security

Closely associated with the uses of food to promote interpersonal relationships and to raise one's status is the use of food to promote security. The individual, as explained through the Maslow theory, who knows where his or her next meals are coming from is on the way to acquiring security. A feeling of security is associated with orderliness or a lack of anxiety and tension over whether food will be forthcoming. Certain foods foster security more than others, even apart from their ability to satisfy hunger. For many people, milk is the primary security food. Many of us watched the Red Cross handing glasses of milk to soldiers returning from the Asian Theater of World War II almost before they had come off the gangplank. The eagerness with which these men—long deprived of family and familiar foods—took this milk gave ample proof of its meaning to them. Harriet Bruce Moore said: "The unhappy, suffering, far-from-home-and-loved-ones soldier looks back to *milk* as in many ways expressing the comfort, security, and contentedness of life as it was at home." Milk, because of its association in early life, may foster security for some; but other people, when questioned, name foods such as potatoes or meat. Sweets must have a rather deep meaning for many, as evidenced by the liberal use of them during times of tension.

In times of crises, familiar foods are even more highly valued. During World War II, the quartermaster's corps conducted extensive research to determine the meanings of specific foods to the men in the Armed Forces. The value of food in maintaining morale was well understood.

During the summer of 1966, the author asked a class at the University of Hawaii what food signified security. The immediate answer was "rice." As is well known, the Chinese and Japanese predominate ethnic groups in modern Hawaii. These students then told of the hoarding of rice when a shipping strike threatened to reduce its importation.

Relieving Tension

The use of food to relieve tension is commonly known. Research has shown that as many as 75 percent of a group studied said that they ate more when under tension; the 25 percent who tended not to eat under tension admitted that they *sometimes* did use food to relieve boredom. Such use of sweets, even in young children, is well known. This dietary habit has been credited by some to be basic to the problem of obesity in the affluent countries. The fact that from one-fourth to one-third of many people's calories come daily from snacks may result not so much from hunger as from relieving boredom or tension. Increasing interpersonal sociability certainly plays a part in the heavy snacking pattern of Americans.

Influencing the Behavior of Others

Another use of food is to influence the behavior of others. Some mothers express their love of family through the preparation of food. It has been sarcastically said that the mother who is angry may serve liver, spinach, and bread pudding, but when she wants to please her husband or her family, she may serve steak, baked potatoes, and ice cream.

Sweet foods often are used as rewards, even as a personal reward, when a day has been especially hard. Generations of children have been admonished to eat their vegetables so they could have dessert. Some physicians give a child an all-day sucker for being good.

Young children learn very early that to eat or not eat their food is an easy way to elicit a reaction from anxious parents. In fact, many children are past masters at controlling adults through their eating. Food also can be a powerful weapon for punishment, either by the withholding of eagerly sought food or by the forced eating of unwanted food.

Adolescents often find the use of food a good way to express rebellion. Many people who work with this age group believe that some overeating, with the resulting obesity, is the result of parental conflict and the child's rebellion.

In business, clients are sometimes entertained with expensive and luxurious meals. This makes it difficult for the client to refuse a request. Some commercial companies have made a rule that food and drink may not be accepted as gifts from customers or prospective customers. The reason for this is obvious.

Abraham Maslow in *Motivation and Personality* (1970) discussed human needs. His classification is useful in considering why people eat as they do. He classified human needs as: (1) physiological, (2) safety, (3) belongingness and love, (4) esteem, and (5) self-actualization.

Hunger, here meaning an urgent need for food, is one of the most dominant of the physiological needs; it is a survival need. When a person is truly hungry, his or her need for food dominates their entire being. In the extremities of hunger, one thinks only of oneself, having forgotten even family and loved ones. It is useless to ask people to think of anything else until their hunger is satisfied at least to the extent that they are again physiologically comfortable. Maslow said: "For the man who is extremely and dangerously hungry, no other interests exist but food. He dreams food, he remembers food, he thinks about food, he emotes only about food, he perceives only food, and he wants only food." It is easy to understand why politics, community welfare, and even love of fellow people are of no immediate concern to the truly hungry person. (See also page 200.)

The next needs in this hierarchy, the safety needs, may be considered also as *security* needs. Once a person's hunger has been satisfied at least temporarily, he or she can become interested in attaining the security that will insure the next meal today and tomorrow and in the days ahead.

Maslow discussed the infant's need for undisrupted routine or rhythm as an illustration of the safety need. This is a basic reason why regular meals are necessary for a happy child. The antisocial behavior of hungry slum children is largely due to the lack of satisfaction of this basic need. The on-and-off programs for relief of hunger often are upsetting to a hungry group for the same reason. Security, as we have said before, can be obtained by the storing of food so that future meals are assured. As the economic situation of the individual improves, he or she may move upward in the satisfaction of food needs. Yet in times of disaster, they become anxious over their future food supply. The hoarding of sugar during or just before food rationing went into effect during World War II is proof that people are soon brought back to fear for the security of their food supply. The overloading of American cupboards, pantries, and freezers perhaps may be traced to this motive and gives evidence that the need has not been fully satisfied. The fact that the insecure individual chooses a familiar over an unfamiliar food may well be explained by the need for a feeling of safety.

When the physiological and safety needs are fairly well satisfied, as Maslow said, the needs for belongingness, for love, and for affection appear. Food is used constantly to satisfy belongingness needs. Members of closed groups carefully guard their food habits to remain "in" or to "get in." All of us worry what to serve at a meal if we do not wish to deviate from a group's expectations, especially when we do not know what they expect. As people become more and more secure, they can dare to serve what they want to; they can substitute lower-calorie fresh fruits for the rich, high-calorie desserts usually served.

The esteem needs next in the hierarchy are well illustrated by the "best cooks" contests. We have already discussed food to attain or maintain status; promoters of contests to see who is the best cake or cookie baker in the country must be well aware of the strength of this motivation. Perhaps the use and promotion of proficiencies in the preparation and presentation of food is a commendatory way to build a sagging ego in the adolescent.

The last need in this hierarchy of needs was called *self-actualization* by Maslow. Some students studying food and society have been found to understand the term *self-realization* better than the term used by Maslow. At this stage, the individual dares to make up his or her own recipe, to serve exotic foods, and to indulge in complicated procedures of food preparation. Townsend's 1928 statement expresses what we are trying to say: "The educated cosmopolite does not hesitate to try strange foods. Not so, the savage, the child, the ignorant. In these three classes, food prejudices often curious and irrational abound." Perhaps we should add that the savage, the child, and the uninformed are not secure in their sense of belonging, nor have they attained a fixed status among their often hostile associates. Therefore, they dare not be different in what they eat. Children who have unusual foods at home are the most venturesome in trying new foods at school. There probably is no age limit on being a gourmet if one dares to be one. Evidence of the increasing popularity of foods from other countries probably bespeaks the fact that increasing travel increases belongingness and raises self-esteem, perhaps even gives great satisfaction to the security need. For the further discussion of this classification of human needs and how Maslow interpreted the satisfaction of them, the student is referred to his *Motivation and Personality*, 1970 edition.

Some students have found the following terms and the diagram helpful:

disaster direction ↓ normal direction ↑

self-realization	—social need
esteem or status	—social need
belongingness	—social need
security	—physiologic and social need
survival	—physiologic need

The arrow pointing downward in the hierarchy of needs diagram was put there to remind us that our surplus food in an affluent society could be wiped out in a disaster such as a nuclear holocaust; we would then be brought down rapidly to the survival stage. One is reminded of the letters-to-the-editors and popular opinions expressed in the press some years ago when there was a campaign to stock bomb shelters with food. Some people said they would not assume responsibility for any except their own families.

Expressing Creativity

Although we have mentioned creativity several times in relation to food, it probably warrants more discussion. Whenever a person's hunger and need of food for security are both satisfied, he or she then dares to use creative abilities in preparing food and to try new foods and combinations of them.

The history of the Romans is replete with stories of excessively extravagant feasts for the wealthy class. The development of complicated methods of preparing food in history and in modern times often puzzles the student. Perhaps the fact that everyone eats, except in fasting, and also that food is an intimate part of daily life leads some to degrade food preparation as a lowly task. Yet chefs of renown and those who can create beautiful and delicious foods are well rewarded in most modern societies. The ancient Romans and Greeks gave special recognition to good chefs.

Cookery can be an art. In late 1966, *Time* (November 25) used a cover picture and story on Julia Child, whose TV cooking program had become a rage. Many of the newly published cookbooks are written to appeal to those who want to be creative in food preparation. In 1977 it was reported that the *Better Homes and Garden Cookbook* (first published in 1930) had sold 19 million copies, with 328,144 copies sold in 1976 to outsell all other cookbooks that year.

Mothers often show their impulse to create or to show love for their family through food preparation. They prepare an especially delicious dish, serve a meal of a meaningful pattern, or have an appropriate food for a special occasion. Families come to expect a particular food on special occasions, and deep meanings thereby come to be attached to it. Thus, the love of the mother is associated with certain foods, and these are often lifetime favorites in spite of the children's wandering far from the parental home.

SYMBOLISM AND PRESTIGE FOODS

A complete body of symbolism has surrounded foods both in historical and modern times. Bread, commonly called "the staff of life" in societies where it is a staple food and not just an accompaniment, assumes high prestige. In some of these cultures, bread is used in religious and social rites; it is placed as an exhibit or decoration at a banquet. In the Lord's Prayer, we say, "give us our daily bread," meaning all food. An old proverb says, "as good as bread." In groups where bread is highly regarded, even crumbs are precious and always are carefully gathered up when they fall on the floor. The story is told of a group of United States senators each being given a loaf of bread upon leaving a Greek island by boat and of the great insult inflicted when one threw his overboard because he felt he did not need it.

Nizzardini and Jaffee, writing in the mid-1940s on Italian food patterns for the Committee on Food Habits, said that in the group where Italian bread is eaten every day and every meal, an emotional tone surrounds it. These people consider it wrong to waste any food but sinful to waste bread; and the *thrifty* housewife gets this appellation because she uses much bread rather than other accompanying foods.

Bread is a prestige food for some people. In some cultures, it must be white to enjoy the highest prestige. White sugar also has enjoyed a long history of prestige. Meat is a prestige food with many people. Roast beef in England was long regarded as food for land owners and the wealthy, so it was small wonder that ration points were carefully hoarded in war time so that the Englishman could buy his Sunday roast. In the United States, roast beef and steak dinners often command and get the highest prices at many restaurants. The finest of caviar has such prestige that in 1978, it was being sold at a rate of $79.01 per pound in Seattle, Washington.

Molded cooked peacocks with feathers replaced in elaborate pastries, as Cussler and DeGive reminded us, showed, "how culinary artifice assumed prestige in sophisticated Roman society." They also said that *"changing the appearance of food* usually involves complex techniques proportionate to the degree of civilization, so that highly milled and refined foods hold an approved position." It must be pointed out that an adverse reaction to highly processed foods may later begin. Now in the United States whole-grain breads often command a higher price than white bread. Bennett said that foods of "in groups" acquire prestige and those of "out groups" affect the attitude toward them. Foods used at ceremonial functions—for example, weddings, picnics, family gatherings, holidays—acquire high prestige. He believed that foods are more important as symbols than as carriers of nutrients; that symbolic interest in food operates largely as a way of relieving tension.

In some cultures, certain foods are supposed to have magical qualities and be influences either for good or evil. Not all this association is from primitive cultures or from early times. Even recently, those who opposed pasteurization of milk were heard in public testimony to endow *raw* milk with the ability to turn gray hair back to black. Certain foods, like the fertilized duck egg, which is regarded highly by some groups in the Philippines, are said to possess aphrodisiac qualities. It is a rather common belief, although untrue, that visceral meats are less "energy giving" than muscle meats. Many Americans have a revulsion concerning eating the brains of animals.

A discussion of the meaning of food cannot bypass the question of food taboos. These taboos usually surround animal foods such as meat, eggs, fish, and milk. Many of these culturally imposed dietary restrictions are connected with sex and reproductive function. Some foods are taboo for women, some for boys just entering adolescence, some for fathers or prospective fathers. There are numerous tribes who restrict menstruating women from even coming in contact with some foods. Many of these restrictions concern milk and cows, whose welfare is thought to be inimical to that of women. There are also restrictions concerning the foods pregnant or lactating women may or may not eat.

Some taboos may have been based on valuable experience, whereas others have arisen from superstitions, myths, and folk tales. In his *African Notebook,* Albert Schweitzer presented cases of individuals who unknowingly broke taboos and died within a short time.

Another aspect of foods is interesting to contemplate because it is related to the symbolism of food. Norman Cameron, in *The Psychology of Behavior Disorders,* said:

> Our language is full of ambiguous allusions to social acceptance and rejection, to verbal assaults, to gastric need for food, and to the spiritual need for sustenance. Thus we eat our words and swallow our wrath, the Lord spews us forth, we sink our teeth into a problem, drink in a message, find an explanation indigestible, and reject it with biting comments. When the human being, with all of his verbal ambiguities in his behavior, becomes confused, he often acts out as social operations what was intended to be only verbal metaphors.

In many ways, our English language would be weaker did we not use words basically concerned with food and eating where there is no connection with food. Harriet Bruce Moore said: "Every one has 'his taste' and from infancy until death he concerns himself with seeking and enjoying the kinds of food that are most pleasurable to him." She went on to explain this need by the frequency and naturalness "with which we use our eating sensations to categorize and describe other experiences." She summed this up thus:

> We speak of "taste" in many areas of flavors to describe people and situations—spicy, flat, sour, sweet, delectable, and so on. We speak of sensation associated with food—of coolness, bland, tart, smooth as cream, an oily personality, and so on.

We also tend to categorize our foods in ways only some of which have rational meaning. The meaning of the terms "hot" and "cold," when applied to foods by such people as those of India, are difficult for Americans to fathom or connect with their use of the term hot meaning spicy or hot in degrees of temperature. Foods such as meat are said to be strength giving. Foods are luxury or essential, primary or secondary, homemade or "store" foods. Some foods such as peanut butter, milk, and cooked cereals are children's foods, while steak, potatoes, and pie are traditionally men's food, and casserole dishes, salads, vegetables, and cakes generally are more appealing to women.

The meanings of food are usually consistent and stable within a group, and the individuals in the group understand these meanings and make the same interpretations.

The symbolism of salt is one of the fascinating stories in lore concerning food. It has been said that since it was our earliest condiment the hunger for it is almost universal—it is well documented that human settlements were made close to the sources of salt. Some primitive people obtained a salt mixture from ashes when they could not get salt from mining it or evaporating sea water. Many North American Indians, unfamiliar with our salt, used alkaline potash instead. Some say that the word salt is derived from the Greek word for "sea." Homer referred to salt as "divine" and separated those nations that knew salt from those that did not.

Salt was once eagerly sought and even used as money. The Roman salt cellar was the symbol of hospitality and friendship. In ancient days, salt was used as a form of purification, as a medicine, and in embalming after death. Wars have been fought for salt rights. Traeger said: "In some places salt is so scarce that it is considered as much a treat as children in our own culture regard sugar candy." He also says that "little cakes of salt, each stamped with the likeness of the emperor, were once used as money in China." Pepper also soared in ancient times to heights of fame, and reparations after wars often were made partially in payments of pepper.

Jean A. S. Ritchie, in 1950, in her classic presentation in the FAO Bulletin, *Teaching Better Nutrition,* has summed up the cultural significance of food. She says:

Because of its fundamental role in the struggle for existence, food has acquired a significance in human society beyond that of providing nourishment for the body, which is reflected in many patterns of human behavior. Food may be closely associated with feelings of security and prestige. It has an important place in religious observations. It is linked with countless superstitions and prejudices. Thus, it can arouse many emotions—pleasure, envy, confidence, and even violent fanaticism. Their relationships must be taken into account in attempting to alter food consumption.

Jennie I. Rowntree said it just a little differently:

Food is eaten for enjoyment, for emotional release, for social prestige, and for attention, adverse or otherwise. Food is refused because of such unconscious emotions as the pleasure of paining others and showing self-assertion.

Poppy Cannon, in the article in *Saturday Review* entitled ''Revolution in the Kitchen,'' said:

Never was a cliché more fatigued—or truer—than the one that bids: Tell me what you eat and I'll tell you what you are. Not only biography and genealogy but the whole field of anthropology could, if one knew the code, be deduced from food. Food is a mirror that reflects a thousand phases of personal, national, and international history. Geography is reflected in the food; so is climate, the local flora and fauna, religion, superstitions, and taboos; wars, victories, defeats, invasions. The food remembers where people traveled, who their grandmothers were, and from what part of the world their ancestors hailed.

FESTIVALS AND FEASTS

The story of a people could also be written in terms of their feasts and those who attended the celebrations. In general, feasts have been held from pagan times until now to:

1. Celebrate a particular religious event.
2. Celebrate a harvest in the fall of the year.
3. Offer appeasement and glory to a god at the winter solstice when in early times the people feared the sun would desert them.
4. Bless the sowing and celebrate the bursting of spring.
5. Honor the dead and pay homage to ancestors.

Other feasts, peculiar to one cultural group or nation, celebrate certain important national happenings such as the winning of independence. Certain foods come to be associated with each type of feast. Thus, at the time of harvest festivals, traditional and meaningful foods are used. Wild turkeys were used by the Pilgrims in Massachusetts as perhaps their best fall source of meat. This set a precedent for us in the United States in the use of turkey for our Thanksgiving dinner. Long before the Christian era, our present harvest festivals had their counterparts in pagan countries where the gods of the harvest were worshipped with curious and varied rites. Although residents of the United States may think of Thanksgiving as our special festival, practically all European countries have a similar one. These are celebrated there more frequently in the rural than in the urban areas. When the President proclaimed Thanksgiving as a national holiday, it became more of a national festival than it is in most other countries.

In the old calendar, the sign for the winter solstice was a circle with a dot in the center. This represented the sun. A symbolic cracker, called a bretzel or pretzel, was made at this season in the form of a circle with a cross in the center to represent the four seasons. The present pretzel is somewhat of a variation of this original form, but no longer is this food used so symbolically, at least in general.

Many winter holidays are gay with lights as well as foods, as is St. Lucia Day in Sweden, Divali in India, and the religious holiday at Christmas all over Christendom. Often a meat fairly heavy with fat, such as goose, forms the traditional food for Christmas. Foods that take long and loving preparation are used in many countries at Christmas and other winter festivals. In Virginia, which has been "Christmas making" for 350 years, the ways of celebrating are as steeped in custom as are the mince pies in spirits. Mince pie, a Christmas food in England since ancient times, is made from ingredients from the East that symbolize the gifts of the Wise Men to the Infant Jesus. The name, at first "shrid pye" or "shredded pie," later was changed to "minced or mince pie." At first, these were made in the form of the manger. It is said that when the upper part or upper crust was solid, it was called the coffin. But when it was cross latticed, it was supposed to represent the hayrack of the stable. Later, mince pies became known as "idolatry in crust" because of their association with the Church of Rome.

The Ukrainian housewife sprinkles straw under her best embroidered tablecloth for the Christmas table. She also strews straw on the floor and places a sheaf of wheat in corners of the room. It is said that these rites are very old and may represent Christ's humble birth, but some of them may even date back to pagan harvest festivals.

The use of wine and Christmas turkey fat to sprinkle on the Yule log is an old English custom. The Croats and Serbians are said to have sprinkled corn and wine on the Yule log while uttering wishes for an abundant harvest the next spring.

Marian Schibsby, writing for the American Council for Nationalities Services on the old-world Christmas customs of many ethnic groups, told an interesting story of the Armenians. She said that after the Church service it is the custom to make visits; these are known as "hand-kissing visits" because the young folks are supposed to kiss the hands of their elders on whom they call. These visitors bring gifts of fruit: oranges for the women and lemons for the men. Also on that day, children bring gifts of poppyseed bread, pastry, and roast chicken, among other things, to their godparents, who reward them with gifts of money or handsome new clothes.

Schibsby mentioned a custom of the Czechs and Slovaks who, like many groups, use December 24 as a fast day. Some groups are admonished not to eat until they see the first star. The Czech and Slovakian children are urged to abstain from food until evening so that they may see the "golden pig," but Schibsby did not say what this is. Perhaps the highly prized baked carp is what they were to wait for. This meal, which takes weeks of preparation, is said to be well worth waiting for. The table decoration is made of dried fruit with loaves of special Christmas bread called *Vanocka* after the word for Christmas, *Vanoce*.

The traditions centering around Easter are similar to those which, in pagan times, honored the Goddess of Spring. The very word "Easter" is said to come from the name of this goddess, Eostre or Ostara. The spring holiday foods are often young lamb and fresh, newly grown vegetables if available. These are symbolic of youth, no doubt.

In many religions, feasts to honor the dead include the setting of foods which, after the supposed departure of the spirits, are eagerly consumed by the needy living.

Too many feasts may become a threat to good nutrition in several ways. One is, of course, overeating. In some cultures, so much food is saved for feasts that undernourishment in between is common. In general, foods used for feasts are:

1. Scarce—which puts a high priority on them.
2. High quality—the best jar of pickles saved for Christmas dinner.
3. Often expensive—which makes them desired.
4. Difficult and time consuming to prepare—where the love of the cook can be demonstrated.

Abstinence from some kinds of foods before a festival has been practiced throughout recorded history in many different settings. Many people abstain from certain foods, usually animal foods, until the first star is seen the evening before Christmas. Abstinence from animal foods before the spring festival is found in a number of cultures as it is in Lent before the Christian Easter. Denying oneself the favored animal food is considered good self-discipline and increases one's devotion to a belief. It has been said that authoritative religions all use the denial of the gratification of appetites in order that one may live above carnal desires and escape the fear of complying with instincts.

It has been said that among the most valued gifts the immigrant brought to the United States were their folkways and folklore. The best and finest of their customs and traditions associated with their festivals now have become woven into the culture of the United States. Many people are now working to preserve these differences in ethnic foods and customs.

STUDY QUESTIONS

1. Explain how food patterns are culturally oriented.
2. What differences in your own food patterns have come from your own family background?
3. How can the Maslow hierarchy of needs be used to explain food practices?
4. Why is a study of festival foods important in understanding the culture of a group?
5. On page 134, Poppy Cannon is quoted. Can you justify her statement with illustrations from the literature?

TOPICS FOR INDIVIDUAL INVESTIGATION

1. Describe in detail the food habits of one ethnic group of people, pointing out similarities as well as differences from the food habits and foodways with which

you are most familiar. Give the background or reasons for the difference wherever you can.

2. Plan in detail a program to improve the food habits of a particular group of people using the Willerman-Lewin method.
3. Describe a program where making a food or several foods available caused a real change in food habits.
4. Trace the changes in consumption of five foods in the United States during the first seven decades of the twentieth century. Give basic reasons for these changes.
5. Show how a group of people such as the Amish influence the foods of their neighbors. Also show how these distinct patterns of ethnic groups settled in a defined area are influenced by their neighbors.
6. Use any popular American cookbook to try to discover foods introduced by some immigrants.

REFERENCES AND SUGGESTED READING

A.H.E.A. *Family Holidays Around the World.* Washington, D.C., 1964.

Babcock, C. G. Food and Its Emotional Significance. *J. Amer. Diet. Assoc.,* 24:390, 1948.

Bennett, John W. Food and Social Status in a Rural Society. *Am. Soc. Review,* 8:561–69, 1943.

Bowker. Library and Book Trade Information, 22nd edition. R. A. Bowker, New York, 1977.

Bruch, H. Obesity in Childhood and Personality Development. *Amer. J. Orthopsychiatry,* 11:467, 1941.

Burgess, A. and R. F. A. Dean, Eds. *Malnutrition and Food Habits.* Macmillan, New York, 1962.

Cajanus 8 No. 1, 1975 from Jelliffe, D. B. Child Nutrition in Developing Countries, p. 62, AID, Washington, D.C.

Calder, R. *A Starving World.* Macmillan, New York, 1962.

Cameron, N. *Psychology of Behavior Disorders—A Biosocial Interpretation.* Houghton-Mifflin, Boston, 1947.

Campbell, Sadie. Folk Lore and Food Habits. Newsletter (*Cajanus*) Institute, 8, No. 4, 1975.

Cannon, P. Revolution in the Kitchen. *Saturday Review,* p. 54, Oct. 24, 1964.

Cassel, J. Social and Cultural Implications of Food and Food Habits, *Amer. J. Pub. Health,* 47:732, 1957.

Committee on Food Habits. *Manual for the Study of Food Habits.* National Research Council Bull. 111, National Academy of Sciences, Washington, D.C., 1945.

Committee on Food Habits. *The Problem of Changing Food Habits.* National Research Council Bull. 108, National Academy of Sciences, Washington, D.C., 1943.

Cussler, M. and M. DeGive. *Twixt the Cup and the Lip.* Twane, New York, 1952.

Deutsch, R. M. *The New Nuts Among the Berries.* Bull Publishing Co., Palo Alto, Calif., 1977.

Dodd, P. C. and P. D. Starr. Chapter 2, Characteristics of the Community. *Nutrition in the Community* (edited by D. S. McLaren). John Wiley & Sons, New York, 1976.

Dupont, Jacqueline, Ed. Dimensions of Nutrition-Proceedings of the Colorado Diet. Assn. Conference, Fort Collins, Colorado, Associated University Press, 1969.

English, O. S. Psychosomatic Medicine and Dietetics. *J. Amer. Diet. Assoc.*, 27:721, 1951.

Eppright, E. Factors Affecting Food Acceptance. *J. Amer. Diet. Assoc.*, 23:579, 1947.

Fliegel, F. C. *Food Habits and National Background*. Pennsylvania State Univ. Agr. Exp. Sta. Bull. 684, University Park, Pa., 1961.

Food for Peace, Annual Report on Public Law 480. U.S. Government Printing Office, Washington, D.C., 1965.

Galdston, I. Motivation in Health Education. *J. Amer. Diet. Assoc.*, 25:747, 1949.

Galdston, I. Nutrition from the Psychiatric Point of View. *J. Amer. Diet. Assoc.*, 28:405, 1952.

Golden, H. *Only in America*. World Publishing, New York, 1958.

Graubard, M. A. *Man's Food—Its Rhyme or Reasons*. Macmillan, New York, 1943.

Hollinger, M. and L. J. Roberts. Overcoming Food Dislikes: A Study with Evaporated Milk. *J. Home Econ.*, 21:923, 1929.

Hottes, A. C. *Christmas Facts and Fancies*. A. T. DeLaMare, New York, 1954.

Jelliffe, D. B. Parallel Food Classification in Developing and Industrialized Countries. *Amer. J. Clin. Nutr.*, 20:279, 1967.

Jelliffe, D. B., and F. J. Bennett. Cultural and Anthropological Factors in Infant and Maternal Nutrition. Proceedings of Fifth International Congress of Nutrition, *Fed. Proc.* 18:185, 1961.

Jelliffe, E. F. Patrice-*Cajanus Newsletter of the Caribbean*. Food and Nutrition Institute, Mona, Kingston, Jamaica, Vol. 4, No. 3, 1971.

Jensen, Lloyd B. *Man's Food. Nutrition and Environments in Food Gathering Times and Food Producing Times*. Garrard Press, Champaign, Ill., 1953.

Kane, H. T. *The Southern Christmas Book*. David McKay, New York, 1958.

Khurody, D. N. *What's Behind a Bottle of Milk,* 3rd Ed. Government Central Press, Bombay, India, 1958.

Khurody, D. N. *The Retrospect and Prospect of Bombay's Milk Supply*. Government Central Press, Bombay, India, 1958.

Kluckhohn, Clyde. *Mirror for Man*. Fawcett Publications, Inc., Greenwich, Conn., 1974.

Lee, D. Cultural Factors in Dietary Choice. *Amer. J. Clin. Nutr.*, 5:166, 1957.

Lowenberg, M. E. Food Preferences of Young Children. *J. Am. Diet. Assoc.*, 24:430–434, 1948.

Maslow, A. H. *Motivation and Personality*. Harper & Row, New York, 1970.

Masouka, Jitswichi. Changing Food Habits of the Japanese in Hawaii. *Am. Soc. Rev.*, 10:759–765, 1945.

May, J. M. The Geography of Food and Cooking. *Int. Record Med.*, 170:231, 1957.

Mead, M. Dietary Patterns and Food Habits. *J. Amer. Diet. Assoc.*, 19:1, 1943.

Mead, M., Ed. *Cultural Patterns and Technical Change*. UNESCO, Paris, 1953.

Mead, M. Factors of Food Habits. *Ann. Amer. Acad. Pol. Sci. Soc.*, 225:136, 1943.

Moore, H. B. Psychologic Facts and Dietary Fancies. *J. Amer. Diet. Assoc.*, 28:789, 1952.

Nizzaridini, G. and N. F. Joffe. *Italian Food Patterns and Their Relationship to Wartime Problems of Food and Nutrition*. Committee on Food Habits, National Research Council, Washington, D.C., 1943.

Perl, Lila. *Rice, Spice and Bitter Oranges*. World Publishing Co., New York, 1967.

Pike, Magnus. *Food and Society,* John Murray, London, 1971.

Pirie, N. W. *Food Resources Conventional and Novel*. Penguin Books, Baltimore, Md. 1969.

Radke, M. and E. K. Caso. Lecture and Discussion as Method of Influencing Food Habits. *J. Amer. Diet. Assoc.*, 24:23, 1948.

Radke, M. and D. Klisurich. Experiments in Changing Food Habits. *Science Monthly,* 43:193, 1936.

Renner, H. B. *The Origin of Food Habits.* Faber & Faber, London, 1944.

Ritchie, Jean A. S. *Learning Better Nutrition.* FAO Nutritional Studies No. 20, FAO, Rome, Italy, 1967.

Ritchie, Jean A. S. Teaching People Better Habits of Diet. *J. Amer. Diet. Assoc.,* 26:94, 1950.

Roberts, Lydia J. *The Dona Elena Project.* Univ. of Puerto Rico, Rio Piedras, P. R., 1963.

Rowntree, Jennie I. The Human Factor in Nutrition Study. *J. Home Econ.,* 41:433, 1949.

Schibsby, M. *Foreign Festival Customs.* American Council for Nationalities Service, New York, 1951.

Seifrit, E. Changes in Beliefs and Food Practices in Pregnancy. *J. Amer. Diet. Assoc.,* 39:455, 1961.

Simoons, F. J. *Eat Not This Flesh.* Univ. of Wisconsin Press, Madison, Wis., 1961.

Spicer, D. G. *Feast Day Cakes From Many Lands.* Holt, Rinehart and Winston, New York, 1960.

Stacy, Sandra. Who Should Learn What? Health Education Amongst Traditionally Oriented Australian Aborigines. Paper presented 7th International Congress of Dietitics, Sydney, Australia, May 5, 1977.

Sumner, W. G. *Folkways.* Mentor Books, New York, 1960.

Sweeney, Mary. Changing Food Habits. *J. Home Econ.,* 34:457, 1942.

Traeger, James. *Foodbook.* Grossman Publishers, New York, 1970.

Todhunter, E. N. *The History of Food Patterns in the U.S.A.* Proceedings of the Third International Congress of Dietitics, Newman Books, London, p. 13, 1961.

Townsend, C. W. Food Prejudices. *The Scientific Monthly,* 27:65, 1928.

United Nations Education and Scientific and Cultural Organization. The Milk Conservation Program—An Appraisal of UNICEF/FAO Assisted Milk Conservation Programs. Private Communication, 1948–1960.

U.S. Office of Education. *A Study of Methods of Changing Food Habits of Rural Children in Dakota County Minnesota.* Nutrition Education Series Pamphlet No. 5, 1944.

Wellin, E. Cultural Factors in Nutrition. *Nutrition Reviews,* 12:129, 1955.

World Food Program, Committee on Food Aid-Interim Evaluation Report, April, 1976. India Project No. 618. Milk Marketing and Dairy Development.

Young, C. M., B. G. Waldner, and K. Berresford. What the Homemaker Knows About Nutrition. *J. Amer. Diet. Assoc.,* 32:218, 1956.

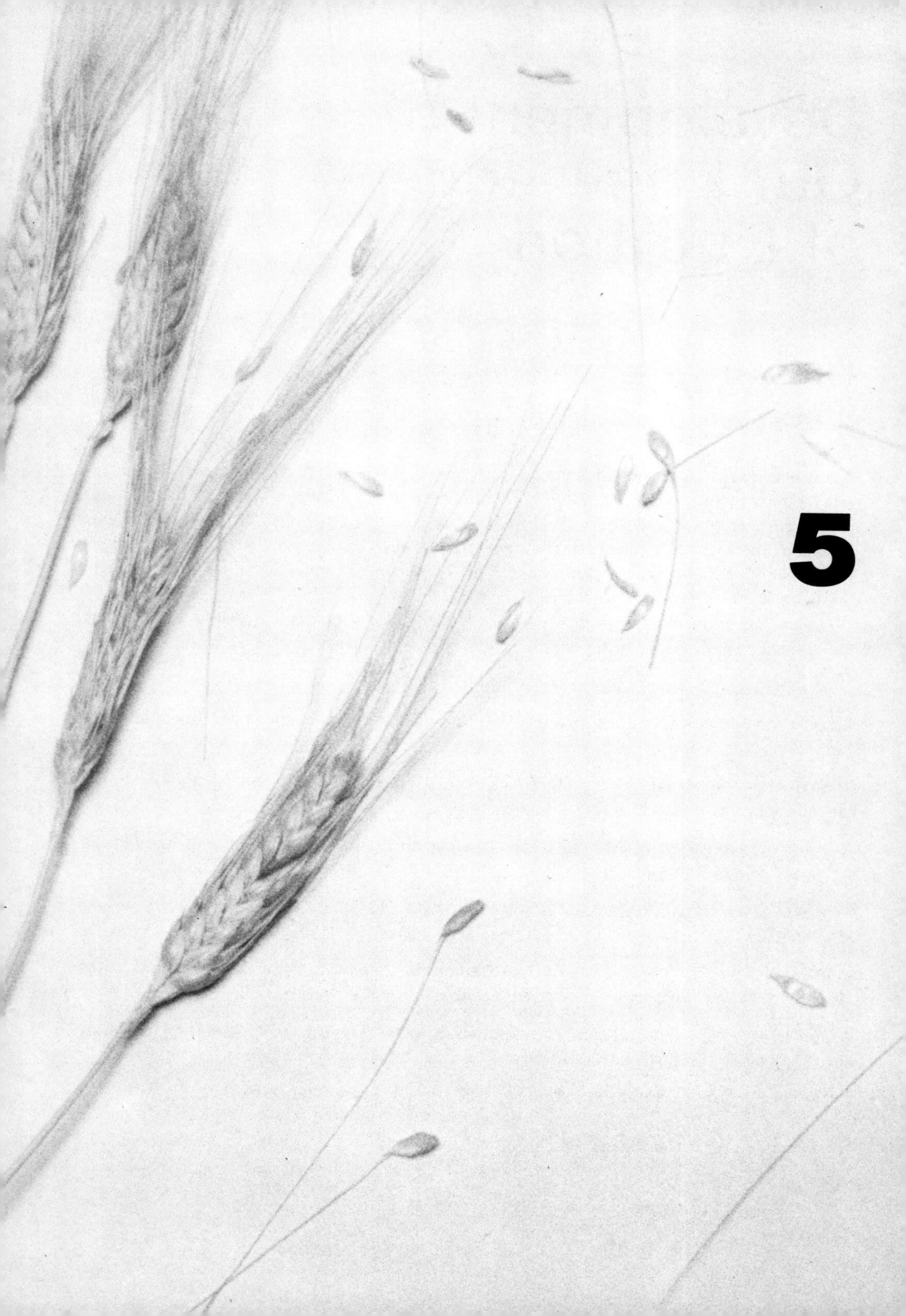
5

Development of Our Knowledge of Nutrition

Our concern is with people and their food. Let us first look at man* himself. What is man? This question has been asked throughout the ages. Philosophers and theologians have argued about the question. Scientists in medicine, anatomy, and physiology have dissected man, experimented on him, and treated him to see how he is put together. Social scientists have analyzed him to see how and why he behaves as he does. Educators have worked with him to discover how he learns.

Man has been classified in many ways. One's view of man probably depends on one's background of education, training, and experience. Here is one viewpoint on man. He is:

Aggressive—explorations, discoveries, and long history of wars speak for this characteristic.

Compassionate—the generous, sometimes self-sacrificing nature of what man will do for his fellowmen is attested to throughout history.

A reasoning, thinking being—the advances in science and our rich stores of knowledge are proof of this feature.

Creative—art, literature, music, architecture, and the inventions we are heirs to are results of this creativity.

Inquisitive—were it not for man's inquisitiveness, exploration of the earth and outer space and all the discoveries of science never could have been made.

A spiritual being—man's belief in some force, power, spirit, or God has placed him above all other creatures in the world.

Gregarious—family, home, community, and city life are evidence of this.

*Man is used here in the genetic sense of all human beings.

Communicative—powers of speech and written language, further developed into all the mass media of communications, are an essential part of man and his progress.

A physiological being—much of what man is and his actions depend on his physical structure and its physiological functioning.

At different periods in history, one or another of these characteristics of mankind has tended to be predominant. But always the physiological nature has expressed itself. The hunger drive is basic to a person's existence. Food determines survival because food nourishes the body. There are many kinds of food, and they differ widely in their nutritive value. Knowledge of the nutritive value of food is a twentieth-century achievement. Throughout the ages people ate what they could get. Undoubtedly it was by trial and error that civilized people gained some understanding of how foods differed; they learned from experience that certain kinds of food were necessary for health. But not until this century did people identify the different nutrient constituents in foods and learn how they were used physiologically for the highly complex processes in the body.

Always man's inquiring mind has asked: "What is it?" "Why?" "How?" His search for the answers to these questions about food in relation to health is the story of the development of the modern science of nutrition. Today, the basic concepts* are summarized in the simplest terms as follows:

1. Nutrition is the way the body uses food. We eat to live, to grow, to keep healthy and well, and to get energy for work and play.

2. Food is made up of different nutrients needed for growth and health. Nutrients include proteins, carbohydrates, fats, minerals, and vitamins. All nutrients needed by the body are available through food. Many kinds and combinations of food can lead to a well-balanced diet. No single food has all the nutrients needed for good growth and health. Each nutrient has specific uses in the body. Most nutrients do their best work in the body when teamed with other nutrients.

3. All persons, throughout life, have need for the same nutrients, but in varying amounts. The amounts of nutrients needed are influenced by age, sex, body size, activity, state of health, and heredity.

4. The way food is handled influences the amount of nutrients in food, its safety, quality, appearance, taste, acceptability, and cost. Handling means anything that happens to food while it is being grown, processed, stored, and prepared for eating.

WHY HISTORY?

History gives meaning to the present. Through knowledge of the past, we gain understanding of what is happening today. History has more than a utilitarian purpose; it is

*Statements made by the United States Interagency Committee on Nutrition Education, 1972.

the record of the progress of human endeavors and work, ideas, visions, failures, and achievements. Athena sprang full armored from the head of Zeus, according to Greek mythology, but knowledge never has sprung full fledged from the brain of humans. It has been acquired step by step.

The history of nutrition is the story of men and women with questioning minds at work on the problems that affect the lives and health of all people. This is an exciting story interwoven with medicine, anatomy, physiology, chemistry, bacteriology, and agriculture. Scientists of almost every nationality contributed to the story because, as Pasteur said, "science knows no national boundaries." They were people of different temperaments and personalities, some with little formal education and others of high specialization; they were physicians, chemists, sailors, explorers, tradesmen, rich aristocrats, teachers, pharmacists, and lawyers. But they were all individuals with curiosity and a will to find the answers to questions that arose in their minds.

This chapter deals with some of the high points of discoveries that have brought us to our present state of knowledge. We are not quite sure when the story began, but reliable records date back to early Greek and Roman times. The story can be pieced together through study of Babylonian and Egyptian tablets, ancient scrolls and papyri, journals of explorers and early voyagers, records of wars and famines, diaries and letters of people in all walks of life, scientific papers, and medical records.

Nutrition as a science is a twentieth-century development. Since nutrition is vital to our life and well being, why should nutrition be so late in developing? The answers are several:

1. Nutrition is dependent on the isolation and measurement of nutrients, which could be achieved only after the development of modern chemistry and the invention of scientific instruments for the quantitative study of minute amounts of chemicals present in food and the human body.
2. Nutrition deals with the living organism and its physiologic functions. Therefore, progress was dependent on advances in the biological sciences.
3. Much that is known about nutrition and health was learned from the study of disease, so progress in clinical medicine had to come first.
4. Concern for others, rather than concern for science and technology as such, is a development of the twentieth century.

History without dates is meaningless. Dates help to put events in a time sequence and to relate them to other events. Use them as a guide to increased understanding of human progress in acquiring knowledge of food and its nutritional significance to health.

THE BEGINNINGS OF MODERN SCIENCE

The story of the history of modern nutrition begins with the seventeenth century, often called the Golden Age of Science, when modern science began to develop because instruments were invented to make experimentation and measurement possible.

The Greeks and Romans believed in using diet in the treatment of disease, although they had no understanding of which foods were really helpful or why. An early Greek physician introduced the idea of four elements: fire, water, earth, and air. These four elements made up the four qualities: hot, dry, cold, and wet. But science could not progress far on such concepts as these. In the second century A.D., Galen, a physician from the Greek kingdom of Pergamos, dissected animals and wrote on human anatomy. He wrote many books on medical topics with so much authority that for the next 1200 years his teachings and writings were accepted as the final word on the subject.

From the time of the downfall of the Roman Empire (476 A.D.) through the Middle Ages was the period of the spread of Christianity, and there was little attention to medicine or science. Voyages of exploration, particularly the discovery of America by Columbus (1492), turned people's thoughts to broader horizons. The invention of movable type in the fifteenth century made the printed word available to more people and thus helped the wider spread of knowledge and ideas.

And now for the seventeenth century. Elizabeth I, or "good Queen Bess" as she was sometimes called, died in 1603, and the reign of the Stuarts began in England. The period of ocean voyages and land discovery was now to be joined by a new type of discovery—scientific discovery. No longer were people willing to accept what Galen said; the voice of authority gave way to the experimental approach. Galileo (1564–1642) in Italy made a telescope to study the stars. Anton Leeuwenhoek (1632-1723), the Dutch tradesman, spent his time grinding lenses and making a kind of microscope so that he was the first to see "little animals" in pond water. He studied all kinds of plant and animal tissue; he was a careful, patient observer who wrote simple, honest accounts of what he saw; and he was a man who described himself as having "a craving after knowledge which, I notice, resides in me more than in most men."

William Harvey (1578–1657) proved, by demonstration and carefully planned experiments, that the blood circulates through the body (1628), going from the heart by way of the arteries and returning by the veins. Harvey thus laid the foundation for later understanding of how food materials are transported to every cell in the body. Robert Boyle (1626–1691), the "father of chemistry," experimented for the joy of finding out things and invented an air pump. Sir Isaac Newton (1642–1727) gave us the theory of gravitation and wrote his great work on mathematics.

The experimental method, crude though it was at first, was now being used. Scientific societies were formed and had their scientific journals for reporting results of experiments. The *Mayflower* arrived in 1620 in what was to become the United States of America; Harvard College was founded in 1636. These are some of the high spots of the seventeenth century, the beginnings of science and freedom for men to use their inquiring minds and to test their ideas.

HOW FOOD IS CHANGED INTO THE HUMAN BODY

Ham and eggs eaten by Susie Jones for breakfast are on their way to becoming Susie Jones. Magic? No—it is a process whereby the chemical constituents of food are rearranged within the body to form the chemical constituents that make up a human being. The complex and intricate processes are well understood today, but current knowledge has been achieved only by patient study through the centuries. Sanctorius (1561–1636), an Italian physician, probably was the first person to do nutrition studies on humans. For weeks he weighed himself, his food, and all body excretions. But neither the equipment nor the basic information in science was available to help him solve the problem of differences between his body weight and what he ate and excreted. One hundred years passed before the next steps were taken to discover how food is changed into the human body.

Digestion

How could solid food be changed in the stomach or some other part of the digestive tract and then get into the blood stream to be circulated in the body? Many wondered about this problem. But how little it was understood is illustrated by the following statement:

> Some physiologists will have it that the stomach is a Mill—others that it is a Fermenting Vat—others again that it is a Stew-pan—but in my view of the matter it is neither a Mill, a Fermenting Vat, nor a Stew-pan—but a stomach, Gentlemen, a Stomach.

This was the way John Hunter (1728–1793), English surgeon and lecturer, informed his students and colleagues that he did not know what the stomach did.

A few men found some ways to try to answer the question. One of these was René Réaumur (1683–1757) of France. He was educated in law but could financially afford to study what interested him most, and that was natural science. He had a pet bird, a kite, which could regurgitate food after swallowing it. Réaumur made some metal cylinders and placed food inside them. Then he put wire grating at each end so that the food could not fall out but would still be exposed to the action of digestion in the stomach when swallowed. Meat was put into the tubes; when regurgitated by the bird, it was found to be partially dissolved. There was no odor of putrefaction and the tubes showed no evidence of crushing or pressure, thus disproving the current theories that digestion was a grinding action or was putrefaction. Réaumur also put sponge in some of the tubes; in this way, he soaked up some of the gastric juices, He found that this juice was acid in nature and would partially dissolve meat in a test tube. New theories are slow to be accepted. Although Réaumur's evidence did not change current ideas, he had introduced a new method of investigation.

Twenty-five years later, Lazzaro Spallanzani (1729–1799) of Italy continued the work and methods begun by Réaumur, and he also experimented on himself; he swallowed small linen bags containing meat and bread. He confirmed Réaumur's findings and wrote a book that showed that digestion was a chemical process and not fermentation.

The next big step forward came in 1822. It was the result of an accident, but a man with vision, curiosity, and scientific interest was there to take advantage of the unusual occurrence. The accident happened to Alexis St. Martin, a French Canadian trapper who was shot in the chest and abdomen. The young Army surgeon who treated him was William Beaumont; the place was a frontier village in northern Michigan; the time was 1822. Although the injury was believed to be fatal, Beaumont's treatment and care of the patient brought about his recovery. However, a small hole in the abdominal wall and into the stomach remained open. Through this opening, Beaumont could insert a thermometer and measure the temperature; he could also see what foods and conditions stimulated the flow of gastric juice and the rate at which different foods were digested. He made 238 observations and experiments, and many of his inferences still are considered to be correct today. Undoubtedly Beaumont could have learned even more about the digestive process but, understandably perhaps, Alexis did not enjoy being studied in this way and went back to Canada.

Chemistry developed rapidly in the nineteenth century. Soon chemists were able to identify the acid in gastric juice as hydrochloric acid, but they also found that some other agent was responsible for the actual process of dissolving food. This agent was found to be an enzyme that was named pepsin (1835).

Advances from that time forward were comparatively rapid, and the chemistry and physiology of digestion are well understood today. Also, much has been learned of the psychological influences on the digestive processes.

Calorimetry

What happens to food once it is absorbed and circulating in the blood stream was even more puzzling than the question of digestion. At about the time Spallanzani was doing his experiments, this question was receiving the attention of Antoine Lavoisier (1743–1794) in Paris. Other scientists (Priestley and Scheele) had discovered oxygen but did not understand it or correctly identify it. Lavoisier discovered the true nature of oxygen. Moreover, he had the vision to interpret and the ability to systematize the knowledge of his time so that modern chemistry could develop. At the height of his scientific career, Lavoisier was a victim of the French Revolution and was beheaded on the guillotine. The work he started was continued by others. Lavoisier showed that accuracy in weighing on analytical balances and exact measurements were essential in science. And above all, his experiments laid the foundation for understanding the processes going on inside the human body. For this he has been called the "father of nutrition."

Breathing is natural to everyone; without air, we all die. This was an ancient discovery. But what does air do and what is it? Scientists of the seventeenth century had studied the problem and found that a lighted candle enclosed in a vessel was soon extinguished. Others enclosed a mouse in a jar of air over water and found that when part of the air was used up the mouse died. Lavoisier's experiments and his keen mind for interpreting what he found showed that breathing or respiration is a chemical process that uses oxygen; the process is called oxidation. Oxygen is essential for the changing of food nutrients into the body structure of man. The sum of all these many chemical processes is metabolism; Lavoisier was the first to measure metabolism in people. He measured the amount of oxygen consumed by his laboratory assistant when sitting at rest and also the amount of carbon dioxide he breathed out at the same time. From these and other measurements on animals, Lavoisier was able to show that oxidation within the body is a source of heat and energy. Lavoisier's experiments also showed that more oxygen is used when one eats food and when one exercises or does work. This was the beginning of calorimetry or measurement of heat and work in the body, which eventually led to the meaurement of calorie values of foods.

Other scientists soon added to the foundations of knowledge established by Lavoisier. The center of research passed for a time to a group of German scientists who first built a calorimeter large enough for a dog to be enclosed in and then one in which a person could be enclosed. The oxygen used and carbon dioxide exhaled could be measured precisely, as well as the body heat at all times and under differing conditions of diet and of work. Graham Lusk (1866–1932) of Connecticut studied calorimetry in Germany. When he returned to the U.S., he had a calorimeter built and then investigated the metabolism of healthy and diseased animals and children.

NUTRIENTS IN FOOD

The search for Protein

Although a scientist discovered the gas called nitrogen in 1772, it was not known that this element had anything to do with nutrition until 1816. At that time, a French physician and teacher of physiology, Francois Magendie (1783–1855) published some of his research findings. When he fed dogs single foods such as sugar and water or olive oil and water, the animals died. Magendie concluded that animals needed nitrogen in the diet. He knew that both body tissues and many foods contained nitrogen, and he suggested that the nitrogen of the tissues probably came from food. The nitorgen-containing foods were called albuminous foods; just 22 years (1838) after Magendie's work, a Dutch chemist, Mulder, gave the name *protein* to the nitrogen-containing material in these albuminous foods.

The word protein comes from the Greek word meaning first. But protein does not take first place in nutrition. No nutrient is first because nutrition requires that there be adequate amounts of a number of nutrients. However, protein is essential, and children stop growing when it is not supplied in their diets. In many countries today, especially those dependent upon cereals and root crops, good quality protein is lacking and the health and vigor of the people are impaired. Kwashiorkor (described in Chapter 9), a disease of children, is associated with lack of protein and calories in food.

A new pathway was opened by this work on nitrogen-containing foods. Chemists began to identify the various constituents or building blocks that make up different proteins; these blocks are called amino acids. Some 22 amino acids have been identified in food. Some of these amino acids can be synthesized in the body from nitrogenous material supplied in the diet. Others must be supplied preformed in food; these are called the essential amino acids.

Chemical analysis and animal feeding experiments have been the methods for learning about proteins. Albino rats have been used most frequently in the twentieth century because they are small, easily handled, grow rapidly and therefore show any deficiency quickly, and eat almost any kind of food mixture. Advances in chemistry make it possible to separate the pure constituents of food. By feeding these in varying combinations, the essential nutrients for an adequate diet were identified. The amount of protein needed by animals or people can be measured. The amount of nitrogen is determined in the food that is eaten, and similar analysis for nitrogen is made on excreta. If what is consumed equals what is excreted,then there is obviously a balance and the diet is adequate. If more is excreted than is being eaten in food, then the body is losing protein and more must be eaten to meet the body's needs. Using these basic methods, rapid advances in knowledge of proteins have been made in the last 50 years. But research is still continuing on the amino-acid makeup of foods, the amounts needed, and the various ways in which protein foods may be combined in the diet to provide all the amino acids. Although foods of animal origin are the best sources of the essential amino acids, recent studies have shown that a judicious mixture of different plant proteins can be made and that mixtures of cereals and other plant foods can be prepared that are nutritionally adequate (see Chapter 10).

Is Fat Necessary?

Carbohydrates—starches and sugars—form the basis of the diets of people the world over, except for the Eskimos in the Arctic regions where these foods will not grow. Cereals (wheat, rice, corn, oats, rye, and barley) and tropical root plants are the easiest and cheapest of all foods to grow. Their great value is that they are a cheap source of calories, and calories are necessary to satisfy hunger and provide energy.

Fat was one of the earliest food substances to be recognized because of its oily or greasy nature. The fat on meat is readily seen, as is the cream on milk. Oil, which is liquid fat, is found in nuts and the seeds of many plants such as cottonseed and soybean. These foods are usually more expensive to produce than are the cereals and root crops.

By the middle of the last century, scientists were beginning to look much more critically at proteins, fat, and carbohydrates and to question how they were formed in the body, where they came from, and whether they were necessary in food. At first it was thought that the fat of an animal's body was obtained from fat in food. But farm animals grew fat eating grass, and grass certainly had little fat in it. Using the method of feeding diets of known food composition, Boussingault, in France, fed diets that were free from fat to geese; the geese grew well and stored fat in their bodies. He obtained the same results with ducks. In other countries, similar experiments with fat-free diets for dogs and farm animals gave clear evidence that the animal body can synthesize fat from carbohydrate. The same is true for human beings. If the body is given more carbohydrates, that is, more calories, then are needed for work and body functions, the excess is changed chemically in the metabolic processes to fat and is stored in the body as fat.

This does not mean that fat itself is unnecessary in the diet; fats are high in energy value, providing two and one-fourth times as many calories per unit of weight as do carbohydrates or proteins. Fats are enjoyed because they give flavor and palatability to food. Some fats carry certain vitamins and also an essential unsaturated fatty acid. (Unsaturated fatty acids are ones in which two or more pairs of carbon atoms in the carbon chain of the molecule can add additional hydrogen atoms.)

Mineral Elements

In the early 1800s, three classes of foodstuffs were recognized and called saccharine, albuminous, and oleaginous substances; these are now known as carbohydrates, proteins, and fats. The nineteenth century was a period of rapid discovery of the chemical nature and properties of these substances and of the other elements necessary for growth and health. Chemical analysis and feeding experiments with animals were the techniques used to discover a new group of substances, the ash constituents or mineral elements, essential for human nutrition.

When plant material was burned, it did not disappear entirely; some ash always remained. Chemists at this time (1800) began to look at this ash and try to find out what it was composed of. They were also curious about the chemical nature of bone, blood, and other body fluids. At the same time, other investigators were using the new technique of feeding experiments with farm animals. One of these investigators was Boussingault (1802–1887), the French chemist, physicist, and mining engineer, to whom reference has already been made. He is credited with being the first to apply knowledge of chemistry to the feeding of farm animals. In his experiments, he compared the growth and health of animals when one lot was fed a diet containing ordinary salt and another lot received no salt. Salt made an obvious difference in the appearance and well-being of the animals. In similar types of feeding experiments, he found that iron was essential in the diet.

Other investigators found that calcium and phosphorus were needed for skeletal growth. Iodine was discovered in the thyroid gland of humans. Sheep died unless cobalt was present in the soil on which their food grew. Many scientists in many places identified new mineral elements necessary for life, and new discoveries still are being made. At least sixteen of these elements are now known to be part of the body structure or the body fluids, and they must be supplied in the daily food intake. Some of these, such as copper, zinc, and manganese, are present in such small amounts that they have been called trace elements or microelements.

One more group of food nutrients had yet to be discovered—the vitamins. Although they were the last group of nutrients to be isolated and named, their story is perhaps the longest and started earlier in history than that of any other food constituent.

DEFICIENCY DISEASES AND DISCOVERY OF VITAMINS

The history of humanity has been marked by the struggle to obtain food and to ward off disease. Until this century, hunger, famine, and disease were major factors in keeping down the numbers of the population in many countries. Much disease has been eliminated or controlled since the discovery of the bacterial origin of disease and the development of sanitation, drugs, and antibiotics.

Another group of diseases is being eliminated through knowledge of nutrition; these diseases are called the dietary-deficiency diseases because they are caused by the lack of vitamins or other nutrients in the diet. Some of these diseases such as scurvy, pellagra, and rickets have been known for many years. Since 1912, the vitamin associated with each has been discovered; that is the story told here. Other dietary-deficiency diseases include beriberi, endemic goiter, and kwashiorkor. These are discussed in Chapter 9.

Scurvy

Scurvy has been known for centuries. Because it affected sailors on long voyages, it has been called the scourge of sailors. However, this disease has been just as much a calamity for soldiers, explorers, and civilian populations when they have been deprived of fresh foods, especially fruits and vegetables.

It is always easier to look back and see how and why problems existed than it is to understand them at the time. So it is natural to ask why there is no mention of scurvy in Columbus' voyage of discovery across the Atlantic in 1492. He had three ships with a complement of 88 men. They sailed on September 6 and reached the West Indies October 12—a voyage of little over one month. They also stopped at the Canary Islands for repairs, fresh water, and food. Healthy men on a voyage of that length did not succumb to scurvy. But on longer voyages scurvy took its toll.

Vasco da Gama, the great Portuguese navigator, sailed from Lisbon in 1497 to the East Indies. He lost 100 out of 160 men while on a voyage around the Cape of Good Hope because his men were continuously at sea for four months without fresh food of any kind.

Jacques Cartier, the French explorer, is well remembered in the history of scurvy because he learned from the Indians how to cure it in his crew on their voyage during 1535 and 1536 to Canada.

During this period there died to the number of twenty-five of the best and most able seamen we had, who all succumbed to the aforesaid malady (scurvy). And at that time there was little hope of saving more than forty others, while the whole of the rest were ill, except three or four.

Cartier saw an Indian walking about in good health whom he had seen ten days earlier ill with the same disease his men suffered from. The Indian told him that he "had been healed by the juice of the leaves of a tree and the dregs of these, and that this was the only way to cure sickness." Cartier obtained some branches of the tree and prepared the drink from it for his men.

As soon as they had drunk it, they felt better, which must clearly be ascribed to miraculous causes; for after drinking it two or three times, they recovered health and strength and were cured of all the diseases they had ever had . . . in less than eight days a whole tree as large and as tall as any I ever saw was used up, and produced such a result, that had all the doctors of Louvain, and Montpelier been there, with all the drugs of Alexandira, they could not have done so much in a year as did this tree in eight days; for it benefited us so much that all who were willing to use it, recovered health and strength, thanks be to God.

The particular tree used has not been identified with certainty. Some thought it to be the sassafras tree, others the hemlock. Leaves and twigs of pine, willow, and evergreens have been analyzed and shown to be good sources of vitamin C, the vitamin that cures scurvy.

Practical experience worked well for some voyagers. John Woodall, ship's surgeon, wrote a book in 1617 in which he gave advice for preventing scurvy: "The use of the juice of lemon is a precious medicine and well tried, being sound and good." But Lord Anson, who sailed in 1740 with three ships to explore the Pacific and also to raid and capture Spanish galleons, paid no attention to such suggestions. He had a force of 961 officers and men; within a year 626 were dead, most of them from scurvy.

No matter how exciting the stories, descriptions, or folklore about foods or treatment of disease, science rightly demands experimental evidence before accepting statements. In the case of scurvy, this evidence was provided by Captain James Lind in his book, *A Treatise of the Scurvy,* published in 1753. Lind was the son of a Scottish merchant. He studied medicine, entered the Royal Navy, and became a ship's surgeon and then physician in charge of a Royal Naval hospital. He was a man noted for his clear thinking, knowledge, and ability. In his book, we have the description of the first clinical experiment carried out under controlled conditions. It still stands today as a model of careful planning of a nutrition experiment with control of all conditions, completeness, and conciseness and accuracy of recording. It is worthy of study not only for its place in history and its information but also for its style. Lind wrote:

On the 20th of May 1747, I took twelve patients in the scurvy, on board the *Salisbury* at sea. Their cases were similar as I could have them. They all in general had putrid gums, the spots and lassitude with weakness of their knees. They lay together in one place, being a proper apartment for the sick in the fore-hold; and had one diet common to all *viz.,* water-gruel sweetened with sugar in the morning; fresh mutton-broth often times for dinner; at other times puddings, boiled biscuit with sugar; and for supper, barley and raisins, rice and currants, sago and wine, or the like. Two of these were ordered each a quart of cyder a-day. Two others took twenty-five gutts of *elixir vitriol* three times a-day, upon an empty stomach; using a gargle strongly acidulated with it for their mouths. Two others took two spoonfuls of vinegar three times a-day, upon an empty stomach; having their gruels and their other food well acidulated with it, as also the gargle for their mouth. Two of the worst patients, with the tendons in ham rigid (a symptom none of the rest had), were put upon a course of sea-water. Of this they drank half a pint every day, and sometimes more or less, at it operated, by way of gentle physic. Two others had each two oranges and one lemon given them every day. These they ate with greediness, at different times, upon an empty stomach. They continued but six days under this course, having consumed the quantity that could be spared. The two remaining patients took the bigness of a nutmeg three times a-day, of an electuary recommended by a hospital surgeon, made of garlic, mustard seed, balsam of Peru, and gum myrrh.

The consequence was, that the most sudden and visible good effects were perceived from the use of the oranges and lemons; one of those who had taken them, being at the end of six days fit for duty. . . . The other was the best recovered of any in his condition; and being now deemed pretty well, was appointed nurse to the rest of the sick. . . .

As I shall have occasion elsewhere to take notice of the effects of other medicines in this disease, I shall here only observe, that the result of all my experiments was, that oranges and lemons were the most effectual remedies for this distemper at sea. I am apt to think oranges preferable to lemons, though perhaps both given together will be found serviceable.

Despite this clear-cut evidence of the value of citrus fruit for curing scurvy, it was not until 50 years later that the Royal Navy adopted the regular practice of daily provision of lemon or lime juice for all sailors. And this is the origin of the term "limey," so long applied to British sailors and sometimes even today to anyone from England.

The Gold Rush days of California, 1849 to 1850, brought a sudden increase of 100,000 persons to that part of the country. Food shortages, especially of fruit and vegetables, developed quickly; the deaths from scurvy in the mining camps have been estimated conservatively at 10,000. The last part of the overland trail to California was marked with the graves of those who died of scurvy. It is of interest that scurvy and the

Gold Rush were factors in starting the citrus industry of Southern California; the demand for lemons led some pioneers in 1849 to plant large orchards of citrus fruit.

Acceptance of new knowledge is sometimes very slow. Military forces apparently thought of scurvy as a sea disease and did not provide protection against it. Consequently, throughout Europe and America, the story of wars is also a record of scurvy. In the American Civil War, 30,714 cases of scurvy were reported and 338 deaths were attributed to this disease. In the Franco-Prussian War of 1870 to 1871, the besieged city of Paris suffered severely from scurvy. In the Russo-Japanese War, half the garrison of 17,000 soldiers suffered from scurvy after the siege of Port Arthur. In World War I, 1914 to 1918, thousands of troops were incapacitated by scurvy; it affected the armies of Russia, Turkey, Romania, Germany, Austria, Italy, and France. The troops from India fighting in Mesopotamia with the British army had 7500 cases of scurvy in a 19-week period.

It has been said that "science knows no national boundaries." The same is true of scurvy and other dietary-deficiency diseases. Lack of an essential nutrient in the diet affects anyone regardless of nationality, color, occupation, place of living, age, and sex. Scurvy often affected men more than women because the men were absent from home and regular meals, and their hard work produced the effects more quickly. Today scurvy is not unknown in infants whose mothers fail to give them orange or other fruit juice. It is also seen in men and women who fail to use fruits and vegetables in their diets because of poverty or because they live alone and do not take the trouble to obtain an adequate diet.

In 1907, two Norwegian investigators, searching for the cause of beriberi found that guinea pigs fed a diet of only grain and water developed scurvy but that this could be cured by feeding them greenstuff. This was one of those "lucky chances" in research because guinea pigs, monkeys, and humans are practically the only creatures that must have vitamin C-containing foods supplied in their diet. Almost all other animals can synthesize this vitamin in their bodies. This discovery with guinea pigs opened the way for a quick and easy means of studying foods as a source of vitamin C. Finally, in 1932, an American scientist, C. G. King at the University of Pittsburgh, crystallized pure vitamin C from lemon juice. And at the same time, Szent Gyorgy in Hungary was making the same discovery using sweet red peppers. This vitamin is now named ascorbic acid and can be synthesized in the laboratory.

Pellagra

Pellagra is a disease somewhat more recently recognized than scurvy because it occurs mainly where people use corn (maize) as a staple of the diet, and corn was introduced into Europe after the discovery of the Western Hemisphere. Pellagra was described first by Gaspar Casál of Spain in 1735; he attributed it to faulty diet after observing its occurrence among poor peasants who lived chiefly on maize. The disease was common in Italy in the eighteenth century and continued to occur in that country until wheat and other foods were introduced into the high-maize diet. The Italians named the disease pellagra, meaning "rough skin," because this is one of the characteristics of the disease. In the nineteenth century, pellagra was common in Romania, Hungary, Turkey, Greece, and Egypt; it still exists where large amounts of cornmeal are eaten.

One of the earliest descriptions of pellagra was in 1907 by a physician at a mental institution in Alabama. Pellagra increased in the southern states among low-income families, both white and black, until in 1917 there were 170,000 cases recorded and many deaths. The United State Bureau of Public Health appointed Joseph Goldberger to investigate the cause of this malady. Many physicians thought it was an infectious disease, but Goldberger found that doctors and attendants in asylums where the disease frequently occurred were free from pellagra. Moreover, he was unable to transfer the disease from pellagrins to himself. He did not find pellagra wherever the diet included meat, milk, and eggs. All the evidence pointed to a poor diet, high in cornmeal, as the cause. By feeding experiments on animals and humans, Goldberger showed this to be true. It was first thought that something in good-quality protein foods such as meat, milk, and eggs prevented pellagra and that a pellagra-preventive vitamin would be found in these foods. Although this was not quite the answer, these proteins were found to contain an amino acid, tryptophan, which could be changed into the pellagra-preventive vitamin within the human body. The vitamin was discovered through studies with dogs which suffered from a disease called black tongue which is similar to pellagra in humans. In 1937, Elvehjem of the University of Wisconsin found that nicotinic acid would cure black tongue in dogs. Clinicians then used this nicotinic acid on pellagra patients, and they were cured of the disease.

Rickets

Rickets is rarely seen today but was once a common disease of children in England and Europe. Bowed legs were the most visible signs of rickets, but many other parts of the bone structure also were affected. Rickets was most frequently observed during the middle of the eighteenth century when the industrial revolution began in England, and the rapidly increasing number of textile mills employed many women and children. Cities became crowded, slums developed, many families never saw sunlight, and rickets began to occur in children.

What was the cause of rickets? By some happy chance, cod liver oil was found to be beneficial. The Manchester Infirmary began using cod liver oil, 50 to 60 gallons annually, for treatment of rickets, joint diseases, and rheumatism. The oil took from four weeks to six months to have any effect. Many theories were given for the action of cod liver oil; some thought it was the iodine in the oil, other that it was the fatty acids. Not until 1922 was the answer found—a vitamin.

Where there is plenty of sunlight, there is no rickets. At the end of World War I, children in Vienna and Berlin were found to have severe rickets; they were treated by exposing them to lamps that produced ultraviolet rays, the same as those from sunlight. This process is called irradiation. Experiments with animals that were fed diets that produced rickets showed that it was just as effective to irradiate the food before giving it to the animals as to irradiate the animals. The puzzle was a complicated one. Rickets occurred where there was poor hygiene, crowded living conditions, and poor diet. Cod liver oil cured rickets and so did sunlight or the ultraviolet light from lamps.

In the 1920s, with knowledge of other vitamins as a guide, vitamin D was found in cod liver oil. Certain foods, and also the human skin, contain substances called sterols. When these sterols are exposed to sunlight or ultraviolet rays, one of the sterols is changed to active vitmain D. Thus, two centuries of experience with the disease of rickets finally yielded the answer: vitamin D is necessary so that the body can use the minerals calcium and phosophorus to form normal bone. Today it is approved practice in the United States to give all infants some form of vitamin D such as irradiated sterol or the pure vitamin in solution. Infants and children are given milk to which vitamin D has been added. Thus, another of the dietary-deficiency diseases has been eliminated for all who use the knowledge of nutrition.

Discovery of Vitamins

It was in 1906 that Frederick Gowland Hopkins, biochemist of Cambridge University, England, and Nobel Prize winner, reported that there was an unknown something in food essential for life and health. By 1912, he was able to support this statement with experimental data. He fed milk to young albino rats and they grew well. But when he fed them the purified constituents from milk, the animals not only failed to grow but soon died.

Another investigator, Casimir Funk, a Polish chemist working at the Lister Institute in London in 1911, was trying to find the substance present in the outer coating of rice which was known to be a cure for beriberi. His reading, thinking, and experimenting led him to believe that beriberi, scurvy, and rickets were all caused by something that was lacking in some diets. These substances, present in certain foods, he named *vitamines* in the 1912 publication; this name was later changed to *vitamins*. Funk was not the first to propose that there was something in food essential for health, but he was the first to express clearly this idea so that it received attention in the scientific world. The name and idea of vitamins soon captured public interest.

The time was ripe for such an idea. But why had there been such a long delay in acceptance of the possibility of dietary deficiencies such as vitamins? It is not easy to explain why an idea presented at one time gains immediate acceptance and at another time is rejected or unnoticed for years or even centuries. In the second half of the nineteenth century, Louis Pasteur, the great French scientist, clearly demonstrated to all the world that diseases were caused by microorganisms. At the same time, Robert Koch of Germany identified many bacteria and showed how to fix and stain them for study under the microscope. Pasteur and Koch founded the science of bacteriology. In a world that had just awakened to the concept of disease caused by invading organisms or bacteria, it was not easy to accept an idea that was the complete reversal of this, namely that disease could be caused because something was *not* present.

Acceptance of the vitamin theory could not be delayed very long after 1912. Since 1907, Dr. Elmer V. McCollum and co-workers at the University of Wisconsin (and later at Baltimore) had been trying to find exactly what were the constituents of an adequate diet for cattle. The first interest of these investigators was to help farmers; only when the first vitamins were discovered did McCollum realize their significance for human health and become one of the great leaders of the day in human nutrition. McCollum and Marguerite Davis used synthetic diets, ones made up of purified materials. When lard was used as the source of fat in the diet, the experimental animals ceased to grow. But if fat from butter or fat extracted from egg yolk was used, growth was normal. Many experiments of this type led to a scientific report in 1913 showing that a special factor was present in some types of fat and not in others. Two years later, continued research provided evidence that there were two different factors essential for normal growth, one associated with fat and the other with milk sugar. McCollum called these factors "fat-soluble A" and "water-soluble B." McCollum also introduced the term "protective foods." This term clearly expressed the newly developing ideas of nutrition that foods differed in their value in the diet. In 1918, he wrote: "Milk and the leaves of plants are to be regarded as protective foods and should never be omitted from the diet."

At the same time that McCollum and Davis were making their first vitamin studies, similar investigations were being carried on independently by Osborne and Mendel at New Haven, Connecticut, and were in agreement with McCollum's findings. Thus, the first two vitamins, A and B, were proven to exist. Then many investigators in various countries took up the search for further information about these vitamins and for other vitamins. Soon vitamin C, the cure for scurvy, and then Vitamin D, associated with the prevention of rickets, were described. Vitamin E, necessary for reproduction in animals, was added to the list in 1922.

By 1926, what had been called vitamin B was shown to consist of at least two separate factors. Although investigators did not know the chemical identity of these vitamins, they knew that they existed because of the effect on animals when foodstuffs containing these vitamins were withheld from the diet. Experiments were conducted using rats, mice, guinea pigs, monkeys, hamsters, chickens, pigeons, and farm animals. Studies with dogs led to the discovery of the vitamin that prevents pellagra. The physiological effect of the different vitamins, the comparative vitamins in different foods, and the effect of heat, cooking, drying, and other treatments on the vitamin content of foods were measured by feeding experiments. Search for other vitamins also continued. Microorganisms such as yeasts, molds, and bacteria were used because they too needed vitamins for their growth. Because the microorganisms grew much more quickly than animals, results could be obtained in a few days or hours instead of the weeks for animal studies.

The most recent vitamin to be discovered was vitamin B_{12}, or cyanocobalamin, which was identified in 1948 and found to be essential in the prevention of pernicious anemia.

While biological assays were going on in the animal laboratories, chemists were at work seeking to extract the vitamins from food, purify them, obtain the pure crystalline material, and determine the chemical formula for each. In 1926, a Dutch worker (Jansen) obtained crystals of vitamin B_1, which prevents beriberi. But it was not until 1936 that Robert R. Williams, who had spent a lifetime in the search for this vitamin, was able to produce it in quanity and determine its formula. The chemical structures of all the known vitamins now have been determined; they can be manufactured in the laboratory for use in research and medical treatment. However, the best way for every individual to obtain vitamins is from food. Meals that include meats, milk, fruits, vegetables, cereals, and butter or margarine can supply all the needed vitamins for the normal individual. Foods wisely chosen have the advantage of supplying not only vitamins, but also the other essentials for health, namely energy or fuel value (measured in calories), protein, and minerals.

NUTRITION IN HUMANS

Chemical analysis and feeding experiments have shown what nutrients are needed and in what quantities. But how to find out what goes on inside the human body was for a long time a puzzling question. How could one see inside people? Then, in 1934, a new tool become available that made this possible, at least indirectly. Harold Urey, a chemist at Columbia University, discovered "heavy hydrogen," and for this he was awarded the Nobel Prize. Heavy hydrogen, now called deuterium, has all the properties and reactions of ordinary hydrogen except that it has a different weight or mass. This means that an atom of heavy hydrogen can always be identified wherever it is in food or the body tissues.

A young biochemist, Rudolph Schoenheimer, took some of the heavy hydrogen and placed it by chemical procedures in certain fatty acids and fed these to mice. After a period of this feeding, the animals were killed and analyzed, and the amount and location of the heavy hydrogen were determined. In this way, it was found that the heavy hydrogen had become part of the fat tissues of the body, even in those organs and areas that were believed to be fat-storage depots. This work introduced a new concept into nutrition—that there is a constant state of change within the cells of the body. There is a dynamic state in the body with constituents from food rapidly exchanging places with similar constituents already in the cells. This same type of experiment also was done with heavy nitrogen and the proteins. Many chemical changes were followed in the body by this method. It was as if a label were tied to nutrients in the food and they could be followed in their chemical processes throughout the body. Radioisotopes now serve the same purpose. These can be located in the body, its tissues, fluids, or bony structure because of their radioactivity. Thus, the biochemists have a new tool with which they can follow what is happening to food nutrients in the body; in other words, they can "see" inside people.

Learning from Eating Experience—Dietary Studies

In the last decades of the nineteenth century, careful studies were made of what different people ate. The reasoning was this: People who were able to work hard and appeared to be in good health must be eating the kind of food they needed. Therefore, food of such people was weighed and measured; the calories, total protein, fat, starches, and sugars also were calculated. Nothing was known then about vitamins or differences in protein; the calories were thought to be the all-important item. It is of interest that the calorie intakes calculated in these diet studies were almost the same as the caloric needs determined in the calorimeter studies done in Germany. Dietary studies were made for many groups in this country around 1900 by W. O. Atwater, "father of nutrition," in the United States. Atwater designed a bomb calorimeter, so called because of its shape. It was a tightly sealed container in which small weighed amounts of pure foodstuffs could be placed, ignited by an electric spark, and burned in oxygen. All the heat produced in this way by the oxidation of the food could be measured. Thus were obtained the familiar calorie values of food: four calories for each gram (about one-thirtieth of an ounce) of protein and of carbohydrate and nine calories per gram of fat. These calorie values of foods were used, and are still used today, to calculate the calorie value of a day's diet.

Dietary studies are currently used as one way of finding out if individuals are obtaining all the nutrients they need in desired amounts. The amounts of protein, fat, minerals, and each vitamin, as well as calories, are calculated. Dietary studies are a useful and practical tool in nutrition investigation.

Quantitative Requirements for Nutrients

What are the constituents of food that are essential in the diet? This was one of the first questions that challenged investigators, but science is quantitative. How much of each nutrient is needed was the next question. This is more difficult to answer, and research still is going on to determine amounts needed of some of the vitamins and mineral elements. The basic technique is the same as that already described for animal feeding. Purified diets are used, and for the nutrient studied, the amounts are varied to find how much is needed for growth and health of experimental animals. Then similar experiments are made on humans. Here there are many difficulties encountered. Amounts of nutrients needed differ with age and rate of growth, with activity, body size, and a number of other influencing factors including biochemical individuality.

Summary of Achievements in Nutrition

People have progressed from food for survival to knowledge of nutrition for health. The four nutrition concepts given at the beginning of this chapter summarize in elementary terms where we stand today with regard to what is known of the science of nutrition.

Knowledge of nutrition as a science was negligible until the nineteenth century and has developed fully only in this century. Its growth has been dependent largely on chemistry, physiology, and medicine; nutrition had to wait for these sciences and the concept of the experimental method to develop. Also there had to be available the kind of labo-

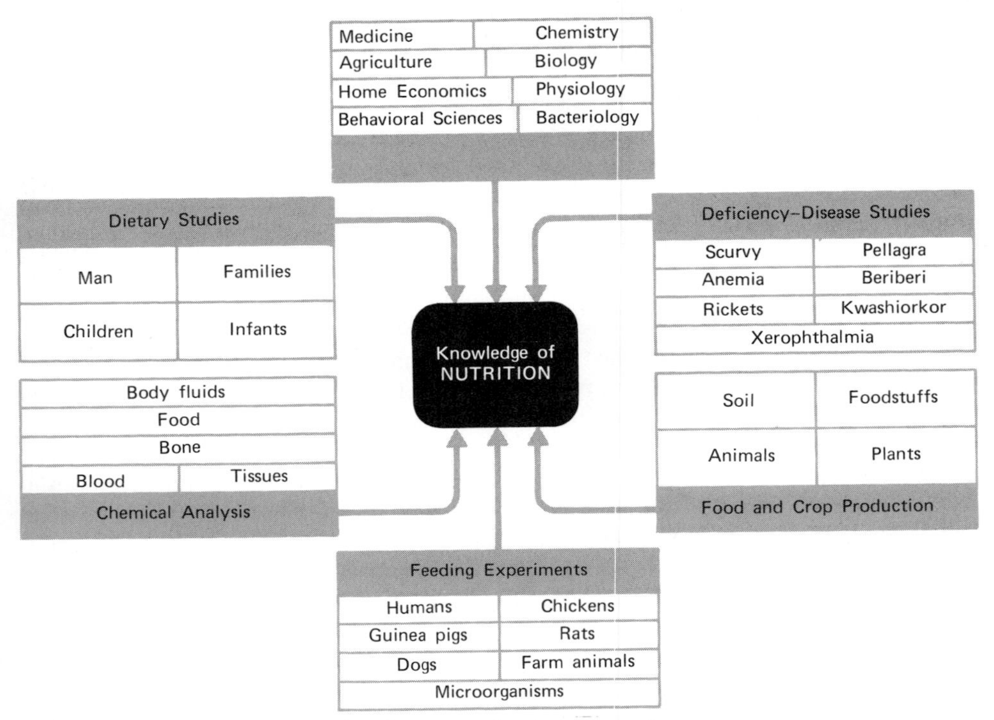

Methods and areas of investigation that led to the development of the science of nutrition.

ratory apparatus and equipment necessary for quantitative measurements. People, ideas, and tools at the right time and place have been the essential ingredients for progress and scientific discoveries. The figure above is a graphic summary of some of the many and varied studies that have led to present knowledge of the science of nutrition.

It is now known that nutrition is essential for growth, health, and well being of all people. However, it must be added that nutrition alone cannot guarantee good health because many other factors are involved (hygiene, freedom from infection, accident, and other health hazards).

Progress in nutrition science is a continuing process, but there is an immediate challenge now. This challenge is how to make available to all people everywhere enough food of the right kind, and how to educate all people to select and enjoy foods for nutritive value.

The story of the history of nutrition shows how we have acquired our present sum of knowledge. Nutrition affects people's health, ability to work, behavior, and learning ability. But knowledge is not enough; use of knowledge is not always guided by reasoning ability. Many other factors influence how and to what extent people use their nutrition knowledge and put it into practice in food selection. Some of these influencing factors are shown in the preceding diagram and are discussed in chapters throughout this book.

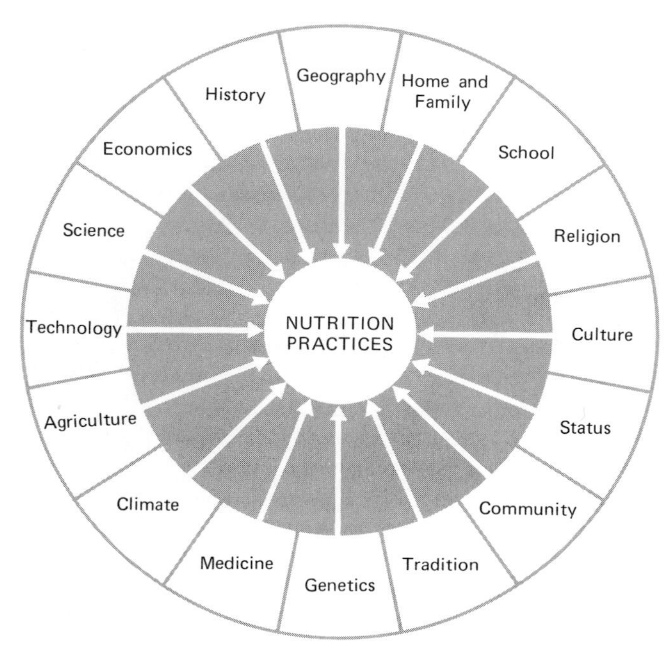

Chart of human nutrition practices.

STUDY QUESTIONS

1. In the nineteenth century, chemical analysis could not measure all the nutrients present in food. Why was this and how was the problem solved?
2. This chapter has stressed some problems encountered in the development of nutrition science. List these and others you find in your reading. Explain why these were major problems at that time.
3. Scientists of the past were seeking for the unknowns about food values and nutrients in relation to health. What can you envision as unknowns in this field that should be explored today?
4. Read the journals of some early explorer of land or sea or the diaries of early American colonists. How would you evaluate their food and its nutritional value?
5. What were the chief nutritional problems at different periods in American history such as the early colonial days, the overland trail period, the industrial expansion era, and the growth period of large cities?

6. Prepare a chronological chart showing major discoveries in nutrition and other events happening at that time. What are the relationships between nutrition progress and other historical events?

TOPICS FOR INDIVIDUAL DISCUSSION

1. Describe your concept of man and how much he can or should be influenced by nutrition. Develop in depth your concept of a well-nourished individual.
2. In what ways does the history of nutrition help you understand other events in history? Choose one of these events and develop the relationship.
3. Choose one of the nutrients and critically trace its history of discovery; or choose one of the discoverers in nutrition science and describe and evaluate the work in relation to his or her life and personality.
4. Polar explorations have failed many times because of nutritional difficulties. Select a polar expedition, describe its preparations and route, and then evaluate the nutritional problems, why they occurred, and whether or not they were inevitable at that time.
5. In what ways has the stage of nutrition knowledge influenced the outcome of wars or exploration? Choose one of these events and trace the relationship between the event and nutrition.

REFERENCES AND SUGGESTED READING

General

Aykroyd, W. R. *Conquest of Deficiency Diseases*. F.F.H.C. Basic Study No. 24, WHO. Geneva, 1970.

Biggar, H. P. *The Voyages of Jacques Cartier*. Published from the original translations, notes, and appendices, by authority of the Sec. of State under the direction of the Archivist, Ottawa, Canada, 1924.

Drummond, J. C. and A. Wilbraham. *The Englishman's Food. A History of Five Centuries of English Diet*. Jonathan Cape, London, 1939.

Essays on the History of Nutrition and Dietetics. Amer. Diet. Assoc. Chicago, 1967.

Galdston, I., Ed. *Human Nutrition Historic and Scientific*. N.Y. Academy of Medicine Monograph III. International Universities Press, New York, 1960.

Hill, Mary M. ICNE Formulates Some Basic Concepts in Nutrition. *Nutrition Program News*. U.S. Dept. of Agr. pp. 1–2, Sept.–Oct. 1964.

Lusk, G. *Nutrition*. Paul Hoeber, New York, 1933.

McCollum, E. V. *A History of Nutrition*. Houghton-Mifflin, Boston, 1957.

McCollum, E. V. *From Kansas Farmboy to Scientist, The Autobiography of Elmer Verner McCollum.* University of Kansas Press, Lawrence, Kans., 1964.
Orr, J. B. *Feast and Famine, The Wonderful World of Food.* Rathbone Books, London, 1957.
Todhunter, E. N. The Story of Nutrition. *Yearbook of Agriculture.* U.S. Dept. of Agr., p. 7, 1959.
Todhunter, E. N. Some Aspects of the History of Dietetics. *World Review of Nutr. and Diet.* 5:32, 1965.

Scurvy

Hess, A. F. *Scurvy Past and Present.* J. B. Lippincott, Philadelphia, 1920.
Lind, J. *Treatise of the Scurvy.* Edinburgh Univ. Press, London, 1753. Reprinted as a Bicentenary Volume, C. P. Stewart and D. Guthrie, Eds. Edinburgh Univ. Press, 1953.

Pellagra

Parsons, R. P. *Trail to Light—A Biography of Joseph Goldberger.* Bobbs-Merrill, New York, 1943.
Roe, D. A. *A Plague of Corn: the Social History of Pellagra.* Cornell University Press, Ithaca, N.Y., 1973.
Sebrell, W. H. Biography of Joseph Goldberger. *J. Nutr.* 55:3, 1955.

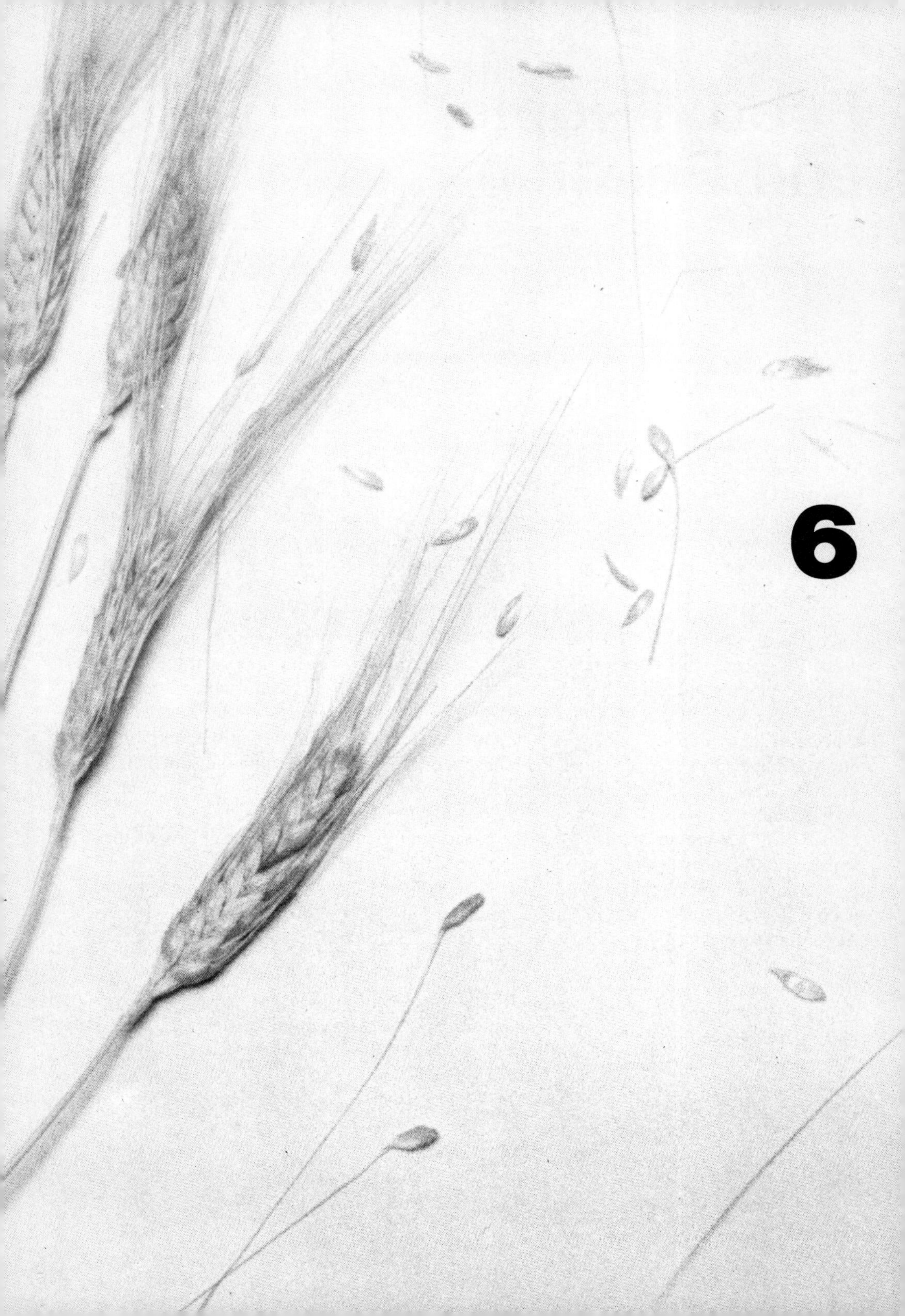

6

Food, People, and Religion

The various religions of the world have a profound influence on peoples' dietary practices and customs. Over the centuries of recorded and unrecorded human history, many religions have decreed what foods people could or could not eat, what foods they could or could not eat on certain days of the year, and frequently how certain foods must be prepared for consumption. Many of these dietary habits have become symbolic of the religion itself.

What are some of these religious influences on diet? What are the religious bases for these dietary practices? How did they develop? What is the significance today of these influences? These are a few of the many questions that seem important to examine when developing a deeper understanding of the relationship between food and people.

It has been said that religious beliefs and practices are perhaps the least understood aspects of the cultures of other peoples. On casual examination the various religions of the world appear widely different. Each has its own beliefs concerning the supernatural, its own sacred objects, its own symbolism, its own priests, ministers, or holy men, its own seemingly mystical rituals and prescribed activities, and its own moral values. However, if a more detailed study of the world's religions is undertaken, many of these apparent differences dissolve and a large number of similarities appear.

What is meant by the term religion? It undoubtedly has different meanings to many people. No attempt is made in this section to discuss all the intricacies of this subject. According to Webster's dictionary, religion is the service and adoration of a god through worship in obedience to divine commands found in the sacred writings and through the following of a way of life regarded as incumbent on true believers. It further states that religion is a conviction of the existence of a supreme being or some supernatural influence that controls the destiny of all.

Brown, in *Understanding Other Cultures,* states that every religion provides ways by which people can try to relate to a supreme being or some supernatural force. Many of the practices and beliefs of the various religions of people are attempts to explain those things which people themselves cannot understand or control. Each religion has evolved certain rituals or customs that are important to the members of that religion. The observance of these rituals and customs is believed to be mandatory since they express and reaffirm the various beliefs of the religion.

Food, which was early peoples most precious and often scarce possession, has become associated with many of these religious rituals or customs. The practice of giving food or abstaining from food has provided people in their everyday life with a symbolic way to indicate devotion, respect, and love to a supreme being or supernatural power. Furthermore, the act of giving or abstaining from food has been used to insure the good will and protection of the all powerful on behalf of the individual. The religious practices of most religions are deeply imbued with many symbolic meanings; without an understanding of this symbolism, the practices of the religion by themselves may seem strange and peculiar. Brown gives an example of this. To a Christian, the symbolic meaning of the bread and wine in the Communion Service is clear. But to someone totally unfamiliar with this symbolism the words, "This is my body broken for you . . . This is my blood . . . ," which are recited before the bread and wine are consumed, might indeed seem very peculiar.

FIVE MAJOR RELIGIONS

In this chapter, five major religions of the world and the relationship between these religions, food, and people are discussed. These religions are Christianity, Judaism, Islam, Hinduism, and Buddhism. The areas of the world where these religions predominate are shown on the map. Relationships between food and other religions such as Shintoism, Confucianism, and various tribal religions undoubtedly exist and would be interesting topics to pursue. However, based on available figures (1976), these five major religions together were estimated to encompass about 60 percent of the world's population (see graph on page 169); and for this reason, they were selected as the basis for this discussion.

Christianity

Christianity is the most widely spread of all the major religions in the world today. Its adherents numbered in 1975 some 954 million—approximately one out of every four people in the world. Of these 954 million Christians, 57 percent were Roman Catholic, 34 percent were Protestant, and 9 percent were Eastern Orthodox.

It is not possible in this book to discuss in detail the influence of all the Christian religions on the food habits of their adherents. Almost everyone is familiar with the ruling of the Roman Catholic Church, which until recently required Catholics to observe certain fast days and to abstain from eating meat on Fridays in remembrance of the sacrificial death of Christ. However, in 1966, the United States Catholic Conference abolished this church law; now Catholics are required to abstain from eating meat only on the Fridays of Lent.

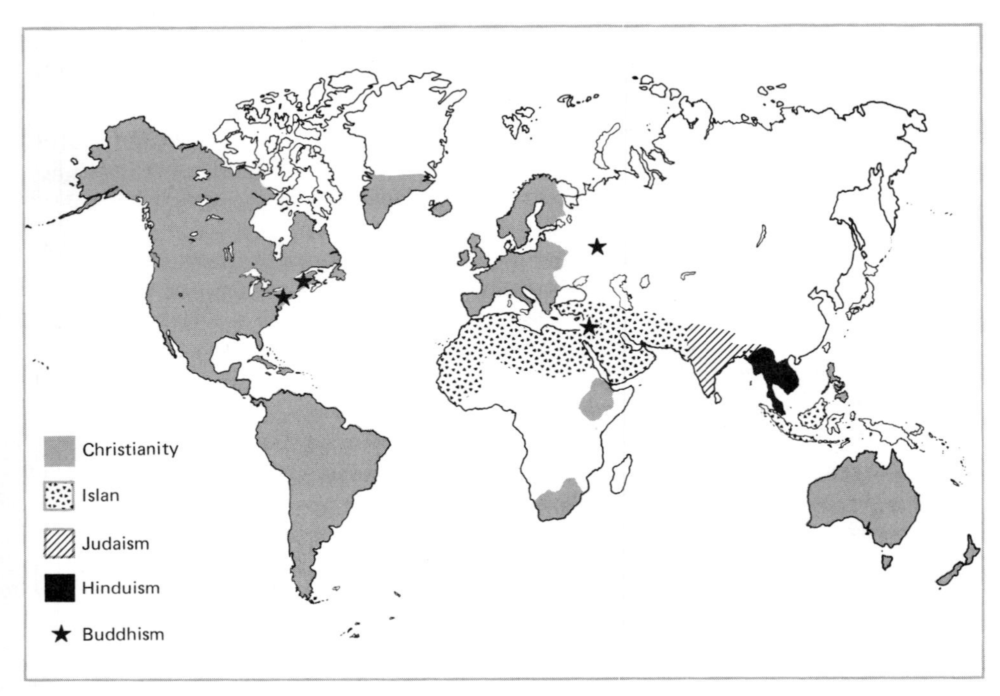

Map—distribution of five major religions in the world.

Among some Protestant denominations, such as the Seventh-day Adventists and the Church of Jesus Christ of the Latter-day Saints, certain dietary practices exist that are an integral part of their religious beliefs. The Seventh-day Adventists comprise the largest single body in the Adventist movement that is, those who believe in the imminent second coming of Christ. The world membership was approximately 2.5 million, with over 480,000 reported to be residing in the United States as of 1976. The church is active in world-wide evangelistic preaching, maintains 48 publishing houses, and conducts over 5000 schools ranging from elementary schools to colleges and universities. It has the third largest parochial school system in the United States. In addition, the church operates 128 sanitariums and hospitals, medical, dental and physical therapy schools and 37 nurses' training schools in many countries. It also sponsors a welfare organization actively involved in disaster relief through the distribution of food and clothing. The funds needed for these extensive operations are obtained by a 10 percent tithe of the membership plus additional voluntary contributions. The institutions sponsored by this church are indeed numerous considering the total membership of the denomination.

Seventh-Day Adventists Church.. During the early part of the nineteenth century, a world-wide interdenominational resurgence occurred in the belief that the second coming of Christ as foretold in the Bible was near at hand. In the United States this movement was led by the Millerites, followers of William Miller, who predicted originally that Christ would return to earth on October 23, 1843. When Miller's prediction failed, many of his followers abandoned this belief; but others held fast to the idea. From one segment of these believers, the Seventh-day Adventists Church developed and was officially organized in 1863. The present Seventh-day Adventists believe that the exact time at which Christ will return to earth cannot be predicted, but that it is not far away.

One of Miller's converts to Adventism in 1840 was a young woman named Ellen G. Harmon. This woman, who was later to become the wife of James White, an Adventist preacher, was to have a profound and lasting influence on the Seventh-day Adventists Church. Mrs. White's eminent position in her church as one of the principal founders and guides was the result of over 2000 prophetic visions and dreams she was reported to have had over a 70-year span beginning in 1844. Seventh-day Adventists believe that Mrs. White had a prophetic gift and that through her God gave his inspired message to them. Although Mrs. White's formal education ended when she was only nine years old, she is reported to have written over 100,000 manuscript pages by hand describing the substance of her visions and dreams. Many of her writings have been

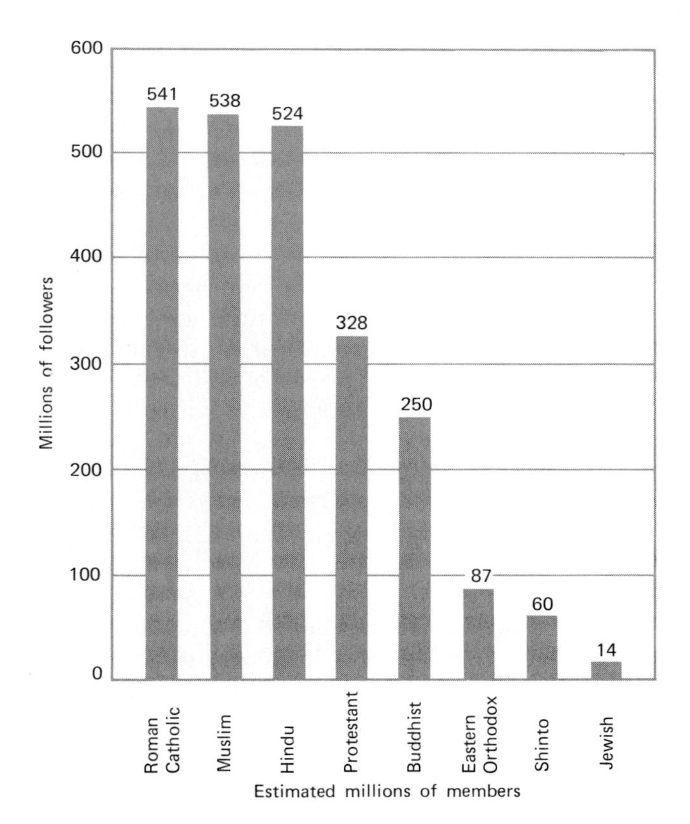

Chart—estimated millions of members of followers of selected world religions, 1976.

compiled into such books as *The Ministry of Healing, Counsels on Diet and Foods, Counsels on Health*. Over 50 books containing her writings are available today. Basically, the Seventh-day Adventists practice the principles of Protestantism but differ in their belief regarding the imminent coming of Christ and his 10,000 year reign and in the divine inspirations of Mrs. White. One of Mrs. White's early visions contained the warning that man should worship God on the seventh day or Sabbath as originally stated in the Fourth Commandment and not on Sunday; so as their name implies, they observe Saturday, the seventh day of the week, as the Sabbath—a day of rest and prayer. Like many Orthodox Jews, they may prepare the Sabbath meal on Fridays and wash the Sabbath dishes on Sunday. The practice of footwashing is observed prior to the celebration of Holy Communion, which occurs four times a year. The Bible is the ultimate and absolute authority on matters of faith and practice and the true word of God. To the Seventh-day Adventists, the Ten Commandments are to be taken literally and provide the basis of a person's duty on earth. Mrs. White's writings are considered to provide a clear explanation and commentary on God's word for modern people.

An all important concept of the Seventh-day Adventists' beliefs is that of healthful living. The biblical reference for this is taken from Corinthians 3:16–17:

> Know ye not that ye are the temple of God and that the Spirit of God dwelleth in you.
>
> If any man defile the temple of God, him shall God destroy; for the temple of God is holy, which temple ye are.

In 1863, Mrs. White wrote of a vision she was given:

> I saw that it was a sacred duty to attend to our health, and arouse others to their duty. . . . We have a duty to come out against intemperance of every kind, intemperance in working, in eating, in drinking, in drugging—and then point them to God's great medicine; water, pure soft water for diseases, for health, for cleanliness, for luxury. . . . I saw that we should not be silent upon the subject of health, but should wake up minds to the subject.

Shortly after this vision, the Western Health Reform Institute was established, the first of many such world-wide institutions sponsored by the church. This first institute was later to become the world famous Battle Creek Sanitarium in Battle Creek, Michigan.

To the Seventh-day Adventist, good health is a treasure, and violation of the laws of health surely leads to sickness. One's lifestyle should be directed toward maintaining and preserving health through eating the right kinds of foods in moderation and in getting a sufficient amount of exercise and rest. Accordingly, the Seventh-day Adventists believe that the original vegetarian diet prescribed by God is the best diet for health. They believe that the simpler one eats, the better his body will function and that, in the consumption of grains, fruits, vegetables, and nuts, one can find all the required food nutrients. With very careful planning of menus to include a variety of these foods, this belief is probably true, with the exception of vitamin B_{12}. Most Seventh-day Adventists are lacto-ovo-vegetarians, but some consume no milk or eggs; others, at the opposite end of the spectrum, consume meats. The book *Counsels on Diet and Foods,* published in 1938, contains a compilation of Mrs. White's writing about this subject. Seventh-day Adventists rely on legumes such as lentils, soybeans, garbanzos, and peas in addition to nuts, whole grain cereals, cottage cheese, eggs, and milk to provide enough good-quality protein in their diet. In the *Ministry of Health,* Mrs. White advocated the use of nuts in place of flesh foods, the substitution of olive oil for animal fats, and the consumption of bread made from whole-wheat flour and not refined flour.

The Seventh-day Adventists reject flesh foods for many reasons. The rejection is partly related to the statements in the Bible that forbid man to eat certain unclean foods, such as the swine and also to the writings of Mrs. White, who pointed out that the consumption of meat could cause various diseases and could make people more animalistic and less sympathetic to the needs of others.

Tea, coffee, alcoholic beverages, and tobacco are all considered harmful to the health of the individual due to their stimulating action on the body. Water is considered the best liquid, especially if soft, and should be consumed at room temperature or slightly cooled either before or after a meal, but never with a meal.

The meals served in a Seventh-day Adventists' home are not highly spiced. Condiments such as mustard, pepper, and others which might be harmful to the stomach are avoided. Breakfast is usually a substantial meal, and the noon meal is the largest of the day. Supper is light in order to avoid overtaxing the digestive tract. A typical lacto-ovo-vegetarians' breakfast might consist of fruit juice, brown rice with honey and milk, stewed prunes, whole-wheat toast with margarine, and a cereal-base coffee substitute. The main meal at noon might contain Dinner Cuts, a baked potato, lentils, carrots, whole-wheat bread with margarine, milk, and a fruit such as watermelon. (Dinner Cuts are a commercially prepared vegetable protein product containing essentially wheat protein, produced by the Loma Linda Foods of Riverside, California. This company, as well as the Worthington Foods of Worthington, Ohio, produces a wide variety of processed foods from wheat and soybeans which may serve as meat analogs in the diet.) Supper or the evening meal may consist of a soup and salad with cottage cheese or peanut butter on whole wheat crackers. Eating between meals is discouraged in order to allow the digestive tract proper time to digest and assimilate the food eaten at meal times. Mrs. White recommends that five to six hours should lapse between meals.

Eastern Orthodox Church. To the average westerner, the Eastern Orthodox Church is probably the least familiar branch of Christianity and thus merits a closer look. Historically, Orthodox Christian Churches were established in the Holy Lands before Christianity spread to Rome. But by 300 A.D., the two principal centers of Christianity were Rome and Constantinople, and they had already begun to compete with each other for absolute power and authority over all Christians. In 1054 A.D., this power struggle culminated in a division of the followers of Christianity into the Church of

Rome and the Eastern Orthodox Church. Some main points of disagreement between the two groups were the origin of the Holy Spirit, the use of unleavened bread in the Communion Service, and clerical celibacy. The Eastern Orthodox Church believed that the Holy Spirit originated completely from God the father, that leavened bread should be used in the Communion Service, and that priests should be allowed to marry prior to ordination. The followers of the early Eastern Orthodox Church were the Christians of the Middle East, the Balkans, the northeastern Mediterranean area, and Russia. Eastern Orthodoxy is the state religion in many of these same countries today. All of the state churches are independent of each other and have their own separate patriarch or archbishop. But they acknowledge as their spiritual leader the Patriarch of Constantinople. The world membership in 1975 was estimated at 87 million; 4.1 million adherents resided in the United States.

In the Greek Orthodox religion, numerous fast days provide ample opportunity for people to prove that they do not live by bread alone but that the soul can rule the body. With only two exceptions, every Wednesday and Friday of the year are considered fast days to commemorate the betrayal of Christ and His death upon the cross. In addition, there is a 40-day fast called the Great Lent that precedes Easter and there is another 40-day fast called Advent which begins on November 15. Two shorter fast periods in June and August also are observed.

On these fast days, no meat or animal products including milk, butter, and cheese can be eaten; fish, with the exception of shellfish such as clams, shrimp, and oysters, also cannot be eaten. Abstinence from olive oil although not olives, is observed by the more devout older Greeks. Because the olive and its oil are important staples in the diets of Greeks, the denial of olive oil represents a true sacrifice and an outward symbol of one's devotion to God. Another possible reason for abstinence from the oil is that many years ago olive oil commonly was stored in casks lined with the stomach of the calf; thus, the olive oil was contaminated in a religious sense by having been in contact with an animal product. Moreover, in earlier times olive oil was thought to increase sexual desire. Since every fast day is supposed to be a day of sexual abstinence, this may be another explanation of the avoidance of olive oil. A popular common meal in Greece on fast days is dried bean and lentil soup.

Easter, the most important event in the calendar of the Orthodox Church, occurs on the first Sunday after the full moon, which occurs on or immediately after March 21, but it may not precede the Jewish Passover. Thus, in some years Easter is postponed to the first Sunday after the Jewish Passover. The 40-day Great Lent period is preceded by a three week prelenten period of preparation and repentance. The third Sunday of this prelenten period is called Meat Fare Sunday (Apokreos). All meat in the house is consumed or disposed of on this Sunday and during the week following. On the following Sunday, Cheese Fare Sunday, all cheese, eggs, and butter in the house are consumed. On the next day, "Clean Monday," the family is ready to begin the true Great Lent and abstain from all animal foods until Easter Sunday. Fish is allowed on two days during this fast—on Palm Sunday and the Annunciation Day of the Virgin Mary. The Great Lent fast is in memory of the Lord's 40-day fast in the desert and of Holy Week. Lentil

Children of Greek Orthodox Church with baskets of red eggs in preparation for Easter Sunday (*Courtesy Jack Kirland, Knoxville News Sentinel, Knoxville, Tennessee*).

soup is always eaten on Good Friday to symbolize the tears of the Virgin Mary. The lentil soup often is served with vinegar to recall that Christ on the cross was given vinegar instead of the water He requested.

The Orthodox Easter fast traditionally is broken after the midnight Resurrection Service on Easter Sunday with mageritsa, a soup made with the internal organs of the lamb such as the tripe, liver, pancreas, lungs, and heart. Lamb is the traditional food on Easter. Another traditional Greek custom is the baking of thick, round, leavened loaves of Easter bread decorated with colored, hard-boiled eggs. The eggs are always dyed bright red, symbolic of the blood of Christ which redeemed the world. The eggs are dyed only on Holy Thursday and Saturday and are considered tokens of good luck in the home. The eggs are placed on the top of the bread dough, and then the bread is baked. The red color is used as a sign of mourning, and the egg symbolized the tomb of Christ. The breaking open of these eggs on Easter morning symbolizes the opening of the tomb of Christ and is an outward sign of belief in the resurrection of Christ. One person says, "Christos Anesti" (Christ is risen) the other person replies "Alithos Anesti" (Indeed, He is risen), and each cracks his or her egg against the other's egg.

All members of the Greek Orthodox Church are encouraged to receive Holy Communion every Sunday at the celebration of the Divine Liturgy. The altar bread used for this service is called Prosphoron, meaning the bread of offering. These round loaves of leavened bread are usually prepared by the women in their own homes from the purest ingredients. The bread must be free of all shortening, milk, sugar, and eggs. The preparation of Prosphoron serves to involve the laywoman of the church actively in an all-important religious rite because it is believed that the Holy Spirit descends during a particular prayer in the service and changes the bread into the body of Christ and the wine into His blood. As the dough of the Prosphoron rises for the second time, a Prosphoron seal is placed on top of the dough and left there until the bread is ready to bake. The Prosphoron seal marks the bread as indicated in the drawing below. The center portion of the loaf represents a lamb and is the part of the loaf that becomes the body of Christ. The abbreviations IC and XC indicate Jesus Christ and the letters NIKA mean conquers. The priest at the Communion Service removes this section of the Prosphoron and places it on a paten along with the ten smaller triangular pieces. The larger triangular piece on the left of the center portion is in memory of the Virgin Mary; the nine pieces on the right are in commemoration of the Angelic Hosts and Saints of the Orthodox Church. The Prosphoron offering is brought to the altar before the service with two lists of names. One list is composed of the names of living friends or family members and the other list of dead ones. During the service, the people named in the lists are remembered; good health is wished for the living and pleasant repose for the dead.

Boiled whole grain wheat (Koliva) plays an important role in memorial services for the dead. It is customary in the Greek Orthodox Church to offer Koliva before the altar three, nine, and forty days, as well as six and twelve months, after the death of a family member. It also may be offered whenever desired thereafter. The Koliva symbolizes the resurrection of Christ. The offering of Koliva on the third, ninth, and fortieth day after death is related to the recorded appearances of Christ on earth after his crucifixion. The boiled wheat, symbolizing everlasting life is mixed with parsley, chopped walnuts, zweiebach biscuits, spices, sugar, raisins, blanched almonds, sesame seeds, and pomegranate seeds. The raisins and the pomegranate seeds are used as symbols of sweetness and plenty. A leveled mound of the mixture is placed on a silver tray and sprinkled heavily with powdered sugar. The sugar covering symbolizes the wish of the living that the departed will have a sweet and blissful life in heaven. In the center of the Koliva a cross is made with brown sugar or Jordan almonds. Beneath the cross, either the name or the initials of the deceased is placed by using either toasted almonds, brown sugar, or raisins. The Koliva is blessed by the priest at the morning service and is later distributed to friends of the deceased.

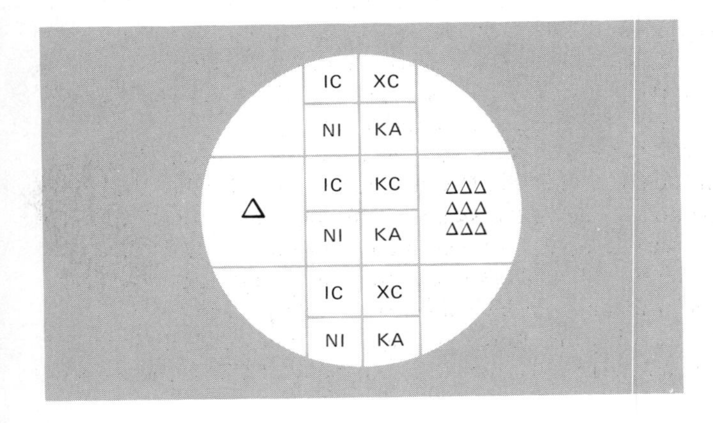

The Prosphoron seal marks the altar bread.

Judaism

The ancestors of the Hebrews, who can be traced back to about 2000 B.C., were seminomads roving the lands of Egypt, Syria, and Mesopotamia. The beginnings of Judaism, God's covenants with Abraham and later with Moses, are recorded in the first five books of the Old Testament. As God's chosen people, the Jews were commanded to denounce idolatry and polytheism, to worship only the one true God, and to ascertain and obey His will in all matters. The Torah, composed of the books of Genesis, Exodus, Leviticus, Numbers, and Deuteronomy, is the most sacred writing of Judaism and contains the basic laws that express the will of God to the Jew. The Torah, meaning guidance and direction, is considered by the Orthodox Jew to be the ultimate authority regarding all human conduct. This guiding principle of Judaism is read aloud at every Sabbath service in the synagogue; the entire five books are read in a year.

Other sacred books, such as the Talmud, were written at later times. Over the centuries, the early rabbis attempted to interpret, amplify, and adapt the teachings in the Torah to make them more meaningful to people in their daily lives. These interpretations

Table illustrating the seder plate containing matzo and the other symbolic foods associated with Passover (*Courtesy of the B. Manischewitz Company, Newark, N.J.*).

Orthodox Jewish family observing the first night of Passover (*Courtesy of the B. Manischewitz Company, Newark, N.J.*).

of the Torah became known as the body of oral law and were passed down from generation to generation by word of mouth. Sometime in the latter part of the sixth century A.D., the body of oral law finally was committed to paper and became known as the Talmud. The teachings from the Torah and the Talmud range all the way from the Ten Commandments and the Golden Rule to detailed instruction regarding the proper attire to wear on the Sabbath.

Throughout most of their history, the Jewish people suffered persecution, isolation, enslavement, and, on several occasions, near extermination. Yet each time they survived and were delivered from their oppressors. To the Jew each of these experiences represent a reenactment of the deliverance of the Jewish people from bondage in Egypt centuries ago and serves to strengthen his belief that the Jewish people truly are chosen people of God.

As the chosen people, the Jews have certain responsibilities to God. Judaism teaches that people are capable of perfection and that they alone are responsible for their actions. People have a choice between what is right and wrong. Sin is attributed to innate human weakness; no one can completely escape it. Although Judaism recognizes the existence of a hereafter, its main concerns are with people in this life and the ways to guide them in fulfilling their moral responsibilities to God.

For the Jew, the Torah makes a distinction between those animals considered clean and are thus permitted to be eaten and those considered unclean and thus forbidden. Leviticus, Chapter II, and Deuteronomy, Chapter 14, give the Biblical basis for many Jewish dietary practices. Animals classified as clean are those that chew their cud and whose hooves are divided (cloven). If an animal satisfies only one of these crteria, it cannot be considered clean. Thus the cow, sheep, ox, and goat are clean but not the pig since he does not chew the cud. Although the camel chews its cud, it is unclean because it does not have cloven hooves. Also forbidden are most winged insects, reptiles, creeping animals such as the mouse, and birds of prey. Only fish with both fins and scales are permitted to be used for food. Thus all shellfish and eels are eliminated from the diet of an Orthodox Jew. Any meat from animals that have died either from natural causes or disease is considered unfit.

Blood is a sacred substance and is taboo for human consumption. Several references in Leviticus, Chapter 17, which give the basis for this dietary practice, are, "I will set My face against that soul that eateth blood" and "For the life of the flesh is in the blood." To the ancient Jews, killing was synonymous with the shedding of blood; the blood was thus considered the vital life of the animal. The internal fat of an animal is also taboo. Thus, only those soaps and scouring powders that do not contain animal fats may be used for washing dishes. Detergents are permitted.

Another Jewish dietary practice that can be related to Biblical teaching is that which prohibits eating meat and dairy foods together in the same meal. The exact reason for this practice is not clear, but it may be the result of the three statements in Exodus and Deuteronomy that warn not "to seethe a kid in its mother's milk." Not only can meat and milk not be eaten at the same meal, but meat cannot be prepared or served in the same dishes used for preparing and serving foods containing milk and other dairy products. Thus, in Orthodox Jewish homes, two sets of dishes, silverware, and cooking utensils are needed, one for use with meats and the other for use with foods containing milk and other dairy products. Each set of dishes and utensils must be washed separately and carefully handled so that one set does not become mixed with the other. An Orthodex Jew will wait six hours after eating meat before eating milk or any dairy food, but only a one-hour interval is necessary if milk is consumed prior to meat. This dietary regulation prevents anyone who has meat in a meal from having such things as cream in coffee, dessert containing milk, or even butter on vegetables.

The attempts of the early rabbis to interpret and expand the Torah in more specific terms, as mentioned earlier, resulted in the Laws of Kashrut as written down in the Talmud. The term *kosher* refers not only to those foods that are permitted by the Bible but also to foods that have been processed and prepared in the prescribed manner. Trayf is the term used to indicate either a food that is unclean according to the Bible or one which has not been prepared according to the ritually correct method.

A rabbi must supervise the slaughtering of all animals for them to be considered kosher. In fact, only one other ritual in the Jewish religion actually requires the participation of a rabbi, and that is divorce. The actual slaughter of the animal is done by a trained person called a shocket. One swift deep slash at the throat of the animal makes him unconscious immediately and allows the blood to drain from his body as completely as possible. The meat from animals so slaughtered is carefully inspected and then stamped with the seal of the shocket to indicate its ritual purity.

Meat to be truly kosher must also be treated further to ensure the complete removal of blood. Meat is soaked in cold water for thirty minutes and then allowed to drain on a slanting board. The meat is then generously sprinkled with salt. After one hour it is washed in cold water; then it is ready to be cooked. In the past, this task was usually performed in the home but it is now possible to purchase meat that has been treated in this fashion.

Although no Biblical reference can be found to justify the practice, the Jew is forbidden in the Talmud to eat the sciatic nerve of an animal. According to Epstein, kosher butcher stores in the United States sell only forequarters of meat; the ligaments and nerves of the hindquarters are very difficult to remove and must be removed if the meat is to be considered kosher.

From the earliest times, rabbis have devoted considerable time to determining what was acceptable as kashrut and what was not. The increasing number of processed foods appearing on the market in recent years has made this problem perhaps even more difficult for the Jewish homemaker. The problem has been alleviated somewhat by the use of certain symbols on the labels of processed foods. The commonly used symbols are U or K which refer to the Union of Orthodox Jewish Congregations and the O. K. Laboratories, respectively. The presence of these symbols on a label indicates that the food is kosher and that it has been processed following the Laws of Kashrut. The introduction of such products as margarine and nondairy cream substitutes has made it possible for the Jew to circumvent the dietary restriction regarding the use of meat and dairy products in the same meal. A nonanimal "gelatin" was put on the market which enables the Orthodox Jew to have congealed salads and desserts.

The Jewish holy days and festivals are rich in symbolical meanings, and food plays a major role in much of this symbolism. Every Sabbath is truly a day of rest and spiritual reunion in an Orthodox Jewish home. In most homes, Friday is spent preparing for the Sabbath, which begins at sundown and continues until sundown on Saturday. The Sabbath dinner on Friday evenings is prepared with great care. All food that will be eaten on the Sabbath is prepared and cooked ahead in accordance with the belief that the Sabbath should be a day of rest. The traditional items on every Sabbath table are two loaves of bread called challah. The custom of serving challah on the Sabbath goes back many centuries to the ancient practice of placing twelve challah loaves on the altar of the Temple in Jerusalem; each loaf represented one of the original tribes of Israel. The use of two challah loaves today is in remembrance of the double portion of manna which God provided the Israelites on Friday for the Sabbath during the 40 years they spent wandering in the wilderness.

The ten most solemn holy days of the Jewish year begin with Rosh Hashanah, the Day of Judgment, and end with Yom Kippur, the Day of Atonement. On Rosh Hashanah, the challah is also made but it is decorated with ladders or birds baked on the top to carry symbolically the prayers of the family to heaven. Bread and slices of apple are dipped in honey as a symbolic wish for sweetness in the new year. Yom Kippur is a day of complete fasting for all except children under thirteen years of age.

The symbolic role of food in the Jewish faith is perhaps most evident in the traditional practices observed during the eight-day Festival of Pesach (Passover) which commemorates the flight of the Israelites from Egypt as described in Exodus. The story of the liberation of the Jews is relived by all members of the family, especially at the seder meal, which is eaten on the first evening of this festival. The preparations in an Orthodox Jewish home for Passover are many. According to ritual laws, none of the foods used every day in the kitchen can be used during Passover. Especially prepared foods marked Kasher L'Pesach (Kosher for Passover) must be used.

No leavened bread can be eaten during this time in obedience to God's command to Moses. For centuries, the Jews have made an unleavened wheat bread called matzo. It was made especially for Pesach and prepared ahead of time in large enough amounts to last throughout the entire eight-day festival. This preparation was usually a project of the whole community; detailed instructions for its preparation are given in the Talmud. Today matzo is commonly prepared commercially under rabbinical supervision. It is possible even to obtain a special kind of matzo that has been prepared under the most exacting, ritually correct conditions, the wheat having been constantly washed during harvesting, milling, and baking. This latter type of matzo is used by some of the more pious, older Orthodox Jews.

Flour and other grains cannot be used in cooking during Passover. In place of flour, the Jewish housewife uses finely ground matzo called matza meal. No leavening agents or malt liquors may be used during Passover. In fact, it is a custom for an Orthodox Jew prior to Passover to write out a bill of sale and sell all the leavened products he owns to a non-Jew for the duration of the Passover. The sale is proposed with the understanding that the goods will be returned to the original owner after the holiday. The rabbi handles the transaction for the members of his congregation at their request. All leavened products in the house are either eaten or discarded prior to the beginning of Passover.

Many Jewish homes have separate sets of dishes that are used only during the Passover. If everyday utensils have to be used during Passover, there is prescribed ritual for purifying them.

The seder plate is usually used twice a year, on the first and second nights of Passover. A seder plate is shown in the picture on page 175. It has various containers for the traditional foods that, over the centuries, have become symbolic of the Jewish exodus from slavery in Egypt. In the boatlike containers would be placed a roasted egg and a roasted lamb bone. The roasted egg is generally considered to be a symbol of the burnt offerings made in the Temple at Jerusalem; the lamb bone symbolizes the Paschal lamb which in ancient times was sacrificed at the Temple. The containers carried by the two women would be filled with maror and karpas, respectively. The maror (bitter herb such as horseradish) recalls the bitterness of slavery; the karpus (usually parsley or celery) represents the poor quality of diet the Israelites were fed during their years of slavery. During the seder meal, the karpas would be dipped into the container of salt water held by the hatted man and then eaten in remembrance of the tears shed by Jews while in bondage. The wheelbarrow pushed by the other hatted figure would contain charoset, which is a combination of finely chopped apple, nuts, cinanamon, and wine. The consistency of the charoset is likened to that of the mortar which the Israelites used in constructing buildings for the Egyptians. On top of the commanding figure of Moses in the center of the seder plate would be placed a wine cup called the cup of Elijah. According to tradition, the prophet Elijah would announced the coming of the Messiah on the seder night. Under the top of the seder plate are three shelves; on each shelf a piece of matzo, the bread of affiction, would be placed to represent the three divisions of Israel—priests, Levites, and laymen. The picture shows a father and his children celebrating Pesach and singing songs written in the Haggadah which contains the history and ritual of the Pesach festival. The seder plate is much simpler than the one from the last century, but all the symbolic foods are present.

The world Jewish population in 1976 numbered almost 14.3 million, making it the smallest of the major religions in terms of numbers. Within the last century, the Jews gradually emerged from the ghettos of Europe and emigrated to the United States in large numbers. Slightly over 6.1 million Jews now live within the boundaries of the United States mainly in the northeast.

As Jews became more a part of the outside world, it became increasingly difficult for them to carry out many of the numerous ancient customs of their religion. The end result of this conflict between modern everyday life in Western Europe and United States and the necessity of following the rigid rules of Orthodox Judaism was the division of the Jews into three groups: Orthodox, Conservative, and Reform. All three groups are agreed on most matters of basic theology but differ in their interpretations of the ancient rituals and the value received from observing these rituals in today's world. The Reform Jew conforms least to the old customs and rituals such as those described. He does not practice the various dietary restrictions or obey the Laws of Kaskrut. In addition, various changes have occurred in the Reform Sabbath service. The Reform Jew rejects the use of prayer shawls and skull caps. The Torah is read in English as well as Hebrew. Organ and choir music are allowed, and men and women are allowed to sit together in the Reform Temple. The Conservative Jew is a blend of Orthodox and Reform Judaism. He still observes and practices some of the ancient rituals, including the eating of only kosher foods. But he has forsaken many of the other practices of the Orthodox Jew. Accurate figures on synagogue membership in the United States are difficult to obtain. It has been estimated that each of the three branches of Judaism has about 1 million members. However, many Orthodox congregations are not affiliated with any national organization; thus the number of Orthodox Jews may actually be higher than the number of Reform or Conservative Jews.

To Orthodox Jews, the ancient practices and customs that regulate his diet are intended to test their piety and love of God. To them, they are part and parcel of the Jewish way of life and are some of many acts that God has directed his chosen people to perform. Until the last 100 years or so, these dietary practices unquestionably made it extremely difficult for the Orthodox Jew to have social and cultural relations with non-Jews. The Jews were prohibited in the Talmud from eating bread baked by a Gentile or even buying from him such items as milk and wine. The Laws of Kashrut, however, gave to the Jewish people a common bond which was visible to all and served to identify them as a particular group. This common bond no doubt has helped to unify and unite them in years past. To Reform Jews, the Laws of Kashrut are outdated and archaic and a reflection of totemism. They believe that the customs that reflect the principles of the religion should change with the times. However, Reform Jews have not introduced any new customs to reflect these principles.

Islam

Islam, the youngest major religion in the world, is both a religion and a way of life for over 538 million people. It is the second largest religion in terms of numbers of adherents. Islam is perhaps almost as widely spread throughout the world as Christianity. It is the major religion of Saudi Arabia, its birthplace, and the surrounding Arab countries of Iraq, Jordan, Syria, Turkey, and Iran. In the course of some 1300 years since its foundings, Islam has spread south to the African continent. Today it embraces the majority of the Egyptians, Algerians, Moroccans, Libyans and many other people south of the Sahara such as Nigerians and Ethiopians. The teachings of Islam moved eastward to Asia; today it is the major religion in Pakistan, Indonesia, and Malaya. The Islamic Center in Washington, D.C., reported in 1976 that the Muslim population of Europe was approximately 17 million and that in North and South America and Australia there were slightly more than a million adherents. Fifty-seven countries in the world are reported to have over a 50 percent Muslim population.

Mohammed, the founder of Islam, was born in Mecca, Saudi Arabia, in 751 A.D. During Mohammed's early years, he came in close contact with both Jews and Christians and was impressed with their belief in one god as contrasted with the many gods of the Arabs. Although a successful trader and merchant, Mohammed was prone to spend many days and weeks in solitude in the hills surrounding Mecca. One night while Mohammed was meditating on the nature of life and the destiny of man, God spoke to him through the Archangel Gabriel. Mohammed, convinced he was mad, attempted to kill himself but was stopped by a voice saying "Thou art a prophet." The initial doubts of Mohammed were alleviated by later visitations of the Archangel; Mohammed became convinced that he was truly a prophet of Allah, the one true God.

At first, the teachings of Mohammed extended only to his family and friends, but gradually he began to voice his teachings in the market place of Mecca. At that time, Mecca was the crossroad of two great caravan routes, the spice route from Southern Arabia to Syria and the route from Persia to the Nile Valley. It was also to Mecca that many Arab pilgrims came to worship at the numerous shrines. These visiting pilgrims and the caravan traders helped in time to spread the teachings of Mohammed to the outlying areas. However, the merchants and wealthy people of Mecca, afraid that Mohammed's teachings of submission to one god would curtail the number of pilgrims who came to the city, ridiculed and ostracized him. In 622 A.D. Mohammed fled from Mecca to Medina with some of his loyal converts. It is from this date that the Islamic calendar begins. Mohammed united the tribes of Medina and became their spiritual as well as political leader. After a few military battles, he conquered Mecca. On his triumphant return, he destroyed all the idols and declared the shrine of Mecca to be a place holy to the one true God.

Mohammed taught that there was only one God, Allah, and that all must submit completely to His will. The word Islam means submission, and the word Muslim refers to one who submits. The God of Judaism, of Christianity, and of Islam are all basically similar because the Arabs trace their origin back to the early Hebrews through Abraham's son Ishmael. Neither Christ nor Mohammed are considered divine by the Muslim—only spokesmen of God. Mohammed is, however, the greatest since he was the latest and the last of the great prophets of God.

The followers of Islam acknowledge the divinity of the Old and New Testaments but believe that the Bible is not the final expression of the will of God. The most sacred writing of Islam is the Koran. This sacred book, although probably not written during the lifetime of Mohammed, is believed to contain the words spoken to Mohammed by Allah. It is thereby the most authoritative and final expression of the will of God; it supersedes the earlier Biblical writings. The Koran consists of 114 suras or chapters which all (except one) begin with the sentence "In the name of Allah, the Beneficent, the Merciful." Parts of the Koran are read daily in all Moslem schools and mosques. One of the longest suras is the second one, entitled "The Cow" or the little Koran. It contains the main points of all the revelations made to Mohammed as well as instructions regarding the dietary regulations, the need for fasting, pilgrimages, and correct morals.

In the years following the writing of the Koran, scholars and other religious-minded people atempted to analyze and interpret the Koran and relate it in a more meaningful way to the daily life of the faithful followers. A growing list of traditions developed over the years based on what Mohammed either said or did or was reported to have done. These traditions became the patterns or guidelines for every Muslim to follow in almost every conceivable facet of life—a situation analogous to the Jewish Talmud.

The religious practices of those who profess to Islam are often referred to as the Five Pillars of Islam. The first of these is faith. All Muslims repeat once a day the creed "I bear witness that there is no God but Allah and that Mohammed is the Prophet of Allah." Allah is considered to be in complete control of everything. He has determined the fate of every person; whatever happens is the will of Allah. On the day of final resurrection, all will be judged worthy of either heaven or hell.

Prayer is the second pillar. All Muslims are taught to pray five times a day; at dawn, noon, midafternoon, sunset, and nightfall. The call to prayer can be heard at these times in any Muslim city. A crier climbs to the balcony at the top of the minaret of the mosque and calls out the words by Mohammed, enjoining the faithful to prayer. Regardless of where a Muslim is, he is supposed to offer prayer. If he is not able to go to a mosque, he spreads down his prayer rug, thereby making that spot sacred, turns his face toward Mecca, and prays. Friday is the day of public prayer and sermons are delivered in the mosque after the noon prayer.

Before praying Muslims must first wash as an act of purification. This is usually done at a running fountain in the courtyard of a mosque. In recent years, particularly in the large cities, the pressures of industrialization and commercialization have made this practice of praying five times a day very difficult and observance of this custom is declining.

Alms giving is the third pillar. Muslims are expected to give 2.5 percent of their net savings in money or goods. The alms or Zakat were originally used to help the poor. Several passages in the Koran describe the benefits gained by giving money to the poor, orphaned, and aged. Today the Zakat is given to the ministry of religion in Muslim countries or to local mosques or schools in countries where Islam is not the predominant religion. Additional Zakat is also expected to be paid at the end of the Ramadan Fast (described below) so that the poor may participate in a major religious festival called Id al-Fitr which breaks the four week Ramadan Fast. The second religious festival called Id al-Ad-ha occurs during the time of the Pilgrimage to Mecca and involves the sacrifice of an animal and sharing the food with the poor.

Fasting is the fourth pillar. The Koran promises rewards beyond bounds for fasting for God's sake. The Koran commands all faithful Muslims to observe the fast of Ramadan; Ramadan is the ninth month of the lunar Muslim year. Since Mohammed received his first revelation on the twenty-seventh day of this month, he declared in the Koran that the entire month should be one of complete fasting from sunrise to sunset. The fast includes abstinence from water and smoking as well as food. During Ramadan, it is believed that "the gates of Heaven are open, the gates of Hell closed, and the devil put in chains." The faithful observance of the Ramadan fast is believed to result in the remission of sin. In many of the larger cities in the Arab world, a cannon is fired several hours before sunrise to warn the people that the hour to begin fasting is approaching. The cannon is fired again at sunset to announce the end of the day's fast. The meals eaten after sunset are supposed to be light. A special type of leavened bread is eaten during this month. The observance of the Ramadan fast is perhaps the most strictly adhered to of all Islamic practices. This may in part be attributed to the numerous community activities involved in the observance of this fast, which place a strong pressure on all to conform. To fast during Ramadan is considered a yearly reaffirmation of one's allegiance to Islam; nonobservance of the fast could bring social disapproval or perhaps ostracism. Since the Muslims follow a lunar calendar, the month of Ramadan occurs at different times during the year. When Ramadan occurs during the summer and temperatures reach 100 or more, the self-discipline required to refrain from taking even a sip of water must be very great. Several other fast days exist for the Moslem, but none have as great a significance as that of Ramadan. The Koran exempts young children, the aged and sick, travelers, and nursing or pregnant women from the Ramadan fast; however, days missed because of travel, pregnancy, or lactation must be made up at a later time.

The last pillar of Islam is the pilgrimage or haji to Mecca. This trip is the height of religious exhilaration for the Muslim. Every year thousands come to pay homage at the great shrine; the vast majority come from Saudi Arabia, but many journey from countries all over the world. The area surrounding Mecca for 100 square miles is closed to all who are not Muslims. The Great Mosque of Mecca, which can hold over 35,000 people in its court, also contains the holiest shrine of Islam, the Kaaba. The southeast corner of the Kaaba contains the Black Stone, which is believed to have been given to Abraham and Ishmael by the Archangel Gabriel.

The Koran and the traditions, like the Jewish Torah and Talmud, contain statements that inform the Muslim of the clean and proper foods to eat and how they should be eaten. Animals that are forbidden are any that die of disease or strangulation or are beaten to death. Blood is forbidden as well as swine. Islam like Judaism adopted the rejection of the pig; four passages in the Koran forbid the eating of pork. The pig is so abhorred that in some places even the word pig is avoided, and the animal is referred to as "the black one." Simoons, in his book *Eat Not This Flesh,* reports that a pious Muslim killed by a wild boar is said to remain in the fires of hell for 500 years to become purified. Muslims are also forbidden to partake of wine or other intoxicating beverages.

No animal food except fish and locusts is considered lawful unless it has been slaughtered according to the proper ritual, which is similar to that used by the Jewish shocket. The person killing the animal must repeat at the instant of slaughter, "In the name of God, God is great."

Among the Islamic traditions one finds statements regarding how one should eat. For example, the Muslim is commanded "to eat in God's name, to return thanks, to eat with the right hand and with shoes off, and to lick plate when meal is finished." Islam makes no distinction between people regardless of wealth, social position, race, or color and encourages the practice of all types of people eating together. All are united in the worship of the one and only true God.

One cannot help noticing the similarity between some of the ritual practices of Islam and Judaism. This may be attributed to the fact that the two religions developed in the same part of the world and to the close contact of Islam with Judaism during the formative years of Islam.

Hinduism

Hinduism, considered by some the oldest living religion, originated in India approximately 4000 years ago. Its adherents in 1976 numbered some 524 million, with the vast majority of these people living in the Indian subcontinent. Although to many of us it may appear that the Hindu worships several hundred deities, this is not strictly true. These numerous gods and goddesses are all manifestations of one supreme being the Hindu calls Brahman—the Universal Spirit. According to ancient Hindu mythology, Brahman appeared in the form of the god Brahma and created the universe. Then in the form of the god Vishnu, Brahman sustained the universe for a period of 432 million human years; eventually, in the form of the god Shiva, Brahman destroyed the universe. The universe to a Hindu is cyclic. The present world was created by Brahma. It is now approximately 425,000 years from the time when Shiva will cause the destruction of the world, thus enabling another world to be reconstructed by Brahma. The Hindu believes that nothing that once existed is ever completely destroyed, it merely undergoes a change in its form.

Intimately involved in the Hindu way of life and religion is the caste system. From ancient times, the caste system has provided a means of dividing society into unalterable levels of social status depending on birth. An individual born into a caste was destined to remain a member of that caste throughout his or her life regardless of efforts to advance to a higher caste. In all societies, birth undoubtedly influences one's social status, but it was usually possible for individuals to improve their social position by one means or another. Not so with the Hindu. According to the early religious writings, four social orders or castes of Hindu society arose from the different parts of the body of Brahma. From his mouth were created the priests and teachers called Brahmins; from his arms sprange the warriors and rulers, the Ksatriyas; from his thighs came the farmers and traders or Vaisyas; and from his feet, the menial laborers, the Sudras, were born. All individuals born outside these four orders were considered to have been created from the darkness that Brahma discarded in the process of creation. These people were called outcasts or untouchables. Since 500 B.C., when the caste system was known to have been in effect, the four original castes have subdivided within themselves so that today nearly 3000 different castes are said to exist.

The word caste in Sanskrit means the equivalent of race, suggesting that the caste system may have originated from the racial pride and color prejudice of the Aryan conquerors of India thousands of years ago. Whatever its origin, the caste system became a basic institution sanctioned by the religion and woven into the Hindu way of life.

The members of each caste had a moral duty to perform that was unique for that caste. For each caste, definite rules and regulations existed, dictating to the members whom they could marry, what they could eat, and with whom they could socialize. The Brahmins occupied a privileged position in the Hindu society and were considered the highest caste. Originally the Brahmins were not permitted to engage in any type of work other than study and religious teachings. People in the other castes were expected to support and sustain the Brahmins with gifts of food or money. The ancient laws and writings sacred to the Hindu encouraged the giving of these gifts to the Brahmins, promising great benefits or merit to the giver. For example, the gift of a cow or a piece of land to a Brahmin ensured that the giver would go to heaven. In more recent times, many Brahmins have abandoned the old idea of not working; today many Brahmins are engaged in the professions of law, medicine, and business. Many have positions in the government and in universities. However, they still retain their esteemed social position and rigidly follow many of the ancient practices regarding their social and home life.

The Ksatriyas, as the kings and soldiers, originally were obligated to protect the community and willingly give their lives to protect the Brahmins as well as the most sacred animal to the Hindu, the cow. The members of this caste were allowed to kill for food and were meat eaters. The duties of the Vaisyas were to make money and to improve the economic situation of the country. They were particularly encouraged to give gifts to the Brahmins and money for the building of temples. The moral duty of the Sudras was to serve the three higher classes with diligence and humbleness. This class in particular developed numerous subdivisions based mainly on various occupations such as carpenters and weavers; the profession of a Sudra had an important influence on his social status. In these early times, the outcasts or untouchables were considered so lowly that they were not even allowed in the villages and towns except to do the most menial of labor. These people were not allowed to own land or to build houses and lived under wretched conditions.

The caste system of India has been likened in many ways to the social structure of Medieval Europe; the princes, feudal lords, merchants, and peasants of that period are comparable with the four main castes of India. The Industrial Revolution contributed greatly to the dissolution of Europe's caste system, but India's caste system has remained relatively unchanged over the centuries. However, in 1949, as a result of the vigorous efforts of Gandhi, the Indian government declared untouchability illegal and expressed opposition to the social barriers of caste. Social changes of this nature are accepted slowly; the caste system is still a forceful factor, particularly in the villages, and affects the lives of millions of Indians. Whether the caste system can survive the increasing industrialization of India and the increasing mobility of Indians from the villages to the cities is a question that cannot be answered at the present time.

Fundamental to the Hindu religion are the ideas of reincarnation and destiny. To a Hindu, his or her present existence is but one of many. After death, his soul is liberated and eventually takes birth again in another form. Thus, the Hindu goes through endless cycles of birth, death, and rebirth. The ultimate goals of the Hindu are to attain liberation from this cycle and to gain complete self-identification with the Universal Spirit, Brahman. The form the soul takes at rebirth is the direct consequence of a person's actions during his previous life. If a Hindu, of whatever caste, performs his or her moral duty well and is pious during his or her present life, the individual may be reborn in a higher caste. On the other hand, if he does not behave according to his moral code, he may be reborn at a lower level of existence, either human or animal. Thus, every thought and deed committed by a Hindu are his or her own responsibility and he or she alone must reap the consequences. This philosophy justifies to the Hindu all the inequalities of life, including the caste system. What a Hindu is in this life is the direct consequence of his or her actions in a previous existence, and the next life will be largely determined by their present actions.

To the orthodox Hindu, Brahman is all and everything. All living things contain a part of this divine spirit. Thus, all life is sacred. To take the life of even the smallest creature is tantamount to causing harm to a part of Brahman. The belief in reincarnation also contributes to the Hindu's abhorrence of the taking of life since he could never be sure that any animal he killed did not contain the soul of an ancestor reborn as that animal.

Of the numerous writings sacred to the Hindu, the Code of Manu contains many references that have an influence on the diet of the Hindu. A few examples follow:

> Wound not others, do not injury by thought or deed, utter no word to pain thy fellow creatures.

One should cease from eating all flesh. There is no fault in eating flesh, nor in drinking intoxicating liquor, nor in copulation, for that is the occupations of beings, but cessation from them produces great fruit.

Meat can never be obtained without injury to living creatures, and injury to sentient beings is detrimental to the attainment of heavenly bliss.

There is no greater sinner than that man who, though not worshipping the gods or the manes, seeks to increase the bulk of his own flesh by the flesh of other beings.

Most pious Hindus, especially those of the Brahmin caste, are strict vegetarians who follow the nonviolence attitude and strict rules of the Code of Manu. The more devout Brahmins deny themselves eggs as well as all forms of meat since to eat an egg would be equivalent to taking a life. The members of the other castes may eat meat other than beef, but prejudice against this practice increases the higher the caste. The particular god which a family worships may influence whether they eat meat. Although the avoidance of pork and chicken in the diet is undoubtedly influenced by the religious attitude of the sanctity of life, it is also due in part to the idea that these animals are scavengers and thus unclean. Fish is consumed by some Hindus, particularly those in the area of Bengal.

Although all animals contain a part of Brahman and are sacred, the cow has been singled out as a particularly sacred animal. The exact reason for this is not clear. Records dating back hundreds of years before the birth of Christ indicate that cattle were slaughtered and eaten in India. However, the code of Manu, written sometime between 100–300 A.D., listed the slaying of cattle as an offense requiring penance. One can at best only speculate on the reasons for this change in attitude. It has been suggested that the cow took on a sacred aura because of its years of faithful service in helping man till the soil and providing him with food to feed his family as well as fuel, in the form of dried cow dung, to heat his home and cook his food. It also has been suggested that the killing of cattle was prohibited to encourage the development of agriculture and the planting of crops for food.

According to Hindu mythology, the cow was created by Brahma on the same day as the Brahmins and thus is an animal to be venerated above all others. In fact, one of the several Hindu heavens is named after the cow. The cow has become the symbol of motherhood in India. Mahatma Gandhi referred to the cow as a poem of pity and the mother to millions of Indian mankind. The early scriptures admonish "all that kill . . . cows rot in hell for a many years as there are hairs on the body of the cow." Thomas reports that no devout Hindu will pass a cow without touching it and then touching his own head. The act of feeding a cow brings great merit to a Hindu. The cow is sacred to all sects of Hinduism and to all castes. Cows wander at will through most towns and cities of India, often causing considerable damage to crops. In 1956, India had 159 million cattle, one-fifth of all the cattle in the world. Many of these cattle were diseased and unproductive; perhaps of even more serious consequence, they were either consuming or destroying food needed by the people. Every conceivable means is used in India to protect the cattle from harm and slaughter. The Indian government in 1965 supported sixty-two special farms for old, infirm, and unproductive cattle.

The kitchen in a devout Hindu Brahmin home is sacred. Since all food contains a part of the Universal Spirit, Brahman, it must be prepared and consumed with proper reverence. The women who prepare the meal, as well as any who partake of it, must purify themselves by means of ritual bathing of the entire body and often by putting on clean clothes. A Brahmin usually does not accept cooked food from a member of any lower caste but he will accept uncooked food. Even the shadow of a lower caste person falling on the food of a Brahmin is said to render it unfit for eating.

Ghee (clarified butter) and milk coming from the cow are sacred foods. These ritually pure foods cannot be contaminated even by the touch of someone from the lowest caste. Thus, a Brahmin may accept milk or any food provided it is cooked with ghee from a Sudra. This sacredness of milk is evidenced also by the fact that in some Indian villages milk is sprinkled inside a house in which a child had died of smallpox. The purifying effect of the milk is believed to make the house safe.

Ghee is preferred over all other animal fats. Although the Sepoy rebellion in 1857 was due to many factors, one cause was the aversion that the soldiers had to other animal fats. A new rifle requiring greased bullets had been introduced into the army. The tips of these bullets had to be bitten off before the gun was loaded, and the soldiers rebelled at the taste of the animal grease.

The coconut is another food considered sacred. It is used as a symbol of Shiva, the three eyes of the coconut being associated with the three eyes of Shiva. To be successful, all new enterprises should be started by breaking a coconut.

Meat, especially beef, is not the only food that is taboo to the orthodox Hindu. The code of Manu forbids to the higher castes the eating of domestic fowls, onions, garlic, turnips, mushrooms, and salted pork. The association of blood with the color of some lentils and tomatoes has made these vegetables unacceptable to some castes.

The Hindus have many days of fasting and prayer called Vratas. On these days, they are expected to observe either a complete fast or at least to abstain from eating cooked foods. The Hindu has no weekly day of rest comparable to Sunday in the Christian religions, but actually every day of the week is a holy day dedicated to one or another of the many gods. Brahmins and most women of the higher castes observe Vratas on certain prescribed days each month. To break the fast, a Brahmin has to be fed. Women of the lower castes can feed a Brahmin either ghee, coconuts, fruits or some uncooked food.

Buddhism

Buddhism originated during the sixth century B.C. and in many ways was an outgrowth of Hinduism. Siddhartha Gautama, who was to become Buddha—The Enlightened One—was raised as a Hindu, the son of a wealthy Himalayan chieftain. At the age of 29, discontent with his luxurious life and deeply troubled with the misery and suffering of humanity, he renounced his worldly possessions and assumed the role of a beggar.

He wandered throughout India seeking the advice and counsel of the wisest teachers and scholars as to the universal cause of misery and how it could be removed. For six years he denied himself friends and the comforts of adequate food, shelter, and clothing while he devoted his time to meditation on how misery and suffering could be abolished. On a night in May on which the moon was full, he seated himself under a bodhi tree and passed into deep meditation. Legend has it that he was overcome by a deep mystic rapture that lasted 49 days—enlightenment was captured and Gautama became Buddha. In the Deer Park of Sarnath near Benares, India, Buddha delivered his first sermon on "Setting in Motion the Wheel of Righteousness." For the remainder of his life, he traveled throughout India teaching the Middle Way. In 250 B.C. Buddhism was made India's state religion. Although today less than 1 percent of India's population is Buddhist, Buddhism is the predominant religion in Sri Lanka, Burma, Thailand, Laos, Cambodia, and Japan. Its adherents numbered some 250 million in 1976. In the United States there are 60 Buddhist churches, mostly concentrated on the west coast, which have a membership of over 100 thousand.

Buddha taught that ignorance produces selfish desires that are the cause of rebirth and it is this rebirth that causes sorrow and suffering. People pass through many cycles of birth, growth, decay, and death. These teachings are embodied in the Four Noble Truths, which state that:

1. Existence is suffering.
2. This suffering is due to selfish desires.
3. The cure of suffering is to destroy these selfish desires.
4. This cure can be accomplished by practicing the Eight-Fold Path: right belief, right thought, right speech, right action, right means of livelihood, right exertion, right remembrance, and right meditation.

By following this Eight-Fold Path, people gradually can in the life after life on earth attain liberation from rebirth with its inevitable suffering and finally reach Enlightenment or Nirvana.

Basic to the understanding of Buddhism is the doctrine of Karma. Karma means literally "action or deed," but it implies both cause and effect. Briefly it means that what a person is today is the result of the sum total of their actions or deeds in a previous existence. This is the Buddhist's answer to the apparent injustices of his or her present life. If a person is born a cripple or poor or rich, he or she must simply suffer or enjoy the consequences because he or she alone is responsible. Every person is thus the master of the life to come. In order not to be reborn in a lower form or as a nonhuman, but rather in a higher state moving slowly toward Nirvana, Buddhists vow to follow the Eight-Fold Path including "right action." They vow to abstain from killing or doing injury to any living being, from stealing, from falsehood, from drinking intoxicating beverages, and from sexual misconduct. By the practice of "right action," the Buddhists gain and

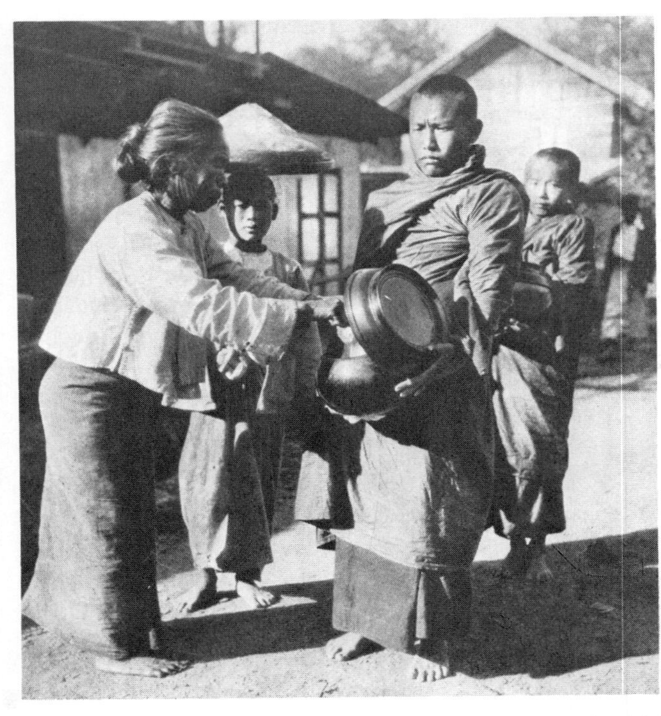

Buddhist monks are completely dependent on voluntary contributions of food from the village people (*collection of the author*).

acquire the merit that will help them progress toward a higher existence in the next life. The accumulation of merit is paramount in the life of a devout Buddhist. Violation of these vows brings demerit. If demerit is accumulated in excess of merit, it may result in rebirth at a lower level.

The building of merit is accomplished through voluntary gifts without thought of immediate personal gain. By making a self-sacrificing gift to a beggar, the Buddhist shows that he is concentrating on someone other than himself and is not overly concerned with the accumulation of worldly goods.

Buddhist monks hold a very special role in the attainment of merit. The Burmese monk is considered by the villagers of Upper Burma to be the embodiment of all that is good and noble in people and one who is definitely on a higher level of existence. Thus, the custom of helping to feed and support a person of such exemplary conduct is considered natural and a high form of merit-making (Kutho). The Buddhist monk vows not to eat after midday although he is allowed to drink tea and coconut milk. He pledges to remain aloof from all women. His worldly possessions are the three cloths that he wears, a begging bowl, a razor, a needlecase, a mat, and a small cloth used to filter his drinking water. Buddhist monks are completely dependent upon voluntary contributions of food and clothing from the people. Every morning the yellow-clad monks with their iron or brass beggar's bowls silently make the rounds of the houses in the villages. The monks are not allowed to announce their arrival in any way or give any thanks for food received. The woman of the house gives the very best of what rice, curry, or fruit she has available. (See the picture opposite.)

In the cities or larger towns in Thailand, the monks' meals may be prepared from food sent to the monastery by wealthy Buddhists. Some village households may send additional food to the monastery for the monks' midday meals. In fact, one hour before noon, a temple drum may be sounded to warn those who want to send food that the hour is approaching. Many families might not normally eat a meal at noon themselves but still would prepare food to be sent to the monks. In some northern Thailand villages, the monks no longer beg for their food each morning. Instead, a section of the village, consisting of 16 or so households, is assigned the responsibility of providing sufficient food for the monks on a particular day. The food is brought to the monastery early in the morning by the women and girls of the households. The monks are served by temple boys. Additional food also might be sent to the monastery on special holy days, and the monks might be invited to eat with a family on important family occasions.

The cost of maintaining the monks might represent an economic hardship in the eyes of a Westerner. DeYoung estimates that there were probably 400,000 Thai males in monasteries in 1955. Village boys in Thailand usually become temple boys at about the age of ten. In this capacity, they act as attendants to the monks and, in return, are taught to read and write and to learn some of the Buddhist scriptures. Many boys remain in the temple and qualify for novicehood. In Burma, parents are expected to sponsor their sons for novicehood. This is one of the highest forms of earning merit; the boys are encouraged to enter the monastery in order to provide their parents with the opportunity to obtain merit. The length of stay in the monastery may vary from only a few days to several months or a lifetime.

DeYoung estimates that the amount of food contributed to the monastery by each household in a Thai village in a year's time is probably equivalent to the cost of feeding one additional person for a year. Assuming that an adult male consumes approximately 1 pound of rice a day, this amounts to at least 365 pound of rice a year.

Kutho, or merit, in lesser amounts can be obtained by giving food to nuns and beggars. Food is always offered immediately to a visitor in a Burmese home. Not to offer food is thought of as not the right action and is a source of Akutho or demerit.

The vow to abstain from taking life is reflected in countless ways in Buddhist countries. The growing of rice and other crops is regarded as the right livelihood because it does not directly involve the taking of life. Attempts to introduce the growing of ground nuts have been successful for this reason, whereas attempts to increase the production of livestock, such as pigs and chickens, have met with limited success. Pigs raised by villagers in Thailand usually are sold to a Chinese dealer for slaughter and marketing. In Thailand, a villager must buy a permit to slaughter a pig. Chickens are raised for sale by nearly every farm household in Thailand, but most farm families do not eat more than four or five chickens a year.

However, the vow to abstain from taking life is not rigidly adhered to, as evidenced by the fact that fish is a common supplement to the Thai rice diet. According to Pfanner, Thai villagers reason that they do not kill the fish, they simply remove them from the water. In a Burmese village, a government program to control rodent destruction of ground nuts by use of rodent poison was accepted. In anticipation of resistance to the program, the government declared that any Akutho earned by killing the rats would come to the government and not the farmer. Most farmers, however, adopted the attitude that killing the rats was necessary; that by doing this, more money would be earned from the sale of ground nuts. The increased income could then be used to help acquire Kutho, thus balancing any Akutho gained by killing the rats.

POSSIBLE ORIGINS OF RELIGIOUS DIETARY PRACTICES

From the discussion of the five selected religions, it can be seen that they all prohibit some food either completely or on certain days. In every case, these foods are of animal origin. For certain groups in the Hindu society and for Buddhists, no meat of any kind can be eaten; for all Hindu castes, beef is especially tabooed. The eating of pork or blood is considered despicable to the Orthodox Jew or Moslem. If the adherents of the Eastern Orthodox Church abstain from meat, fish, and dairy products on all the indicated days of fast, these foods cannot be eaten on about 186 days out of the year.

In almost every religion, statements of one type or another pertaining to diet can be found in the sacred books and writings. Because these dietary regulations were actually written down in these sacred books, which were often considered the word or will of the supreme being, the regulations have been preserved and perpetuated over the centuries. The religion itself has encouraged and contributed to the continuing observance of these dietary habits from the earliest times. However, this does not explain why the particular dietary practice came to be a part of the sacred writings of the religion. The real origins of these dietary practices are lost in antiquity; today one can only suggest possible reasons as to why these practices developed.

The environment prior to the development of each religion and the writings of the sacred books must surely have influenced the people's dietary habits. The founders of the various religions may have incorporated already existing dietary habits into the religion. Primitive people were oppressed by hunger and consumed almost any food that they could obtain. Usually no choice was involved. It was more a question of food for survival. Simoons suggests that the original prejudice against the pig developed among the pastoral peoples living in the arid regions of Asia. The pig was not a commonly eaten animal in their group but was in the diet of those who settled permanently in the area. Contempt for the food of the rival group may have made the pastoral people ridicule the eating of this animal; thus, the prejudice was established and may then have been incorporated into the sacred writings. The similarity between the dietary practices of Islam and Judaism suggests that Mohammed may have been influenced by the existing practices of the Jews.

An example of a religious festival that was practiced before the Old Testament was written and is still practiced today is the Jewish Pesach. The origin of the present-day Pesach festival, as related by Schauss, is really the combination of two festivals that were observed by nomadic Jews long before their deliverance from Egypt. The Festival of the Shepherds was one of these. It was observed in the spring when the kids and lambs were born. On the night of the full moon just before dusk, a sheep or goat was sacrificed and the animal roasted whole. All the family members had to consume the animal completely that night since it was forbidden to have any of the uneaten meat left by daybreak. One ritual associated with this festival was to mark the tent posts of all who partook of the feast with the blood of the slain animal. The other early festival was called the Festival of Matzos (unleavened bread). This festival also occurred in the spring at the time of the cutting of the barley and lasted about seven weeks, until the wheat was harvested. Prior to the harvest of the barley, the Jews removed from their homes any old bread or fermented dough. The first barley cut was given to the priest as a gift to God. This latter festival was a command festival conducted in a place of worship.

Schauss states that, over the centuries, as the Jewish people settled in towns and cities, the meanings and relevance of these early customs became obscure to the new generations. The Jews retained the old customs but reinterpreted them and gave them new meaning and emphasis. Pesach thus became the festival that allowed each Jew to commemorate and relive the deliverance of the Jewish people from bondage in Egypt. Thus, the eating of the matzos during Pesach is retained, but not to assure a good harvest of wheat. Instead it is eaten to commemorate the fact that the Jews did not have time to allow bread dough to rise and so baked unleavened bread on the night they fled from Egypt. It seems inevitable that this sort of reinterpretation and reevaluation of the many customs and rituals in all religions must have occurred over the centuries since their founding. The decree that allows Roman Catholics to eat meat on Friday if they so choose is an example of the reevaluation process.

The fear of disease has been suggested as a possible reason why the early Jews, Moslems, and Hindus rejected the pig. This animal was a scavenger and may have been considered unfit as food since it ate all kinds of filth. The relationship between trichinosis and the eating of pork is well known to us today, but it is doubtful that early people knew of this relationship. It is possible that they did recognize a connection between the eating of pork and vomiting and diarrhea, which are early symptoms of trichinosis. But Simoons points out that these symptoms of trichinosis occur in only about 5 percent of the cases. Undoubtedly the problem of preserving meat and dairy products for the early Hebrews and Moslems was great, particularly with the climatic conditions of their environment. Spoiled meat was inevitable if it was not consumed rather quickly, but this would be true of all meats and not just pork.

Early man, as well as many groups of primitive people today, worshiped and regarded as sacred certain animals. This practice is referred to as totemism. Why a particular animal is singled out is unknown. It may be through fear or because of the pleasant association people have with a certain animal. The latter reason is the one most often suggested as to why the cow is a sacred animal to the Hindu. In some African tribes, cows usually are not killed and eaten but are kept as status symbols and an indication of wealth.

Certain dietary practices may have developed as a means of separating one religious group from another. Simoons suggests that the rejection of pork by the Moslems was adopted by Mohammed to distinguish Islam from Christianity. As pointed out earlier, various dietary practices may have originated to provide an effective way of holding the members of a religious group together. The observance of these practices in their everyday life gave a common bond to the group which, in turn, strengthened their religious beliefs.

THE FUTURE RELATIONSHIP

Since the early beginnings of each of the five religions discussed in this chapter, food has played an intimate role in the manner by which people have attempted to relate to a supreme being or supernatural power. For hundreds of years within each religion, the numerous symbolic ways of using food has had deep meaning to people. It is perhaps not surprising that food, so necessary for physical well being, should also have been used to attain spiritual well being.

Most of the discussion in this chapter has been concerned with the relationship of religion, food, and people as it has existed in these religions. But what of today and tomorrow? Are these religions having as great an impact on the dietary practices and habits of their adherents as they had in the past? The abolishment of the church law directing Roman Catholics to abstain from eating meat on Fridays and other fast days, the large number of Reform Jews in the United States who do not observe the Laws of Kashrut, and the custom of many Greek Americans to observe only a 7-day fast before Easter and Christmas instead of the 40-day fast suggests that, in the United States at least, the influence of certain religions on the dietary habits of their adherents is not as strong as it was. The situation in other countries is difficult to determine. If in the future the role of food in religion decreases, will people need to replace the spiritual values they once received from the observance of certain religious dietary practices with something else and, if so, with what?

STUDY QUESTIONS

1. What similarities and differences have the religions discussed made on the food practices and customs of their adherents?
2. What are the religious bases or reasonings for the various food practices and customs listed in Question 1?
3. What values have certain religious dietary practices had in the past to their adherents? Do you think that these values are important today? Why?
4. Roman Catholics have been given the opportunity to choose some other way of doing penance than abstaining from meat on Fridays. What are some of these

choices? How widely have these other ways of doing penance been adopted by Catholics?

5. Why is the cow a sacred animal to the Hindu?

TOPICS FOR INDIVIDUAL INVESTIGATION

1. Examine in detail the religious influences of Shintoism and Confucianism on the dietary habits of their adherents.
2. Discuss how the tribal religions of various American Indian tribes influenced their dietary habits and agricultural practices.
3. Discuss the influences that some tribal religions of Africans have had on the production, distribution, and consumption of food.
4. Interview a Hindu, a Moslem, an Orthodox and a Reform Jew, a Seventh-day Adventist, a member of an Eastern Orthodox Church, and a member of the Church of Jesus Christ of the Latter-day Saints to determine what influence their religions have on their own dietary habits. Does the observance of these practices have certain values for them? If so, what? What are some difficulties they encounter in following these practices?

REFERENCES AND SUGGESTED READING

Ali, M. *The Religion of Islam.* Ripon Printing Press, Lahore, Pakistan, 1950.
Ansubel, N. *The Book of Jewish Knowledge.* Crown, New York, 1964.
Bancroft, A. *Religions of the East.* St. Martin's Press, New York, 1974.
Brown, J. C. *Understanding Other Cultures.* Prentice-Hall, Englewood Cliffs, N.J., 1963.
DeYoung, J. E. *Village Life in Modern Thailand.* Univ. of California Press, Berkeley, 1955.
Engle, F. and G. Blair. *The Jewish Festival Cookbook.* Paperback Library, New York, 1966.
Epstein, M. *All About Jewish Holidays and Customs.* KTAV Publishing House, New York, 1959.
Firth, R. Religion in Social Reality. *Reader in Comparative Religion* by W. Lessa and E. Z. Vogt. Row, Peterson, White Plains, N.Y., 1958.
Fitch, F. M. *Their Search for God—Ways of Worship in the Orient.* Lothrop, Lee and Shepard, New York, 1947.
Fitch, F. M. *Allah, The God of Islam.* Lothrop, Lee and Shepard, New York, 1950.
Gaster, T. H. *Customs and Folkways of Jewish Life.* William Sloane Associates, New York, 1955.
Gaster, T. H. *Festivals of the Jewish Year.* William Sloane Associates, New York, 1952.
Herndon, B. *The Seventh Day.* McGraw-Hill, New York, 1960.
Hughes, T. P. *A Dictionary of Islam.* W. H. Allen, London, 1935.

Karay, M. P., Ed. *Hellenic Cuisine*. Saint Helen's Philoptochas Society and Saints Constantine and Helen Parent-Teacher Association, Detroit, 1957.

Khaing, M. M. *Burmese Family*. Indiana Univ. Press, Bloomington, 1962.

Life. The World's Great Religions. Special Edition for Young Readers. Golden Press, New York, 1958.

Life. The World's Great Religions. *Time*, New York, 1957.

Nash, M. Burmese Buddhism in Everyday Life. *Amer. Anthropologist*, 65:285, 1963.

Nash, M. *The Golden Road to Modernity: Village Life in Contemporary Burma*. John Wiley, New York, 1965.

National Geographic Society. *Great Religions of the World*. National Geographic Society, Washington, D.C., 1971.

Pfanner, D. E. and J. Ingersoll. Theravada Buddhism and Village Economic Behavior. *J. Asian Studies*, 21:341, 1962.

Rice, E. *The Five Great Religions*. Four Winds Press, New York, 1973.

Schauss, H. Pesach: Its Origins. Reprinted from *The Jewish Festivals*, Union of American Hebrew Congregations, Cincinnati, 1938. *Reader in Comparative Religion* by W. Lessa and E. Z. Vogt. Row, Peterson, White Plains, N.Y., 1958.

Siegel, R., Strassfeld, M., and Strassfeld, S. *The Jewish Catalog*. The Jewish Publication Society of America, Philadelphia, 1973.

Simoons, F. J. *Eat Not This Flesh*. Univ. of Wisconsin Press, Madison, 1961.

Spence, N. *The Story of America's Religions*. Holt, Rinehart and Winston, New York, 1957.

Stephanou, E. *Belief and Practices in the Orthodox Church*. Minos Publishing, New York, 1965.

The Bulletin of the Islamic Center, Vol. 6, No. 1, August 1977. Islamic Center, Washington, D.C.

Thomas, P. *Hindu Religion: Custom and Manners*. D. B. Taraporevala Sons, Bombay, India, 1956.

Vanos, F., and L. Prichard. *Can The Greeks Cook*. Dietz Press, Richmond, Va., 1950.

Von Grunebaum, G. E. *Mohammedan Festivals*. Henry Schuman, New York, 1951.

White, E. G. *The Ministry of Healing*. Pacific Press Publishing Association, Mountain View, Cal., 1905.

White, E. G. *Counsels on Diet and Foods*. Review and Herald Publishing Association, Washington, D.C., 1938.

Women of St. Paul's Greek Orthodox Church. *The Art of Greek Cookery*. Doubleday, New York, 1963.

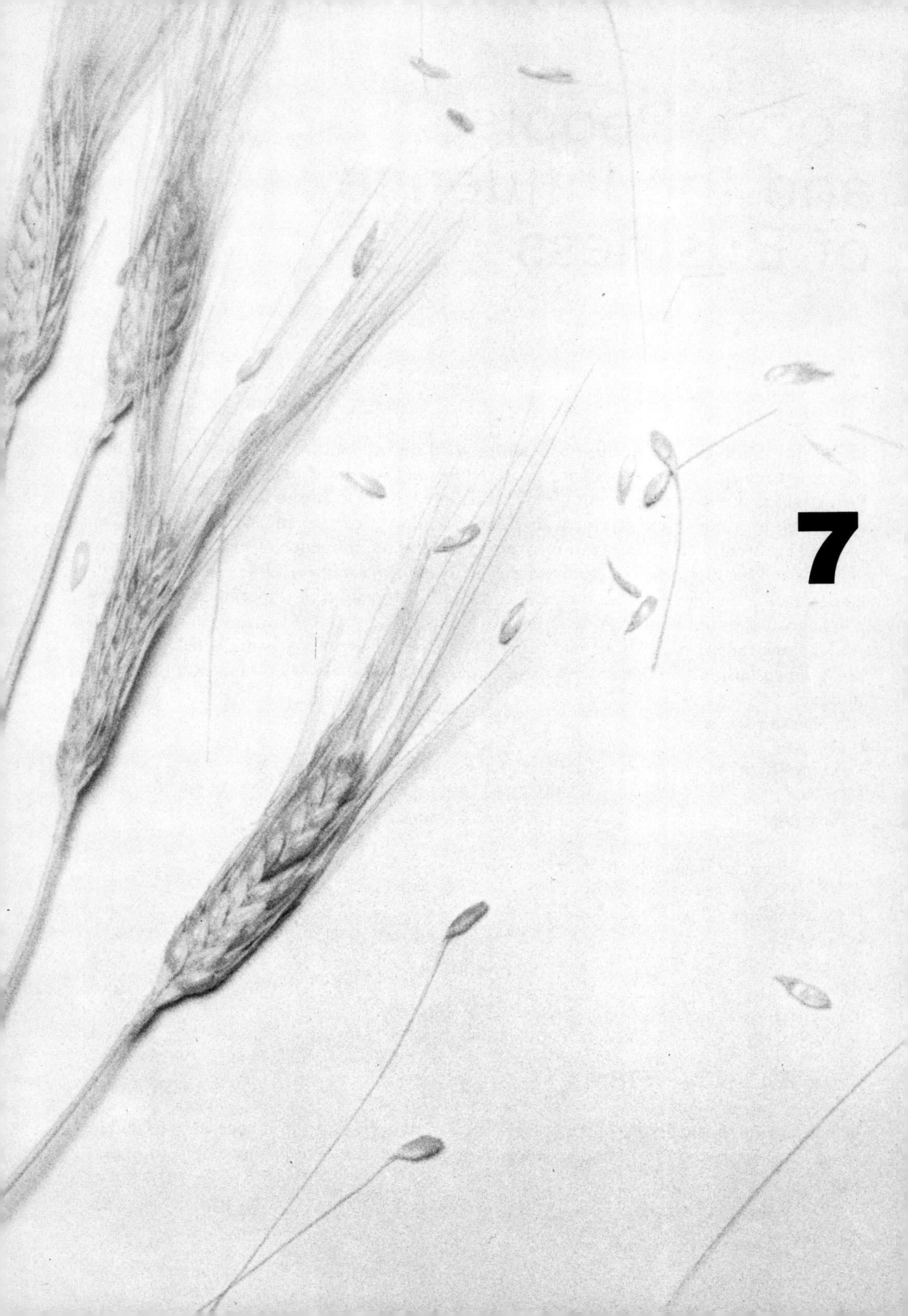

7

Food, People, and the Influence of Business

Up to this point, people's physical need for food and some of the cultural, social, and individual reasons for its selection, preparation, and use have been considered. These factors alone do not totally explain modern people's relationship to food. What is it that causes us, as a nation, to consume millions of dollars worth of sugar-coated cereals or frozen pizzas each year? The answer is not clear, but the influence of business is clearly at work and has helped to make these products and thousands of others part of our everyday eating habits. How did business come into its position of importance? How does it influence consumers in their food buying habits?

To answer these questions and begin to understand how food is marketed, we must break down business influence into the discrete parts that make it up, and examine them in detail.

These parts are:

- Business firm
- Product
- Promotion

The product can further be broken down into:

- The product itself
- Brand
- Package
- Price
- Retail outlet

THE BUSINESS FIRM

In order to understand why people behave in a certain manner, it is necessary to understand their background. The same holds true for business. We cannot begin to understand why businesspeople in general, and food marketers in particular, act the way they do if we do not know about the problems and opportunities they face.

The Function of Business

The function of any business is to produce goods or supply services. It does this to generate profits for its owners. Any business, large or small, engages in three activities in order to operate:

1. Financing itself
2. Producing goods or supplying service
3. Marketing

For example, if a native in West Africa decides to produce a cash crop, he must obtain capital to buy seed and other needed raw material. Many times the money is borrowed from a cartel run by a powerful head—often a woman—that buys the crops once they are harvested. The business system in this example is quite simple. Financing and marketing are taken care of by the cartel, and the native sees to it that his wives tend the fields to produce the crop.

The picture is quite different when we look at the way a large corporation functions. It gets the capital it needs by issuing stocks or bonds or borrowing from financial institutions. This money is used to help build plants and buy machinery to produce its line of products. The marketing strategy employed by this form of business probably includes the use of both national advertising and a large number of sales agents.

Note that both of these businesses engage in the three basic activities mentioned earlier. Corporations in the United States—especially the very large ones—have developed these activities to such a degree that their complexity and sophistication are seldom equalled anywhere else in the world. The development and refinement of these activities can be traced through our economic history. Each has held the limelight at some point in our development.

Soon after our nation was founded, it faced a scarcity of goods and services. More people called for more and more products. In order to produce the needed goods, this period, which lasted until the end of the nineteenth century, was characterized by successful attempts to increase production efficiency.

Increased production efficiency was usually characterized by the introduction of machines to take the place of a number of people. But machinery and raw materials were expensive, and large amounts of capital were required to buy them. The great financiers came on the scene to satisfy this need. These men were experts in raising the capital that was needed to keep business producing, prospering, and growing.

The final activity left for refinement—marketing—came to a dominant position soon after World War II, and it has continued to hold its position of central importance. We have become a nation characterized by abundance. As Philip Kotler points out in his book *Marketing Management Analysis, Planning, and Control:*

The economy is marked not by a scarcity of goods, but by a scarcity of markets. The major problem of most firms is to find sufficient customers for their output.

People in the United States and in other developed nations find themselves in a position vastly different from the situation that faces the people in less developed nations. The situation can be viewed in light of the *Hierarchy of Needs* concept presented by Maslow. As stated in a previous chapter, Maslow classified all human needs into physiological needs and social needs. The idea behind this theory of human motivation is that a minimum satisfaction of one need is necessary before the person can move up to seek satisfaction of the next need in the hierarchy. People in many countries of the world engage in the daily struggle to satisfy basic physiological needs or, perhaps, have "advanced" up to obtaining some level of security or safety in their lives. On the other hand, people in the United States and other developed countries, are sure that their physical needs will be satisfied and are attempting to be loved by their peers and, in many instances, have advanced to seeking esteem.

As Kassarjian and Robertson said in their book *Perspectives in Consumer Behavior:*

In middle-class America, most individuals seem to be attempting to satisfy their love or esteem needs. If advertising at all reflects the American need structure, this becomes evident from a casual perusal of present-day ads. Seldom does one see an advertising message like "Crispy crackers fill your stomach fuller than other products"; more typically one sees "Serve Crispy crackers with exotic cheese and impress your friends."

Comparison: Less Developed Nations versus Developed Nations Their Relative Levels of Realized Needs

Maslow's hierarchy of needs	**Less-developed nations**	**Developed nations**
The Need for Self-Actualization		
Esteem Needs		
Belongingness-Love Needs		
Safety Needs		
Physiological Needs		

In developed countries, marketing continues to overshadow the other two principal activities of business in terms of importance and will continue to do so. This point was brought out quite clearly in a National Association of Manufacturers Symposium when a participant said:

In this exciting age of change, marketing is the beating heart of many operations. It must be considered a principal reason for corporate existence. . . .

No longer can a company just figure out how many widgets it can produce and then go ahead and turn them out. To endure in this highly competitive change-infested market, a company must first determine what it can sell, how much it can sell, and what approaches must be used to entice the wary customer. . . .

Enticing the wary customer is a very difficult task—and an expensive one. Food manufacturers and retailers spend millions of dollars each year on research designed to tell them what the customer wants in the way of products and services. And the people in the business of marketing listen to their audience, or face the possibility of going out of business.

If one read and believed many of the popular books that purport to "expose" the deceptive methods used by business to foist worthless products on an unsuspecting audience, then one would have to conclude that consumers are complete dullards, unable to think for themselves. But I am a consumer, and you are too, and I am sure that neither of us thinks we are pawns in the hands of corporate researchers. And we are not.

Research does tell business what consumers want and what is on their minds. The majority of this feedback is used in a way that helps, not hurts, consumers. For example, a report in *Progressive Grocer's 44th Annual Report of the Grocery Industry* showed that 65 percent of the homemakers interviewed felt that they were using cents-off coupons more in 1977 than in 1976; 59 percent believed that they were more conscious of exact prices in 1977; and 35 percent were shopping in more stores per week to take advantage of weekly specials. Also, another segment of this study showed that 68 percent of the shoppers interviewed almost always made a list, while only three percent almost never made a list before shopping.

In light of this information, a corporate executive would be making a big mistake by assuming that today's shopper would buy whatever was produced at whatever price was put on it.

This does not mean that some unscrupulous corporations, or people within corporations, do not try to deceive consumers. It happens, but it occurs with much less frequency than one might imagine because of the number of safeguards built into our system. Governments at the local, state, and federal levels have divisions such as the FTC designed to protect the consumer. Private organizations, such as the Better Business Bureau and groups of concerned citizens, are constantly on the watch for deceptive practices. Finally, companies themselves engage in massive efforts to make sure that what they do is not deceptive, because once their name and image is tarnished it is very hard to win back the public's trust and confidence.

Marketing Defined

Marketing, as defined by the American Marketing Association, is the performance of business activities related to the flow of goods and service from producer to consumer in order to satisfy consumers and achieve the firm's objectives. Striving towards consumer satisfaction is the basic philosophy of modern marketing. If a company that is dependent upon the consumer to buy its product does not live by this philosophy, it will fail.

A bread manufacturer might feel quite smug. After all, people must have carbohydrates in their diet in order to survive. Yes, they need carbohydrates, but do they need bread? Bread is not the only source of carbohydrates. Even if it was, the manufacturers bread is not the only one on the market. The customer in the typical supermarket can choose between a vast assortment of bread put out by a variety of manufacturers. Today's customer doesn't "need" a particular brand of bread. The people wheeling their shopping carts down the aisle may not realize it, but when they pick up a loaf of bread they have said to one company "You have done well—I like your product" and have shown their indifference or displeasure to the other manufacturers by not choosing their products.

Steurart Henderson Britt in his book *The Spenders* summed up the philosophy that marketing specialists in our age of abundance must live by: *the consumer is king.*

THE PRODUCT

The business firm in our society recognizes its dependence on the consumer for its continued existence. It manifests this recognition through its marketing efforts. One of the primary tools available to the marketing specialist in his or her attempt to satisfy the consumer is the product their firm sells.

What Is a Product?

When a shopper goes to the local supermarket, he or she sees thousands of products on the shelves. Crackers are an example. What is a cracker? According to the list of ingredients on the side of the box, it is flour, shortening, salt, leavening, and perhaps various other things such as sesame seeds. It is also a particular brand of cracker with a distinctive name, packaged in a box or carton, and sold for a certain price in the store the shopper selected. A cracker is also intangible to the extent that the consumer not only buys the physical attributes contained in the product but also the psychological ones attached to it.

According to Ernest Dichter, President of the Institute for Motivational Research, in his *Handbook of Consumer Motivations:*

Crackers are psychologically a sort of quick, lazy bread and are consumed as snacks or informally at social gatherings. A good part of their appeal

Bread, fresh from the oven is just beginning its journey to the hands of the ultimate consumer (*Courtesy Interstate Brands Corporation*).

comes from their tactile variety and taste. This implies the rhythmic sound and the sensation they have for the tongue and palate. Together with other products such as nuts or cereals, crackers signify the importance of emotional elements in the food field other than taste.

While thinking about crackers, we can turn our attention to a product that is often used to spread on them—peanut butter. This protein-rich food, which will probably continue to be popular and to serve as a basic part of youngsters' diets, is at present made up of peanuts, dextrose, salt, and hydrogenated oil. Peanut butter is symbolic of youth. Kids usually love the stuff—or are made to believe that they love it. Sidney J. Levy told of one interesting incident in an article titled "Symbols by Which We Buy":

One little 6-year-old boy protested in an interview how he had never liked peanut butter, but that his mother and sister had always insisted that he did, and now he loved it. Apparently a violent bias in favor of peanut butter is suitable to little boys, and may be taken as representing something of the rowdy boyishness of childhood, as against more restrained and orderly foods.

Crackers—Just flour, shortening, and so on—or more? (*Courtesy Nabisco Inc.*).

The imagery and symbolism connected with crackers, peanut butter, and all the other foods we eat are just as much a part of them as are their physical ingredients. It is for this reason that a product should be defined much like William J. Stanton did in his book *Fundamentals of Marketing* when he wrote that a product is a complex of tangible and intangible attributes, including packaging, color, price, manufacturer's prestige, retailer's prestige, and manufacturer's and retailer's services, which the buyer may accept as offering satisfaction of wants or needs.

Brand

Students of the American West—via reading or devotion to television and motion picture westerns—are familiar with the concept of branding. Ranchers brand their cattle to prove ownership. Branding, however, began long before our nation was founded. The guild system, which flourished between 1200 and 1700, perfected its use. Each article produced by a guild member bore the guild mark or brand. Severe and often cruel penalties were enforced against "industrious" individuals who forged a guild's mark. This early form of branding achieved the same results as the modern version.

Definition. According to the American Marketing Association, a brand is a name, term, symbol, or design or a combination of them that is intended to identify the goods or services of one seller or group of sellers and to differentiate them from those of competitors.

The term brand is comprehensive in that it actually represents a number of more specific terms. A brand name consists of words, letters, or numbers that can be vocalized. Jell-O, Campbell's, and Green Giant are examples of brand names. Brand marks appear as symbols, designs—things that can be recognized but not expressed when a person pronounces the brand. Examples of a brand mark are the friendly *Jolly Green Giant* and the *Morton Salt Girl* and her ever-present umbrella.

The word trademark is often used synonymously with brand. This is technically incorrect because a trademark is actually a legal term that includes only those brands or brand marks that the law designates as trademarks.

Brand Images. Brands, like products, produce images in the minds of consumers. Marketing specialists attempt to make these images "positive" so that their brand will be preferred over the others that are available.

The evolution of a brand mark (*Courtesy Morton Salt Company*).

Herta Herzog, when speaking to a group of marketing educators, said that a brand image

. . . is the sum total of impressions the consumer receives from many sources: from actual experience and hearsay about the brand itself as well as its packaging, its name, the company making it, the types of people the individual has seen using the brand, what was said in its advertising, as well as from the tone, format, type of advertising vehicle in which the product story was told.

All these impressions amount to a sort of brand personality which is similar for the consuming public at large although different consumer groups may have different attitudes toward it. . . .

The brand image contains objective product qualities. . . . These qualities themselves have rational as well as symbolic meanings which merge with the meanings created by all the other sources through which the public meets a brand.

What Do We Call It? The problems a couple encounter in trying to determine the name for their forthcoming baby are similar to those experienced by the marketing specialist attempting to determine the "correct" name for a product. Some names just came into being by accident. Hannah Campbell, in her book *Why Did They Name It . . . ?* tells how the brand name Maxwell House came into being:

In 1873 Joel Cheek was a traveling salesman with a wholesale grocery firm. Though he sold a variety of grocery products, coffee held a greater interest for him than any of the others from the very beginning. While on the road he often thought about trying his hand at developing his own blend of coffee. . . .

Several years later he got his wish. . . . At first he limited his experiments to his spare time, but gradually they demanded more and more of his working day. . . . In 1882 he quit the partnership . . and after more years of experiments, found the blend of coffee that had fired his imagination.

One of the South's finest hotels at this time was the Maxwell House in Nashville. . . . Joel Cheek went to this hotel one day and proudly offered them the new blend of coffee. The management decided to try it and within weeks the guests in the magnificent dining room were talking about the marvelous new coffee. "This Maxwell House coffee, sir," they said, "is superb!"

Although business has undergone a radical change since Mr. Cheek developed his blend of coffee, many companies still leave the choice of a brand name up to chance and hope for a flash of inspiration. Other, more realistic, firms do not leave names up to chance. They realize that a brand's name is extremely important to its performance in the marketplace. As stated by Lippincott & Margulies, Inc. in their article "The Name's the Thing," which appeared in *Design Sense 24:*

> As products, services, even companies have become more alike in function, and appearance, the name has assumed new significance. Often it is the sole tangible, differentiating element between one brand and another. In many cases, it is the only permanent tool which advertising, promotion, publicity and packaging can use to create the . . . brand identity . . . the product image.

There is a great degree of latitude available in terms of selecting a name, but as was stated in the Lippincott & Margulies article, it will not do its job unless it possesses three basic elements:

1. The appeal of both sight and sound.
2. The prospects of long-term consumer equity.
3. The expression of a specific unique image.

Sight appeal simply means that the name has to look good if it is to appear on packages, in ads, and on signs. Sound appeal, according to Lippincott & Margulies, is even more important than sight appeal; methods of word reproduction may change, but the sound of words does not. Marketing specialists may turn to the science of language—philology—for guidance. If a hard-selling message is desired, then hard, abrupt consonants such as *b*'s, *t*'s, and *k*'s should be used. To make a soft impression, sibilants such as *s, ch,* and *z* should be used. Long-term consumer equity simply means that the customer will never tire of the name. It will come about naturally if sight and sound appeal and a positive product image are attained.

One other element should be added to the list—protectability. In light of the tremendous amount of time and money invested in the development of a brand and its image, the manufacturer makes every effort to ensure exclusive rights to it. The Lanham Act of 1947 aids the manufacturer in this regard. If the brand mark and/or name complies with a number of requirements, the manufacturer will be allowed to register them in the United States. They then become legal trademarks and are made the legal property of the manufacturer. The manufacturer, therefore, must come up with a name that meets the Lanham Act's requirements in order to protect his investment.

One of the great fears of any manufacturer is that a product's name will become generic—descriptive of a type of product—and the manufacturer will lose legal rights to it. In cases such as this, the courts can rule that the name has lost its distinctiveness and become part of the public domain. Shredded wheat, for example, was once a name owned by the National Biscuit Company, but the courts ruled that it had become generic in nature and therefore no longer protectable under law.

Private Brands. Private or store brands account for a very sizeable portion of food products sold. They are an especially important factor in canned goods. Most of the larger chain stores have had products produced under their own brand names for quite some time.

Several factors have accounted for the popularity of these brands. One is the fact that the stores can make a higher profit on the products carrying their own brand name than they can on manufacturer's brands and still sell them for less.

The consumer plays an important role here, also. Many shoppers are aware of the fact that the store's brand is usually produced by large, well-known manufacturers. Consumers have also become more sophisticated; they are beginning to depend on their ability to determine the quality of a product regardless of the brand name it carries. When asked "How would you compare brand name canned goods to private label canned goods?" in a survey done by the Chicago *Tribune,* one shopper answered:

Pricewise a private label is cheaper, but the quality is the same or close to it. You actually pay for the advertising of the brand name, whereas for the private label you don't.

Nevertheless, manufacturer's brand names still account for the largest portion of total sales. People continue to prefer them. As one respondent to the *Tribune* stated when asked the same question:

I think the name labels taste better. I am used to the brand name and when I change I don't like it as well. The brand name would be a higher price and has a better quality.

Packaging

The idea of placing products in containers to move them from one place to another has been with us since ancient times. Skins or leaves probably served as the first form of container. As civilization developed, so did human development and use of materials for holding and transporting goods.

The beginning of modern packaging is generally attributed to a Parisian chef and confectioner, Nicholas Appert. In 1808, motivated by Napoleon's offer of 12,000 francs for a method of preserving food to feed his army, Appert developed a process that involved the use of a glass container.

The advent of mass production in centralized locations and the subsequent shipping of products to distant distributors heralded the need for new and better packaging. This need was not immediately met. Well into the twentieth century, most products were still packed in bulk containers.

We can all picture what it must have been like in the "good old days" around the general store. Everything had to be counted out or weighed. The cracker barrel, the flour sacks, the big old pickle barrel—a part of the past we are much better off without.

The crackers in the barrel were often stale long before the consumer purchased them; the flour sacks attracted rodents; and who knows what dropped into the pickle barrel!

A New Area. Although packaging has its roots deep in the past, the greatest growth in terms of innovation in the field has taken place in the last 30 years. The prime stimulus for this growth was the development of the supermarket. Inherent in the operation of the supermarket is the concept of self-service. The friendly grocery store clerk that gathered all the things the customers wanted while they waited for them is a thing of the past. The customer is now on his or her own. Business executives realize that the package now is an important marketing tool, for it acts as an instore sales agent. The package must get the customer to stop and pick it off the shelf from among a number of competing products. The package does not work alone, for it is only part of the entire product, but it plays an extremely important role.

What Consumers Want. Consumers have some very definite ideas about what they want a package to do for them. According to Curt Kornblau in a paper delivered to the American Marketing Association:

> . . . above all the consumer seems to want convenience and utility.
>
> Consumers expect the package to protect the contents and keep them at their flavorful best. They want packages that are easy to open, easy to use and easy to close. They are less than happy with pry-off tops, set-in lids, cans that open with a key, packages that leak, . . . "Press here to open" directions which seem entirely unrelated to the facts.
>
> Consumers want packages that will fit on the shelves of the average home and won't topple open because of poor design. They want information on the package that will help them decide whether to purchase the product and, having purchased it, how to use it.
>
> Consumers want honest value. They are not favorably impressed, for example, with misleading information as to the number of servings in a package.

Business Answers. Marketing specialists are well aware of what consumers demand in the way of packaging, and they are making every effort to give it to them. New and better methods of packaging are constantly being developed. Before the end of World War II, meats and produce were seldom packaged for the consumer. Today, with the widespread use of plastics for bags and shrink-pack plastic films, the majority of meats and a large portion of the produce is sold in premeasured quantities, thereby making this part of the shopping trip much easier and more convenient.

Caution Needed. Consumers do not necessarily accept all innovations as being good. This is especially true of packaging in the food area. People take eating very seriously. Consequently, they are often wary of changes. This caution is generated by the product, their feelings toward it, and the package.

While packaging of produce, for example is being done in more and more stores, many customers are not too happy about it. Their discontent varies by product. A *Progressive Grocer* consumer dynamics study found that, while 78 percent of the shoppers interviewed preferred to have their carrots prepackaged, only 52 percent liked to buy lettuce that was already packaged and only 14 percent liked their peaches in some form of package. Walter P. Margulies discussed this factor in relation to ketchup bottles in his book *Packaging Power:*

> Look at ketchup bottles. Could a container be less utilitarian? However delicious, the contents are stubbornly molasseslike at cool temperatures. The amount of ketchup we might want is difficult, if not impossible to measure accurately in advance.
>
> Designers have naturally addressed themselves to the problem of the ketchup bottle. The difficulties are obvious and many solutions are easy to reach. But in spite of higher utility, and economic and aesthetic superiority, new designs have been market failures. Ketchup that isn't in a ketchup bottle is viewed with suspicion by the public.

Beyond Convenience and Utility. Marketing specialists are concerned with giving the customer what he or she wants in the way of packaging. The wants and needs of the consumer, however, go beyond the physical aspects of the package and its features.

The package, like all the other elements of the product, plays an important role in shaping the image the consumer has of a particular brand. As was stated earlier, the package has been playing a much more important role in shaping the image of the brand in the consumer's mind due to the increase in self-service in supermarkets. In other words, the package must act as a communicator to the consumer. As Burleigh B. Gardner, President of Social Research, Inc., said in "The Package as a Communication":

> When we talk about a package as a communication, we are referring to a complex set of reactions in the mind of the beholder, all of which contribute to a feeling about the product inside. The nature of this feeling can contribute to the anticipation of what the product will be like and the satisfaction it will provide. In the case of many food and beverage products the package may actually affect the sensory response to the product. Thus the same soft drink in different bottles may taste different. With high volume consumer items, where there are many competing brands, even subtle differences in package communication can have an important impact on sales.

According to Gardner, there are four factors that affect a package's ability to communicate:

1. Material used
2. Form or shape
3. Colors used
4. Label

The Material. Gardner stated that

> . . . There are distinct differences in the meanings and imagery evoked by different materials. Thus, metal arouses feelings different than plastic, paperboard or glass. Each evokes a different set of associations ranging from descriptive realism, i.e., hard, brittle, to the nonrational, emotion-laden ideas such as purity or warmth.

The Form. The consumer perceives and often accepts or rejects products on the basis of the physical shape of their package. Ernest Dichter in his book *Handbook of Consumer Motivations* tells about a test designed to determine the consumers' preference for various shapes of meat packages:

> Ground beef was put into three different types of packages. One was a well-structured rectangular package; the second was semistructured, flat, broken, and circular; and the third was completely unstructured, an amorphous-appearing mass. All three types were wrapped in the same material. The packages were arranged in random order and the housewives were asked to indicate their first and second choices. The overwhelming preference was for the structured package.

The Color. Color is an extremely important factor in communication to the consumer. As Walter Margulies states in his book *Packaging Power:*

> . . . Color is not only a visual perception, but a multisensory experience. People "feel" color as well as see it. Indeed, some people even hear color.
>
> Green is the symbol of abundance and health. . . . Green offers a perfect example of package color reflecting product in its almost universal application to green-vegetable containers.
>
> Orange is perhaps the most "edible" color, especially in its brown-tinged shades. It is evocative of autumn, pumpkins, and harvest; of things well cooked and good to eat.

The Label. The label is generally considered to be part of the package. Its primary function is to communicate to the consumer facts about the product inside the package;

but as Gardner points out, the label also portrays a visual communication in two dimensions: form and color. The colors interact with the form to present a total configuration.

Packaging and the Public Good. As was stated earlier, consumers demand honest value. They are particularly unhappy with what they consider to be either misleading or inadequate information.

The government has taken steps to make sure that consumers are given all the information they need to make rational decisions. Most of the government's efforts in this area are embodied in the Fair Packaging and Labeling Act of 1966 and amendments to this Act. This law provides for the Food and Drug Administration and the Federal Trade Commission to set packaging regulations they believe are necessary. It also makes labeling mandatory and allows industry voluntarily to adopt packaging standards that limit the multiple weights and measures that were being used. Further, the law requires food made of two or more ingredients to have those ingredients listed by their common or usual names in order of their predominance in the food.

While these were steps in the right direction, many concerned individuals and groups pointed out that the consumer still did not have enough information to make a rational choice. These individuals, encouraged by the hard won fights of consumerists on other fronts, made themselves heard. Their efforts resulted in a number of new or revised practices in the industry, including unit pricing, open date coding, and nutritional labeling.

The concept behind unit pricing was the consumer's need to have some way to

Today's fast moving self-service shopping environment requires a product's package to be an in-store sales agent (*Courtesy of Proctor and Gamble Company*).

make price comparisons on the multitude of brands and sizes that confronted them on the average grocer's shelf. Short of carrying an electronic calculator on each shopping trip, the average shopper found it very difficult to determine if one brand in a four ounce package selling for 78 cents was a better buy than another brand in a six ounce package selling at $1.26.

Unit prices appear in addition to the regular package prices, usually immediately below the shelf facings for the brand. If the consumers use the unit pricing method they would find that the four ounce package used in the example given above would offer the best value based on price because the price per ounce is 19.5 cents versus 21 cents per ounce for the brand in the six ounce container.

Another positive practice instituted on a broad basis because of consumer action was open date coding. This coding was designed to help consumers determine the freshness of the perishables they were purchasing. Before this practice was instituted, manufacturers relied on a secret, or "closed," system to alert them to pull the products off the shelf. Now that the pull date is clearly stamped on perishable products the consumer no longer has to wonder how long the product has been sitting on the grocer's shelf, or how long it will last in the refrigerator. Store owners and manufacturers have also benefitted from open date coding. Customers no longer feel that it is necessary to squeeze every loaf of bread on the shelf to find the freshest one, or rummage through a grocer's freezer to pull out the package at the very bottom of the case.

Another change brought about through consumer action was a revision of nutritional labeling regulations. All products that are fortified as well as those that make nutritional or dietary claims on their labels or in advertising must comply. Use of nutritional labeling is still voluntary for all other food products. The following information must appear on the labels of products required to post information concerning nutrition:

- Servings in the container and the size of the servings.
- The amount of calories, protein, carbohydrates, and fat in each serving.
- The percentage of the U.S. Recommended Daily Allowances (U.S. RDA) of protein, vitamins, and minerals in each serving. The vitamins and minerals that must be listed if the product contains more than 2 percent of the U.S. RDA are: vitamin A, vitamin C, thiamine, riboflavin, niacin, calcium, and iron. The list may also include vitamin D, vitamin E, vitamin B_6, folic acid, vitamin B_{12}, phosphorous, and iodine.

All the reforms discussed above, unit pricing, open date coding, and nutritional labeling, reflect consumers' need to know more about the products they buy. In many instances, business people were reluctant to institute these changes. They argued that the costs associated with these reforms would be greater than the potential gain realized by the consumer. Further, they argued, consumers would not use the new information.

The first point, cost versus benefit, is impossible to quantify. But information on the second point, the use of new information on the second point, the use of new information, is available and clearly shows that consumers do use these decision-making tools. According to research data discussed in the *44th Annual Report of the Grocery In-*

dustry by *Progressive Grocer,* 75 percent of the shoppers surveyed used unit pricing occasionally, frequently, or almost always, while only 25 percent of the shoppers either never heard of unit pricing or almost never used it.

Open date coding has met with even a better reception by consumers. The report mentioned above showed that fully 78 percent of the shoppers surveyed almost always use this information, while only three percent have never heard of the practice or almost never use it.

The only reform mentioned above that has not received a forceful commitment from shoppers is nutritional information. Although 40 percent of the individuals surveyed by *Progressive Grocer* believed that this information was very important, 9 percent considered it unimportant, 15 percent viewed it as slightly important, and 34 percent considered nutritional labeling to be somewhat important.

One must wonder if it is a lack of interest, or a lack of understanding and ability to comprehend that has created this situation. In light of the complexity of the topic, it would seem that the latter conclusion is more realistic and this points up the tremendous need for consumer education. Until a widespread, comprehensive program of education on this topic is instituted, people will continue to ignore nutritional information on labels and rob themselves of the benefits that could be their's for the reading.

It is impossible to leave this topic without discussing one of the more controversial issues confronting manufacturers, stores, and consumers: the UPC. The UPC, or Universal Product Code, can be found on almost every product sold in today's supermarket. The Universal Product Code is a numbering system designed in a manner that allows each item in a store to be identified by a unique and universally applied ten digit number. The first five digits identify the firm that manufactures or distributes the product; the last five digits identify the product and specific information, such as size or weight, that distinguish one product from another in the manufacturer's line of products.

Although this system might appear simple, it took a great deal of cooperative effort on the part of all interested parties. Representatives from all types of retail food operations, wholesalers, and manufacturers all worked to develop this system. McKinsey & Company, a management consulting firm, worked out the details of the system and brought it to industrywide use in 1973.

When you look at a product in the supermarket, you will see ten digits at the base of a series of thirty-one parallel lines or bars. These bars can be machine read, so the actual numbers never need to be read. When this symbol is passed by an electronic scanning device at a checkout counter, a computer in the store or at some central location is triggered and records the name of the product and other information, such as price, automatically at the checkout register.

Grocery industry representatives hailed this process as a revolutionary method that would facilitate inventory control, cut costs and the length of checkout lines, eliminate errors made by checkers in recording prices, and cut the noise level in the area surrounding the checkout counters.

Consumer groups were impressed by some of the advantages of the system, but were concerned that the process could be used in a way that would not be in the consumers' best interest. More specifically, they were concerned that individual prices on grocery items would be eliminated because prices could be programmed into the computer. This move would force the consumer to rely on shelf prices. Further, computerized pricing could create its own system of errors. For example, wrong prices could be entered into the computer, or shelf prices might not be updated as quickly or correctly as the prices fed into the computer.

Consumer advocates campaigned against computerized pricing and won victories in many states. For the most part, all grocery stores are required to mark prices on individual products whether or not they have a computerized inventory system. These and other activities by concerned consumers have significantly slowed the movement toward a fully automated checkout system, and have caused store owners to think twice before making the heavy investment in new machinery required by such a system.

Price

The fourth factor that goes into making up the consumer's image of a product is the price he or she must pay to obtain it. Every consumer, to some extent, is concerned with prices for they act as limiting forces upon the consumer's unlimited wants. Alfred Oxenfeldt, et al. in *Insights into Pricing* reveal that attitudes about prices (actually the money that they represent) are formed in very early childhood long before the individual really understands their significance. These attitudes are very strong. Young children often look forward to a visit by an uncle or aunt who usually rewards them with a shiny dime or quarter. Children can also sense the tension that may arise in a family because of a lack of money. The emotionalism of the situation is communicated to them.

The adult consumer's attitudes toward money and prices are based on the ones they formulated quite early in life. Some lead to miserliness, others to extravagance—but they are always strong. For this reason, some people place price at the forefront in their decisions concerning the purchase of a product, while others relegate it to a much lesser position.

The Economist. When price is discussed, it is natural to think of turning to economists, for this is their area of specialization. They should have the answers. They do—to a point. The economist generally considers the consumer to be an economic person—an individual who possesses all the information available in order to make a decision, based solely on rational motives devoid of any emotion. Unfortunately, the consumer rarely has all the information available on any given product and emotion often plays a very important part in the decision to buy a product.

Information. Food as a general category is one area where consumers usually have a great deal of information. They buy products each week so they have a chance to determine the quality of one brand over another to a certain degree. But even in areas of assumed expertise, the consumer is often lacking in information and therefore turns to some other measure of quality.

Numerous studies have shown that consumers consider the price of a product to be an indicator of quality. In a study conducted by J. D. McConnel, subjects were given numerous chances over an extended period to select among three brands of beer. The beers were identical except for prices and their hypothetical brand names. The majority of the people involved selected the higher priced beer over the other brands and gave it the most favorable ratings in terms of quality. Obviously, the saying "you only get what you pay for" is applied as a guideline by consumers in a great number of buying decisions.

Psychological Factors. Why does this or that product cost 98¢? Obviously, the price reflects the cost of producing, shipping, and marketing the product along with a profit margin for everyone involved in the process. But psychological factors are also taken into consideration. In "The Psychological Aspects of Price," Chester R. Wasson discussed three psychological aspects of price:

1. Quantum effects
2. Reverse direction perception
3. Fair price comparisons

Quantum Effects. Wasson states that:

This phenomenon takes its name from a principle long known in physics: under certain conditions, the effect of light energy is not continuous, but sometimes has to build up to a certain point to work, then causes a disproportionate end result. A parallel price effect phenomenon is familiar to every supermarket operator. A given product may not move at $1.05 but a package containing only four-fifths as much, clearly labeled as to quantity will readily sell at 98¢. One dollar is a quantum point as far as its customers are concerned.

Reverse Direction Perception. Numbers often seem to possess magical qualities because of the manner in which people perceive them. As Wasson states, a $2.95 price may look cheaper to the buyers than a $2.45 price, a 29¢ price may look like less than 24¢. A price that is actually higher on the numerical scale often proves to be lower on the consumer's psychological scale.

Fair Price Standards. Consumers attempt to gain as much information about a product as possible. Often there is very little available. In order to come to a decision, consumers may determine psychologically what they believe a fair price to be and often will not pay more—or less—for it. Wasson gave an example of a product originally priced at $1.19. The manufacturers decided that sales were not high enough, so they tried an experiment with the price. They selected three groups of stores. In one group, the product was priced at $.89; in another, at $1.09; in the third, at $1.29. The stores selling the product for $1.09 sold far greater quantities than the stores with the lower and higher prices. Consumers felt that $1.09 was the "right" price. They probably considered the $.89 price too low to be a quality item and the $1.19 or higher too much money for that particular product.

The Retail Outlet

The words "retail outlet" in today's food industry are almost synonymous with the term supermarket. There is good cause for this equation. *Progressive Grocer's* 44th Annual Report of the Grocery Industry shows that 75 percent of all grocery sales in 1976 were made by supermarkets. The supermarket is actually a relatively new method of retailing food. According to Rom J. Markin in his book *The Supermarket: An Analysis of Growth, Development, and Change,* prior to the 1920s, the grocery business was the most backward form of retailing. Consumers had to go from one specialized shop to another for the products they desired. This meant trips to the butcher shop, the bakery, and the produce store. But things began to change in the 1920s because of changes in the environment.

The people of our nation were beginning to move from the farms to the cities in search of jobs. As a result, the market for products in geographically small areas was expanding, and the jobs in the cities generated higher incomes. As incomes rose, tastes for new and different foods came into evidence. Home refrigeration by electrical means did much to change the environment. The consumer no longer was forced to shop every day for perishable products. In addition, the automobile was to a large extent responsible for the development and rapid growth of of the one-stop, complete food market. No longer were people confined to their immediate vicinity. The automobile allowed them to go to new shopping areas and make larger purchases.

As Markin points out, the supermarket evolved slowly through time. A number of distinct concepts helped to develop it into the institution we know today. One of these early concepts was cash and carry. This was an unusual departure from the accepted system. Normally customers ran weekly and monthly accounts, and even small orders were delivered. Another important innovation was self-service. Improved packaging methods and quality control made this method of shopping acceptable to the consumer.

As the supermarket became the accepted retail outlet for food, the small, independent grocery stores that at one time could be found in every neighborhood began to close their doors. They could not compete with the vast selections and low prices of the larger stores.

It is interesting to note that one of the strong points of the supermarket when it began—convenience—has caused a resurgence of the neighborhood store in a new form. The idea of going to a supermarket and standing in check-out lines for a loaf of bread or a carton of soft drinks is not very appealing to the consumer. Neighborhood stores—or more correctly convenience stores—that are often run by a husband and wife team have stepped in to fill this void. Located in high population areas, these stores stay open long hours—sometimes 24 hours 7 days a week—in order to serve their customers. The benefits to be derived from frequenting this type of store are valued by the consumer, as indicated by their growing numbers and increased sales. In 1960 there were only 2500 convenience stores and total sales amounted to 357 million dollars. In 1970 their numbers had grown to 13,250 and sales were almost two and one half billion dollars. In 1976 the number of stores had doubled over the 1970 figure and stood at 27,400 and sales had reached nearly seven and one half billion dollars.

What the Shopper Looks for. In all metropolitan areas shopper are confronted with a large number of grocery stores. Yet invariably there is one store that they patronize more than any other. The reasons for selecting one store over another will vary based on the shopper's age, income, and a host of other demographic and psychological factors, but certain generalizations can be drawn. When Burgoyne, Incorporated, a Cincinnati based research firm, asked food shoppers in cities across the United States in 1974 to identify the factors they considered most important in selecting a favorite supermarket, the following list of factors, in order of importance, emerged:

- Low prices on groceries
- Quality and freshness of meats
- Convenient location
- Quality and freshness of fruits and vegetables
- Variety and selection of grocery merchandise
- Attractiveness and cleanliness of the store
- Good store arrangement—ease of shopping
- Fast checkout service
- Friendliness of store people
- Better parking facilities
- Trading stamps

No one reason can be selected as *the* determinant in store selection. The following quote from a Chicago *Tribune* study of food shoppers in the Chicago area shows how interrelated the factors are in the final choice of a store.

I know where things are. It seems to carry all the brands that I like. It is closer to me. Because of the drugs and all their other little departments, like household things, I'd say they have a wide variety of things, of not only foods. It also has a mail box close to it and that's a dumb reason, but I always have something to mail; and because they cash checks there.

Store Image. The factors given in the Burgoyne study are evaluative in their nature. They are used by the consumer for comparing one store with another. Theoretically, an objective study could compare stores based on these criteria, and one would emerge as the "best." This would ultimately result in the "best" store receiving all the customers while neighboring stores would be forced to close their doors. Yet in many areas, competing stores all manage to obtain a certain percentage of the available consumers and all survive. This occurs because the consumer's perception of a store—the image that it generates—may be quite different from its "score" if it were subjected to an objective evaluation.

In their book *Consumer Behavior,* Engel, Kollat, and Blackwell gave six factors that help to form a store's image in the mind of the consumer. They are:

1. Price
2. Advertising
3. Product and service mix
4. Store personnel
5. Physical attributes
6. Store clientele

Price. The price level for a given store or chain is one of the determinants of the image it produces in the mind of the consumer. Price is an objective factor, yet the price level perceived by the customer and the objective or actual price may be quite different. As Engel, Kollat, and Blackwell state, consumers often form their image about a store's prices more on the basis of advertising, displays, advertising specials, and physical layout than from the actual level of the store.

Advertising. The late Pierre Martineau pointed up the importance of advertising in image production in his book *Motivation In Advertising* when he stated:

> Whether he (the retailer) realizes it consciously or not, all of his advertising is creating an image of his store. One of the most important functions in the housewife's role is to know the stores. She learns to single out certain cues in the advertising which will tell her about the store's status . . . its general atmosphere, its customer body, even its physical qualities; and then she decides intuitively whether this is where she fits in.

Product and Service Mix. The products and services offered to the shopper help to determine the image that it generates in the mind of the consumer. In a recent interview, a shopper was asked why she picked one store over another that was closer to her home. She replied that the one closer to home carried a number of different brands "nice for people that feel that they must have this kind of canned corn or that kind of cake mix" but that their prices were higher and she refused to pay the difference because her family would "only eat the same old things week after week—no chance to get fancy."

Store Personnel. Engel, Kollat, and Blackwell state that:

A store sometimes takes on the character of the clerks, stock boys, and those management personnel who are seen by customers. The way clerks react to customers sometimes characterizes a store as friendly, impersonal, helpful, up-to-date, or disinterested.

Physical Attributes. The physical attributes of the store tend to reinforce the consumer's perceptions of other image-producing factors or cause them to be questioned. When considering the exterior of the store, Walters and Paul in their book *Consumer Behavior An Integrated Framework* stated that:

The architecture, signs, and windows and doors, as well as the general condition of the building, all speak to consumers. The architecture of the exterior sets the image theme. Materials such as steel and aluminum still tend to be viewed as modern but cold. Concrete and glass are seen as modern but warm building materials.

The interior of the store must be coordinated with the exterior in order to present one image to the consumer. The arrangement of shelves, islands, special displays, the color of the walls and floors, and the type and intensity of lighting all go into making up the store's image. Through these factors, a store can create the image of being bright, clean and modern or become classified as crowded, dingy, and dirty.

Store Clientele. Consumers are very much aware of their fellow shoppers. Since individuals tend to belong to distinct social groups, it is only natural for them to choose the grocery store they shop at in light of the influence exerted by the group members. These influences tend to help form the image of the store in the minds of the consumers and allow them to know in which store they do and do not "belong."

PROMOTION

Promotion is the last major factor that must be covered to complete our overview of the influence business has on people and the food they eat. Kernan, Dommermuth, and Sommers define promotion as any identifiable effort on the part of a seller to persuade buyers to accept the seller's information. They go on to state that:

the central element in this definition is persuasion. Would-be buyers must be persuaded of both the meaning and the value of seller's products or services. This requires communication of information—either directly from the seller to the buyer or from the seller to some intermediary who can be expected to influence the buyer.

Promotion of food is undertaken by both the original seller of the products—manufacturers—and intermediaries—the grocery stores.

Types of Promotion

The word promotion is used to denote a number of different "tools" that are available. In the food industry, the two primary tools used by both manufacturers and retailers are advertising and sales promotion.

Advertising. According to the American Marketing Association, advertising is

> . . . any paid form of nonpersonal presentation and promotion of ideas, goods, or services by an identified sponsor. It involves the use of such media as the following:
>
> Magazine and newspaper space
> Outdoor (posters, signs, skywriting, etc.)
> Direct mail
> Radio and television
> Programs and menus
> Circulars
>
> This list is intended to be illustrative, not all inclusive.

Manufacturers of food products that are distributed nationally and have wide appeal to a multitude of consumers may use all or most of the media listed above in an attempt to persuade consumers to buy their products. The stores, however, limit the types of media they use because their market is local rather than national in scope.

The primary medium used by grocery stores is newspaper advertising. This medium evokes immediate response by the reader. Most advertising by grocery stores in newspapers plays on this sense of immediacy. Each week, usually on Wednesday, a large number of retailers have their ads displayed. According to the Supermarket Institute, 63 percent of their total members advertising is placed in Wednesday's paper. The ads are usually quite crowded and are price oriented. They are designed to shout "sale" to the consumer and allow for price comparisons.

Not everyone in the food industry is convinced that this creative strategy is the correct one to follow. In *Chain Store Age,* D. Parson's keynote address to a National American Wholesale Grocers Association meeting was quoted as follows:

> Supermarket ads are directed at the consumer audience of 35 years ago, and talk to the housewife as if she were on relief.
>
> But the days of dramatic price comparisons (with the corner grocery) are long since gone, now that supermarket is competing against supermarket.

Creative strategy is changing, but it is taking place very slowly. As Markin pointed out in his book:

> . . . Greater attention is being placed on the selection of the items, size of advertisements, art work, and other factors. Some operators, in a bid to gain increased customer acceptance and appeal in their food advertisements, are moving rapidly to the use of color in newspapers.
>
> Others in an effort to increase the effectiveness of their newspaper advertisements, are going to the dramatic use of illustration, increased white space, variety of type sizes, and humorous cartoons.

The second most important medium for local retailers is handbills and circulars. They can be tailored to the store's creative strategy and be distributed to people in the immediate vicinity of the store—the most likely customers.

Radio is also used as a medium, but it has some distinct drawbacks for the retailer. He can only advertise a limited number of products in a given commercial and must pay for "deaf ears" since many listeners are distant from the store and do not represent potential customers.

Television suffers from the same drawbacks that radio does in the eyes of the individual retailers. The problems are actually magnified in the case of television because the audience is usually larger and more geographically scattered. Nevertheless, television and radio are used and often quite effectively by chain stores that have a number of stores throughout a viewing or listening area.

Sales Promotion. The American Marketing Association defines sales promotion as

> . . . those marketing activities other than personal selling, advertising, and publicity that stimulate consumer purchasing and dealer effectiveness, such as display . . . demonstrations, and various nonrecurrent selling efforts not in the ordinary routine.

According to Markin, the most often used forms of in-store supermarket promotion activities are: in-store displays; premiums; trading stamps; and contests.

In-Store Displays. It is difficult to enter any grocery store without being visually bombarded by in-store displays. Special displays can usually be found in any area that might be left vacant—along windows, on the end of aisles, and often in the aisle itself—along with special displays in the regular display areas.

There is a reason for all of these displays. Most importantly, these displays catch the consumer's eye, and it has often been proven that they lead to a tremendous increase in the sale of the displayed product. As Markin points out, some of the other reasons for their increased use are:

- To increase sales of related product lines
- For decorative purposes; enhance the appearance of the store

- To create a buying psychology on the part of the customer through psychological techniques of mass, color, and arrangement
- To create a "price" atmosphere

The manufacturers, through their sales agents, help the retailer plan and set up store displays. They furnish posters, racks, and so on, to aid the retailers and thereby aid their own cause.

Premiums. Another form of sales promotion that is usually inspired by the manufacturers is the use of premiums. Open up any magazine and you will find a coupon allowing a bargain price on some product. Coupons are also given in newspapers or sent to the consumer's home. Retailers look upon this tool with mixed emotions. Although premiums or coupons increase their sales, they have a great deal of paperwork associated with them—paperwork that takes up time.

Trading Stamps. The concept of giving trading stamps was developed around the turn of the century, but it was not until the mid-1950s that they really came into their own. Retailers in search of an added incentive to give to customers saw the trading stamp as the answer. Store after store employed stamps because they did not want their competitors to lure customers away. The use of stamps, however, has declined dramatically since the 1960s because consumer demand for lower prices has forced retailers to make a choice: continue giving stamps and keep margins higher, or drop stamps and pass the savings on to the consumer. Most retailers have chosen the second alternative.

Contests. Contests, like trading stamps, are attempts by the retailer to keep present customers and to lure new ones into the store. Just as in the case of trading stamps, store after store tends to jump on the contest bandwagon when one store or chain introduces the concept into a particular area.

The consumers of today, however, look on contests with mixed emotions. They accept them, but in our cost-conscious world, most of them would rather have a decrease in the prices they pay than a miniscule chance of winning a trip to some far off place in the sun.

STUDY QUESTIONS

1. What are the basic elements of a business enterprise?
2. Why has the consumer become a "king" in the eyes of business executives?
3. Identify and discuss the various levels in Maslow's Hierarchy of Needs.
4. What is marketing?
5. Differentiate between a brand name, a brand mark, and a trademark.

6. What elements should be considered by a businessperson when naming a product?
7. What elements must be considered when choosing the packaging for a product?
8. Do people always act rationally when evaluating the price of a product? Discuss.
9. The "best" supermarket from an objective perspective is not always the one chosen by the consumer. Why?
10. What types of promotion are used by supermarket owners to promote their stores and the products in them?

TOPICS FOR INDIVIDUAL INVESTIGATION

1. Study the history of business in the United States in greater detail. Show how each phase in its development helped to build the system to its present state.
2. Organize a debate in class and use the following statement as the basis for discussion: Resolved: the supermarket industry in the United States takes unfair advantage of the consumer.
3. Pretend that you are a particular product and point up the things that consumers look for—and avoid—when selecting "you."
4. Think up a name for a new snack food based on the guidelines given in this chapter.
5. Go into a supermarket and interview customers on a variety of topics of interest to you. (Be sure to obtain the manager's permission.) Potential topics for research include:
    a. Store selection criteria
    b. The reasons for choosing one brand over another
    c. The use of consumer aids such as unit pricing and nutritional information

REFERENCES AND SUGGESTED READING

Alexander, R. S., Compiler. *Marketing Definitions. A Glossary of Marketing Terms.* American Marketing Association, Chicago, 1960.

All About Food—The Chicagoland Woman and Her Grocery Store, Chicago Tribune Company, 1970.

Britt, S. H. *The Spenders.* McGraw-Hill, New York, 1960.

Britt, S. H., Ed., and J. L. Lubawski, Collaborating Ed. *Consumer Behavior in Theory and in Action.* John Wiley, New York, 1970.

Buell, V. P., Ed. and C. Heyel, Coordinating Ed. *Handbook of Modern Marketing.* McGraw-Hill, New York, 1970.

Buskirk, R. H. *Principles of Marketing. The Management View,* 3rd Ed. Holt, Rinehart & Winston, New York, 1970.

Campbell, M. *Why Did They Name It . . .?* Fleet Press, New York, 1964.

Chisholm, R. F. *The Darlings, The Mystique of the Supermarket.* Chain Store Age Books, New York, 1970.

Consumer Dynamics in the Super Market. Progressive Grocer in cooperation with the R. H. Donnelley Corp. and The Kroger Co., New York, 1956.

Dichter, E. *Handbook of Consumer Motivations. The Psychology of the World of Objects.* © 1964 by E. Dichter. Used with permission of McGraw-Hill Book Company, New York.

Dirksen, C. J., A. Kroeger, and F. M. Nicosia. *Advertising Principles and Problems,* Fifth Edition. Richard D. Irwin, Homewood, Ill., 1977.

Engel, J. F., D. T. Kollat, and R. D. Blackwell. *Consumer Behavior.* Holt, Rinehart and Winston, New York, 1968.

Engel, J. F., H. G. Wales, and M. R. Warshaw. *Promotional Strategy,* Revised Edition. Richard D. Irwin, Homewood, Ill., 1971.

Fair Packaging and Labeling Act, Public Law 89–755, 89th Congress S. 985, Nov. 3, 1966.

Gardner, B. The Package as a Communication, in M. S. Moyer and R. F. Vosburgh, *Marketing For Tomorrow . . . Today. 1967 Conference Proceedings.* American Marketing Association, Chicago, 1967.

Gist, R. R. *Marketing and Society A Conceptual Framework.* Holt, Rinehart & Winston, New York, 1971.

Herzog, Herta. Behavioral Science Concepts for Analyzing the Consumer, in Duncan, D. J., Ed. *Proceedings—Conference for Marketing Teachers from Far Western States.* University of California, Berkeley, 1958.

Kassarijian, H. H. and T. S. Robertson. *Perspectives in Consumer Behavior.* Scott, Foresman, Glenview, Ill., 1968.

Kernan, J. B., W. P. Dommermuth, and M. S. Sommers. *Promotion An Introductory Analysis.* Copyright © by J. B. Kernan, W. P. Dommermuth, and M. S. Sommers 1970. Used with permission of McGraw-Hill Book Company, New York.

Kornblau, C. Packaging and Supermarkets: The Package in the Market Place, in G. L. Baker, Jr., Ed. *Effective Marketing Coordination. Proceedings of the 44th National Conference.* American Marketing Association, Chicago, 1961.

Kotler, P. *Marketing Management Analysis, Planning and Control.* Prentice-Hall, Englewood Cliffs, N.J., 1967.

Levy, S. J. *Promotional Behavior.* Scott, Foresman, Glenview, Ill., 1971.

Levy, S. J. Symbols by Which We Buy, in Stockman, L. H., Ed., *Advancing Marketing Efficiency. 41st National Conference.* American Marketing Association, Chicago, 1958.

Lubawski, J. L. The Consumer in the Marketplace, J. C. Penney's *Forum* Spring/Summer, pp. 18–19, 1971.

Mandell, M. I. *Advertising,* Second Edition. Prentice-Hall, Englewood Cliffs, N.J., 1974.

Margulies, W. P. *Packaging Power.* Copyright © 1970 by Walter P. Margulies. Reprinted by permission of The World Publishing Company.

Markin, R. J. *The Supermarket: An Analysis of Growth, Development, and Change,* Revised Ed. Washington State Univ. Press, Pullman, Washington, 1968.

Martineau, P. *Motivation in Advertising.* Copyright © 1957 by P. Martineau. Used with permission of McGraw-Hill Book Company, New York.

McConnel, J. D. The Price-Quality Relationship in an Experimental Setting. *Journal of Marketing Research* Vol. 5, pp. 300–303, 1968.

Miracle, M. P. Market Structure in Commodity Trade and Capital Accumulation in West Africa, in R. Moyer and S. C. Hollander, *Markets and Marketing in Developing Economies*. Richard D. Irwin, Homewood, Ill., 1968.

New Look for Chain Ads. *Chain Store Age* Vol. 45 pp. 66–67, April, 1969.

Oxenfeldt, A., D. Miller, A. Shuchman, and C. Winick. *Insights into Pricing from Operations Research and Behavioral Science*. Wadsworth, Belmont, Cal., 1965.

Peak, H. S. and E. F. Peak. *Supermarket Merchandising and Management*. Prentice-Hall, Englewood Cliffs, N.J., 1977.

Preston, L. E. *Markets and Marketing An Orientation*. Scott, Foresman, Glenview, Ill., 1970.

Preston, L. E., Ed. *Social Issues in Marketing*. Scott, Foresman, Glenview Ill., 1968.

Robertson, T. S. *Consumer Behavior*. Scott, Foresman, Glenview, Ill., 1970.

Stanton, W. J. *Fundamentals of Marketing,* 3rd Edition. McGraw-Hill, New York, 1971.

Super Market Institute, *The Super Market Industry Speaks. Eighteenth Annual Report*. Super Market Institute, Chicago, 1966.

The Name's The Thing. *Design Sense 24*. Lippincott & Margulies.

Tomorrow's Corporate Marketing Operations. A Symposium. Marketing Committee, National Association of Manufacturers, December 1968.

Wasson, C. R. *The Economics of Managerial Decision: Profit Opportunity Analysis*. Appleton-Century-Crofts, 1965.

Walters, C. G. and G. W. Paul. *Consumer Behavior an Integrated Framework*. Richard D. Irwin, Homewood, Ill., 1970.

White, C. Ecology Switches Signals for Food Package: "Self-destruct." Reprinted with permission from the November 1, 1971 issue of *Advertising Age*. Vol. 42, No. 44, p. 54. Copyright 1971 by Crain Communications, Inc.

Wish, J. R. and S. H. Gamble, Eds. *Marketing and Social Issues: An Action Reader*. John Wiley, New York, 1971.

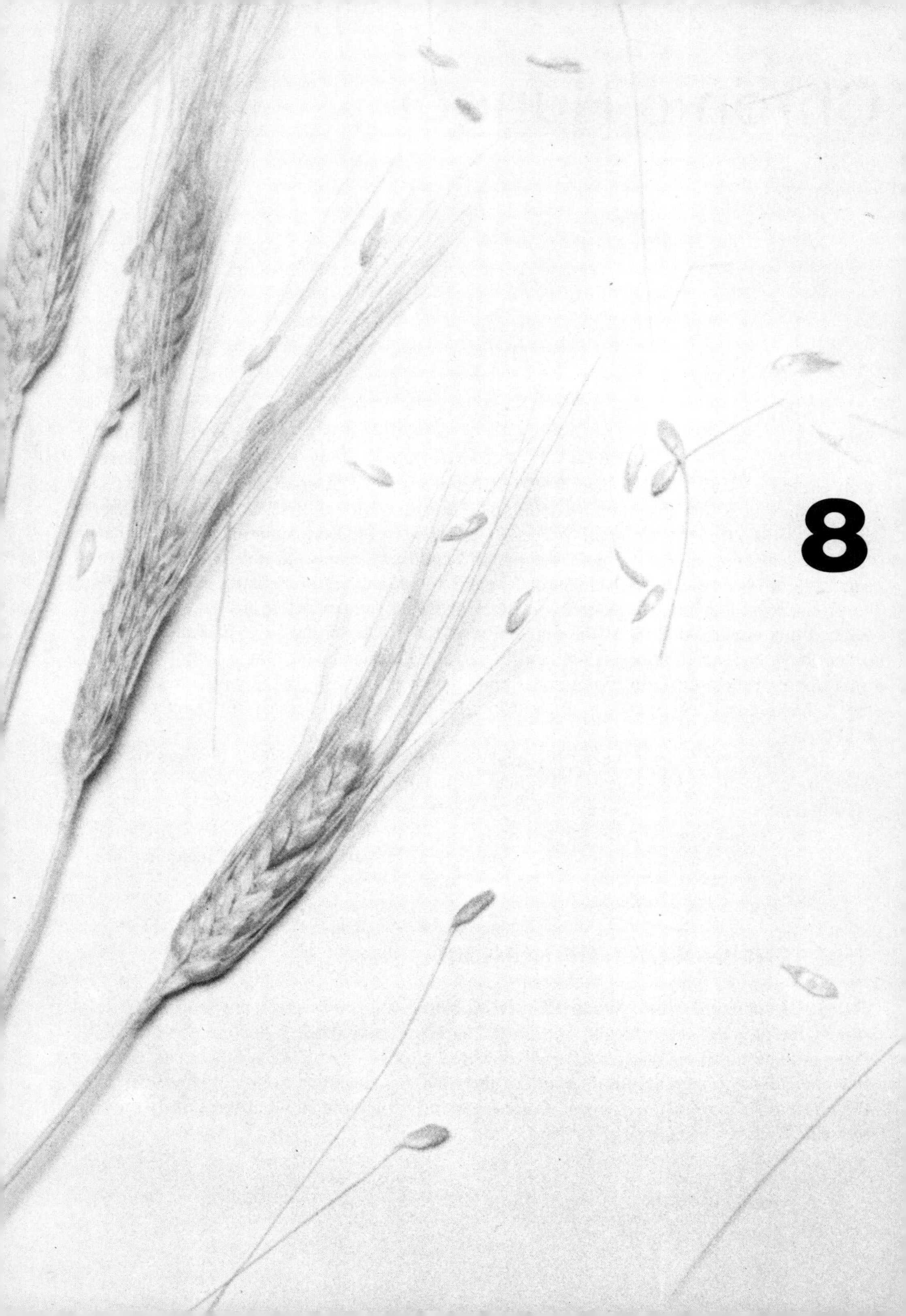

8

Chronic Hunger

Hunger is a condition of misery and suffering, a condition of human degradation. The effects of it reach around the world—to those who suffer its wretchedness and to those who escape it as well—for hunger is the concern of people of good will everywhere.

Hunger is not an uncommon condition. In preparation for the World Food Conference in 1974, the United Nations reassessed the world food situation, finding that "Millions of men, and even more women and children, simply do not have enough to eat. Definitions of undernourishment differ, and a wide variety of statistics can therefore be produced in support of this or that assertion. But, even on a cautious view, it is estimated that about a quarter of the population in the Far East, the Near East and Africa do not have enough food to enable them to perform their ordinary human activities. The total figure of those suffering from undernourishment in the developing world (excluding the Asian planned economies such as China) amounts to the horrifying total of 460 million people."

The effects of hunger on the physical condition of individuals, on changes in the structure of the brain (as observed in studies with experimental animals), also, the possible influences of hunger on behavior and on mental development, the recurrence of famines, and chronic hunger in the United States are dealt with in this chapter. Causes for the existing prevalence of hunger and proposals for combatting its high incidence are discussed.

THE TERMINOLOGY OF HUNGER

Hunger is sometimes used synonymously with undernutrition. Both are interpreted to signify the effect of the intake of an insufficient quantity of food. When there is hunger, there is undernutrition. However, undernutrition may be from causes other than insufficient food—for example, an infection of intestinal parasites that nourish themselves on the nutrients of the host can in some cases prevent normal intestinal absorption. Almost inevitably where there is poverty there is hunger.

When there is an inadequacy in the nutritional quality of the diet and deficiency of certain nutrients such as protein, minerals, or vitamins, the term used is malnutrition. Undernutrition and malnutrition are not mutually exclusive; people who are undernourished may also be malnourished. In the literature the three terms, hunger, undernutrition, and malnutrition seem to be used indiscriminately. Malnutrition is discussed in Chapter 9.

EFFECTS OF HUNGER ON PHYSICAL STATUS

The effect of hunger on individuals is variable. The response depends on the duration and severity of the lack of food on the one hand and on the capacity of an individual to adjust to the deprivation on the other.

Growth

Failure to thrive is a sensitive indicator of undernutrition in the young. Children who grow in spite of hunger grow less and so are smaller than well-nourished children of the

Hunger—a condition of misery and suffering of human degradation (*Courtesy Agency for International Development*).

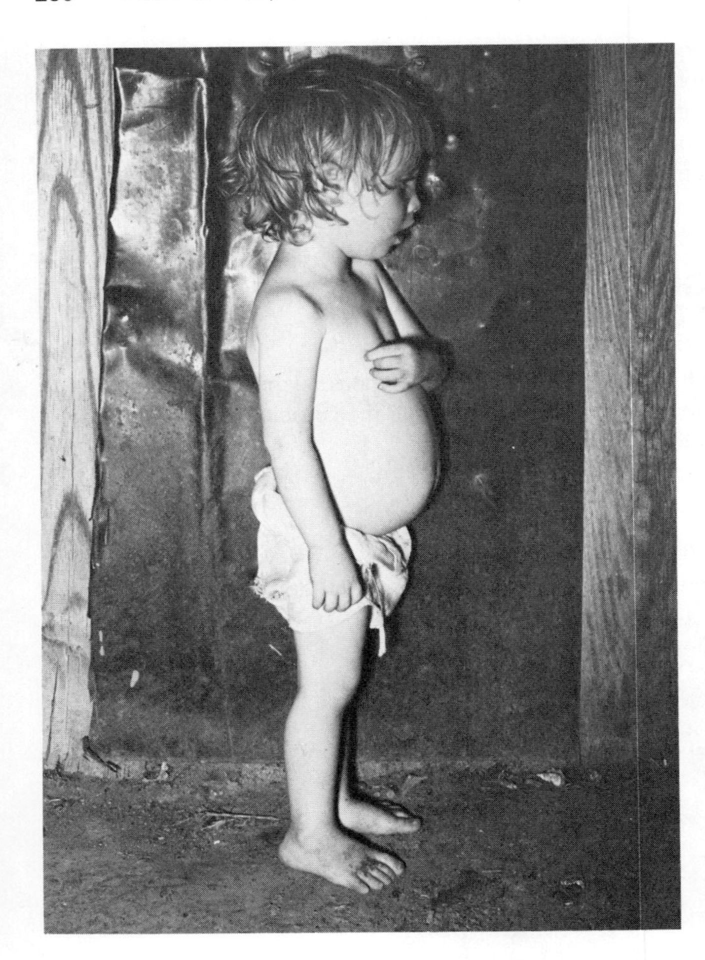

Malnutrition in a child of a family of day laborers on farms (*Courtesy FSA-HEW*).

same age. Economically disadvantaged children, children, who live where there is a shortage of food, and children who suffer the results of war and disaster reflect the stunting effect of insufficient food. Meredith of the University of Iowa examined a dozen research studies dealing with growth and economic level. The pattern common to all was that the children of higher-income families were taller and heavier than their counterparts in the lower-income groups. Thus, the children whose parents were in professional and managerial positions were larger than the less economically well-off children of the unskilled and semiskilled workers. And the children who were in school in the better residential districts were larger than the children in schools in the poorer residential areas.

Infants and young children in less developed countries present dramatic, even though at this moment rather indirect, evidence of the effect of nutrition on growth. Breast-fed infants in less developed countries grow in the early months of life at a rate within the norms established in the United States. However, a break in the growth rate occurs after six months of age, with the rate falling below the United States standards. The cause is believed to be lack of proper food. This pattern was observed in the children of Lebanon. A survey of child-feeding practices in all parts of Lebanon revealed that at six months of age 90 percent of all infants were at the breast. By one year of age many had begun to sample adult fare. These foods were lower in nutritive value than breast milk and often were carriers of infectious microorganisms.

Experimental studies with animals extend our information on the physical effects of hunger. It is always a question of whether these findings apply to humans, but they at least can be considered indicative. When the diet of experimental animals is restricted so that the body weight is held constant, certain parts of the body are found to persist in growth. In studies using dogs as the experimental animal, the dogs were found to grow longer and taller and leaner. In recent studies with pigs and chicks, McCance and his coworkers in England found the weight of the bones, the heart, and the brain to increase in spite of the stationary body weight.

There is the continuing question as to whether restriction of food intake in early life affects the ultimate size attained. The recovery growth of eight children of ages ten months to three years under treatment for marasmus and kwashiorkor was observed by Ashworth in Jamaica. During the recovery period, the children grew 15 times as fast as

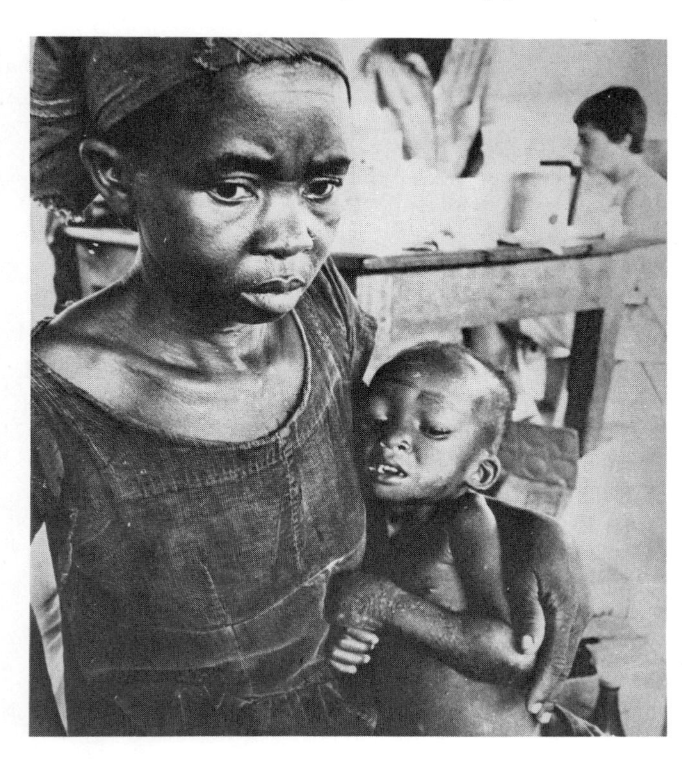

A worried mother brings her child to be treated for malnutrition (*Courtesy Agency for International Development*).

normal children of the same age and five times as fast as normal children of a similar height and weight. These children attained the expected weight for height; when they reached this size, their food intake fell abruptly and their growth rate dropped to a level comparable to that of normal children of that height and weight. Further follow-up studies are needed to know the firm answer to the question of the permanence of stunting early in life.

Body Composition

During hunger, there is a loss of fat and protein from the body and an accumulation of water. In the classical Minnesota study of Keys and his co-workers on the effects of semistarvation, 32 young men consumed a diet of 1570 kcal over a period of 24 weeks;

Table 8-1 Composition of Body Weight Loss at Successive Periods of Undernutrition (Mean Values)

	Percentage of total loss in		
Days	**Fat**	**Protein**	**Water**
	Experiment—53 days		
1–3	27	9	64
4–6	40	10	50
7–12	53	13	34
	Experiment—54 days		
1–3	25	5	70
11–12	69	12	19
22–24	85	15	0

From: A. Keys, "Undernutrition," in Duncan: *Diseases of Metabolism,* 5th Ed. W. B. Saunders, Philadelphia, p. 681, 1964.

fat and protein were lost from their bodies. During the first few days of the restricted diet, there was considerable water loss. This loss decreased with the progress of the experiment, reaching a point where there was water retention (Table 8-1). It has been observed that in severely malnourished infants the water content is approximately 85 percent of the body weight, whereas the normal is around 65 percent.

Bones also change in composition with hunger, becoming more fragile. Radiographs of 95 infants and children hospitalized in Guatemala City with protein-calorie deficiency showed a picture of juvenile osteoporosis. It is the type of weakening observed in animals with experimentally produced protein-calorie deficiency.

Pregnancy

Fertility does not appear to be impaired by undernutrition. Casual observations indicate this situation, and demographic studies give circumstantial evidence of it. In the less developed countries where hunger exists, the annual birth rate was estimated to be about 40 per 1000 population in 1963. In the other countries of the world, the annual birth rate was estimated to be about 17 per 1000 population.

When the deprivation was near starvation level in Rotterdam and The Hague in the winter of 1944 and the spring of 1945, amenorrhea developed in about one-half of the women, with a consequent fall in the birth rate due to a lower rate of conception. A fairly quantitative relationship between food availability and fertility was established using the records kept in Holland during the famine and immediately following (1944–1946). When the average daily rations were less than around 1500 kcal (6,276 kj), a change of 100 kcal (418 kj) daily would effect a change of 241 births monthly.

If fertility persists in spite of hunger, it is logical to question the effect on the infant born. The infants born to severely deprived mothers in Holland in 1944 to 1945 were thin but not short. In general, it seems that the baby of an undernourished mother is on the whole surprisingly normal but lightweight. The socioeconomic level is reflected in the birth weight within ethnic groups (Table 8-2). Although other factors are involved, it seems safe to conclude that the amount of food eaten by the mother is important in the difference between the birth weights of babies of the well-to-do and the poor.

Some babies are small at birth (2500 g or less) because they are born prematurely; others are full-term and are small because they have suffered intrauterine malnutrition and are termed small-for-gestational age. Thirty-nine percent of the almost 4000 consecutive live-born infants observed at the Royal Victoria Montreal Maternity Hospital

Table 8-2 Mean Birth Weights According to Socioeconomic Status

Place	Population	Subjects	Mean birth weights (grams)
Madras	Indian	Well-to-do	2985
		"Mostly poor"	2736
South India	Indian	Wealthy	3182
		Poor	2810
Bombay	Indian	Upper class	3247
		Upper-middle class	2945
		Lower-middle class	2796
		Lower class	2578
Calcutta	Indian	Paying patients	2851
		Poor class	2656
Congo	Bantu	"Very well nourished"	3026
		"Well nourished"	2965
		"Badly nourished"	2850
Ghana (Accra)	African	Prosperous	3188
		General population	2879
Indonesia	Javanese	Well-to-do	3022
		Poor	2816

From: World Health Organization. *Nutrition in Pregnancy and Lactation.* Tech. Rept. Series No. 302. Geneva, Switzerland, p. 14, 1965.

(1961–1962) by Scott and Usher were small-for-gestational age. The predisposing factors were identified to be low material weight and poor antenatal care. Either small birth weight or nutritional deficiency was the basic or associated cause for 57 percent of the 35,095 deaths of children under 5 years analyzed by Puffer and Serrano in the Inter-American Investigation of Mortality in Childhood. The children who do survive grow at subnormal rates.

Nutrition in childhood as an influence on the incidence of stillbirths among women is suggested by Thomson and Hytten, who use demographic data of Britain as their guidelines. They begin with the 1930s when there was a period of substantial unemployment; malnutrition was prevalent among the poor. During the subsequent war years, the rate of stillbirths fell from 38 per 1000 in 1940 to 28 per 1000 in 1945. During this period, there was food rationing, and pregnant and lactating women were given priority on supplies of protective foods, cheap or free milk, and vitamins. The authors believe that the good diet accounted for the fall in the rate of stillbirths. During the ten years following World War II, there was little change in the rate of stillbirths. There was economic austerity after the war, but the authors believe that the nutritional status of women during pregnancy and lactation did not suffer. In recent years, the stillbirth rate in Britain has been falling rapidly again.

Thomson and Hytten do not present an explanation for the current fall in the rate but do offer an hypothesis. The basis for their proposal rests in part on the findings of an earlier work of Thomson in which he studied 489 women in Aberdeen, Scotland. He divided them into two groups: those with normal and those with abnormal clinical histories. Undernutrition was not found to be related to obstetrical performance; however, there were indications that stature of the mother did bear a relationship. The authors hypothesize that girls who are reared under favorable conditions and have a good diet "attain a high level of health and physiological efficiency" by the time they bear children; on the other hand, those who are stunted due to malnutrition fail to attain their full adult size. Thomson and Hytten point out that the mothers of the 1960s grew up after World War II. They are taller and heavier than those who grew up before that time. Other earlier studies have shown also that short women have higher rates of stillbirths than do tall women.

One last point about pregnancy of particular importance for undernourished women is the capacity of the body to use more efficiently the food nutrients provided to it during this period. As indicated from studies of the nutrients protein, calcium, and iron, a higher percent is absorbed from the gastrointestinal tract and more retained in the body by the pregnant woman than by the woman who is not pregnant. Such studies have not been done with the undernourished woman. However, it is safe to assume that there are minimal levels of need that, if not provided, would harm the mother or the unborn child.

Work Capacity

Significant anywhere, but particularly in less developed countries, is the adverse effect of hunger on work capacity. The debilitation of undernutrition has been observed under naturally occurring conditions and has been explored under conditions imposed in the experimental laboratory. Hunger lessens the work capacity of people.

Keller and Kraut studied the coal miners of the Ruhr district of Germany during and immediately following World War II. In 1939, when the rations provided an average of 4500 kcal (18,828 kj), approximately 2300 kcal (9,623 kj) of this amount remained for work after the requirements for basal metabolism and other activities were fulfilled. The daily amount of coal removed by each miner was 1.9 ton. In 1944, when only 1900 kcal (7,950 kj) were available for work, 1.65 ton of coal per man were mined. Workers in a steel plant were also studied. In 1939, when the worker's rations supplied 1900 work kcal (7,950 kj) daily, the steel production amounted to more than 120 tons per man per month. However, in 1944, when only 1150 kcal (4,812 kj) were available daily for work, production was less than 80 ton monthly per man.

The men in the experimental study of semistarvation carried out by Ancel Keys and his co-workers at the University of Minnesota suffered a marked loss of physical strength and endurance during the 24-week deprivation period. Voluntary exercise became less with the progress of the study. The men felt weak and tired. Although they moved cautiously, they bumped into objects and tripped over things.

The behavior of troops on short rations while in field operations reveals the incapacitating effect of too little food. Kark tells of the controlled study carried out in 1942 in the Canadian Arctic as follows:

One company was given an excellent ration, the others lived on calorically deficient rations. By the end of the week it was obvious to us that those living on the poor rations were deteriorating, but all the measurements we made could not distinguish between the three companies. Then after a particularly grueling day they came into the bivouac area for the night, cut down spruce trees for their shelter, ate supper, and bedded down. The next morning, after they had left, we found that each platoon of the well-nourished troops had built proper shelters to protect them from the wind and the cold. The platoons of the next best nourished company started to build shelters, but halfway through they were so tired that they stopped. The most caloric deficient soldiers were so tired when they came into the bivouac area that they just took spruce branches, laid them on the ground, and slept unprotected.

Infection

An affliction of the undernourished is infection. Where the incidence of hunger is high, infections are common. The outcome of the combination is more grave than for either alone. Infections that cause the undernourished to be acutely ill often have only a minor effect on the well-nourished.

Infections lessen the appetite, increase the loss of nitrogen from the body and decrease absorption of nutrients from the intestine, thus worsening the state of nutrition.

It is a vicious cycle because the poorly nourished have a lowered resistance to infections. Resistance to infection is mediated through the immune response. The immune systems are less efficient in undernutrition: specific antibody synthesis is frequently impaired. There is evidence that immunication of the severely undernourished child may not be effective. The number of lymphocytes that form antigen sensitive cells is lower than normal; for example, tuberculin sensitivity after B.C.G. vaccination and cutaneous reaction to diphtheria toxoid antigens are impaired.

Infantile diarrhea is an example of causal relationship of hunger to disease. The undernourished child is more susceptible to diarrhea than the well-fed child. The diarrheal condition then increases the severity of the undernutrition because the rapid passage of material through the intestine decreases the already limited absorption of nutrients.

Diarrhea, the primary cause of death of children under five years of age in less developed countries, increases markedly in incidence at the time of weaning. This almost

Table 8-3 Mortality Rates per 1000: May 1959–April/May 1963

	Mortality rate	
	Age 6–18 months	**Age 19–36 months**
Santa Cruz Balanya (control)	96.6	25.2
Santa Catarina Barabona (feeding)	30.3	10.4

From N. S. Scrimshaw. Primary Deterrent to Human Progress. *Pre-School Child Malnutrition.* National Academy of Sciences, National Research Council, Washington, D.C., p. 70. 1966.

universal association has led to the adoption of the term "weanling diarrhea." The replacement of mother's milk by food less nutritionally adequate and likely a carrier of infectious microorganisms is believed to be a causative factor. Further evidence of the role of nutrition was the decrease in the incidence of diarrhea among children under five years of age when supplementary food was given to them. In the Mayan Indian highland village of Santa Catarina Barabona, Guatemala, the children received four days each week a supplement of milk, a banana, and a special cereal mixture fortified with yeast, calcium, and vitamin A which supplied an additional fifteen grams of protein and 450 kcal (1,883 kJ). The mortality rate of the children of this village was notably less than that for the children of Santa Cruz Balanyz who received no supplements (Table 8-3).

The incidence of diarrhea in undernourished children is not only higher than in normal children but fatalities from it are also higher. In 1956 in Mexico City, the fatality rate in children hospitalized with diarrhea was 14 to 15 percent in those without evidences of undernutrition and as high as 52 percent in those severely undernourished.

In seeking some solution for the tremendously high incidence of infant mortality from diarrhea in less developed countries, Sabin looked back into the history of this malady in the United States. As late as 1920, the death rates due to diarrhea in New York City were comparable to current rates in many Latin American countries. An extraordinarily low level of diarrheal death in infants, however, was achieved in the United States and Canada by 1955. This reduction was associated more with other improvements in the standard of living than with the mere provision of pure water and sanitary disposal of excreta in the homes because these sanitary installations were already in existence in New York City before 1920. Sabin, searching for an explanation, says:

> . . . it is necessary to ask, therefore, what public activity is most likely to contribute to a significant reduction in infantile diarrheal mortality before the great improvements in the general standards of living are achieved in the parts of the world now plagued by poverty, hunger, ignorance, and disease.

He concludes that:

> . . . if malnutrition during the first two years of life could be largely eliminated, and breast-feeding could be supplemented and followed by feedings free from heavy bacterial growth, there is reason to expect a very significant reduction in the current, tragic infantile mortality, even though 'dirty hands' might continue to transmit infectious agents for a long time to come.

Organisms capable of causing diarrhea can be recovered from fecal samples in the early months of life without clinical diarrhea occurring; later, diarrhea does occur. It is proposed that the status of nutrition worsens after weaning, causing greater susceptibility.

There is need for exerting efforts to maintain conditions as sanitary as possible. A rather unexpected observation is that in the majority of the infantile diarrheas no pathogenic organism can be identified. It is hypothesized that intestinal organisms normally present and normally nonpathogenic may become pathogenic and cause diarrhea when present in abundance, as is commonly the case when the sanitation of the environment is poor.

ADAPTATION

The discussion thus far has examined some of the physical effects of hunger. Hunger causes stunting of growth and changes in body composition. It decreases the capacity to work and increases susceptibility to infection. But how is it that persons consuming diets grossly inadequate can live and work? Actually, the body makes adjustments to maintain normality in its composition and its functioning. Cannon, the physiologist, originated the word "homeostasis" to describe "the types of arrangements by which this stabilization is accomplished." Distinguished students of the subject, Mitchell and Keys, have written extensively about it. For example, when the energy intake is inadequate, body movements are diminished. The basal metabolism per square meter of body surface is reduced. And as a consequence, the total energy expenditure is lessened and the amount of energy needed is decreased. Keys indicates that, when the weight is reduced by around 20 percent from a previously normal weight, it is possible to maintain the body on a diet of approximately 50 percent of the energy value of the previously normal food intake. The mineral and vitamin intakes were in the general range of the National Research Council Recommended Daily Allowances, with the exception of the intakes of riboflavin and vitamin A, which were about one-half the recommendations (1948). This relationship between weight loss and energy reduction "explains why the rate of weight loss progressively decreases when a normal person chronically subsists on an inadequate diet and why life may be maintained for very long periods of time on a greatly reduced food intake." In the case of protein, minerals, and vitamins, when the intake is limited, the body eliminates less and retains within the body a higher percent of the amount provided in the diet.

HUNGER AND BRAIN STRUCTURE AND FUNCTION

Of serious concern to scientists and laypersons alike is the effect of early malnutrition on the structure and chemistry of the developing brain and consequent behavior. Evidence of the relationship between hunger and mental development comes from observations of the malnourished and from experimental studies with animals.

By the age of two years, the human brain has approached its adult size, weight, and cell number. The period of most rapid growth of the brain, commonly called "growth spurt" begins in mid-pregnancy and continues to around 18 to 24 months after birth. During the period of rapid growth the developing brain is notably more susceptible to injury from inadequate nutrition than at any other time.

In experimental studies with rats, Winick and Noble established that during growth there is first a phase in which the number of cells increases in number, followed by a phase in which the cells increase in size; the two phases overlap to some extent. Nutritional deprivation during the first phase leads to a permanent reduction in cell number; however, the reduction in cell size because of deprivation is not permanent. Dobbing proposes, however, that the cell number-cell size concept that is well established for homogeneous tissues such as liver and muscle may not apply as well to the brain because of the heterogeneity of its cells. A deficit in the number of brain cells found at autopsy of young children who had been undernourished Dobbing believes indicates a deficit of cells in the supporting substance (glial cells) rather than a deficit in brain cells themselves. Dobbing makes this supposition because nutritional deprivation in the children came at a time when only glial cells were being formed. Biochemical changes with early malnutrition have been observed in animals with reduced content in the brain of some enzymes, proteins, glycoproteins, and lipids.

A consequence of early malnutrition is its interference with normal behavior and cognitive development. Undernourished children behave differently from the well-nourished. Observations made by Chavez and Martinez of children from birth to two years of age clearly delineate some of these differences. One group of 17 mothers nursed their infants, giving them no supplementary food, according to the custom in this Mexican village. Mother's milk alone was not sufficient so the infants became under-nourished. Another group of 17 mothers, as similar as possible in socioeconomic and other respects to the first group, were given from the 45th day of pregnancy a supplement of vitamins and minerals and 64 g of powdered milk. The infants born to the supplemented mothers were breast-fed and were given supplements of milk and baby foods in amounts sufficient for the infants to maintain normal weight. As early as the 24th week of life, differences in behavior between the children with and those without supplements were observable. Those with supplements slept less during the day and played more. Those without supplements were sick more often and their illnesses were more severe and more prolonged. These illnesses may have contributed, at least in part, to the greater passivity of the nonsupplemented children and their greater dependence on their mothers—to carry them, for example, instead of playing alone or walking with her. They were predominantly negative, withdrawn and timid; at certain ages they were apathetic but at the same time showed anxiety when separated from their mothers. The children receiving supplements were more playful, bold, and mischievous—also, they were more demanding, disobedient, and aggressive with their mothers. The investigators indicated that they wished to explore further a question raised by this study: "Did the supplement—that is to say, nutrition—only serve to accentuate the basic character of the child, or did his character change?"

In animals also, there is a difference in the behavior of the underfed and the well-fed. Barnes and his co-workers and others have done research bearing this out. Even though it is impossible to extrapolate to the human, some animal studies do provide leads for research in the human. The undernourished are apathetic and lacking in curiosity. In one study using baby pigs, Barnes and his co-workers placed a new object in the form of a brightly colored metal ball in a test chamber to which the pigs were accustomed. It took only two minutes after the well-nourished pigs were placed in the chamber for them to contact the ball and begin playing with it. On the other hand, it took the undernourished pigs 12 minutes after entering the chamber to contact the ball and they played with it very little.

The influence of early undernutrition on cognitive development has been studied in children and in animals. Underfed rats and pigs were found by Levitsky and Barnes to utilize information less well than the well-nourished control animals. In the experiment, the animals were taught to respond to a certain signal, such as a light going on, in a certain way in order to receive a reward or to avoid punishment. After the animals had learned to respond to this signal, another signal, such as the sound of a buzzer, was introduced simultaneously with the original signal. After being exposed to the two signals simultaneously for a period of time, the buzzer alone was used. The undernourished animals responded to the buzzer less well than did the controls. Rehabilitation improved the response of the underfed but never did they attain the proficiency of the well-nourished.

It has been questioned whether or not the improvement in behavior of severely undernourished children undergoing medical rehabilitation might not be due in part to the general stimulus of the milieu of the institution. The longitudinal study of Yatkin in Beirut of 55 infants suffering with severe protein-energy-malnutrition tested this supposition. The infants entered the Rehabilitation Unit when they were between 2½ and 19 months of age. In order to study the factor of stimulation, half of the infants were kept in the usual environment of the clinic (the unstimulated group); the other half was given extra awareness and emotional stimulation (the stimulated group). The room in which the stimulated group (*S*) was housed was colorfully decorated, equipped with a variety of toys for the children to play with and there was music for them to listen to. Also attentive nurses took care of the *S* children, playing and singing with them. The standard nursing and medical care for the two groups (*US* and *S*) was the same. In addition, a control group of 30 healthy children was selected from the same community, matched as to age and sex with the experimental groups. Both the *US* and *S* groups improved consistently and significantly, as measured by the Griffith Mental Development Scale. This scale embodies a general development quotient (DQ) and measures five mental functions: locomotor, personal-social, learning and speech, eye and hand coordination, and performance. The stimulated group, however, improved significantly more than the unstimulated group. At the end of the four months' of treatment, both experimental groups still achieved lower than did the well-child controls.

To know if early undernutrition would cause irreversible changes in human beings, Monckeberg did a follow-up study on 14 infants who came to the hospital early in life with severe marasmic undernutrition caused by adverse socioeconomic conditions in the home. After discharge from the hospital, each child received free a total of 20 liters of milk each month with a similar amount for all other infants and pre-school children in the family. The children were followed year after year. When they reached between 4 and 7 years of age, their clinical examinations and blood analyses were found to be normal. However, the average intelligence quotient of the group was significantly lower than the average for Chilean preschool children of the lower socioeconomic class.

Winick summarizes the findings on hunger and cognitive development as follows:

The sum total of the numerous studies carried out in deprived populations would suggest that early malnutrition coupled with all the social ills that such a child endures will result in long lasting effects on cognitive development.

By contrast, when malnutrition occurs in an 'enriched' environment, such as children with cystic fibrosis or pyloric stenosis, the behavioral effects are less marked and disappear. These data have suggested that there might be an interaction between early nutrition and lack of environmental stimulation which leads to the behavioral changes observed later in life. [*Nutrition Notes* (AIN) 12(2) 4 1976)]

Experiments that produced hunger in adults, such as the Minnesota experiment, gave researchers an opportunity to observe the deterioration in social relationships and personal adjustment with the progress of hunger. Actually, two criteria for the selection of the young men were good mental health and the ability to get along reasonably well with others.

Hunger changed the behavior of these young men. The clamor of it distracted them from their attempts to continue their cultural interests, normal activities, and studies. There was preoccupation with food. And when it did arrive at the two meals per day, they were torn between gulping it and consuming it slowly. There were changes in emotional reactions and attitudes. The stresses of this semistarvation regime caused instability. Periods of depression were common; gloominess permeated much of their lives; they seldom smiled. There was little humor, and the negative approach to things was the common attitude.

The discrepancy between what they had once been able to do physically, wanted to do now, and were unable to accomplish was a source of great frustration to them. It was necessary to rest when ascending stairs; it was even difficult to lift the feet high enough to avoid stumbling on uneven sidewalks.

An attempt was made to relate changes in social behavior with loss of body weight. With increasing loss of weight, the behavior changed from slight disorder and strife to very serious disorder, then receded to slight disorder and finally to none.

Percentage loss of body weight	Civil disorder and strife
5	Slight
10	Moderate
15	Serious
20	Very serious
30	Moderate
40	Slight
50	None

Although most of the time the men were silent and sad, as the deprivation progressed there were periods of a few hours or a few days when they felt elated. Some thought that they finally had adjusted to the ration and expected that the state of elation would continue. But it did not. The weather affected moods notably. Warm, sunny days brightened the spirits; cold, damp, cloudy days caused greater depression.

The sociability of the men changed greatly. In general there was a feeling of animosity toward strangers; there was a special dislike for those who had food. It became "too much trouble" or "too tiring" to contend with other people, so the men became more withdrawn and alone. Personal appearance and grooming deteriorated as stress progressed.

The pressure of hunger was more than some of the men could take, even though all were of the finest character. One person not only bought food but stole it as well; he was not able to continue the experiment.

The intellective capacity, as measured by psychological tests, did not change during the starvation period nor the subsequent period of rehabilitation. However, it was difficult for the men to concentrate on the intellective task at hand because of preoccupation with food. The men described themselves during the stress of hunger, in contrast to their previous well-fed condition, as lacking in self-discipline and self-control, indecisive, restless, sensitive to noise, unable to concentrate, and markedly nervous.

During the rehabilitation period, many of the behavior symptoms of the starvation period persisted for several weeks. Similarly, it is reported that after relief had come to the Belsen concentration camp in 1945 the inmates continued to steal, hide, and hoard food. At the beginning of the rehabilitation, the inmates in the Minnesota project complained "without spirit, hopelessly—but later as their condition improved, their complaints became fierce, bitter, and resentful." One man in the Minnesota experiment characterized the difference between starvation and rehabilitation as "the difference between old age and adolescence."

FAMINES

Throughout human history, famines have existed. The literature on famine, as reviewed by Dando, reveals that:

> rarely did one factor directly cause a famine (particularly a drought); famine duration has varied greatly in the past; famine regions differ significantly in time, size and intensity; famine deaths or deaths related to famine ranged from the thousands to the millions; famines were not restricted to certain cultural areas; and famines did not occur more frequently in selected racial groups.

Even though famines have existed throughout human history, Mayer believes that "contrary to widespread popular belief, famines are not inevitable"; he points out that we must profit from our past experiences with famine and avert the disaster from occurring by noting warning signs and by keeping up-to-date inventories of background information and local conditions. Also, with particular concern for the recent famine in Ethiopia (1973–1975) with an estimated death toll of 200,000, Gebre-Medhin and Vahlquist also ask, "What can be done for the future to avoid repetition of serious shortcomings and mistakes?" They explained that severe and prolonged drought triggered this outbreak of famine but that the underlying cause was "primitive cultivating methods, archaic land tenure systems, overgrazing, exploitation of peasant farmers, lack of infra-

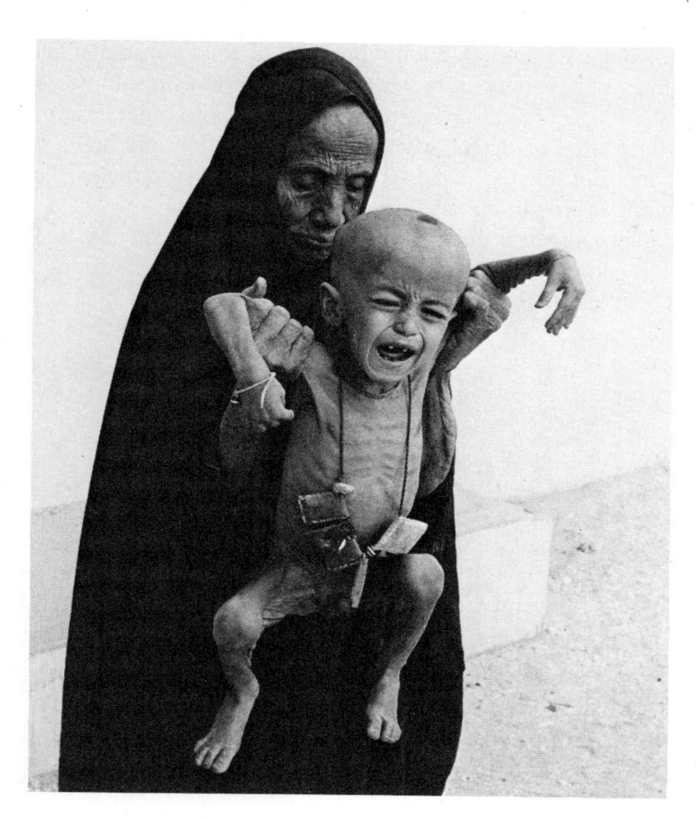

Grandmother and marasmic child—emergency food saved his life (*Photo by Elizabeth Linusson*).

structure and transportation systems, and heavy bureaucracy.'' They conclude that only by overcoming these problems where they exist can there be hope of avoiding the recurrence of famines

Chronic Hunger in the United States

Between May 1971 and June 1974 a Health and Nutrition Examination Survey (HANES) was conducted by the United States Public Health Service. Although health surveys had been conducted previously, this was the first time that an assessment of nutritional status was a constituent part of the survey. Nutrition was included ''to assess and monitor over time the nutritional status of the American people.'' The sample of 28,943 persons between the ages of 1 and 74 years came from 65 different locations within the contiguous 48 states.

The measurement methods employed in HANES to assess nutritional status were intended not only to detect overt signs and symptoms of undernutrition, but also to detect early ''risk'' signals. To obtain information four different kinds of data were sought:

(1) information on the person's dietary intake (kind and quantity of food consumed and its nutritional value), (2) findings of a variety of biochemical tests made on samples of blood and urine to determine the levels of various nutrients, (3) results of clinical examinations by doctors and dentists alerted to detect stigmata of malnutrition and signs or conditions indicative of nutritional problems, and (4) various body measurements that would permit detection of abnormal growth patterns as well as obesity.

Preliminary clinical and anthropometric findings have been published; dietary findings, it is expected, will follow shortly. For assessment of the clinical observations a system of risk categories was adopted: high, moderate (medium), and low. "A high risk sign is assumed to indicate that a person showing this sign has a high probability of either having the deficiency disease or developing it unless he takes more of the lacking nutrient in his diet or as a supplement. A person at moderate or low risk has a moderate or low probability of either having or developing a particular deficiency disease."

The clinical findings showed a generally low or negligible incidence of high risk signs. Moderate risk signs for possible deficiencies of thiamin, riboflavin, niacin, vitamin D, vitamins A and C, calcium, and iodine were generally more common among blacks than whites for the same age-sex-income group.

The anthropometric findings in the age groups 1 to 18 showed blacks in general to be slightly taller and heavier. There were more lean blacks than whites, especially among the men; there were more white obese men than blacks. Obese black women were the highest risk group in terms of high risk to suffer and die from certain diseases (hypertension, heart disease, diabetes).

Of special concern is the state of nutrition of the North American Indians. For the most part, the problems are one of poverty and relative cultural and geographic isolation. In general, their diets are deficient in animal protein, milk, and fruits and vegetables. There are few anthropometric data but the studies available show the average Indian preschool child to be below the average United States white child in both height and weight. From among the 2000 preschool (under 5 years) Navajo Indian children, 616 were admitted to the hospital (Public Health Service Indian Hospital, Tuba City, Arizona) in the 1963 to 1967 period, 15 of them were ill with kwashiorkor and 29 with marasmus. Then, in 1968 infant and child feeding programs were introduced on the reservation. During the period 1969 to 1973 when the intervention food program was in operation, the number of preschool children admitted to the hospital was reduced 18 percent, the number admitted with low body weight for chronological age was reduced 39 percent, marasmus practically disappeared, and the number of cases of kwashiorkor was decreased by 50 percent. Concern is expressed by Van Duzen and her co-workers, who made these observations, that the intervention food programs may not be permanent.

Some Causes of Hunger

The causes of hunger are multiple and interrelated; foremost among them is insufficient food. In some parts of the world, chronic and seasonal hunger are a part of life because of lack of food. Since 1974, when global food reserves were almost completely exhausted, regional crises could no longer be halted with a ready international system of available food. Because of the dangerously low level of food reserves, FAO has been promoting the adoption of an International Undertaking or World Food Security by governments. The objective of the plan is "to ensure adequate world reserve stocks through a scheme of international coordination of national stocks" (Bhattacharjee, 1976).

Actually, for more than a decade total food production has been increasing in both developed and less developed countries and at similar rates. However, the increase has been small per capita in less developed countries because of the rapid population growth. Bhattacharjee, reporting trends in 86 less developed countries over a 15- to 20-year period, stated that in 53 of those countries the supply of food did not meet the domestic demand and even failed to keep apace with the population growth in 34 of them.

Increased production is essential to the solution of the world food problem, especially in the developing countries. For these countries, the World Food Conference of 1974 endorsed greater self-sufficiency in food as a priority objective. The outlook is hopeful, according to Wortman, who believes that "when Fertilization is combined with high-yielding varieties and improved cropping practices, yields can climb quickly and substantially." The prediction is backed up by success stories; for example, in the Punjab, India, agricultural production quadrupled in the mid 1960s. Barriers to farmers' willingness to adopt techniques for increasing production are market facilities that are inadequate and low sale prices. Also, the new highly yielding varieties of crops are more susceptible to pests and require more fertilizer and water than the usual varieties. Wortman challenges governments with one proviso, that "the development efforts of agrarian countries be concentrated less on industry and more on agriculture." From 50 to 60 percent of the people in developing countries are agrarian. Reutlinger and Selowsky in a World Bank publication also note the importance of government. They believe that with realistic assumptions about per capita income growth rates and the possibilities for accelerating food production at prevailing production costs, "that only government intervention specifically designed to subsidize food production or to assist the poor to achieve minimally satisfactory levels of food consumption could lead to the elimination of undernutrition."

For urban dwellers, Lester Brown advocates planting small garden plots indicating that it can make the difference between adequate and inadequate diets. A national program of vegetable gardening has been initiated by Ghana in the rural villages.

An increase in food production to be effectively utilized requires means for its distribution. Provisions for transportation and adequate storage are essential.

Poverty is the universal underlying cause of almost all undernutrition. The basic problem for many of the world's hungry is that they simply do not have enough to eat and lack the purchasing power to buy more. In South India, the poor spend as much as 80 percent of their income on food; the affluent spend as little as 45 percent (Berg). An increase in income is a strong combatant to hunger.

Unavailability of food and poverty are well established causes of hunger—but there are others. Deep-rooted cultural beliefs and customs and also lack of knowledge are additional causative factors. Chandra, from interviews with the mothers of 607 preschool children (21.4 percent suffered severe protein-calorie-malnutrition; only 6.3 percent were of normal weight for age) in Tamil Nadu, India, found that 10 to 18 percent of the mothers thought that the common cold, diarrhea, and undernutrition were natural parts of the child's growth pattern. They believed that eating papayas, mangoes, ragi (a cereal grass), meat, eggs, or pulses (legumes) to be the cause of most illnesses; to them these foods are known as *hot foods* (heat producing). Chandra cited a contrast in that "The agriculturalist has learned to adopt the modern methods of farming, readily and willingly. But yet he is reluctant to change old methods of child rearing."

Similar patterns of malnutrition may result from different causes or combinations of causes. In particular situations it is well to determine the relative importance of the several possible causative factors. Such a study was done by Rawson and Valverde of 250 children under six years of age living with their families in rural Costa Rica. Included in the possible causal factors were: agricultural production, food consumption, domestic economics, childrearing and the cultural aspects of diet and nutrition. The survey encompassed a full agricultural year. The amount of land available to the farmer influenced the nutritional status of the children more than any other variable. When the farmers had access to less than two "manzanas" of land, they usually worked as day laborers and the mothers also worked outside the home. Under those circumstances there seemed to be inadequate management of resources, suboptimal home care and a higher risk of infection and disease. A greater incidence of undernutrition occurred also when there was more than one preschool sibling in the family than when there was one or none.

Causes of hunger differ with specific times and places. Taylor and Taylor point out that in Bangladesh in 1974 the chief causes of hunger were lack of food due to overpopulation and inadequate agricultural production. Added to these were poor weaning practices and a high level of infections. In the Punjab where new procedures had quadrupled agricultural production leading to rapid socioeconomic development, an intensive nutritional and infection control program was carried out between 1968 and 1971. The program resulted in a 50 percent reduction in child mortality and a significant improvement in the weight and height of the children. However, at the termination of the program 17 percent of the children still suffered second and third degree malnutrition. The causal factor that seemed to be responsible for much of the residual malnutrition was large family size and short interpregnancy intervals.

The concluding paragraph of the World Food Conference publication, *Things to Come* (1974), succintly presents the challenge facing the world: "The problems cannot be solved overnight. But it is essential to adopt now a strategy which can gradually set food production moving in the right direction and use foresight to avoid catastrophe. It will not be easy. The issues at stake involve vital national interests, and no international gathering has ever been seen at which these interests were willingly sacrificed. The decisive factor is the political will to face the issues squarely. Unless a positive strategy can be forged to make full use of the world's resources, there can be little alternative to the prospect of hunger on a far larger scale than anything that has been known in the last few centuries."

STUDY QUESTIONS

1. How can it be explained that infants, in parts of the developing world, are better nourished at six months of age than they are at 12 months?
2. What are the two common causes of small birth weight (2500 g or less)?
3. What does research show as to the effect of hunger on the amount and quality of work done?
4. How is it that persons consuming diets grossly inadequate (by accepted standards of daily nutrient intake) can live and work?
5. Is there evidence to support the belief that the improvement in behavior of severely undernourished children being treated in hospitals may be due in part to the stimulus of the hospital environment?

TOPICS FOR INDIVIDUAL INVESTIGATION

1. The body when subjected to the stress of hunger makes physiological adjustment to preserve normality. Enumerate as many of these adjustments as possible.
2. Summarize research available to you on the relationship between hunger and mental development.
3. Cite some of the findings of the first nationwide Health and Nutrition Examination Survey conducted by the U.S. Public Health Service.
4. Discuss some of the causes of hunger and the possible elimination of them.
5. Summarize the behavioral characteristics of children and adults who are underfed.

REFERENCES AND SUGGESTED READING

Abraham, S., F. W. Lowenstein and C. L. Johnson (1974). *Preliminary Findings of the First Health and Nutrition Examination Survey, United States, 1971–1972. Dietary Intake and Biochemical Findings*. DHEW Publ. No. (HRA) 74-1219-1. U.S. Dept. Health, Education and Welfare, Rockville, Md., 1974.

Ashworth, A. Growth rates in children recovering from protein-calorie malnutrition. *Brit. J. Nutr.* 23:835 (1969).

Awdeh, Z. L. Nutrition, infections and immunity. In *Nutrition in the Community*. D. S. McLaren, editor. John Wiley and Sons, New York, 1976, p. 117.

Barnes, R. H. Dual role of environmental deprivation and malnutrition in retarding intellectual development. *Am. J. Clin. Nutr.* 29:912 (1976).

Berg, A. *The Nutrition Factor*. The Brookings Institution, Washington, D.C., 1973, p. 40.

Bhattacharjee, J. P. Population, food and agricultural development. A medium-term view. *Food Policy* 3:179 (1976).

Birch, H. G. and J. D. Gussow. *Disadvantaged Children*. Harcourt Brace Jovanovich, 1970.

Blix, G., Y. Hafvander, and B. Vahlquist (editors). *Famine*. Almquist and Wiksells, Uppsala, Sweden, 1971.

Brasel, J. O. Cellular changes in intrauterine malnutrition. In *Nutrition and Fetal Development*, M. Winick (editor). John Wiley and Sons, New York, 1974, p. 13.

Brown, L. A. Death at an early age. *UNICEF News*, Issue 85 (3):3 (1975).

Brown, L. R. *World Population Trends: Signs of Hope, Signs of Stress*. Worldwatch Paper 8. Worldwatch Institute, Washington, D.C., October 1976, p. 17.

Carlile, W. K., H. G. Olson, J. Gorman, C. McCracken, R. Vander Wagen, and H. Connor. Contemporary nutritional status of North American Indian children. In *Nutrition, Growth and Development of North American Indian Children*, W. M. Moore, M. M. Silverberg, and M. S. Read (editors), DHEW Pub. No. (NIH) 72-26. U.S. Dept. Health, Education and Welfare, Washington, D.C., 1972, p. 47.

Chandra, P. Non-nutritional causes of malnutrition. *Indian J. Nutr. and Diet*. 12:168 (1975).

Chevez, A. and C. Martinez. Nutrition and development of children from poor rural areas V. Nutrition and behavioral development. *Nutr. Repts. Int*. 11:477 (1975).

Cravioto, J. and E. R. DeLicardia. Neurointegrative development and intelligence in children rehabilitated from severe malnutrition. In *Brain Function and Malnutrition: Neuropsychological Methods of Assessment*, J. W. Prescott, M. S. Read, and D. B. Coursin (editors). John Wiley and Sons, New York, 1975, p. 53.

Crosson, P. R. Institutional obstacles to expansion of world food production. *Science* 188:519 (1975).

Dando, W. A. Man-made famines: Some geographical insights from an exploratory study of a millennium of Russian famines. *Ecology Food and Nutrition* 4:219 (1976).

Dobbing, J. The later development of the brain and its vulnerability. In *Scientific Foundations of Paediatrics*, J. A. Davis and J. Dobbing (editors). W. B. Saunders Co., Philadelphia, 1974, p. 565.

Dobbing, J. Nutrition and brain development. In *Present Knowledge in Nutrition*, 4th edition. The Nutrition Foundation, Inc., New York, 1976, p. 453.

Dodge, P. R., A. L. Prensky, and R. D. Feigin. *Nutrition and the Developing Nervous System. The C. V. Mosby Co., St. Louis, 1975, p. 345.*

Eckholm, E. and F. Record. Two Faces of Malnutrition, Worldwatch Paper 9. Worldwatch Institute, Washington, D.C., 1976, p. 10.

Fitzhardinge, P. M. and E. M. Steven. The small-for-date infant. I. Later growth patterns. *Pediatrics* 49:671 (1972).

Food and Agriculture Organization. *Nutrition and Working Efficiency*. Freedom from Hunger Campaign, Basic Study No. 5, Rome, Italy, 1962.

Garn, S. M., C. G. Rohman, M. Behar, F. Viteri, and M. A. Guzman. Compact bone deficiency in protein-calorie malnutrition. *Science* 145:1444 (1964).

Gebre-Medhin, M. and B. Vahlquist. Famine in Ethiopia—a brief review. *Am. J. Clin. Nutr*. 29:1016 (1967).

Gifft, H. H., M. B. Washbon, and G. G. Harrison. *Nutrition, Behavior, and Change*. Prentice-Hall, Inc., Englewood Cliffs, N.J., 1972.

Graham, G. G. The Later Growth of Malnourished Infants; Effects of Age, Severity, and Subsequent Diet. In R. A. McCance and E. M. Widdowson, Eds., *Calorie Deficiencies and Protein Deficiencies*. Little Brown, Boston, Mass., 1968, p. 314.

Hanna, F. M. and R. L. Jackson. Changes in body composition of malnourished infants during repletion. *Annals New York Acad. Sci.* 110:849 (1963).

International Food Policy Research Institute. *Meeting Food Needs in the Developing World: The Location and Magnitude of the Job in the Next Decade*. International Food Policy Research Institute, Washington, D.C., 1976.

Kallen, D. J., editor. *Nutrition, Development and Social Behavior*. DHEW Publication No. (NIH) 73-242. U.S. Government Printing Office, Washington, D.C., 1973.

Kark, R. M. *Food and Hunger in a World of Turmoil*. World Review of Nutrition and Dietetics by G. H. Bourne, Vol. 6. Hafner Publishing, New York, 1966, p. 1.

Keys, A., *et al*. *The Biology of Human Starvation*. Univ. of Minnesota Press, Minneapolis, 1950.

Keller, W. D. and H. A. Kraut. *Work and Nutrition*. World Review of Nutrition and Dietetics by G. H. Bourne, Vol. 3. Hafner Publishing, New York, 1959, p. 69.

Latham, M. C. Nutrition and infection and national development. In *Food: Politics, Economics, Nutrition and Research,* Philip H. Abelson (editor). Amer. Assoc. Adv. Sci., Washington, D.C., 1975, p. 69.

Lechtig, A., H. Delgado, R. Lasky, C. Yarbrough, R. E. Klein, J. P. Habicht, and M. Behar. Maternal nutrition and fetal growth in developing countries. *Am. J. Dis. Child* 129:553 (1975).

Levitsky, D. A. and R. H. Barnes. Nutritional and environmental interactions in the behavioral development of the rat: Long-term effects. *Science* 176:68 (1972).

Lowenstein, F. W. Preliminary clinical and anthropometric findings from the first Health and Nutrition Examination Survey, USA, 171–1972. *Am. J. Clin. Nutr.* 29:918 (1976).

Lubchenco, L. O. Low-birth-weight infant. Outcome. In *Pediatrics,* 15th edition, H. L. Barnett and A. H. Einhorn (editors). Appleton-Century-Crofts, New York, 1972, p. 111.

Mayer, J. Stopping famines before they start. *UNICEF News,* Issue 85(3):18 (1975).

Mayer, J. *U.S. Nutrition Policies in the Seventies*. W. H. Freeman and Co., San Francisco, 1973.

McCance, R. A. *The Bearing of Early Nutrition on Later Development*. Proceedings of the Sixth International Congress of Nutrition. Williams and Wilkins, Baltimore, Md., 1964, p. 74.

McFarlane, H. Nutrition and Immunity. In *Present Knowledge in Nutrition,* 4th edition. The Nutrition Foundation, Inc., New York, 1976, p. 459.

Meredith, H. V. Relation Between Socio-Economic Status and Body Size in Boys Seven to Ten Years of Age. *Amer. J. Diseases of Children* 22:702 (1951).

Monckeberg, F. The effect of malnutrition on physical growth and brain development. In *Brain Function and Malnutrition,* J. W. Prescott, M. S. Read, and D. B. Coursin (editors). John Wiley and Sons, New York, 1975, p. 15.

Morehead, C. D., M. Morehead, D. M. Allen, and R. E. Olson. Bacterial infections in malnourished children. *J. Trop. Ped. and Environmental Child Health* 20:141 (1974).

National Academy Sciences. *World Food and Nutrition Study. Interim Report*. National Academy Sciences, Washington, D.C., 1975.

National Academy Sciences. *World Food and Nutrition Study. Enhancement of Food Production for the United States*. National Academy Sciences, Washington, D.C., 1975.

Niswander, K. R. and M. Gordon. *Collaborative Perinatal Study. The Women and Their Pregnancies,* vol. 1. W. B. Saunders Co., Philadelphia, 1972.

O'Hagan, J. P. National self-sufficiency in food. *Food Policy* 5:355 (1976).

Puffer, R. R. and C. V. Serrano. *Patterns of Mortality in Childhood*. Scientific Publ. No. 262. Pan American Health Organization, Washington, D.C., 1973, pp. 140, 345.

Puyet, J. H., E. F. Downe, and R. Budeir. Nutritional and growth characteristics of Arab refugee children in Lebanon. *Am. J. Clin. Nutr.* 13:147 (1963).

Rawson, I. G. and V. Valverde. The etiology of malnutrition among preschool children in rural Costa Rica. *J. Trop. Ped. and Environmental Health* 22:12 (1976).

Read, M. S. and D. Felson. *Malnutrition, Learning, and Behavior.* DHEW Publ. No. (NIH) 76-1036. Natl. Instit. Child Health and Human Dev., Bethesda, Md., 1976.

Reutlinger, S. and M. Selowsky. *Malnutrition and Poverty.* The Johns Hopkins University Press, Baltimore, 1976, p. 29.

Scott, K. E. and R. Usher. Fetal malnutrition: Its incidence, causes and effect. *Am. J. Obstet. and Gynecol.* 94:951 (1966).

Scrimshaw, N. S. Interactions of malnutrition and infection: Advances in understanding. In *Protein-Calorie Malnutrition,* R. E. Olson, editor. Academic Press, New York, 1975, pp. 353, 360.

Serban, G. (editor). *Nutrition and Mental Functions.* Plenum Press, New York, 1975.

Scrimshaw, N. S., C. E. Taylor, and J. E. Gordon. *Interactions of Nutrition and Infection.* World Health Organization, Geneva, 1968.

Stein, Z., M. Susser, G. Saenger, and F. Marolla. *Famine and Human Development. The Dutch Hunger Winter of 1944–1945.* Oxford University Press, New York, 1975, p. 140.

Taylor, C. E. and E. M. Taylor. Multi-factorial causation of malnutrition. In *Nutrition in the Community,* D. S. McLaren (editor). John Wiley and Sons, New York, 1976, p. 75.

Thomson, A. M. and W. Z. Billewicz. Nutritional status, maternal physique and reproductive efficiency. *Proc. Nutr. Soc.* 22:55 (1963).

Thomson, A. M. and F. E. Hytten. VII. *International Congress of Nutrition Abstracts,* Hamburg 1966, p. 7.

United Nations. *Assessment of the World Food Situation, Present and Future.* The United Nations, New York, 1974.

United Nations. *Things to Come. The United Nations World Food Conference.* The United Nations, New York, 1974.

Van Duzen, J., J. P. Carter, and R. Vander Zwagg. Protein and calorie malnutrition among preschool Navajo Indian children, a follow-up. *Am. J. Clin. Nutr.* 29:657 (1976).

Winick, M. *Malnutrition and Brain Development.* Oxford University Press, New York, 1976.

Winick, M., J. A. Brasel, and P. Rosso. Nutrition and cell growth. In *Nutrition and Development,* M. Winick (editor). John Wiley and Sons, New York, 1972, p. 49.

Winick, M. and A. Noble. Cellular response in rats during malnutrition at various ages. *J. Nutr.* 89: 300 (1966).

Wortman, S. Food and agriculture. *Scientific American* 235: 31 (1976).

Yatkin, U. S. Nutrition and mental development. In *Nutrition in the Community,* D. S. McLaren (editor). John Wiley and Sons, New York, 1976, p. 123.

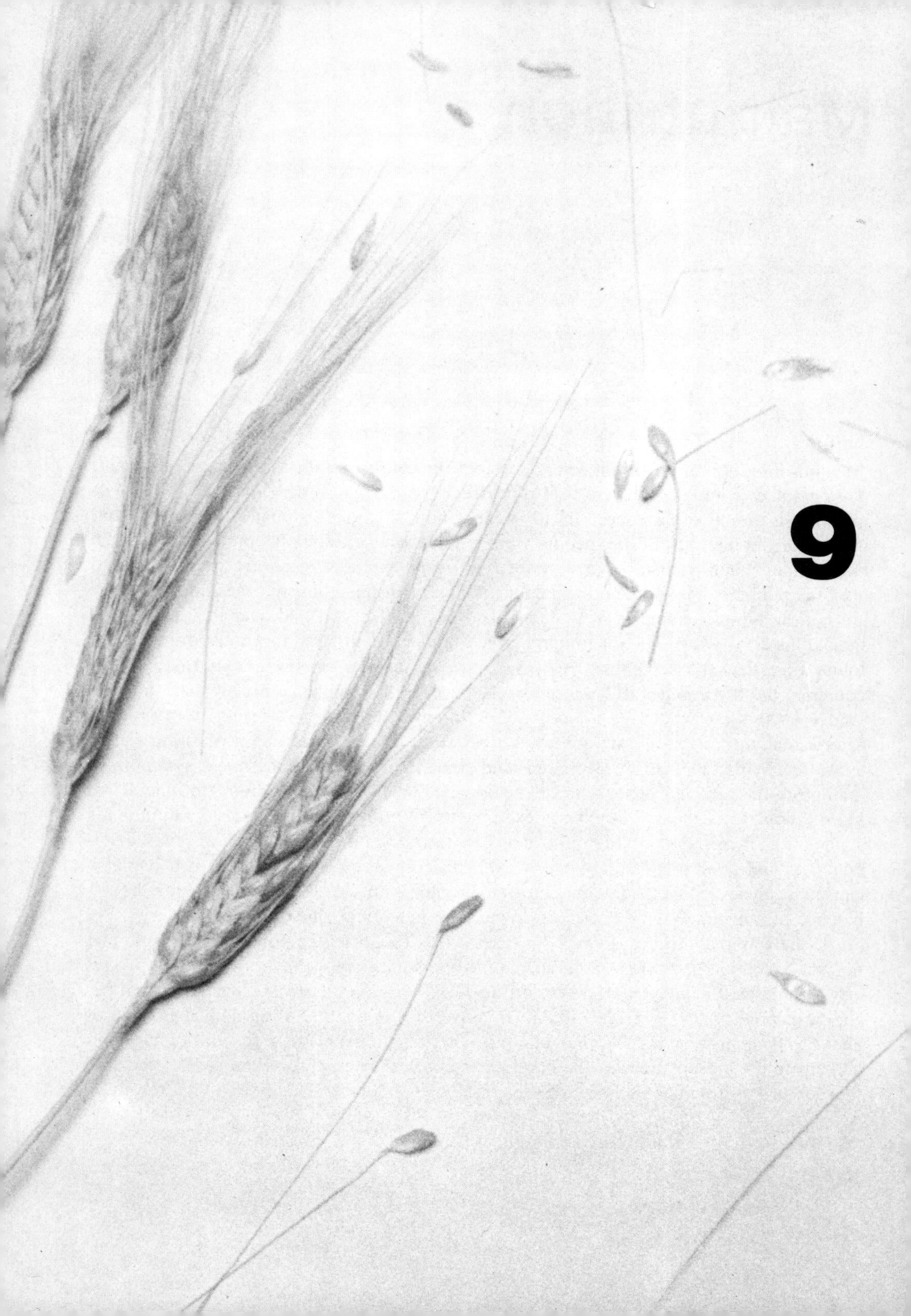
9

Malnutrition

"Malnutrition is more than a medical problem. Its causes are disfunctions in economic, demographic, cultural and ecological processes," said Taylor and Taylor in 1976. Malnutrition is found everywhere. In 1974 the United Nations estimated that about 460 million of the then 3.8 billion people were malnourished. Gershoff pointed out in 1976 that although nutritionists have described and used pictures of severe malnutrition to alert the public to the problem of malnutrition and that these severe cases do exist, they are not the typical examples of malnourished people. He said that over the years when he and his co-workers were examining large numbers of children in Thailand they never found more than 0.5 percent of true marasmus (see page 262). He thought that in some countries the percentages of marasmus and kwashiorkor might be higher than in Thailand yet "the overwhelming majority of children in the world suffering from protein-calorie malnutrition do not demonstrate gross signs of marasmus or kwashiorkor." He, as well as Williams, Jelliffe, McLaren, and others, have given as the major symptom of malnutrition "retarded growth and development," which is "not dramatic unless one knows the ages of the children being examined." Worthy of serious consideration is his statement that the lack of "high prevalence of hard-to-find clinical signs has caused scientists to fail to impress policy-makers with the urgency of the problem." It has also caused agencies concerned with nutrition problems in the world to consider the incidence of nutritional deficiencies far lower than is the real situation.

Where is malnutrition found? In general it is found where poverty is the rule and not the exception and where ignorance and superstition are rampant. "Absolute" poverty was defined in 1970 by the World Bank (UNICEF News 86/1975) as an annual per capita income of $50 or less. "Relative" poverty was defined as an annual income of above $50/capita/year but less than one-third of the national average for the country concerned. In the presentation for the Foreign Assistance Program for 1968, AID* declared that for 400 million people United States foreign economic assistance is a vital resource.

*Agency for International Development of U.S.A.

They said that one fourth of all people on earth exist on incomes of less than $3 per week. It was estimated in 1976 by the World Bank that 645 million people were living in *absolute* or *relative* poverty, with 440 million in Asia.

Surveys have shown that in the United States income level is an important factor although not the only one in less-than-desirable nutritional status. It has been demonstrated that malnutrition in the United States is one cause of the toll that disease takes in the children of migrant workers, the American Indian, and older citizens.

In 1973 an investigation in Latin America by the Pan American Health Organization (see page 308) showed that 57 percent of 35,000 deaths reported in children under five years had malnutrition as either an underlying or associated cause of death.

Cicely Williams (1976) noted that there are many aspects of nutrition that have worsened in the last 30 years in spite of the efforts of all concerned.

Malnutrition leads to disease, either acute or subacute, which can only be diagnosed by medical examination. In the subacute stages of malnourishment, individuals may only be approaching an illness. As is so often seen in the developing countries, an infectious disease such as measles or whooping cough in children or the conditions caused by hookworm or other body-invading parasites precipitates the illness in the person who has been gradually weakened by malnutrition. At the same time, malnutrition may determine not only the incidence but also the progress and severity of the disease. It may favor the invasion of the agent causing the disease and encourage the development of secondary infections, thus delaying recovery.

Illness, with all of its attendant drains on the individual, the family, the community, and even the economy of a nation, would alone justify the world's attention to the problem of malnutrition. The high death rate in most developing countries, though decreasing, still is strikingly illustrated by the average length of life. It was said a few years ago that an infant in some Far Eastern countries had then as much chance to live to be 5 years of age as an infant born in the United States had to live to be 65 years of age. The exact ages in this comparison may vary as situations change, but the relative changes are still strikingly different.

As mentioned previously, inability to work and lack of energy are seen in malnourished people. Although these people often are called lazy, the wonder is not that they do not do more work on their low food intake but that they manage to do so much.

Without fail, growth is depressed when the young body is ill fed. Often this is the first sign of inadequate food. Formerly, we paid little attention to slower physical growth and development in children in some countries; we even accepted, as if it were an innate genetic factor, that a man's wrist bones were the size of those of a ten-year-old boy in the United States. Recent studies in postwar Japan and in many other parts of the world have shown that adequate food during growth can make a difference in the adult size of peoples formerly thought to be predestined to be small in stature.

Within the past several decades severe loss of weight has been seen by most people, either firsthand or in newspaper pictures of people in famine areas. Almost no one presently can be unaware of it as a factor in nutrition.

Within recent years, scientific evidence has increasingly shown that, in severe malnutrition, the potential for intellectual development can be permanently damaged in human beings. Social behavior also has been observed to be changed in some diseases of malnutrition; this is almost universally seen with kwashiorkor, as discussed on page 262.

Gershoff believed that the United States Congress lacks a sense of urgency about malnutrition in the world because it does not have a clear idea of the primary function of the Food and Agriculture Organization (FAO), or its future directions. Neither does the United States Congress understand the 88 intergovernmental organizations that together "with FAO seek to improve world food, agriculture, and nutrition." It is also true that United States policy is made by a score of governmental agencies with no agency having the final authority and responsibility "for making or implementing our policy toward FAO so our policy positions are negative and reactive rather than positive and creative." In concluding his 1976 Trulson Memorial Lecture Gershoff said that billions of dollars are being spent each year on nutrition programs (both international and domestic) with little communication between the many agencies concerned. He emphasized that "the establishment of a nutrition office—at a high level in the executive branch of our government—is essential to coordinate and evaluate existing programs and to point out areas requiring new and more effective effort." This proposal is not new, but those who understand the worldwide needs to deal more effectively with malnutrition will understand its present urgency.

It is difficult to describe the needs for a solution of the problem of malnutrition more succinctly and adequately than is done in "Malnutrition Disease," published by WHO in 1963. It states:

The solution of the problem of the hungry must take into account complex factors affecting almost every aspect of the life of man—climatic, economic, social and educational, religious and cultural. The solution will depend upon achieving cooperation between governments, national and international agencies, and workers in many scientific fields with the active participation not only of people in the developed countries but also the sufferers from malnutrition themselves.

TYPES OF MALNUTRITION

We have chosen to mention 12 of the most prevalent conditions of malnutrition in today's world and to discuss four of these in detail to show how their causes and effects are interwoven into a country's social and economic structure.

The most common conditions of malnutrition in the world today are:

1. Marasmus, a gross chronic calorie deficiency is discussed further on page 262.

2. Kwashiorkor, usually defined as protein-calorie malnutrition is discussed further on page 262.

3. Beriberi.

4. Endemic goiter is discussed on pages 257–262.

5. Anemia. There is little doubt that iron deficiency anemia is one of the most common nutritional deficiencies in the world. Pregnant and lactating women are especially vulnerable to anemia as are growing children. In these individuals, the demands for the formation of hemoglobin, the iron-containing component of blood, are greatest. The maintenance of an optimum blood supply depends on the capacity of the body to generate new cells with sufficient amounts of hemoglobin so that the blood can perform its oxygen-carrying function. As has been shown by repeated surveys anemia affects young children and women in affluent western countries but even a larger percent of *poor* people in underdeveloped countries. Enough iron and high-grade proteins are often not found in poverty-restricted diets to satisfy the needs for building of hemoglobin. In one type of anemia, vitamin C and one of the B vitamins (folacin) are lacking in the diet.

6. Xerophthalmia, a disease of the eye caused by lack of vitamin A and frequently resulting in blindness, has for a long time been considered one of the serious health problems in the world. It is a deficiency disease which, in its most severe form, involves a drying of the membranes of the eye and other changes that cause destruction of the eye, and ultimately blindness. This disease is caused by a lack of vitamin A; young children are most frequently affected, although the disease may be seen in all ages. Young children who have only occasional small pieces of fruit or green vegetable with a diet made up largely of a starchy food fall easy prey to xerophthalmia. In parts of the world where red palm oil, which is high in vitamin A, is produced and consumed, the condition is rarely seen. Night blindness and possibly decreased resistance to infection (though the latter is not well proven) are also results of a diet low in vitamin A.

   Xerophthalmia is a major cause of blindness in several Asian countries; it is also found in Africa, Latin America, and in the Middle East. It is frequently precipitated by infectious diseases such as chicken pox, measles, and gastroenteritis probably because these diseases interfere with the absorption of vitamin A. With low intakes of this vitamin reduced absorption is of course disastrous. Xerophthalmia appeared during World War I when the high price of butter (a good source of vitamin A) forced many people to substitute oleomargarine, then unfortified with vitamin A as it usually is today. Now all skim milk distributed by the United States to Asian countries is fortified with the vitamin A once taken out with the cream. It is thought that before this fortification some of the xerophthalmia in Asia may have been "man-made."

7. Scurvy is mostly seen in drought and famine areas of the arid countries of the Near East. However, some cases were reported in recent years in Canada and the United States, mostly due here to ignorance and most frequently seen in the older people who live alone in the slums of industrial areas. Scurvy occurs when there is a low

intake of vitamin C which is known to be necessary for the formation of collagen, the cementing substance of the cell walls. Vitamin C is also needed for the maintenance of healthy gums and for the functioning of some glands. Growth causes greater need for vitamin C, therefore growing infants and children, and pregnant and lactating mothers show deficiencies most readily.

8. Rickets, seen in North America largely in the 1920s and 1930s, is a disease of infants and young children whose bones are growing rapidly. This disease is caused primarily by a lack of vitamin D, needed for the deposition of calcium in the bones. Vitamin D is found naturally in small amounts in only a few foods such as eggs, cream, and butter and in larger amounts of certain fish. Mostly, however, children do not receive enough vitamin D in foods unless they drink vitamin D-fortified milk as they now do in many parts of the United States. The pro-vitamin of vitamin D occurs in or on the skin and is converted into active vitamin D by the action of sunlight on the skin. Rickets is most severe in children whose diets contain little calcium. Except for the bones of fish and of poultry that are eaten in some parts of the world, milk is the chief food source of calcium. Rickets is found where there is little sunlight or where young infants and children are kept indoors, as sometimes occurs even in sunny, tropical climates because a "pale skin" is valued. Rickets has been known, in the past, to occur in Ibadan, Nigeria, where mothers covered their children to shield them from the sun even though their dark skin would have protected them somewhat from the ultraviolet rays of the sunlight. A survey done in the United States by the Academy of Pediatrics as late as 1960 revealed a surprising number of rickets cases. In 1965, Dale in a survey done in Seattle, Washington, to determine the seven-day intake of 150 children (ages birth through 17 years) showed a great variation of the amount of vitamin D ingested. The vitamin was in the fortified milk as well as in other foods to which it had been added by the manufacturer. A number of preschool children, however, had irregular amounts of this vitamin. She recommended vigilance concerning the levels of vitamin D intake in order to insure the ingestion of enough and not too much.

9. Pellagra is essentially a disease of maize-eating people who are too poor to afford other foods such as meat, fish, or other whole-grain cereals that carry the needed vitamin, niacin, or supply sufficient amounts of the amino acid tryptophan that the body converts into niacin. Large numbers of cases of this disease occurred early in this century in the southern United States; it still is a problem in parts of Africa, India, Egypt, Portugal, Latin America, and Yugoslavia.

10. Ariboflavinosis is, as its name indicates, caused by the lack of riboflavin, one of the vitamins of the B complex. Tissue changes occur in the tongue, mucous membranes of the lips and mouth, and the skin around the base of the nose. Improvement in the diet causes a healing of these lesions. Although this disease is still referred to as a problem, there are fewer data available on its frequency and geography than for many other conditions. The association of this condition with a lack of vitamin A probably increases its importance.

11. Obesity in the affluent countries is currently one of the greatest problems in nutrition. It is said that 10 to 15 percent of the adolescent population can be called obese, with a higher incidence found in girls. The relationship of this condition to heart disease and other degenerative diseases as well as cancer has directed much attention and research to it. Obesity is known to arise from a complex interrelationship of psychological, physiological, environmental, and genetic factors as well as an excess of calories.

12. Dental caries is often listed as a disease of nutrition because its incidence can be reduced by 50 percent with adequate water fluoridation, limited use of sticky, highly sweet foods, and thorough cleaning of the teeth after the ingestion of food. Statistics on the incidence of this disease have caused it to be called the chief disease of nutrition in North America. Its incidence in other parts of the world is variable, being highest where the intake of refined carbohydrates is greatest. The fluorine content of the water supply is another factor in the incidence of dental caries.

Four diseases of malnutrition are discussed in detail.

ENDEMIC GOITER

There are estimated to be 200 million cases of endemic goiter in the world today, according to a World Health Organization (WHO) report in 1960. This disease has been known for hundreds of years, but only in this century has the science of nutrition provided the evidence as to how this disease may be prevented. A century ago a French scientist provided the correct theory about the cause and prevention of endemic goiter, but his contemporaries simply did not believe him. This has recurred throughout science and human history—discoveries have been made but not accepted because the ideas have been ahead of their time.

The major cause of endemic goiter is a deficiency of iodine in the diet. This is a simple statement and one well verified by extensive experiments; by analyses of drinking water, soil, and food; and by clinical data. Study of this disease illustrates how much easier it is to understand discoveries when they fit in with the background of science and what we already know, and how difficult it is to accept that which is new when it is different from current beliefs.

Goiter is no respecter of persons or places (see map). It occurs in some part of almost every region and country of the world, so it is obvious that climate or weather or temperature is not the causative factor. All people, whatever their race, color, creed, or socioeconomic group, are susceptible to this disease. The high incidence of endemic goiter in the United States only 50 years ago led to the experimental studies in the Great

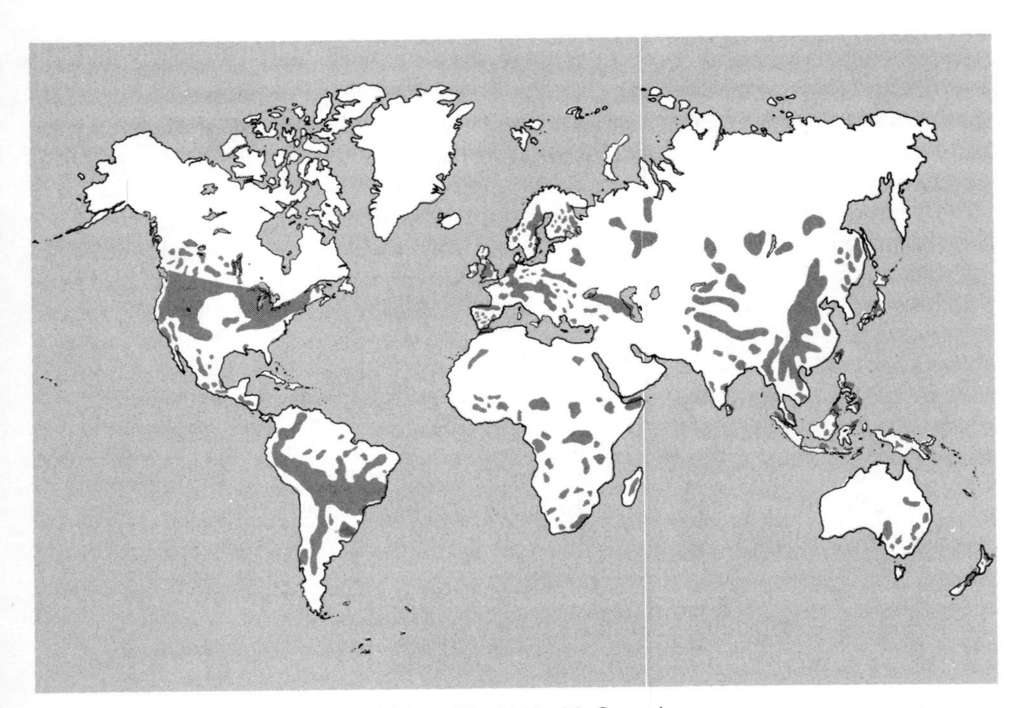

Goiter areas of the world (*Adapted from World Health Organization WHO activities in nutrition 1948–1964,* 1965, p. 25).

Lakes region that demonstrated how this disease could be prevented.

The story of this disease and how to prevent it involves chemical elements and compounds, some physiological terms, and a gland of the body. Definitions and explanations of these terms will lead to fuller understanding of this deficiency disease.

1. *Iodine* is a chemical element first discovered in 1811 by a French chemist, Bernard Courtois, when he was preparing saltpeter for gunpowder for Napoleon's army.
2. *The thyroid,* a ductless gland at the base of the neck, uses iodine to make a hormone needed by the body for its normal processes. The name thyroid was given to this gland by an English physician, Thomas Wharton, in 1646; he was the first to determine the site, size, and weight of the gland.
3. *Thyroxine* is a hormone secreted by the thyroid gland, which must be supplied with iodine in order to make this hormone; Thyroxine was first prepared by Edward C. Kendall of the Mayo Clinic in 1914.
4. *Endemic goiter,* sometimes called simple goiter, is a condition of enlargement of the thyroid. Endemic means that it occurs in a large number of the people in a particular community or location. There are many other types of goiter and thyroid gland disorders that are different from endemic goiter in their effects and causes.

5. *Goitrogenic factors* are ones that produce goiter; the word goitrogenic comes from the Greek root *genic,* which means "giving rise to."

The Discovery of Iodine and the Cause of Goiter

Goiter is believed to have occurred for thousands of years and to have been described by the ancient Chinese, early Hindus, and the Egyptians. Difficulties in language, different meanings of words, and lack of knowledge in early times about the organs of the body leave us uncertain as to exactly how long this disease has been known.

At the beginning of the nineteenth century, biological and medical research had progressed to a stage where more exact and careful studies could be made on goiter. After Courtois discovered iodine (1811), a Swiss physician, Jean Francois Coindet (1820), recommended its use for treatment of goiter. However, the doses used were too large and there were harmful effects, so the use of iodine fell into disrepute. Some 30 years later, a French chemist, Gaspard Adolph Chatin, published results of research where he determined the iodine content of air, water, soil, and plants in many parts of

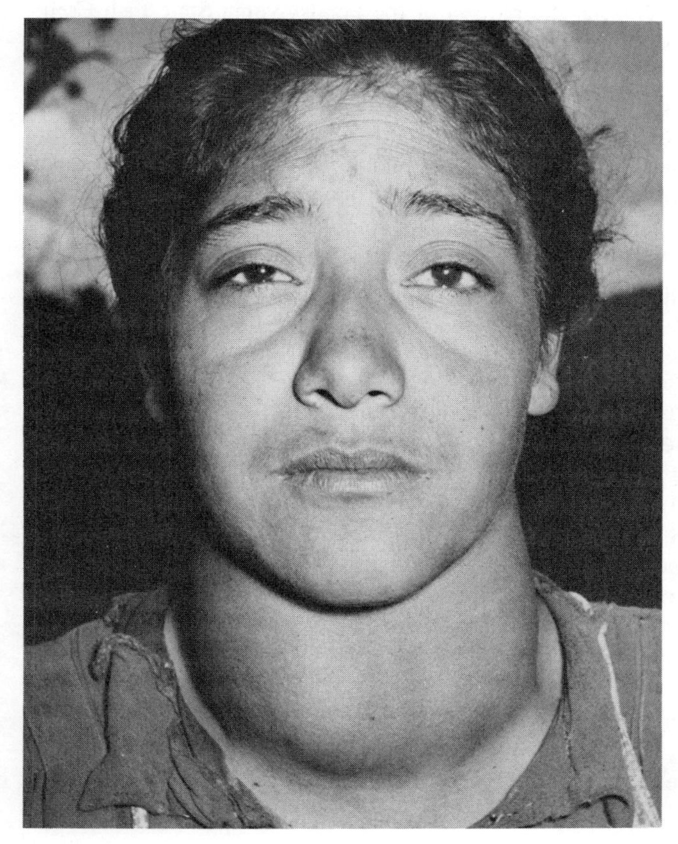

Several million cases of edemic goiter exist in the world today (*Courtesy World Health Organization*).

Europe. He found that in Paris, where goiter did not occur, the people had a daily intake of iodine five times as high as the people of Lyons and Turin, where there was moderate goiter. In the alpine villages where there was much goiter, the people obtained only one-tenth as much iodine a day as the Parisians had. Chatin concluded that iodine deficiency was the cause of goiter, but his contemporaries rejected this idea.

Little progress was made in understanding the cause of goiter until 1895, when Eugen Baumann, a German chemist, analyzed the thyroid gland and showed that it contained iodine in small amounts. At last scientists had a connection between iodine and goiter. However, since goiter was not a fatal disease, it did not attract as much attention or study as did some of the more serious diseases.

In the United States there were serious problems in the cattle industry in various areas of the country, especially in Michigan and in parts of the West. There were heavy losses of young lambs, calves, and colts; piglets were born hairless and were stillborn or died within a few days. At this time (1907), a young medical research scientist, David Marine, in Cleveland, Ohio, began studies on the thyroid that were to lead to worldwide recognition that deficiency of iodine caused goiter. He first analyzed the thyroids of sheep, cattle, and hogs and found a relationship between iodine and the structure of the gland. Then he spent several years, at the request of the Pennsylvania State Fish Commission, investigating the cause of thyroid disease in fish; this disease interfered with the raising of brook trout in the fish hatcheries. He eventually showed that the problem could be prevented by inclusion of iodine in the food of fish.

If iodine prevented goiter in farm animals and in fish, then surely the same must be true for humans; but experimental evidence was essential. Dr. Marine began work in 1916 with school girls in Akron, Ohio. He surveyed all the girls from the fifth to the twelfth grades to find the incidence of goiter. There were 4466 girls examined, and 56 percent had enlarged thyroids. With the approval of the local medical society, the school board, and the school superintendent, treatment by iodine (sodium iodide) was begun in 1917 for all girls who elected to have it. Examinations of the thyroid were made twice yearly. At the end of thirty months, Dr. Marine reported:

> . . . of 2190 pupils taking 2 gm. sodium iodide twice yearly (given in 0.2 gm. doses daily, for ten consecutive school days each spring and autumn), five have shown enlargement of the thyroid, while of 2405 pupils not taking the prophylactic 495 have shown enlargement of the thyroid. Of 1182 pupils with thyroid enlargement at the first examination and who took prophylactic, 773 thyroids have decreased in size, while of 1084 pupils with thyroid enlargement at the first examination and who did not take the prophylactic, 145 thyroids have decreased in size. These figures demonstrate in a striking manner both the preventive and therapeutic effects.

This was one of the first large-scale controlled studies on humans of a dietary-deficiency disease.

Dr. Marine shared his results with R. Klinger in Zurich, Switzerland, where goiter was very severe in some areas. Klinger undertook similar treatments of school children and obtained even more striking results in prevention and improvement of goitrous conditions.

Some investigators believe that there is a relationship between goiter and cretinism and the accompanying feeble mindedness and deaf mutism. However, this has not been clearly defined, and more research is needed to clarify this question.

India is one of several countries that have attacked the problem of goiter. A pilot study was made between 1956 and 1962 to see whether iodized salt would be effective in preventing goiter. Two zones were chosen, and about 5000 people in each were examined for incidence of goiter. One zone received iodized salt and the other received ordinary salt for a five-year period. The people were then reexamined. In the zone where iodized salt was used, the number of goiter cases was reduced from 40 percent to about 17 percent of the population. In the zone receiving ordinary salt, the number of goiter cases remained at the same level it had been. The Indian government followed up this study by arranging to produce iodized salt for the people in several states of India.

Age and Sex Incidence

In areas where goiter is endemic, it may occur in individuals at any age; in highly goitrous areas, babies may be born with goiter. The highest incidence is in girls twelve to eighteen years of age and boys nine to thirteen years old. Pubertal changes appear to increase the need by the thyroid gland for iodine. Females are more susceptible to goiter than males.

Goitrogenic and Other Factors

Iodine deficiency results in goiter, but there may be other factors involved. There are naturally occurring substances in some foods, especially cabbage, rape, rutabaga, turnips, and related plants, which block the utilization of iodine by the thyroid. Certain sulphur-containing drugs act as antithyroid agents, apparently by interfering with the production of thyroxine.

There are genetic differences in susceptibility to goiter. Some research studies also show that infection and contamination of drinking water may be factors in causing goiter.

Food Sources of Iodine

The iodine content of foods depends on the soil in which they are grown; some plants, such as spinach, take more from the soil than others. Seaweeds are rich in iodine because they collect and concentrate iodine from seawater. All seafoods are good sources of iodine.

In general, the vegetables, especially green leafy ones and legumes, contain more iodine than cereals and fruits; meat and milk are between these groups. All foods are highly variable, and foods in the markets were grown in various areas. For this reason, a practical, economical way to make iodine available to everyone is to add it to salt. Iodine, in the form of potassium iodide, is added to table salt in the United States as a public health measure. No one is compelled to use iodized salt; plain salt is also available in the markets. But iodized salt is a wise choice; it is a means of restoring to salt what was present in the original crude substance before it was purified. Continuous educational programs are necessary to remind consumers of the reasons for choosing iodized salt for cooking and for table use.

Many other countries also use some form of iodized salt; a study group of WHO in 1952 recommended that "all food salts should be iodized compulsorily in any country or area in which goiter is endemic." However, many problems are encountered because in tropical countries the crude, moist salt used renders the iodine compound unstable.

MARASMUS AND KWASHIORKOR

These two conditions of malnutrition will be discussed together because at present there is confusion in differentiating the etiology of each, and the specific causes are also somewhat in dispute. That both conditions are important and must be dealt with in international nutrition programs is attested to by Jelliffe who in 1975 estimated that there were then about 10 to 20 million young children with severe syndromes of kwashiorkor or marasmus at one time in the world and that most of them died without treatment.

In 1966 he had defined kwashiorkor saying, "By unofficial international agreement the term kwashiorkor is currently used almost universally for the particular extreme form of protein-calorie malnutrition of early childhood even though there is disagreement about the diagnostic criteria."

In 1935, Dr. Cicely Williams used the word kwashiorkor for a disease for which in a 1933 article she had described the symptoms seen in twenty cases in Ghana (then called the Gold Coast). She said that she used the word merely as a confession of ignorance.

It is known that this disease has had at times some 50 different names all around the world. It had been called "fatty liver disease" or "sugar baby," "m'buoki" in the Congo, "dystrophie des farineux" in French, "mehlnahrschaden" in German, "nutritional distrophy" in India, and "distrofia pluricarencial infantil" in Latin America. The recognition that it was the same in Guatemala, India, or the Congo represented progress in clinical diagnosis of it.

McLaren (1976) said that "generalized malnutrition of the protein-energy type occupies rather a specialized position." He pointed out that it is the infant and preschool children who are primarily affected and he postulated that is much more characteristic of "rural communities or new slum dwellers who have not yet abandoned their dietary habits and infant feeding practices." Others believe that we do not yet have sufficient comparable data to show this to be universally true. It is generally agreed, however, that kwashiorkor is found in weanlings who are largely fed on such foods as cassava, plan-

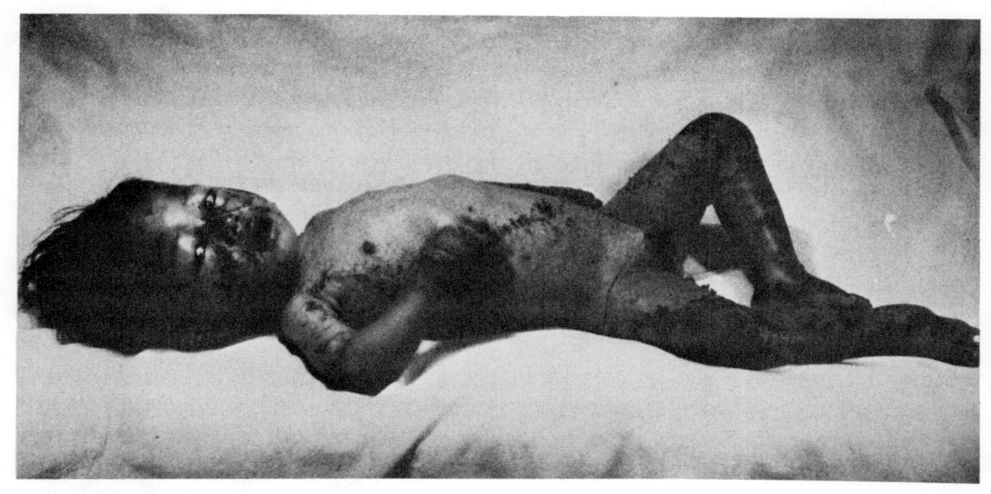

Child with kwashiorkor upon admission to the doctor's care.

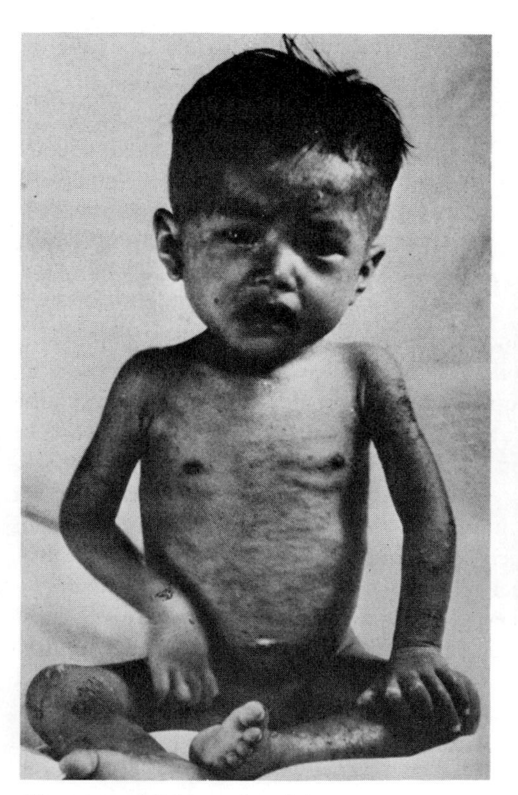

The same child four days later.

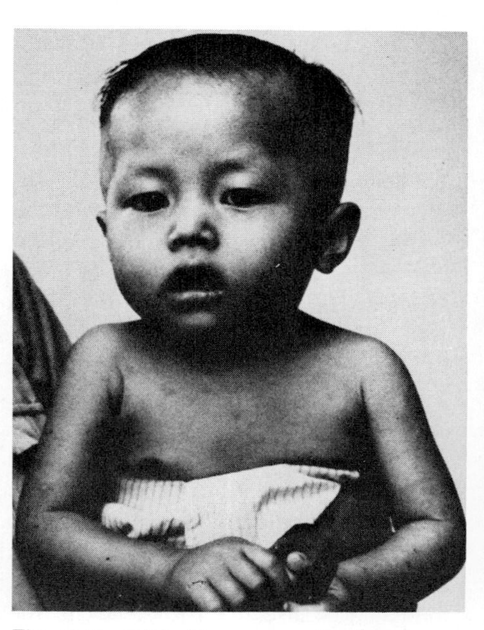

The same child after one month of care.

tains, yams (a large vegetable root), as is true in parts of Africa. Infectious diseases are known to precipitate attacks of kwashiorkor as discussed on page 271.

There is at the present time much confusion as to the relative importance of kwashiorkor and the need for improving the level of protein intake of the world's malnourished children. Recent statistics on malnutrition among the world's poor point clearly to the increase of marasmus in relation to the disease previously described and designated as kwashiorkor. Urbanization where nursing mothers work, the decline of breastfeeding (previously often until the child was two or three years of age), and the use of expensive commercial infant's formulae often overdiluted with water (a source of infectious disease) are universally accepted causes of marasmus that appears frequently in the infant under one year of age. Kwashiorkor or a form of severe protein-calorie malnutrition* as Jelliffe defined it in contrast, appeared in the past and does now in the postweaned child. In countries, such as some African countries, high starch and low protein staple foods such as cassava, yams, manioc, and taro are fed to weanlings. Ignorance on the part of the mother and father of the young child's need for protein in these growing years, a lack of availability of protein-rich foods, and the cost of these must even at present be given at least as important causes for a diet too low in protein to allow children of these ages to grow satisfactorily.

All these foods of the postweaned child have two things in common. They are

1. High in starch and low in needed protein, with these characteristics varying with the different foods.
2. Highly diluted with water.

Why is the weanling not given animal protein foods? In many areas, the family cannot afford meat, milk, eggs, or perhaps even fish; or these foods may actually not be available. In Africa, the tsetse fly, until international organizations such as FAO discovered and used methods for its control, made the raising of cattle practically impossible. In some places, although such foods as milk and eggs are available, the child does not get them because of the ignorance and superstition of its parents. In one tribe, eating eggs is considered a sign of greed because these people think it uneconomical not to let the greater food-producing chicken develop from the egg. In other groups, eggs are said to make girls licentious. The author observed this in a Zulu community during a 1972 food demonstration by a public health nutritionist, as the older women shook their heads and looked distrubed when young mothers were encouraged to eat eggs. In Sierra Leone, eggs are not given to children below the age of five years because they are thought to cause them to steal. In Southern Rhodesia, it is believed that they cause baldness and sterility. When a local African in one area sees a person suffering from what a western observer conceptualizes as inadequate nutrition, the African may believe instead that the disease came about because the child's parents broke sexual taboos. There are kwashiorkor victims in cultures where milk is considered a disgusting food

*Presently referred to by some authorities as protein-energy malnutrition.

because it is a body secretion. In one tribe, only milk from cows of the mother's family's herd is considered fit food for her and her child. It is said that milk is so little valued by certain pastoral tribes in the north of Uganda that the people live on millet and give their milk to their herdsmen. Tribes such as the Masai, who use milk and blood and meat as a food, have no kwashiorkor, whereas their nonmeat-eating and nonmilk-drinking neighbors, the Kikuyu, have a high incidence. This was evident in 1972 when the author observed many Masai and their neighbors the Kikuyu and Mbutu; she saw the large-bellied Kikuyu children along the roadside. Differences in food habits of people living in areas next to each other make the contrast even more noticeable.

UNICEF News No. 2 reports the results of a story of one young Kikuyu mother who improved her family's diet remarkably by cultivation of a kitchen garden and changing old family dietary patterns.

Another cultural factor that operates to promote undernourishment for the preschool child is that his or her order of demand on the scarce food of the family is low. The father, or the breadwinner, has first call, and all other adults get their share before the small child. For example, these people do not know that the growing body demands more good food relative to size than does the adult body. Stories are told that Masai men and warriors eat their fill of the cow they have killed before taking home any for the women and children.

There is no doubt that the picture, as Gershoff has said, is one of "an intertwining web of social, economic, political, and magio-religious, technological, attitudinal, and environmental factors." We cannot, however, discuss here all the factors that make the desirable protein-rich animal foods scarce. The references on page 281 give further information.

Attention was directed in 1971 by the Joint Expert Committee on nutrition of FAO and WHO to the need for an accepted classification and definition of protein-calorie malnutrition before McLaren's article on the "Great Protein Fiasco" was published in 1974. This Expert Committee pointed out that in some countries there are no data on the prevalence of protein-calorie malnutrition and even where data exist they are not comparable with those collected in other countries. They encouraged the extension of studies of prevalence and that the same criteria be used. Not only would a clearer understanding of the prevailing pattern of malnutrition in any region furnish information concerning the nature of the dietary deficiency but it would have a bearing on the preventive measures that would be most appropriate. Some writers have accused the so-called classical theory of kwashiorkor as crediting this disease to a deficiency of protein with a relatively adequate intake of calories, whereas marasmus was said by this theory to have been caused by an overall deficiency of energy and protein. It must, however, be pointed out that Jelliffe and Collis had referred to kwashiorkor as one of the severe forms of protein-calorie malnutrition even before 1970. Gopalan and his coworkers in 1968 in India produced evidence that there are no quantitative or qualitative differences in the diet of children who develop kwashiorkor or marasmus. They proposed that the difference was the capacity of the child to adapt to the deficient diet. It is certain that the problem does differ from the African countries where kwashiorkor had been studied most and India where Gopalan worked. Waterlow in 1971 urged efforts on agreement of a qualitative as well as quantitative classification for use in hospital treatment as well as prevention in the community. He proposed using the percentage of expected weight at the given height calculated from the 50th percentile of the Boston Standard (see reference on page 283.

Almost all workers in international nutrition agree that in kwashiorkor, edema is present because of relative protein deficiency in relation to the calorie intake.

Williams had pointed out in 1931 and 1932 that slight edema of the foot, along with slight flabbiness of the child's flesh, "puniness" and possibly coldness of the extremeties were early danger signals that alerted her when she saw these children in her "Gold Coast" (modern Ghana) clinics. She said in 1975 that as early as 1932 she had surmised a protein or amino acid deficiency and had treated and cured the difficulty with milk. She has questioned the difference of the observations of those physicians who work in clinics seeing many children in a country and those scientists who work in a laboratory.

Some history of the identification of the conditions now called kwashiorkor is necessary as background for the present day controversy.

The word kwashiorkor which Williams gave to this condition comes from the Ga tribe, one of the principal tribes in Ghana. One of her Ga friends said that it was a ritual name given to the second child; there are many "ritual" names in that part of the world. Of course, it is the first child who gets kwashiorkor. Many clinicians have seen this as a disease of the "deposed child"; when a new baby is born, the first child is somewhat "pushed out." Some of the Ga people say that kwashiorkor really means "first-second." Charity Dagadu, a Ga from Ghana, when a student in the author's nutrition class, said that the modern Ga mother uses the word to refer to the jealousy the first child has for the new baby and she said that this belief was prevalent among Ga mothers. Emotional replacement is undoubtedly one factor in the disease in some cases at least, and how much this affects a child's appetite can only be speculated. It is known that where starchy root vegetables are the staple food of a people the "pap" made from these and fed to the "weanling" provides calories but little protein.

Some symptoms now described as a part of kwashiorkor have been described in early literature. As early as 1906 it was suspected that "that disease common in West Africa" was due to a high starch diet. French, German, and Italian physicians had in the early literature stated that this disease in German called "mehlnahrschaden" was due to a high starch diet. In 1959 an older physician in Rome told the author that he did not believe the low protein intake theory. In India it was called "nutritional distrophy," which would scarcely distinguish it from marasmus.

It has long been observed that kwashiorkor, a disease where edema has always been considered to be a common symptom and the distended belly cannot be missed, was to be found more frequently in children two to four years of age. In many countries where this disease has been found in children who were nursed at breast to two or more years until the mother became pregnant with the next. The weanling who then was fed by the mother on a high-starch-low-protein food developed kwashiorkor and often died suddenly with an infectious disease such as measles.

Marasmus described as a disease where the body is as thin as it can possibly be. The wastage of subcutaneous and muscular tissue gives the appearance of extreme gauntness. It is usually found in children under two years of age. During extreme famines it has been seen often but in more recent years it is becoming more common in large urban areas where mothers have substituted overdiluted commercial infant's formulae for breast feeding. Marasmic children are especially prone to gastroenteritis which often proves fatal.

Reliable statistics from the many countries where both marasmus and kwashiorkor are found are not presently available. Questions are, therefore, being raised as to whether urbanization is a real cause in the relative rise of the cases of marasmus in relation to kwashiorkor. Other questions of distinguishing these two diseases are now being posed. It is certain that agreement must be reached on the differentiating symptoms and methods of precise diagnosis as well as the use of comparable data from community to community and country to country.

Many symptoms of kwashiorkor have been described in the literature. An early article from Mexico described a disease with a "snakelike" skin that Williams had characterized as a "crazy pavement" skin. In 1918, reports of a similar condition came from Africa; a similar condition was described in Japan in 1923, in France in 1927, and in 1929 in Cuba. During the next two decades, reports came from Central and South America, from parts of the Caribbean such as Jamaica, from Hungary, from Greece, from India, from the Philippines, from Fiji, and from Spain.

In 1949 a commission of FAO, the "Expert Committee on Nutrition," met to discuss the reports of this disease which was evidently occurring in widely scattered parts of the world and was found to respond promptly and completely when milk was given. This milk was usually provided as skim milk powder. Those on this committee may have remembered the 1933 article that Dr. Williams had written sixteen years before. As a result of the recommendations by the committee for further study of this disease, J. F. Brock and M. Autret made a survey in ten countries in Africa south of the Sahara. They then wrote "Kwashiorkor in Africa," which was issued jointly by FAO and WHO in 1952. Shortly after this similar surveys were done in Central America and Brazil.

Certain characteristics of kwashiorkor have been observed by those who work with these children. In 1966, D. B. Jelliffe classified the clinical features of kwashiorkor into: (1) the constant signs, (2) the usual signs, and (3) the occasional signs. He said that the following signs may be regarded as diagnostic if found in early childhood in areas where the diet in infancy is mainly carbohydrate. They are:

1. Edema
2. Growth retardation
3. Muscle wasting with retention of some subcutaneous fat
4. Psychomotor change

The usual signs, though not necessary for diagnosis, are often present singly or in any combination. They are:

1. Hair changes
2. Diffuse pigmentation of the skin
3. Moon face
4. Anemia

The occasional signs are present in some cases and not in others. They are:

1. Flaky-paint rash
2. Enlarged liver with fatty infiltration
3. Skin lesions such as fissures behind the ears and a "moist groin rash"
4. Associated vitamin deficiency
5. Associated conditioning infections

There is good agreement among those who work with kwashiorkor that retarded growth, showing first in a failure to gain weight before lack of increase in length is evident, is one of the first signs of the disease. This slow rate of growth is now believed to be caused by inadequate food and not a deficiency of a growth hormone.

Some studies have recently shown, as did Ashworth, et al., that children with kwashiorkor can, with adequate feeding, rapidly make up for the defects of body weight in relation to length. When the children they studied reached this stage of recovery there was some mechanism to reduce their appetites. They believe that "following malnutrition there is a stimulus to grow rapidly, but that this stimulus is reduced or removed when expected weight for height is reached." Workers in Africa have reported that children brought to the hospital at the age of eighteen months often show the weight of a normal five- to six-month-old infant. It has been pointed out that if the mothers and all who care for children in these vulnerable countries could be alerted to the seriousness of failure to grow and gain, many cases of the nutritional diseases could be prevented. Additional work is being done now on educating mothers to the need for watching the preschool child's gain in weight. Clinics are concentrating on using new charts such as that devised by Morley (see page 319) and on mothers' education in their use.

Evidence is increasing every day which leads to the belief that, under optimum conditions, growth characteristics are the same in nearly all areas of the world. It is now thought rather generally that racial and genetic factors play only a small part in growth failure.

Another clinical symptom of the disease that is seen in practically 100 percent of the victims of kwashiorkor is *changed behavior*. The child becomes irritable, as Williams pointed out as early as 1933. In extremely severe cases, apathy develops and the child pays little attention to his or her surroundings. This condition was impressed upon the author in a children's ward of the city hospital in Lagos, Nigeria. She saw a change in three days' time in a child with diagnosed kwashiorkor, from total apathy to emitting a whimpering cry. The cry is usually described as one that denotes a thoroughly wretched child, often said to exhibit peevish mental apathy. Brock and Autret in their 1952 report, commented that this clinical aspect has often been neglected. More recently, most authors writing on the subject have mentioned this as one of the prominent features.

Anemia is often associated with kwashiorkor. Adams, studying 148 African and Indian children with kwashiorkor, reported that the anemia found was mainly due to protein deficiency, with deficiencies of iron and folic acid playing a part in the condition.

Skin changes were described by the early writers as "crazy payment" and "snake-like skin." These changes involve a coarsening of the skin in spots, with dark or heavily pigmented areas in some cases and light or dyspigmented spots in others. A change in appearance of the skin, which is more noticeable in Negro children than those of other races, has been called a "flaky-paint" skin. Spots, jet back in color, with sharply defined edges, appear on parts of the body. Erosion of the skin and later ulceration, forming open lesions or sores, may also appear on the affected areas. Secondary infections develop where the skin is broken, especially on those parts of the body that are exposed to the sunlight.

One of the other clinical features of the disease is the change in the color of the hair. The hair may be dyspigmented and become grayish white in color or it may take on a coppery reddish hue, either of which is strange looking in the black hair of a Negro child. The reddish gray tinge denotes a lowered amount of pigment available for the growing hair.

Two types of hair changes may be seen. One shows up in bands of different colors, aptly referred to as "banding" or the "flag sign." This results when the child receives inadequate protein and gives a striking record of the periods of hunger. Brock and Autret told in their 1952 report that when ignorant and uneducated parents in Africa were asked whether the reddish hair was its natural color, they unhesitatingly replied that it was the result of the recent famine. The other type of change of color shows up in tipping of the hair.

Texture changes in hair also occur. The kinky, wiry hair of the African child becomes straight, soft, or even brittle; thin and sparse, it can be pulled out very easily.

Studies focused on the changes in the hair of kwashiorkor victims have shown statistically significant changes in tensile strength and significant differences in the diameter of anterior hair compared with the posterior hair, although the latter differences were not found in normal or even in marasmic children. Other workers have shown severe atrophy of the hair bulb with accompanying construction along the shaft during the short period of a 15-day experimental period of protein deprivation.

All these hair changes have been observed less frequently in Latin America and India than they have in Africa.

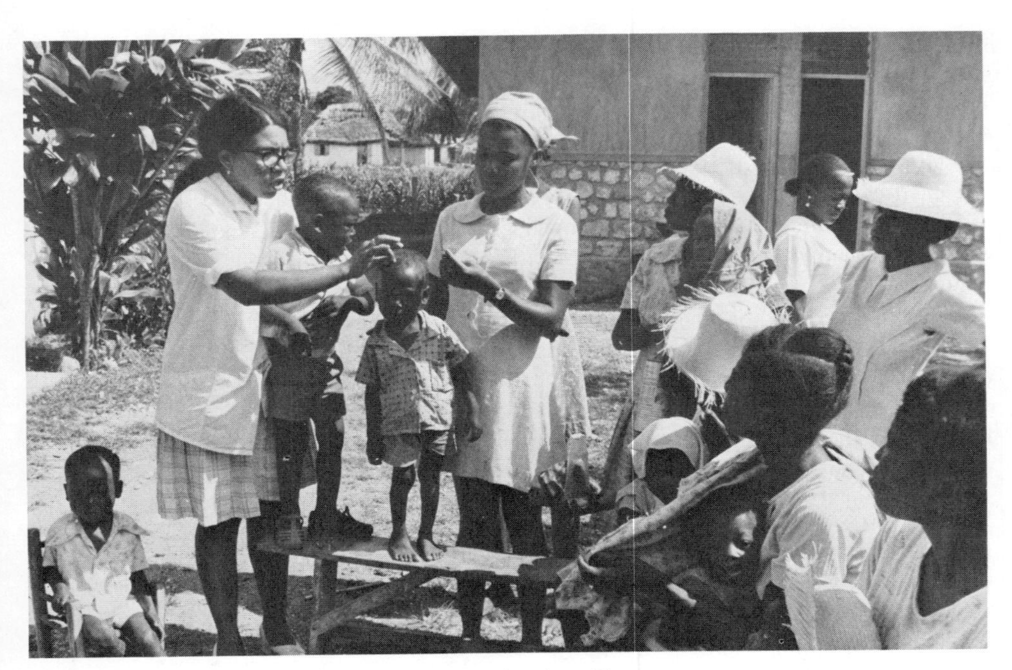

Nutrition worker shows mother telltale signs of malnutrition
—reddish hair.

Nowhere in the literature has the author found any statement concerning the shame that the African mother shows for the reddish tinge causing her to dye the hair black. In 1959 this was shown to her by the prominent pediatrician, Susan Ofori Atta, in a children's hospital in Accra, Ghana. Dr. Ofori-Atta felt that this manifest shame gave her a good opening for teaching the mother how to prevent the reoccurrence of the reddish tinge.

Another clinical feature often found to be present is the enlargement and fatty changes of the liver. Trowell et al reported that in the children they examined who had recovered from kwashiorkor the liver tissue had returned to normal. Abnormality in other internal organs has also been noted.

There is an apparent association of avitaminosis A and kwashiorkor. According to Mahladevans and Ganguly: "The most common and almost inevitable nutritional disorder accompanying kwashiorkor is avitaminosis A." They also say that how kwashiorkor precipitates the vitamin A deficiency is not yet known. It appears that vitamin A is not well carried in the blood plasma of a kwashiorkor victim.

Probably the most alarming change that kwashiorkor may cause in the young child has only recently been recognized. There is an ever increasing body of experimental evidence showing that severe malnutrition such as kwashiorkor, especially in the young infant, may cause irreparable brain damage and therefore a lessening of the potential for intellectual growth.

In 1968 McLaren raised the question of how to classify the large group of cases of protein-calorie malnutrition that could not be labeled, according to him, as either marasmus or kwashiorkor but were known to be "severe primary malnutrition." He and his coworkers have suggested a *Simple Scoring System* that includes three severe forms of protein-calorie malnutrition: *marasmus, marasmic-kwashiorkor,* and *kwashiorkor*.

The Role of Infectious Diseases

Examinations into the causes of death in children in countries where kwashiorkor is prevalent definitely connects it with infectious diseases. In a study of 286 undernourished and malnourished children admitted to a hospital in India in 1957–1960, 123 were diagnosed as kwashiorkor (edematous and fatty type) and 163 as marasmus (wasted type); the mortality was high—23 percent. Within 48 hours after admission 14 percent died, and 5 percent died suddenly in the hospital. The immediate causes of death were given as diarrhea, dehydration, and respiratory infections. It is well known that infection causes a decrease in appetite and water and mineral losses from the body or malabsorption of necessary nutrients from the intestinal tract. Arnold Schaefer observed that 40 percent of the children of Vietnam die from a combination of malnutrition and infectious diseases and that the death rate from measles in Guatemala was 325 times what it is in the United States and in most of Europe.

In south India the maximum incidence of hospital admissions for kwashiorkor was noted to occur during the summer months when there were maximum breeding of the common housefly and maximum incidence of diarrhea. In Central America during a measles epidemic, no children in one village who were receiving supplementary feedings died, but there was a high fatality rate in a neighboring village where no extra food was being given to the children.

It has often been pointed out that the child whose body is weakened by malnutrition cannot withstand a bout of a serious infectious disease. Some have observed that even a vaccination during a period of grossly inadequate protein intake may cause a serious condition. It therefore has been proposed that, in countries where kwashiorkor is prevalent, vaccinations be done before very young children leave the mother's breast.

In Uganda, a pilot system of native nutrition scouts has shown early signs of success. The Uganda Ministry of Health in collaboration with the Pediatrics Department of Makere University and some assistance from UNICEF has set this program up in several steps. They are:

1. A meeting of all the chiefs of an area was called. A committee was appointed to organize the community and to choose eight young people to be the nutrition scouts.
2. These scouts were given training in recognizing the obvious signs of malnutrition and in making simple anthroprometric measurements. Each scout visited 8 to 10 homes a day within a radius of 5 miles of the health center.

3. When indications of malnutrition were found the mother was given very simple advice and urged to take the child to the center for immunizations and health care.
4. Once homes where malnutrition was found were identified they were marked for monthly visits.
5. An experienced nutrition field worker always supervised the work of the scouts.

The overall effectiveness of this plan has and is being studied at all times so the operation can be improved.

Although kwashiorkor has been mainly reported to have been found in tropical countries, some cases of kwashiorkor were reported in the United States in the past decade, one in Kentucky in 1960 and one in the Bronx in 1966; in 1961, three cases were diagnosed in children at a Navajo Reservation. In 1969, Van Duzen and his co-workers made a systematic review of all cases admitted to the Public Health Service Indian Hospital in Tuba City, Arizona over the period of 1963–1967. This hospital was then one of six government hospitals providing health service to the Navajo Indians; the Tuba City hospital provided service to approximately 13 percent of all Navajos. Of 616 children with a diagnosis of malnutrition, 15 had kwashiorkor and 29 had marasmus. These authors belived that these cases were the end result of calorie and protein malnutrition associated with bacterial and viral infections.

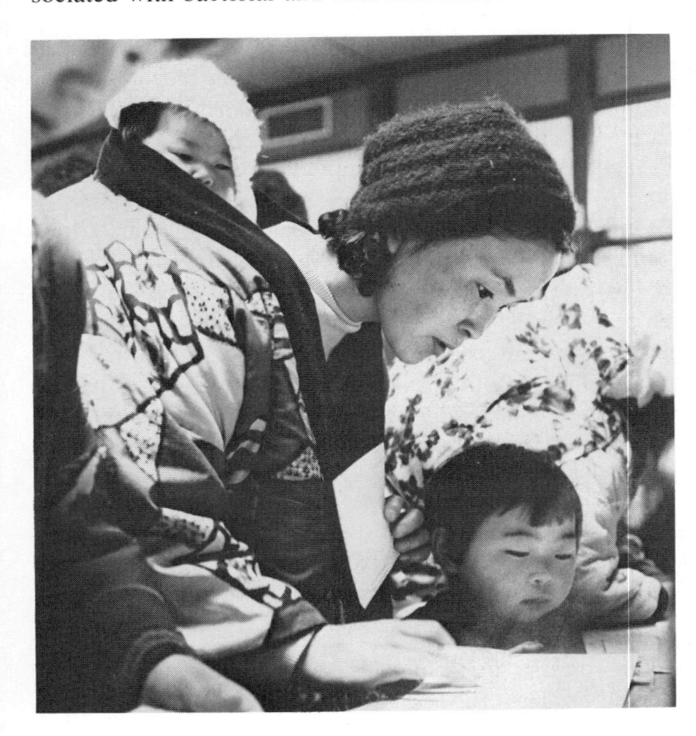

Proper care can prevent malnutrition.

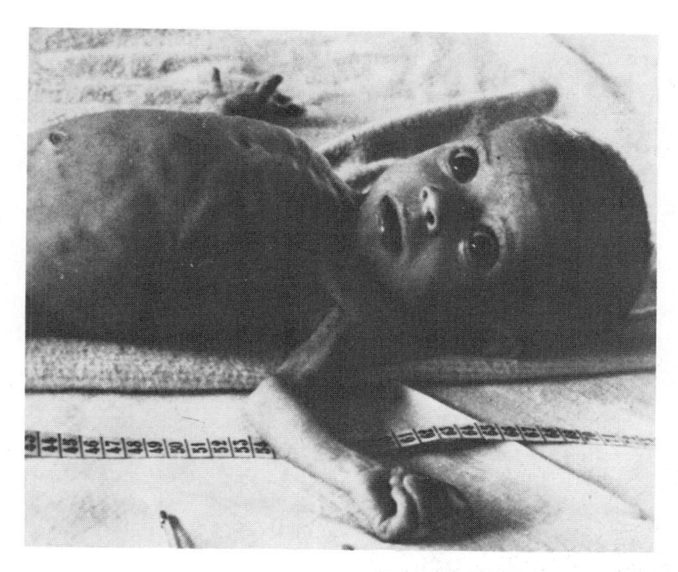

Molab, Iranian girl at four months of age.

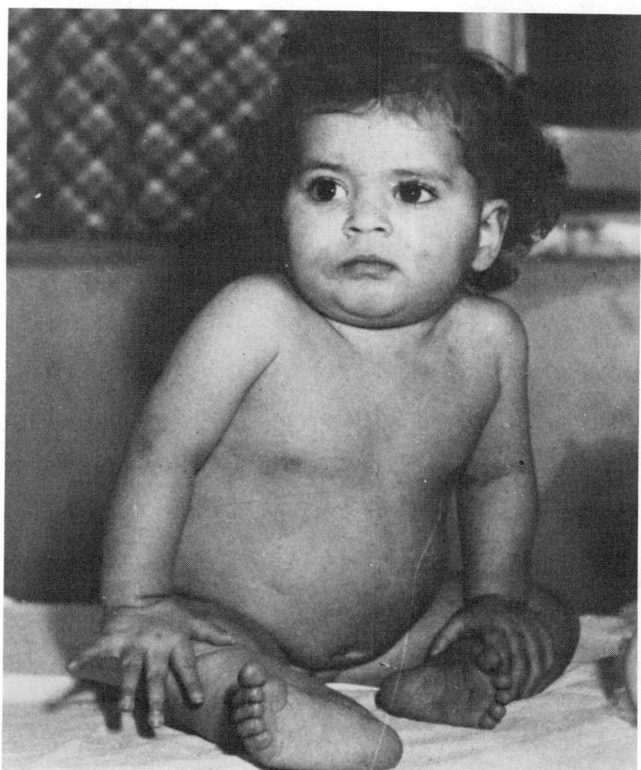

Molab, at ten months of age after care (*Photos Courtesy Food and Agriculture Organization*).

Child enjoying Incaparina (*Courtesy United Nations*).

Jelliffe said in 1975 that with the deterioration of the economic and social situations in many countries of the Third World the numbers of children affected by malnutrition rises especially where famine conditions arise.

McLaren, studying a total of 146 Arab children suffering from protein-calorie malnutrition, found that 28.1 percent of the cases ended in death; and mortality was higher in boys than girls. During the 12-month period of study, 1082 children under four years of age were admitted to the Luzmila Hospital in Amman, Jordan; 43 percent of them had one form or another of protein-calorie malnutrition according to his *Simple Scoring System* described on page 271.

Prevention or Kwashiorkor and Marasmus

Solving the Problem. As can be readily understood, backgrounds of food habits are extremely complicated; yet they must be understood and the extent of the depth of their roots must be probed before any desired changes can be made. There is, therefore, no easy solution for the problem of malnutrition. It has often been pointed out that two types of goals must be set: immediate relief and the long-term goal that looks to prevention in the future. The accomplishment of the short-term goal, however, may prepare the people to attack the larger problem and work toward its ultimate solution. Efforts to have the child weighed frequently during growth to determine its progress have been thought to show great promise.

In most places, especially where medical personnel is extremely scarce, no one knows how many sick children in the community do not come to the attention of a physician for diagnosis. It has often been said that the analogy to an iceberg is pertinent here, and that for every diagnosed case possibly 100 more are undiagnosed and therefore untreated.

Not much help in finding the incidence comes from the examination of records of death. Often the cause of death is listed as measles or some other infectious disease. These diseases undoubtedly cause death because the child's body, so weakened with malnutrition, can not combat the infection.

For both kinds of programs, the cultural backgrounds of food habits and foodways must be understood. Also, parents who control the destiny of the preschool child in the family must be led, through education, to understand the food needs for growth. The demonstration of what protein-high foods can do for a kwashiorkor-ill child had to be used to persuade the father, most of all, that food does make the difference. The problem of reaching the father may be greater than that of re-educating the mother. Often, in the developing countries, the mother accompanies her children to the hospital and stays with them while they are being treated. It is quite fortunate, perhaps, that in many cultures the mother cannot think of abandoning her child to a spotless white hospital with strange people in forbidding-looking uniforms. Most public health workers feel that it is an absolute necessity for the mother to stay with the child so that she may be re-educated while the child is being cured.

It should be pointed out that the poor food the weanling receives probably does, in many cases, also reflect the poor diet of the entire family. A more adequate food intake in general for all members of the entire family is undoubtedly needed. Linsusson found in her work in emergency feeding in Mauretania that she could not give a starving grandmother only food for her grandchild because it was, in mercy, too difficult to watch the grandmother feed the child (see page 243).

Williams believed that the increase in malnutrition was the result of neglecting to provide maternal and child health services and the practical nonexistence of pediatricians in some areas. She also blamed fragmentation of services arising from the modern tendency toward specialization. These problems, in relation to growth in the population and rapid urbanization, have made the dilemma greater. Williams urged more use of the nurse as well as the spread of family-planning knowledge, which she delineates as helping families to have no more children than the parents want. She, as have others, cautioned that all problems of malnutrition cannot be cured, however, by even widespread use of family planning.

Proposed Solutions to Problem of Marasmus and Kwashiorkor. Many people have pointed out that attempts to relieve the problem of malnutrition should be started on many fronts at the same time.

In summary, with no attempt to give an inclusive list, we list some recommendations for the prevention of marasmus, kwashiorkor, and attendant conditions of malnutrition as offered from the published wisdom of the scientific community:

1. National governments must recognize the problems. Most programs succeed better if they emanate from those national governments that build these programs into the national planning for improved nutrition. This is now designated as the formulation and implementation of a national food and nutrition policy. Cook and Yang in 1973 quoted a definition (used by Johnston and Greaves in 1969) of a national food and nutrition policy stated "that such a policy concerns the complex of measures which promote changes in food consumption that lead to adequate levels of nutrition."
2. Infectious diseases, which sometimes precipitate the condition of malnutrition and are the immediate cause of death and certainly always contribute to the illness, must be controlled as much as possible through public health measures.
3. The production of foods, both vegetable and animal, of high nutritive value that are acceptable in the culture of a people must be encouraged. Such production must be promoted in as many programs as possible at the local level.
4. Above all, continuing mass education is needed. Parents must be educated concerning the importance of proper foods in the promotion of health and growth in children. Wherever possible and with whatever means that prove effective, superstitions and traditional beliefs that hamper progress must be broken down, if not immediately, as soon as possible.
5. The small farmer and his wife must be encouraged to plant home gardens and orchards and to raise small animals to produce more and better food for the family.
6. The effective spread of information on family planning is a necessary part of any program to produce healthier children.

The new Basic Services Program of UNICEF, FAO, and WHO, as well as similar programs of other international organizations, are designed to look at the entire community and its needs and to eliminate so-called piecemeal programs except in emergencies.

The programs to attack this problem mostly started after the publication by FAO and WHO of Brock and Autret, *Kwashiorkor in Africa*. But Cicely William's work in West Africa in the 1930s had first brought attention to the problem.

A series of conferences on protein-calorie malnutrition were held in the 1950s and 1960s. The Protein Advisory Group of FAO and WHO was formed and their publications called the attention of the scientific community to the so-called "Protein Gap"—the need for high protein foods to supplement the often high starch protein foods given to weanlings. Incaparina developed at Incap (Institute of Nutrition in Central America and Panama in Guatemala City) which was composed of maize, ground sorghum, cottonseed, flour, yeast, calcium carbonate, lysine, and vitamin A. It was prepared to be consumed as a drink at a relatively low cost per glass. Incaparina in the dry form is used in wheat flour mixtures except bread and also made into puddings and soups. Because of the efforts of Incap the success of this mixture in Guatemala was commendable although distribution seems always to have been somewhat of a problem.

Wade, in 1975, presented a discouraging picture of the success of Incaparina after 15 years of its production and distribution. He says it cannot be considered a success because it did not reach a significant number of people for whom it was designed, its manufacture was not profitable and the impact on the national nutritional status was not noticeable.

Perhaps those who originally worked on it did not expect it to be the total answer, only one part of the solution. Because it was one if not the first of high protein foods to be designed and used for children, it undoubtedly led the way for the manufacture of a large number of such compounds.

In the years following the formulation and use of Incaparina other similar mixtures were devised using indigenous foods in many countries from those in Africa, Asia, and Central America.

Some of the mixtures as Laubina in Lebanon were really compounded and distributed to be used as a supplement to breast feeding or a milk formula, as ''Pablum'' had been used in the United States because local food mixtures could be sold cheaper than imported foods. The combination of vegetable proteins these mixtures used certainly put an emphasis on the direction for future efforts in agricultural food production (see Chapter 10).

Agricultural and nutritional scientists in the United States devised and through a large cereal manufacturer produced and distributed CSM-mix made of gelatinized cornmeal, soy flour, nonfat drymilk, vitamins, and minerals. This powder mixture was intended to be used as a drink for young children after boiling it for one minute with water. United States government and voluntary agencies distributed it abroad.

International Dispute

McLaren in his 1974 article ''The Great Protein Fiasco'' called attention of the scientific community involved in international problems and programs to what he believed was the overemphasis of the need for more protein and the so-called ''Protein Gap.'' He accused reputable nutritionists, international food and nutrition organizations, and committees as well as commercial firms of promoting what he called an ultimate fiasco. He was undoubtedly correct that the form of malnutrition called kwashiorkor as seen in Africa was probably different from conditions of malnutrition evident in some other countries. Jelliffe as well as others had already pointed to the relative increase in the numbers of cases of marasmus in relation to diagnosed kwashiorkor. Jelliffe had since 1959 used the term ''protein-calorie malnutrition'' to cover ''not only the entire clinical spectrum of marasmus, kwashiorkor, and intermediate forms, but also mild and sub-clinical stages.''

Waterlow and Payne pointed out that in kwashiorkor when the appetite wanes, there is a reduced intake of all nutrients. Brock, Collis, and others had also previously used, for the cure of kwashiorkor, increased calories as well as increased protein.

McLaren probably oversimplified the problem of kwashiorkor when he suggested a larger intake of cereals for the weanling. Anyone who has actually fed young children, as the author has, and carefully measured their intake knows of their limited capacity especially where problems of appetite have arisen.

Waterlow and Payne concluded that "One difficulty is that the controversy about the protein gap which represents a genuine difference of scientific opinion is accompanied by another controversy potentially far more dangerous. This arises from the attitude that research on nutritional problems is academic, irrevalent and a waste of time; that we know how to prevent malnutrition and therefore what matters is to use this knowledge." They continue by saying "Perhaps the story of the protein gap shows the arrogance of supposing that we know the answers and illustrates the need for a continuing critical examination of the premises on which action is based."

The wisdom that Cicely Williams gained throughout her years of working directly with families and children where she saw much malnutrition and her years of scholarly endeavor is apparent in her 1976 Preface to *Nutrition in the Community*. She says, "More attention should be given to the multifarious causes leading to the malnourished states, to the production, distribution, selection, and presentation of locally available foods, to the need for education and continuing supervision in hospitals, health centers and homes." She also stated, "Nutrition surveys may identify the nutritional state, but are often incompetent to recognize the many and various causes leading to the malnourished state."

Does the answer to the problems of marasmus, kwashiorkor and the other nutritional deficiency diseases, which follow in the wake of these two, ultimately lie in first discovering the specific problems in a single community discovering mutually agreed on symptoms of the condition of malnutrition, alleviation of the condition of malnutrition through effective treatment, and ultimately exerting efforts to prevent its reoccurrence?

We direct the students' attention to what Cicely Williams said in 1976. "Community nutrition is therefore the whole of the nutritional sciences applied to the consumer as groups or as individuals. It is the interface between food and people and probably some 90 percent of all nutrition takes place in the home. Each culture has always had its special preferred food, food taboos, and food habits."

STUDY QUESTIONS

1. What are the basic causes for some of the problems in malnutrition in:
   a. The American Indian? (choose a particular tribe)
   b. The children of migrant workers
   c. People over 65 in the lower socioeconomic classes

2. How do climate, economics, cultural and social patterns, transportation, communications, education, and religion affect the incidence and severity of malnutrition?

3. Why is xerophthalmia found in greater numbers of children in arid countries? How is goiter related to geography? Why have rickets followed initial industrial development? Why has obesity increased rapidly in modern Europe?

4. Choose a country and describe the steps and procedures you would use to introduce a specific program to improve the nutrition of the children.

5. Why is iron deficiency anemia so widespread in the world?

TOPICS FOR INDIVIDUAL INVESTIGATION

1. Write an article for people who do not have a scientific education, telling the story of pellagra so that they understand the importance of diet in this disease.
2. On a world map, show where each of the six principal sources of calories is consumed in greatest amounts. Indicate the flow of some of these foods from where they are raised to where they are consumed.
3. Discuss the chief causes of five of the most frequent problems in malnutrition in the world today.
4. From reports from UNICEF, FAO, and WHO, list four or five days in which programs in two countries are planned to prevent marasmus/kwashiorkor.
5. Imagine that you are a nutritionist in some African country. Describe what you would need to know before you began a nutrition education program.

REFERENCES AND SUGGESTED READING

Malnutrition

A.I.D. *War on Hunger,* June, 1977, p. 8.

Berg, A. Nutrition and National Priority. *Amer. J. Clin. Nutr.,* 23:1396, 1970.

Berg, A. *The Nutrition Factor.* Brookings Institute, Washington, D.C., 1973.

Birch, H. G. and J. D. Gussow. Disadvantage Children. *Health, Nutrition, and School Failure.* Harcourt Brace Jovanovich, New York, New York, 1970.

Borgstrom, G. *Focal Points.* Macmillan, New York, 1973.

Burgess, A. and R. F. A. Dean., Eds. *Malnutrition and Food Habits.* Macmillan, New York, 1962.

Cajanus. (Newsletter of the Caribbean Food and Nutrition Institute Jamaica Center Mona Kingston, Jamaica, 1975.

Chittenden, R. H. *The Nutrition of Man*. Fredrick A. Stokes, New York, 1907.

Cook, R. and Y. H. Yang. National Food and Nutrition Policy in the Commonwealth Caribbean. *Cajanus,* Vol. 6, No. 2, April–June 1973.

Cravioto, J. Malnutrition and Behavioral Development in the Pre-school Child. *Pre-school Child Malnutrition,* National Academy of Sciences, National Research Council, Washington, D.C., 1966.

Dale, A. N. and M. E. Lowenberg, Consumption of Vitamin D in Fortified and Natural Foods and in Vitamin Preparation, *Jour. of Ped.,* 70:952, No. 6, 1967.

Food and Nutrition Board. Recommendations on Administrative Policies for International Food and Nutrition Programs. National Academy of Sciences, National Research Council, Washington, D.C., April, 1965.

Gopalan, C. *Calorie Deficiencies and Protein Deficiencies* (Eds. McCance, R. A. and Widdowson, E. M.). Churchill, London, 1968.

Gyorgy, P. The Problems, *Pre-school Child Malnutrition.* National Academy of Sciences, National Research Council, Washington, D.C., 1966.

Gyorgy, P. and A. Burgess, Eds. *Protecting the Pre-School Child Programmes in Practice*. J. B. Lippincott, Philadelphia, Pa., 1954.

Howard, A. N., I. McL. Baird. *Nutritional Deficiencies in Modern Society*. Food Education Society of Oxford—A Symposium Held in 1972, Newman Books, London, 1973.

Hundley, J. M. Malnutrition—A Global Problem. *Fed. Proc.,* 18:76, 1959.

International Food Policy Research Institute. *Meeting Food Needs in the Developing World. The Location and Magnitude of the Task in the Next Decade*. Research Report No. 1, Washington, D.C., February, 1976.

Iowa State Univ. Center for Agr. and Econ. Adjustment. *Food, One Tool in International Economic Development*. Iowa State Univ. Press, Ames, Iowa, 1962.

Jelliffee, D. B. *The Assessment of the Nutritional Status of the Community*. WHO, Geneva, Switzerland, 1966.

Jelliffe, D. B. *Child Nutrition in Developing Countries*. U.S. Dept. of Health, Education, and Welfare, Washington, D.C., 1968.

Jelliffe, D. B. The Incidence of Protein-Calorie Malnutrition in Early Childhood. *Amer. J. Pub. Health,* 53:905, 1963.

Jelliffe, D. B. *Infant Nutrition in the Tropics and Subtropics*. WHO, Geneva, Switzerland, 1955.

Johnston, B. F. and J. P. Greaves. *Manual on Food and Nutrition Policy*. FAO Nutrition Studies No. 22, FAO Rome, 1969.

King, C. G. Future Programs. *Pre-School Child Malnutrition*. National Academy of Sciences, National Research Council, Washington, D.C., 1966.

Latham, M. C. Nutrition and Infection in National Development. *Science,* 188:561, 1975.

McLaren, D. S., Ed. Nutrition in the Community. Chapter 3, *Historical Perspectives in Nutrition in the Community*. John Wiley & Sons, Inc., New York, 1976.

Mann, C. V. The Health and Nutritional Status of Alaskan Eskimos, *Amer. J. Clin. Nutr.,* 11:31, 1962.

Manneheimer, E. Programs for Combatting Malnutrition in the Pre-School Child in Ethiopia. *Pre-School Child Malnutrition*. National Academy of Sciences, National Research Council, Washington, D.C., 1966.

Milner, M. Food Technology and World Food Needs. *Food Tech.,* 17:846, 1963.

Myrdal, J. Mood of the Writer. *Saturday Rev.*, Aug. 13, 1966.

Pellett, Peter L. *Marasmus a Continuing Problem in Libya.* Newsletter League for International Food Education, April, 1977.

Poleman, T. T. World Food, A Perspective. *Science.* 188:510, 1975. Nat. Inst. Ch. Health and Human Development, Center for Research for Mothers and Children, D.H.E.W. pub. (NIH) 75–1036, 1976.

Pre-School Child Malnutrition. Primary Deterrent to Human Progress. National Academy of Sciences, National Research Council, Washington, D.C., 1966.

Schaefer, A. Observations from Exploring Needs in National Nutrition Programs. *Amer. J. Pub. Health,* 56:1089, 1966.

Scrimshaw, N. S. The Effect of the Interaction of Nutrition and Infection on the Pre-School Child. *Pre-School Child Malnutrition.* National Academy of Sciences, National Research Council, Washington, D.C., 1966, p. 63.

Scrimshaw, N. S. Present Programs. *Pre-School Child Malnutrition.* National Academy of Sciences, National Research Council, Washington, D.C., 1966.

Scrimshaw, N. S. World-Wide Opportunities for Food Scientists and Technologists. *Food Tech.,* 17:850, 1963.

Scrimshaw, N. S. and J. E. Gordon, Eds. *Malnutrition, Learning and Behavior.* The M.I.T. Press, Cambridge, Mass., 1968.

Scrimshaw, N. S. and D. I. C. Wang. *Protein Resources, Technology Status and Research Needs.* Summary and Research Recommendations, Nat. Science Foundation, Ra-T-75-037, 1975.

Spencer, S. M. The Secret Killer of Children. *Saturday Evening Post,* Aug. 17, 1957.

Taylor, C. E. and E. M. Taylor, *Nutrition in the Community.* D. S. McLaren, ed., Chapter 3, Multi-factoral Causation of Malnutrition. John Wiley & Sons, Inc., 1976.

United Nations International Children's Fund. *The Administrative Aspects of Programmes to Protect the Pre-School Child.* Report of a conference held at Schloss Tremsbuttel, Hamburg, Germany, 1966.

U.S. Dept. of Agr. *The World Food Budget 1962 and 1966.* Foreign Agr. Econ. Rept. No. 4, 1961, rev. 1962.

Williams, Cicely D. Foreward—*Nutrition in the Community,* D.S. McLaren, ed., John Wiley & Sons, Inc., New York, 1976.

Marasmus and Kwashiorkor

Adams, E. B. Anemia Associated with Kwashiorkor. *Amer. Jour. Clin. Nutr.,* 22:1634–1638, 1969.

A.I.D. *War on Hunger,* June 1977, p. 8.

Alleyne, G. A. O., H. Flores, D. I. M. Picou and J. C. Waterlow, Metabolic Changes in Children in Protein Calorie Malnutrition—Chapter 6 of *Nutrition and Development,* Ed. by M. Winick, John Wiley & Sons, Inc., New York, 1972.

The Anemia of Kwashiorkor. *Nutr. Rev.,* 26:273–275, 1968.

Autret, M. *Nutrition of the Preschool Child.* A Consideration of New Approaches. FAO, Rome, Italy, 1964.

Autret, M. and E. F. Horine, Jr. Some Observations on Problems of Planning and Evaluation in Programs for the Control of Malnutrition in the Pre-School Child. *Pre-School Child Malnutri-*

tion. National Academy of Sciences, National Research Council, Washington, D.C., 1966, p. 288.

Behar, M. and R. Bressani. Experience in Development of Incaparina for the Pre-School Child. *Pre-School Child Malnutrition*. National Academy of Sciences, National Research Council, Washington, D.C., 1966, p. 213.

Benoga, J. M., D. B. Jelliffe, and C. Perez. Some Indicators for a Broad Assessment of the Magnitude of Protein-Calorie Malnutrition in Young Children in Population Groups. *Amer. J. Clin. Nutr.*, 7:714, 1959.

Broch, J. and M. Autret. *Kwashiorkor in Africa*. WHO and FAO, Rome, Italy, 1952.

Cajanus (newsletter of the Caribbean Food and Nutrition Institute) Jamaica Center, Mona, Kingston, Jamaica, Campbell Sadie, Food Lore and Food Habits, Vol. 8, No. 4, 1975.

Calder, R. Food Supplementation for Prevention of Malnutrition in the Pre-School Child. *Pre-School Child Malnutrition*. National Academy of Sciences, National Research Council, Washington, D.C., 1966, p. 251.

Dean, R. F. A. *Treatment and Prevention of Kwashiorkor*. WHO Bulletin 9:767, 1953.

Dean, R. F. A. East Africa. *Med. J.*, 37:378, 1960.

Diamond, I. and C. Vallbona. Kwashiorkor in a North American White Male. *Pediatrics*, 25:248, 1960.

Diet in the Treatment of Disease—Part III. Kwashiorkor. *Quarterly Med. Rev.*, Bombay, India, 15:1, 1964.

FAO. *Protein: At the Heart of the World Food Problem*. World Food Problems, No. 5, FAO, Rome, Italy, 1964.

FAO. *Lives in Peril*. FAO, Rome, Italy, 1970.

Gershoff, S. N. Science—The Neglected Ingredient of Nutrition Policy. *Jour. Amer. Diet. Assoc.*, 70:471, 1977.

International Food Policy Research Institute, Washington, D.C., *Meeting Food Needs in the Developing World—The Location and The Magnitude of the Task in the Next Decade*. February 1976, Research Report No. 1.

Jelliffe, D. B. The Incidence of Protein-Calorie Malnutrition in Early Childhood. *Amer. J. Pub. Health*, 53:905, 1963.

Jelliffe, E. F. Patrice. Nutrition Education in the Hospital. *Cajanus-News Letter of Caribbean Food and Nutr. Inst.*, Vol. 4, No. 4, 1971, pp. 292–301.

Joint Expert Committee on Nutrition FAO and WHO Monograph Series No. 522, WHO Geneva, Switzerland, 1973.

The Liver in Protein-Calorie Malnutrition. *Nutr. Rev.*, 27:223–225, 1969.

Mahadevans, P. M. and J. Ganguly. The Influence of Proteins on the Absorption and Metabolism of Vitamin A. *World Rev. Nutr. Diet.*, 5:209, 1965.

Malnutrition and Disease, Freedom From Hunger Campaign Basic Study #12, Part III, Deficiency Disease, Protein-Calorie Malnutrition, FAO, Rome, 1963.

McDowell, Jim. Nutrition Scouts: Another "First" for Uganda. *UNICEF News*. Fighting Child Malnutrition Part II. 86:1975.

McLaren, D. S. Trends in Tropical Child Health (The Rise of Marasmus). *Jour. Trop. Ped.*, 12:84–85, 1966.

McLaren, D. S. Letter to the Editor. *Nutr. Rev.*, 26:256, 1968.

McLaren, D. S., et. al. Short-Term Prognosis in Protein-Calorie Malnutrition. *Amer. J. Clin. Nutr.*, 22:863–870, 1969.

McLaren, D. S. The Great Protein Fiasco. *Lancet*, 2:93, 1974.

McLaren, D. S. (Ed.) *Nutrition in the Community*. John Wiley and Sons, Inc., 1976.
Mental Development Following Kwashiorkor. *Nutr. Rev.*, 27:46–49, 1969.
Morley, David. *Comprehensive Care Through the Under-Five Clinics. Assignment Children.* UNICEF, Jan/March, pp. 75–89, 1972.
Nutr. Rev. The Liver in Protein-Calorie Malnutrition, 27:223–225, 1969.
Objective Measurement of Hair Changes in Kwashiorkor. *Nutr. Rev.*, 26:330–332, 1968.
Recovery Rates of Children Following Protein-Calorie Malnutrition. *Nutr. Rev.*, 28:118–122, 1970.
Scrimshaw, N. S. and M. Behar. Protein Malnutrition in Young Children. *Science,* 133:2039, 1961.
Scrimshaw, N. S. and M. Behar. Worldwide Occurrence of Protein Malnutrition. *Fed. Proc.*, 18:82, 1959.
Taitz, L. S. and L. Fineberg. Kwashiorkor in the Bronx. *Am. J. Dis. of Child.*, 112:76, 1966.
Trowell, H. D., J. N. Davies, and R. F. A. Dean. *Kwashiorkor*. Edward Arnold, London, England, 1954.
U.N. *The World Food Problem—Proposals for National and International Action,* 1974.
UNICEF News, No. 2, Issue 86, 1975, p. 4.
Van Duzen, Jean, et al. Protein and Calorie Malnutrition Among Pre-school Navajo Indian Children. *Amer. J. of Clin. Nutr.*, 22:1362–1370, 1969.
Wade, N. International Agricultural Research, *Science,* 188:585, 1975.
Waterlow, J. C., J. Cravioto, and S. Frank. *Protein Malnutrition in Man*. Academic Press, New York, 1960.
Waterlow, J. C. Classification and Definition of Protein-Calorie Malnutrition, Medical Practice. *British Medical Jour.*, 2:566, 1972.
Waterlow, J. C. and P. R. Payne. The Protein Gap. *Nature,* 258:113, 1975.
Watts, E. Ronald. *Education for Better Nutrition of Children in Tropical Africa. Assignment Children,* UNICEF, Jan./March, 1972, pp. 93–103.
Williams, C. D. Nutritional Diseases of Children Associated with a Maize Diet. *Arch. Dis. Child.*, 8:423, 1933.
Williams, C. D. Kwashiorkor: Nutritional Diseases of Children Associated with Maize Diet. *Lancet,* 2:1151, 1935.
Williams, C. D. The Story of Kwashiorkor-Courier-Central International De L'France. *Paris Courier,* p. 361, June 1963.
Williams, C. D. Malnutrition and Mortality in the Pre-School Child. *Pre-School Child Malnutrition*. National Research Council, Washington, D.C., 1966, p. 3.
Williams, C. D. On that Fiasco—A Letter to Dr. Kalinga Zongo. *Lancet,* 3:793, 1975.
Winnick, M. (Ed.). *Nutrition and Development,* Chapter 6 by G. A. O. Alleyne, H. Flores, D. I. M. Picow and J. C. Waterlow. John Wiley and Sons, New York, 1972.
Wolfe, C. B. and C. B. Stone, Kwashiorkor in a North American White Male. *Pediatrics,* 25:248, 1960.

Endemic Goiter

Endemic Goiter, *Fed. Proc.*, 17 (Part II, Supplement No. 2:57, Sept. 1958.
McCollum, E. V. *A History of Nutrition*. Houghton-Mifflin, Boston, 1957.
Pitt-Rivers, R. and W. R. Trotter. *The Thyroid Gland,* Vols. 1 and 2. Butterworths, Washington, D.C., 1964.

Stanbury, J. B., et al. *Endemic Goiter. The Adaptation of Man to Iodine Deficiency*. Harvard Univ. Press, Cambridge, Mass., 1954.

Stanbury, J. B. and V. Ramalingaswami. Iodine, in G. H. Beaton and E. W. McHenry, *Nutrition, A Comprehensive Treatise*, Vol. 1, Academic Press, New York, p. 373, 1964.

Studies on the Prevention of Simple Goiter. Western Reserve University, Cleveland, Ohio, Bull. No. 7, 1923.

WHO. *Endemic Goiter*. Mono. Series No. 44, 1960. WHO, Geneva, Switzerland.

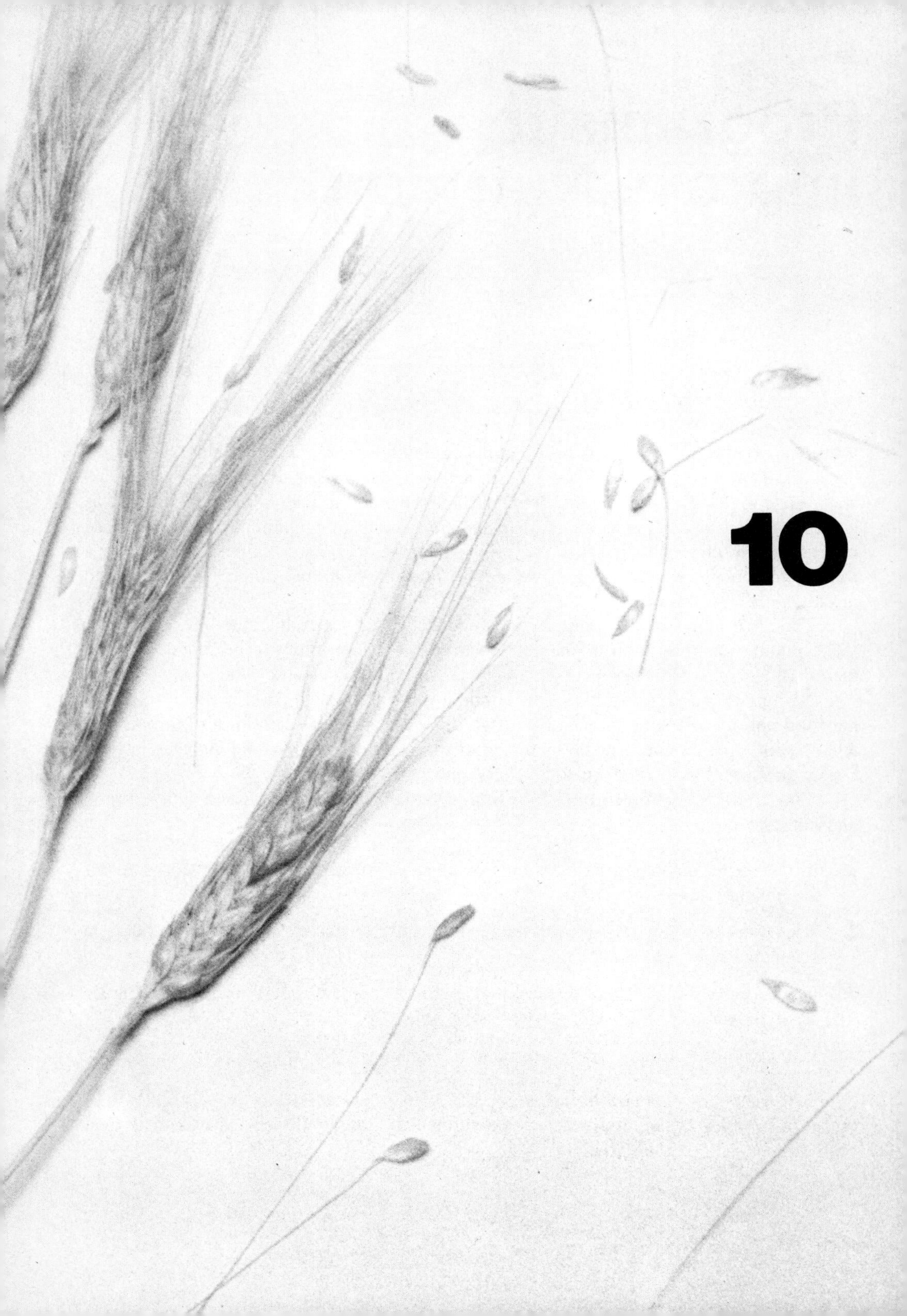
10

Programs to Improve Nutrition

When historian Arthur Toynbee said that the twentieth century will probably be remembered most because it was the first time in recorded history when man dared to use his knowledge to benefit all mankind, he could have been talking about the international as well as national programs to relieve hunger and malnutrition. Although many of these programs have their roots in ideas and proposals from previous centuries, the united efforts of the people working in the twentieth century have brought more immediate and more far-reaching results.

The 1976 report of the International Food Policy Research Institute has a warning, "The number or proportion of malnourished people is not likely to be reduced unless there is major restructuring of income or other means of distributing the food supply."

Nations all over the world are becoming aware of the need for a national food and nutrition policy. Johnston and Greaves gave, in 1969, a simple definition of a food policy: "A food policy concerns the complex of measures which promote changes in food consumption that lead to adequate levels of nutrition."

Cook and Yang outlined in 1973 several necessary characteristics of a national food and nutrition policy:

1. It must be acceptable to the economic planners as a part of the general economic development plans.
2. The terms of the policy should set forth specific objectives with targets and time schedules.
3. It must be based on actual resources available and actual programs and projects already existing.
4. It must be dynamic in order to respond to change.

It is generally recognized that we need a whole new approach to the problems of nutrition in order to get simultaneous measurements of its multiple causes and to deal with the present complex problems.

To determine what measures are needed to combat malnutrition, monitoring of a group is desirable; in forcasting needs, monitoring also can predict probable results in natural disasters such as drought, insect damage and plant disease, wars, and other disruptive influences. Programs to monitor nutritional matters should have four facets.

1. Statistics on the prevalence of a specific nutritional problem.
2. Data on food consumption of various internal population groups.
3. Clear understanding and identification of multifactoral causes of malnutrients.
4. Effect of various preventive and remedial programs on nutritional status and the prevalence of the particular form of malnutrition.

In order to look at the problems of international malnutrition and hunger, we chose to discuss in detail a few of the agencies that deal with these problems. Listed in Appendix 4 are selected and recommended references for those who want information on U.S. agencies.

UNICEF in 1975 reported that children under six years account for one half of the deaths among those living in poverty in Asia, Africa, and Latin America. It was also said then that in Nigeria 180 of 1000 babies still die before their first birthday in India and Pakistan and 130 to 110 in Peru. In contrast, the number of such deaths in Sweden was 11 and 18 in the German Democratic Republic. Berg (1973) said, "Considering how very thin in most countries is the leadership elite on whom rests the burden of these nations' success or failure, such losses [he meant the losses from malnutrition in early life] would seem to inhibit the chances for the development of a group of young leaders to promote economic development." The Center for Research and Development said in 1976 that while only "one or two percent of the world's people suffer from *severe malnutrition* up to one half may suffer from *moderate malnutrition* or *chronic undernutrition*. For the use of the terms of malnutrition see page 254.

Jan Myrdal threw out the challenge in 1966. "In the concrete world in which we live we all know which is the main conflict. The few are rich, the many are poor. The few live long, the many die young. The majority of the population of our world is starving. The majority is downtrodden, trampled upon, exploited. And this majority is becoming conscious. It is questioning the whole structure of the world society."

PROGRAMS OF INTERNATIONAL ORGANIZATIONS

FAO: Food and Agriculture Organization

FAO, with its dramatic design and Latin motto 'Fiat panis' (let there be bread) is the Food and Agriculture Organization of the United Nations. This is the first agency of the

United Nations that was established; it has the major responsibility for helping people the world over to get more and better food. FAO was established in 1945, but it did not just happen on that date. Its purpose and achievements are significant, but an understanding of events leading up to the establishment of FAO are essential if we are to understand human progress toward developing a genuine concern for the well being of others. The story that is the background for FAO had its beginnings some 60 years ago.

For many years, some professional organizations have held international meetings and demonstrated that people of different nationalities could talk together on professional subjects of common interest. An International Institute of Agriculture (IIA) was organized in 1905 mainly through the efforts of David Lubin, a California business executive and farmer. He believed that by collection and dissemination of international statistics about agricultural products the farmers and food producers in various countries could be helped to obtain the best markets for their products. He gained the interest of the King of Italy, who provided housing for the Institute in Rome. However, IIA was concerned with food as a trade commodity rather than in relation to the health and welfare of people.

Wars have brought hunger, famine, death, and destruction to peoples and nations from earliest times, but in this century war has brought forth in many nations the genuine desire to work together for the common good. As a result of World War I (1914–1918), two international organizations were formed: the International Labor Organization (ILO) and the League of Nations, both with headquarters at Geneva, Switzerland. The ILO was organized to deal with problems related to labor such as hours, wages, unemployment, child labor, old age pensions, and sickness benefits. However, in 1935, ILO did concern itself with the nutrition of workers and in 1936 published the report of a study, "Workers Nutrition and Social Policy."

With the establishment of the League of Nations, there was hope that at last a new world order would begin. But political problems eventually became insurmountable for the League; it was handicapped because the United States was not a member. Though the League failed, it did have many successes in the area of social and economic problems, particularly in health and nutrition.

In the Covenant of the League of Nations, it was stated that the League was "To endeavor to take steps in matters of international concern for the prevention and control of disease." A health organization was formed within the League for this purpose, and it was in this health section that the first international programs of food and nutrition had their beginning. In 1925, the Yugoslav delegation to the League requested a study of methods to be recommended in the interests of public health for the regulation of the manufacture and of the sale of food products. But it was not until ten years later that there was any widespread recognition of the need for nutrition studies. In 1935, a report, "Nutrition and Public Health," was published by Etienne Burnet and Wallace Aykroyd in the *Quarterly Bulletin* of the Health Organization. When the Assembly of the League met in September of that year, this report was the basis of discussion. Stanley Bruce of Australia delivered a speech in which he used the phrase "to marry health and agriculture'' and went on to say, ''by so doing, make a great step in the improvement of national health and, at the same time, an appreciable contribution to the solution of the agricultural problem.'' Bruce captured the interest and imagination of those assembled, and a resolution was passed to continue the nutrition work of the health committee and to bring a general report to the next meeting of the assembly.

In 1937, the League published a report, ''The Relation of Nutrition to Health, Agriculture and Economic Policy,'' which became a best seller and inspired many governments to take practical steps to improve the diets of their people. Then World War II came, and the League of Nations was lost, but though it failed in its major goal, there were many solid achievements. And its international work in health and nutrition survived but in a new and different organization.

Preliminary Meeting

While World War II was still in progress, an event of profound significance in the history of mankind took place. This was a conference called by President Franklin D. Roosevelt and attended by representatives of 44 nations. The place of meeting was Hot Springs, Virginia, and the dates were May 18 to June 3, 1943. It was a meeting solely for the purpose of working together to secure lasting peace when the war was ended. Those attending the conference believed this could be achieved by raising the standards of living of the two-thirds of the world's population that was malnourished and in want.

Historic events of this kind come into being from a background of work of individuals—in this case, Frank McDougall. He was in Washington, D.C., in 1942 for discussions on an international wheat agreement; while there, he drafted a memorandum on a United Nation Program for Freedom from Want of Food. This plan was based on a lifetime of experience and on knowledge gained as the Australian delegate to the League of Nations (1929–1939) and as a member of the nutrition committee of the League. In his memorandum, McDougall outlined proposals that would make Stanley Bruce's marriage of health and agriculture a reality.

Freedom from want of food must be given high priority in the actions taken to fulfill the pledges of the United Nations. For not only is food the most essential of human needs but the production of food is the principal economic activity of man . . . one of our most urgent immediate problems is the inability of the lower-income groups to buy sufficient food to maintain good health. Its solution will depend upon economic and social policies designed to increase purchasing power and to reduce the costs of production and distribution. . . . The need is to establish at once a United Nations Organization. . . . A Technical Commission on Food and Agriculture should formulate action programs designed to assist the nations to achieve freedom from want of food. . . . The necessity for immediate action cannot be overemphasized. We must act now if we are to avoid the risk of losing the peace.

Eleanor Roosevelt saw this memorandum and realized that it incorporated some of the same ideas as given by President Roosevelt in his statement a year earlier on the Four Freedoms. She arranged for McDougall to meet President Roosevelt; the outcome was that the President of the United States convened the Hot Springs Conference in May 1943.

The conference recommended that the nations represented establish a permanent organization in the field of food and agriculture and that an Interim Commission be appointed to work out plans for such an organization. Frank McDougall was a member of the Interim Commission and helped to draw up the Constitution of FAO. (He continued to work with FAO in advisory capacities almost to the day of his death in 1958; the McDougall Lecture was instituted by the Council of FAO, Rome, 1958, to commemorate this work.)

FAO Established

The next step, following the work of the Interim Commission after the Hot Springs Conference, was taken in October 1945 when delegates from 42 countries met in Quebec, Canada. They ratified the constitution, which formally established the Food and Agriculture Organization of the United Nations. The preamble to the Constitution of FAO states:

> The nations accepting this Constitution, begin determined to promote the common welfare by furthering separate and collective action on their part for the purposes of:
>
> Raising levels of nutrition and standards of living of the people under their respective jurisdictions,
>
> Securing improvements in the efficiency of the production and distribution of all food and agricultural products,
>
> Bettering the conditions of rural populations,
>
> And thus contributing toward an expanding world economy,
>
> Hereby established the Food and Agriculture Organization of the United Nations.

It takes more than the stroke of pen and signatures on a document to make words become reality. This is especially true when the desired reality is action and change in the lives of people. It takes time, patience, hard work, flexibility, willingness to adjust to the point of view of others, and a determination to overcome obstacles. Of these ingredients, FAO needed a liberal supply. There were barriers, disappointments, frustrations, and conflicting ideas, but the purpose and goal were always kept in sight. There have been some remarkable achievements. At the end of the first ten years of its work, FAO again met in Quebec to celebrate its historic founding and review accomplishments. That year, 1955, two books were published giving authoritative and exciting accounts of the work of FAO: *So Bold an Aim* by P. L. Yates for FAO, and *The Story of*

FAO by Gove Hambidge. Those who read these books will find them extremely worthwhile; here we can give only a few examples of what has been done by FAO up to this time.

Currently FAO consists of 136 governments that work together in a variety of ways to meet the purposes just described. FAO is one of the specialized agencies of the United Nations family. It works closely with other agencies of the UN (especially with UNICEF and WHO), but is an autonomous independent organization with headquarters in Rome, Italy.

FAO is governed by a Conference where representatives of the member nations meet every two years to approve the budget and program of work and to elect new members and a director-general. Each member country has one vote. The Conference also elects a council of 42 member nations that serves as the interim governing board and meets at least once a year. Much of the Council's work is carried out by standing committees. A Secretariat of some 3500 professional workers along with a general service staff carry out the work of FAO. About half the professional staff work in regional offices and in field projects. Regional offices are maintained in Africa, Asia and the Far East, Latin America, North America, the Near East, and in the United National Headquarters in New York.

FAO is a large and complex organization that works through consultation, cooperation, and liaison with international government organizations, intergovernmental organizations, and international nongovernmental organizations. Special studies are made by expert committees, commissions, and panels of experts from various countries. Much money is required to carry out the worldwide programs of FAO. The basic budget for the regular program is voted by the governing Conference and each member nation pays a share related to the economic situation of that country. Funds are also provided by the United Nations Development Program, UNDP, and other sources such as governments participating in special programs; foundations, international and voluntary agencies; the World Bank; and private individual groups or businesses contributing through the Freedom from Hunger (FHH/AD).

FAO plays an increasing role in strengthening national research in developing countries and is one of three international sponsors of the recently organized Consultative Group on International Agricultural Research, CGIAR (see page 326).

Cooperation with other international agencies is a major part of FAO's programs. It has for many years cooperated with WHO and UNICEF on nutrition problems. Now, as an outcome of the 1974 World Food Conference in Rome, FAO is collaborating with UNICEF and WHO is undertaking coordinated supplementary feeding programs for vulnerable groups. These have begun in Bangladesh, India, and Pakistan with the aim of providing food assistance, coupled with nutrition education for over three million pregnant and nursing mothers, infants, and pre-school children.

Another example of collaboration is the program FAO has with the International Atomic Energy Agency (IAEA) that has a panel of experts study the efficacy, wholesomeness, and safety of radiation preservation of certain types of foods.

Freedom from Hunger—Action for Development (FFH/AD)

This is a program within FAO that is regarded as a people's program rather than one carried on by governments. It involves the citizens of various countries and had its origin in 1960 when FAO launched its Freedom From Hunger Campaign. At that time FAO recognized the need to work directly with the people of all countries and not just with governments at their request. People in the industrialized nations needed to understand the problems of world hunger and how hunger might be overcome by united efforts. Since the affluent countries cannot feed the rest of the world, all people of the world needed to be mobilized to participate in a joint effort of war on hunger and poverty. FAO launched its Freedom from Hunger Campaign (FFHC) with support from the United Nations and its specialized agencies. Governments, voluntary agencies, industry, schools and universities, youth groups, and in fact all sectors of the community in many countries responded. Each country was invited to establish its own FFHC committee, and in a short time 80 nations set up their organization and plan of action. These plans were in general directed toward: (1) teaching farmers new skills and teaching mothers better ways to feed their families; (2) demonstrating the results that could be obtained through use of fertilizers, better seeds, irrigation, soil conservation, improved breeds and care of animals, and improved methods of fishing and use of fish ponds; (3) helping to provide teachers, field workers, training programs fellowships for study and funds for seeds and tools.

Action followed quickly. In the United States a Freedom from Hunger Foundation was established and the first cash donation came from the people of the Virgin Islands. Programs provided help here at home for needy groups, as well as projects abroad. The overseas projects included such items as community canneries in Turkey; nutrition and health centers in Peru; demonstration home gardens in Malagasy, and school construction in Brazil, Ghana, and Peru.

Private citizens learned to know more about people of other countries through these programs and it was realized that more than increased food is needed to solve the world's poverty problems. Emphasis was placed on development—improving the living and working conditions in the Third World countries. The Committees have been renamed Freedom From Hunger/Action for Development, FHH/AD. There are now over 100 FFH/AD national committees that work to stimulate fresh ideas about development issues and to involve young people. Projects that are currently planned are ones with a direct answer to local needs and that involve the beneficiaries from the outset and can be continued by local people once outside assistance is terminated.

World Food Program (WFP)

The world food program was begun in 1963 and sponsored by FAO along with the United Nations. It was planned as a means of bringing food to people in developing countries. The stimulus came from the early efforts of the United States to aid starving countries, when in 1954 Congress passed Public Law 480 decreeing that surplus foods could be shipped to other countries as aid. The World Food Program involved more countries in providing support for food and a greater variety of foodstuffs. In this program food is given as a family ration in part-payment of wages to people planting trees, digging irrigation channels, building roads, schools and houses. Thus, it reduces the wage bill, increases employment, and encourages good food habits and so contributes to economic growth. Food is given to settlers on new land until they harvest their first crops and to industrial workers to help build up productivity. Food helps people help themselves. Food is also distributed through hospitals, child care centers, and schools. In this way it helps those most susceptible to malnutrition with its accompanying health defects to achieve better health and become more productive citizens. Food works to improve health and is a force in the social and economic development of many countries. WFP was first established for a three-year trial period. Its effectiveness has been so clearly demonstrated that FAO and the United Nations have decided to continue it for as long as multilateral food aid is found to be feasible and desirable.

UNITED NATIONS INTERNATIONAL CHILDREN'S FUND (UNICEF)

UNICEF, the only international agency whose sole purpose is concern with the needs of children, has accomplished much since the mid 1940s to promote a new hope in families all over the World.

UNICEF is supported entirely by voluntary contributions from governments, organizations, and volunteers.

History of UNICEF

In February 1946, President Truman appointed former President Herbert Hoover to head a survey mission to study the needs of children in war-torn European countries. Following the completion of this survey, Mr. Hoover, supported by other respected public officials, recommended that a special body be created within the United Nations to meet the emergency needs of European children suffering from the ravages of the recent war. In mid-December of the same year, the United Nations International Children's Emergency Fund (UNICEF) was established by the United Nations General Assembly. UNICEF with its own executive board of 30 members from member countries has always had a semi-autonomous status.

An Italian child once explained the word UNICEF as the American word for "cow." Dry skim milk was given to the children of Europe in the early post-war relief program. Undoubtedly, to many mothers and children all over the world, the donations of dry skim milk made by UNICEF have given some relief from hunger and malnutrition. School feeding in Europe was one of the first ways of reaching children. It was early decided, however, that UNICEF should expand its operation to include the world.

Treat for a good cause (*Courtesy* UNICEF).

In 1953, because the United States had a surplus of skim milk powder, UNICEF was able to buy it at a nominal price, and in 1958 and in 1959, the Canadian government made some dry milk powder available. Beginning in 1954, dry milk powder was available free at American ports for the UNICEF overseas child-feeding programs with shipping charges only two to two-and-a-half cents per pound. In three years, beginning in 1957, UNICEF shipped 100 million pounds of this milk annually; in 1959, 5 million children in 62 countries were receiving daily rations of it.

Because various factors reduced the production of milk in the United States and in Canada in the last few months of 1959, there developed uncertainty about the quantity of dry milk powder that would be available, so the milk was then furnished only to vulnerable groups. Efforts were then expended toward helping countries solve their own milk problems. Thus, aid was given to numerous government-subsidized projects such as the Anand Project in India. By the end of 1965, UNICEF had aided milk-conservative programs in 38 countries giving major equipment for 34 milk-drying plants and 64 fluid dairies and auxiliary equipment to another 92 dairies. Also included was training in dairying methods and in quality milk control.

In the first three years of existence, the resources of the Fund were devoted largely to bringing food, medical supplies, and clothing on an emergency basis, to the children of fourteen war-ravaged countries of Europe and China. When it was evident that Europe was recovering, the needs of children in the economically underdeveloped countries created a new demand on the Fund. In 1950, the General Assembly extended the life of the Fund by three years and directed a shift in emphasis from emergency measures to long-term programs in the developing countries. At the end of these three years, UNICEF had established its worth and the General Assembly voted to continue the agency indefinitely. At this time, the name was shortened to the United Nations International Children's Fund, but the well-known initials of UNICEF were retained.

The first Executive-Director of UNICEF was Maurice Pate, an American and an associate in the previous humanitarian activities of Herbert Hoover. Walter Judd, a well-known congressman from Minnesota, proposed that an initial $15 million dollars be contributed by the United States to get this work started. At the outset, the U.S. contributions were more than 70 percent of the total. Maurice Pate continued to give outstanding service until his death in 1965 when Henry Richardson Labouisse was appointed to replace him.

The 1965 Nobel Peace Prize was awarded to the United Nations Children's Fund. Maurice Pate, who had by then become known as Mr. UNICEF because of his great vision, unfaltering dedication, and astute business management of the Fund, had just died. The $54,500 prize was used to train people in the developing countries in fields of service to children as a living memorial to him.

The story of UNICEF Christmas cards is a heartwarming one. In 1949, Jitka Samkova, a seven-year-old girl living in a village in Bohemia, sent her own painting to UNICEF as a "thank you" for the post-war help given to the children of her village. Many will remember her joyful picture with the wreath at the top of a Maypole, which

UNICEF works with mothers whose cooking methods are still primitive (*Courtesy* UNICEF, *Photos by Wolf*).

UNICEF helps promote the teaching of nutrition and eating habits as in this projecting home (*Courtesy Food and Agriculture Organization*).

she said was to show that the line of children being helped was endless. UNICEF used her drawing, and in 1950 sold 130,000 Christmas cards with that drawing on them. This Christmas card project has shown remarkable growth; the number of countries participating increased from 11 in 1950 to over 110 in 1966.

The popular Halloween programs to collect money for UNICEF allows children to have their own fun of being dressed up while collecting and contributing money to be used for the world's needy children. It had a humble beginning when in 1950 a Sunday School class in Pennsylvania contributed $17.

UNICEF Today

The physical and mental growth of more than 100 million youngsters under five years of age is currently in jeopardy due to malnutrition and undernourishment (chronic rather than acute malnutrition) which has increased the past year due to the rising cost of food, fuel and fertilizer.

The above excerpt from Executive Director's 1976 Report to the Board indicated that the situation of children in many parts of the world had deteriorated in 1975. On the increase were the number of children dying from *preventable diseases,* suffering from *severe malnutrition,* and missing the educational preparation for a decent life. Rising costs of imported materials and labor, as well as escalating energy costs, were basic to this situation. The poorest countries continue to suffer the most even though in 1976 there were evidences of recovery from the depression. Malaria, often fatal to children, was reported in 1976 to be spreading.

The disparities in income and conditions of life in many developing countries are becoming more acute. The ranks of the urban poor are swelling because of the migration from poverty-stricken rural areas as the present day tourist can easily observe in bustling Djaharta, Indonesia, whose population has increased, in about one decade, from 200,000 people to 30 times that of 6 million people.

At the 1976 Executive Board of UNICEF, it was reported that their "target population of the developing world living in relative or absolute poverty was assumed to be 900 million of whom 350 million are children." At this board meeting it was decided to endorse priority to aid the young child (0–5 years) but not to exclude children of all ages.

During the 1977 Executive Board Meeting $129.4 million was committed for new or extended assistance in 50 countries and 14 regional or interregional projects. Forty-five countries in Africa, 25 in Asia, 22 in South and Central American countries, and 9 in the Eastern Mediterrean had UNICEF-aided projects. Of all European countries only Turkey was included on the UNICEF aid list.

The first of UNICEF's basic policies today as it always has been is that countries receiving UNICEF aid must agree to use this aid equitably and efficiently on the basis of need without discrimination because of color, creed, nationality, or political belief. UNICEF also emphasizes that once it votes to discontinue a particular project, the country must continue it by its own efforts. UNICEF operates thus no projects of its own within countries; its goals are to encourage and stimulate a local effort by giving the country help that can be used as a lever to mobilize local resources.

Basic Services Program

In order to assist a number of countries to develop essential services for a larger number of children, UNICEF is developing an approach for *meeting the basic needs of children and their families* as an integral part of the development process.

When the U.N. asked the UNICEF Board in 1975 what could be done to expand the Basic Services for children it responded: "Basic Services represent, in essence, a broad-based endeavor to stimulate self-help and to organize human resources for investment in social and economic progress."

This approach is based on the village or urban community setting and uses village or neighborhood workers chosen and supported by the people of the community. These workers are trained in simple techniques to carry out specific limited tasks. Working either full- or part-time they show their neighbors how to improve their conditions. At least part of the expenses are born by the community. The first priority needs are selected by the people themselves so that the problems are solved with enthusiasm by the people concerned. Later, they move naturally on to other projects.

The network of core services in a country becomes a supporting organization for these community workers. Professional people are thus freed to serve as trainers, technical advisors, and supervisors.

The advantages of the Basic Service approach are:

1. The community is involved in identifying its own needs in priority order determined by the people to be benefited. These people also plan and implement the projects.
2. The workers are chosen by the people of the community.
3. Local traditions, customs, and agrarian cycles are taken into account and much time and energy is thus saved.
4. Village-level technologies can adapt modern methods to the needs of the rural countryside.

Care is taken to have the Basic Services planned on a comprehensive and not a piecemeal basis.

The UNICEF Board has pointed out to the General Assembly of the U.N. that:

Basic Services are labour-intensive and therefore provide opportunities for mobilization and productive use of resources abundantly available but substantially neglected, namely human resources.

This approach has importance for the whole development process and is not simply a program for child welfare alone but also supports a more active and skillful adult population.

The 1976 UNICEF Report pointed out that this approach is a proposal for an overall strategy in which governments, United Nation's agencies, bilateral aid programs, NGO (nongovernmental organizations), and others could join. In the Basic Services program UNICEF has promised to continue to support the kind of activities it has long promoted to the limit of its ability. It plans, as it always has, to have each country when it is able to bear its own costs.

During 1975, UNICEF assisted services benefiting children in 109 countries where it is estimated there were 884 million children under 15 years; not all of these children were reached of course but the present programs are attempting to reach more and more of them. In 1975, the sum of $141 million from both governmental and nongovernmental sources represented an increase of 10 percent in real terms—22 percent in dollar terms.

In 1975, contributions of $22 million came from such nongovernmental sources as the sale of greeting cards, Halloween contributions in North America, extension-appeals in Europe, and other collections by national committees (31 countries have these) and other organizations (nongovernmental). The greeting card revenues rose from $5 million in 1971 to $9 million in 1975. Of all the $11,127,213 raised by the U.S. Committee for

UNICEF in 1976, the Halloween contributions were $2,774,654 and the greeting cards brought in $4,757,173.

Alastair Mathison (1975 UNICEF News) reported that "few countries provide grimmer statistics than the Caribbean Nation of Haiti—'the first Black Republic in the World.' " In 1975 the infant mortality in Haiti was 133.8 per 1000 live births, having fallen only by 12 in 5 years. He said that malnutrition seriously threatens the health of Haiti's children. Seven percent of all infants and preschool children suffer from kwashiorkor, 27 percent are gravely malnourished, and 69 percent suffer from some degree of malnutrition. During 1974 an enlightened and concerted effort was made by six United Nations' agencies including UNICEF. It is encouraging that in 1977, although it was difficult to get good statistics, the number of malnourished children seemed to have decreased materially.

Also reported by UNICEF in 1975 is the story of a coordinated service operated in Honduras since 1971 with UNICEF assistance. This project has improved food production as well as provided safe water, better roads, and bridges, and better housing for families and schools. So successful has this project been that UNICEF agreed to invest one million dollars for the period 1971–1978. Twenty million dollars worth of local resources were to be used.

The multifaceted approach to the basic needs and problems of children and their families seems to heed the advice given by Cicely Williams when she said, "More attention should be given to the multifarious causes leading to the malnourished state, to the production, distribution, selection, and presentation of locally available foods, to the need for education and continuing supervision in hospitals, health centres and homes."

UNICEF and the efforts promoted by it now support projects in 60 countries. In 1975 UNICEF spent $3,700,000 to build up social welfare services "helping to equip and staff community centers for children of working mothers and women's clubs, also providing training for local community leaders, social workers, etc." UNICEF is now giving the following services:

1. Health
2. Nutrition
3. Social welfare
4. Education (formal and nonformal)
5. Country planning and project development
6. Emergency aid—long and short term

Although, in its early years of existence, most of the aid was given to projects in health and nutrition, the base of operation is broader today; attempts are being made to assist governments to meet any of the needs of children the particular country considers to be of high priority and for which practical, effective action is possible. During the years of UNICEF's emergency aid maternal and child health services received major attention. The eradication of disease then played a major role in that effort, with special attention given to such diseases as malaria, tuberculosis, yaws, leprosy, and trachoma, all of which were taking a high toll among children.

Emergency aid is always necessary. In 1976, the sum of $100,000 was sent to the regions in Guatemala hardest hit by the earthquake; $150,000 was sent to the Portugese colony of Timor to help meet the needs of the children there who were affected by the hostilities, and $140,000 was sent to Beirut for the same purpose.

Nutrition Programs

In 1975, the program to assist countries to improve the nutrition of their children in addition to the aid given health services provided assistance to family food production and to food storage as well as to supplementary feeding programs in areas of special short-term need. UNICEF gave during that year $15 million to nutrition projects in 67 countries, plus about $9 million in donated foods. This was an increase of $4 million over that given in 1973. In 1975, for emergency relief as well as long-term-child-feeding programs, 32,722 metric tons of children's foods (nearly twice as much as in 1974) were shipped. One-third of this came from the European Economic Community and one-fourth from the United States, 15 percent from the World Food Program, and the rest from other developed countries.

Fortification of foods and distribution of vitamins and minerals to help to combat goiter, certain forms of blindness, as well as anemia has been continued. In the 1976 report, anemia is cited as probably the most widespread nutritional deficiency.

Included now in UNICEF supplies is Oralyte, a rehydrating agent, which at a small cost per child has been found to successfully combat often fatal dehydration.

UNICEF's applied nutrition programs attempt to increase food production for family use, to improve home storage of food, and to provide nutrition education, especially on food preparation for children during weaning. UNICEF also continued to participate in a worldwide campaign to counteract premature weaning.

Current Policies

UNICEF is now urging a nutrition surveillance system as a valuable tool for implementation of food and nutrition policies because children are most vulnerable to inadequate food distribution and consumption. This is in line with the recommendation of the 1974 World Food Conference recommendations that such a system be established by FAO, WHO, and UNICEF.

Assistance to Countries to Establish Foods and Nutrition Policies

In the attempt to help countries to establish food and nutrition policies UNICEF pointed to the need to consider three broad stages:

1. Government intervention programs to prevent or treat child malnutrition.
2. Gradual linkage of planning health, nutrition education, and social welfare services of different ministries to form a mutually supporting system.
3. Development of a national and international ministerial food and nutrition policy.

At the first African Nutrition Congress (Ibadan, Nigeria) in 1975 all African governments were encouraged to develop such policies and to implement them.

Countries Now Assisted

Three groups of countries are now recognized:

Group I. Countries in early stages of development and 29 small countries needing special assistance. The goal is to increase assistance to this group, from general resources to three times the level of Group II in relation to the child population.

Group II. The middle range of developing countries. This group includes 43 countries with 78 percent of all children in the countries assisted by UNICEF.

Group III. Countries at a more advantaged stage of development where projects have less need of UNICEF's material assistance. Assistance to these countries is largely advisory.

Common Needs

The report to the 1976 Board lists the most common needs as:

1. Maternal and child care
2. Family planning
3. Safe water supply and waste disposal
4. Nutritional rehabilitation
5. Local production and consumption of more and better quality of foods
6. Measures to meet basic educational requirements
7. Simple technologies to lighten the daily tasks of women and girls
8. Activities designed to improve family welfare and create opportunities for women's greater participation in community affairs

Proposed Children's Year—1979

In 1976 UNICEF Board also took note of a proposal before the U.N. Assembly that 1979 be designated as the International Year of the Child. This would put emphasis on measures benefiting children on the national level and would focus on the Basic Services at the community level in the developing countries. It is hoped by the U.N. that such a designated year would lead to a permanent higher level of attention and support of services for children.

Sir Herbert Broadley, in a speech to nongovernmental agencies on UNICEF's role in the United Nations, said after discussing the projections of population in the world by the year 2000:

> Thus, members of the United Nations family are faced with immense responsibilities. And of all international organizations, UNICEF perhaps carries the greatest burden, in that to some degree the future civilization lies in its hands. This does not imply anything derogatory to the great work being undertaken by FAO in increasing the world's food supply, by WHO in banishing diseases and improving health throughout the world, or by UNESCO in spreading the benefits of education to the less developed countries. Whatever benefits may occur to the adult population as the result of all these activities, it is the children of today who are the most important in that the future of the world will be in their hands.

The Scope of UNICEF

In summary, the following should be pointed out:

1. UNICEF is the only international agency devoted exclusively to helping children.
2. UNICEF assistance is given only on a government's request after a detailed plan has been submitted setting forth exactly how the aid is to be used and with the assurances of the commitments and responsibilities of the government.
3. Full responsibility for running the health, nutrition, welfare, or education projects rests on the individual government.
4. Every country receiving aid must match UNICEF's contributions. Many do contribute up to two, three, or four times that of UNICEF.
5. UNICEF's aid is given without regard to political belief, race, creed, or nationality.
6. UNICEF is supported entirely by voluntary contributions, approximately 73 percent of which came in 1975 from governments and the balance from organizations and individuals.
7. Each project is planned eventually to become an integral part of the country's health, nutrition, or welfare and education services. The projects should be so planned that when UNICEF aid stops the individual country can and will continue and expand the program.

THE WORLD HEALTH ORGANIZATION (WHO)

In 1977, the World Health Organization Assembly was composed of 150 member states and two associate members. The annual Assembly meeting, usually held in Geneva, Switzerland, establishes policy and decides on the program and budget for the following year.

On May 7, 1966, WHO dedicated a beautiful modern headquarters building on the grounds of the Palace of the Nations in Geneva. This move from one of the original buildings occupied by the post-World War I League of Nations was symbolic of the long history of the international movement to improve and protect world health.

In 1977, more than a century after the first organized efforts to promote international health, there were 5577 staff members including 1239 under the Washington, D.C., office of PAHO, at the WHO headquarters and in 150 countries of the world.

For WHO purposes, the world is divided into six regions. The regional office for Europe, including the USSR, is in Copenhagen, Denmark; for Africa, in Brazzaville, Republic of the Congo; for the Americas, in Washington, D.C.; for Southeast Asia, in New Delhi, India; for the Eastern Mediterranean, in Alexandra, United Arab Republic; anf for the Western Pacific Region, in Manila, Philippines. These regional offices are responsible for planning and operating country projects; the Headquarters' technical staff stand ready to advise and help.

History of the International Health Movement

The international health movement had its inception when Europeans realized that cholera was spreading from country to country. They also began to wonder how disease was related to sanitation, to climate, and to the physical environment in general.

Programs in social welfare arose in Europe when rapid industrialization brought overcrowding, poverty, suffering, and riots to the rapidly expanding urban areas. At this time, privately supported medical missions under newly organized private philanthropic groups began to expand their spheres of action beyond national boundaries. Even in this era of strong nationalism, it became increasingly evident that national governments could not solve their own problems. Because of this, the first International Sanitary Congress was called in Paris in 1851. The progress toward international planning and cooperation in matters of health was not continuous, but the general interest in international health spread and the present humanitarian objectives were coming to the fore. In 1919, at an intergovernmental health meeting, the idea that the masses must accept the need for the proposed health measures and even understand them was brought forth. Following World War I, the newly formed League of Nations included in its covenant a statement calling for international concern for the prevention and control of disease. In 1945, following World War II when the delegates met in San Francisco to form the

What does the future hold for these children in health and nutrition? The proper food can help give them a happy future (*Courtesy Food and Agriculture Organization*).

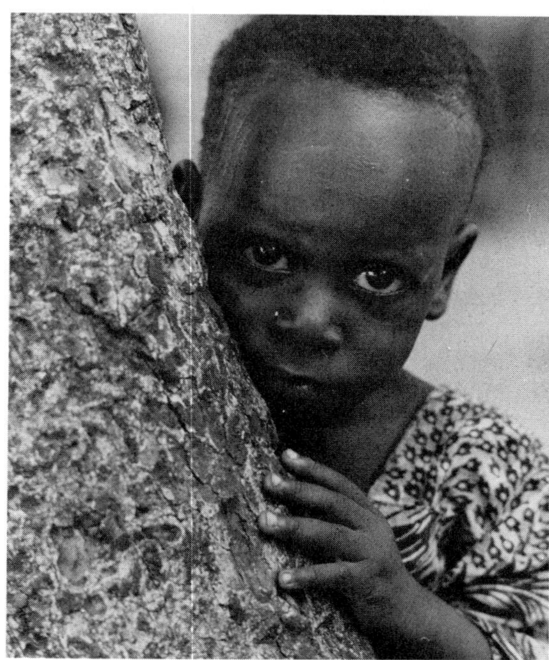

2nd photo in series

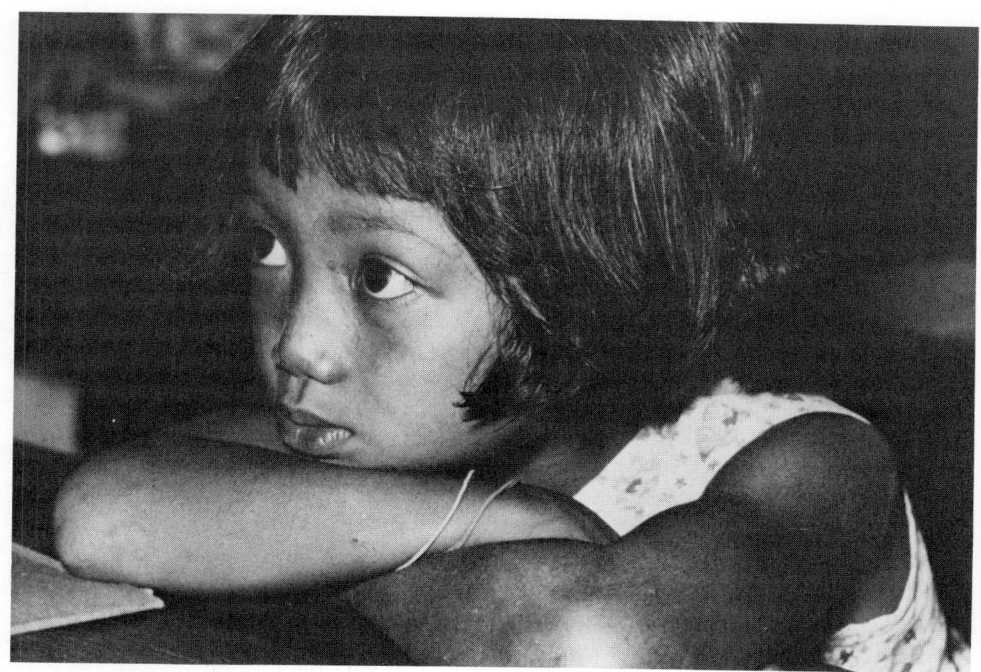

3rd photo in series

United Nations, the will to build the peace on firm foundations and a confidence that the use of existing scientific knowledge in health matters was deemed of paramount importance. Following an International Health Conference held in New York in 1946, the WHO Constitution was drafted; by 1948 fifty countries had ratified it. So on April 7, 1948, henceforth known as World Health Day, WHO was officially launched as an integral part of the United Nations with Dr. Broch Chisholm as its first Director-General.

The opening paragraph of the WHO Constitution says: "Health is a state of complete physical, mental and social well-being and not merely the absence of disease or infirmity." Upon retiring in 1953, in his last address, Dr. Chisholm said that all the principles included in the WHO Constitution "are based on this simple truth: in our shrunken world, health, like peace and security, is indivisible and mankind's fight against illness, its major enemy, can be won only through the concerted efforts of us all."

Nutrition in WHO

From the first, nutrition has been recognized as important in the promotion of good health. In the proposals made for the 1950 program, the Director-General and the executive board of WHO, at the Second World Assembly in 1949, said: "Nutrition is perhaps the most important single environmental factor influencing health." To support this it was stated that discoveries of recent decades show the importance of nutrition in the reduction of the infant death rate and in the incidence of infectious diseases as well as in the productivity of adults.

Because of the gravity of the problems of food production, FAO was started in 1945 three years before WHO. Even before the latter was formed in 1948, observers from the WHO Interim Commission who attended the second annual conference of FAO proposed that a joint committee on nutrition be formed. Thus began the close cooperation between WHO and FAO that has been carried out by the Joint Expert Committee ever since.

In 1925, the Health Organization of the League of Nations began a study of nutrition, but active international interest really only began in 1935, with the circulation to governments and scientific bodies of a report of the Technical Commission. In 1936 a study of the nutritional status of children, of nutritive requirements especially for young children, and of factors influencing nutritive requirements was proposed. Because the needs for nutrition emphasis in public health were already understood, at the World Health Assembly in 1948, nutrition was granted the same high priority as malaria, maternal and child health, tuberculosis, and venereal diseases. A nutrition section was immediately established within the Secretariat of WHO. At the first meeting of the Joint Expert Committee of FAO and WHO in October 1949 and at subsequent meetings, this committee made vital contributions, including:

1. Discussing individual and joint programs of the two organizations.
2. Giving expert advice on problems referred to them.
3. Examining problems of malnutrition of international concern and making recommendations for action to FAO and WHO.
4. Making suggestions for assistance to establish national food and nutrition organization in member countries.
5. Directing attention to training and education of personnel needed in national nutrition activities.

In 1959, some of the practical aspects of cooperation of the two agencies were critically evaluated and an agreement was drawn up, as stated in the book *The First Ten Years of WHO*. WHO agreed to concern itself with "nutrition as it affects health; the objective of FAO is to raise the levels of nutrition and standards of living, and to improve the efficiency of all food and agricultural products."

A specific example of the cooperation of WHO and FAO is shown in the launching of the World Food Program in 1962. This was aimed at making plans for social and economic progress in developing countries and at relieving malnutrition by the organized use of surplus foods. WHO actively cooperated by: (1) examining the health implications as well as those concerning nutrition of the projects proposed, (2) following the progress of these projects, and (3) later evaluating the effects of these programs on the health of the populations involved.

For almost two decades now the Joint Expert Committee has been concerned with the extent of malnutrition and the indices for determining this. Its efforts have pointed to the urgent need for comparability on an international scale of methods of collecting data. Study continues on such problems as assessment of nutritional status and nutritional requirements and assessment of such diseases as goiter, xerophthalmia, nutritional anemia, marasmus and protein-calorie malnutrition, and certain degenerative diseases. The increasing use of food additives led to the appointment, in 1956, of a joint committee to discuss the general principles that should govern their use. By 1964, recommendations for a number of food additives were drawn up. The use of pesticides also was studied by another committee, and principles governing consumer safety were established.

WHO emphasizes nutrition as an inseparable component of health that needs to be integrated by governments into their health plans; this is particularly stressed in the developing countries.

As the result of all of these efforts, more attention is being paid in the developing countries to the teaching of nutrition in the medical schools and to building up contacts between medical schools in the developed and developing countries. Particular emphasis has been given to the need for pediatricians, maternal and child health specialists, and public health physicians to receive specific training in nutrition to enable them to handle the problems of malnutrition in mothers and young children.

For the proposed 1978–1979 budget the following objective was listed:

To collaborate with countries in developing their own capacity for planning and implementation of the activities needed for diagnosis of nutritional problems of public health significance and for prevention and control.

Nutrition Program

The nutrition section of WHO outlined the following as the approach for the proposed programs:

1. Development and testing of methodologies for integrating nutritional objectives into national development plans,
2. Development and testing of methodologies for establishing nutrition monitoring and surveillance systems as a basis for action programmes and for their evaluation,
3. Integration of nutrition activities primarily within maternal and child care, as a component of primary health care,
4. Promotion of and collaboration in measures for the control of endemic goiter,
5. Further development, and the testing under varying conditions of

methods for control of vitamin A deficiency and nutritional anemia,
6. Promotion and support of further studies needed for a better understanding of factors responsible for malnutrition and related problems,
7. Collaboration in training health workers in nutrition.

The program as outlined is to be carried out in collaboration with FAO, UNICEF, and other international and bilateral agencies. This was recommended as a high priority by the 1974 World Food Conference and also strongly endorsed by the Twenty-Eight World Health Assembly.

National health administrators and planners are urged to include nutrition in their plans and to promote the cooperation of the agencies concerned.

Nutrition surveillance is to be tested under field conditions to find simple, easily obtainable, and reliable indicators.

Western Hemisphere Health Programs

Many nations share in the work of the United Nations and specialized agencies, and in the Western Hemisphere, health programs are directed toward meeting the particular needs of the millions of people in Latin America and the Caribbean.

The problems of Latin America are numerous, varied, and in many areas severe; there is a high incidence of infectious diseases, malnutrition and hunger, poor sanitation, poor housing and working conditions, illiteracy, and poverty. No one country has sufficient resources, facilities, and trained personnel to solve all the problems immediately.

Nutrition in the Pan American Health Organization (PAHO)

The regional office of PAHO recently described its work in general and nutrition as follows:

"The PAHO Technical Cooperation Program assists Member Governments in the following priority areas:
1. Prevention or control of disease and disability,
2. Promotion of health and well-being of families,
3. Control of environmental factors affecting health,
4. Promotion and organization of the delivery of health services, and
5. Development of human resources and promotion of research.

In addition to these, PAHO assists in the development of health criteria and standards, and in the collection, synthesis and dissemination of health-related scientific information and public health knowledge.

The technical cooperation activities undertaken by PAHO relate to development and transfer of technology, advisory services, education, and training of human resources, coordination and supporting services.

To carry out such a program, the Organization has five technical divisions. The Nutrition Program is integrated in the Division of Family Health.

The nutrition activities in Family Health are carried out at the regional, subregional, and country levels by the Regional, Area, and Country Advisors, and the multinational centers assigned to the Division. Two of these centers are the "Instituto de Nutricion de Centro America y Panama—INCAP" and the Caribbean Food and Nutrition Institute—CFNI. In addition to the personnel and resources at these centers, the nutrition program now includes three professionals at the regional office and ten at the subregional and country level.

In the program area of *Nutrition,* emphasis is being given to:

1. The integration of nutrition components within primary health services.
2. The development and implementation of national food and nutrition policies.
3. The development of models for nutritional surveillance systems and their testing in selected countries.
4. The development of manpower with special emphasis on the improvement of curriculum development and educational programs for nutritionists/dietitians and on the integration of the nutrition content into teaching programs for physicians, nurses, and auxiliary personnel.
5. The development of World Food Program projects related to health at country levels.

Institute of Nutrition of Central America and Panama (INCAP)

In 1949 a unique scientific organization called the Institute of Nutrition for Central America and Panama was created by Costa Rica, El Salvador, Guatemala, Honduras, Nicaragua, and Panama, the Pan American Health Organization and the W. K. Kellogg Foundation. All of these continue to be involved in INCAP activities.

The purposes in founding this were:

1. To study the nutritional problems of the area
2. To find ways of solving these problems
3. To assist the member governments in applying the measures recommended for this purpose

The government of The Republic of Guatemala provided the necessary buildings in Guatemala City to house the Institute. Dr. Nevin S. Scrimshaw was appointed as the first director, which office he retained until 1961, when the present director Dr. Moises Be'har was appointed to the post.

In 1974 INCAP celebrated its 25th anniversary. During its first 25 years its budget had grown from the modest 1947 sum of $75,000 from the six member countries and $65,000 from the W. K. Kellogg Foundation to $2,250,000 for research and contracts from different sources. The Williams-Waterman Program for Research Corporation and the United States National Institute of Health also contributed to this 1974 fund. The 25th annual report from INCAP acknowledges indebtedness to the Nutrition Foundation of the United States, the Josiah Macy, Jr., Ford, Rockefeller, and Nestle Foundations as well as the International Committee on Nutrition for National Development, the United States Agency for International Development (AID), the International Development Centre of Canada, and UNICEF.

The following accomplishments are reported for the 25 years:

1. Complete and detailed studies of nutritional status and dietary habits of the populations of the six member countries.

2. Completion of a table of the composition of the foods of Central America. This formed the core of the Latin America Food Composition Table.

3. Better understanding of:
   a. The effects of pre- and post-natal malnutrition on growth and development of children, including learning and behavior, and
   b. The interaction of nutrition and work performance of products.

4. Better understanding of epidemiology of protein-calorie malnutrition, including the role of infections.

5. Improved methods for the treatment and rehabilitation of malnourished children including the role of infections.

6. Development and practical application of the principle of combining different plant sources to make highly nutritious, low cost food such as Incaparina (see page 329.

7. Development of original methods of food fortifications, including the iodization of moist, unrefined salt with potassium iodate and fortification of sugar with vitamin A.

8. Utilization of local products and improved management of systems of animal feeding.

9. Development of principles and materials for nutrition education and for teaching nutrition at various levels.

10. Development and application of new methods for assessment of nutritional status of population groups.

Nutrition scouts look for early signs of malnutrition in Uganda (*Courtesy* UNICEF, *Photo by Thorning*).

Although INCAP maintains a primary responsibility for six member nations, it also helps through its advisory services other Latin American countries and the world with its training and research programs by cooperation in PAHO and WHO.

The Caribbean Food and Nutrition Institute (CFNI)

The 1967, PAHO with FAO, the Williams-Waterman Fund, and the University of the West Indies of Jamaica and Trinidad established a Caribbean Foods and Nutrition Institute on the two campuses on which this university is located.

The primary functions of this Institute has been stated as:

a. To train for the area middle-level people, not nutrition specialists. These included nurses, sanitarians, agriculture extension personnel, home economics teachers, and welfare workers.

Seven agencies of the United Nations cooperate to teach Bolivians to raise better potatoes (*Courtesy United Nations*).

b. To coordinate food production and availability with the improvement of nutritional status of the people in the English-speaking area in the Caribbean.

c. To make, as time permits, surveys of food availability and nutritional status.

Cajanus, the publication of CFNI, is especially valuable in its discussions of problems of nutrition and their solution of local Caribbean areas.

Cooperative Relations of United Nations Agencies

Very soon after the creation of FAO, WHO, and UNICEF, it became apparent that committees to handle problems common to all of these organizations would be necessary. In 1960, Maurice Pate, then Executive-Director of UNICEF, said:

> Over the course of the years a network of cooperative relationships has developed between UNICEF and the World Health Organization and also the Food and Agriculture Organization—relationships both of a formal and intimate character—to assure that the available international resources are aligned in the most effective ways possible in helping government projects.

Much of this cooperation has been accomplished through joint-action programs in the developing countries. These commenced in the 1950s as "Expanded Nutrition Programs," which were mainly concerned with school feeding activities. Realizing the potential that practical activities had in nutrition education, in 1961 the International Agencies concerned decided to pay more attention to the food production components of nutrition programs then renamed ''Applied Nutrition Programs.'' These may be defined as:

Coordinated educational activities between agriculture, health and education authorities and other interested agencies with the aim of raising the levels of nutrition of local populations, particularly mothers and children in rural areas.

FAO/WHO/UNICEF Applied Nutrition Programs have been initiated in many countries, and consideration is presently being given to enlargement of their scope through giving more attention to their introduction in areas where specific help is needed.

They have also collaborated in assisting in training personnel from developing countries in food and nutrition.

It long ago became apparent that FAO and WHO should decide on the emphasis each would concentrate on. It was decided that FAO would emphasize production, distribution, and consumption of foods; in WHO it would be nutrition in relation to the maintenance of health and the prevention of disease.

In 1955, FAO, WHO, and UNICEF agreed to collaborate in the Protein Advisory Group (PAG) of the United Nations system. This group changed its name to the Protein-Calorie Advisory Group of the United Nations in September 1974.

This committee was originally set up by WHO to advise on the safety and nutritional usefulness for infants and young children of various protein foods and supplements. The committee was enlarged in 1960 to include FAO and UNICEF.

This group recently defined itself as an interdisciplinary committee of internationally recognized experts who advise the United Nations and its agencies on technical, economic, education, social and other related aspects of global malnutrition problems and the broad programs and new areas of activities needed for combating them. Since 1955 they have emphasized protein-calorie malnutrition (''protein-energy malnutrition'' some believe a more appropriate term) as a primary and continuing threat to the health and survival of infants and young children in the developing countries and they have played an active role in promoting the development of novel and locally available protein resources in the developing world.

McLaren, Waterlow, Payne, and Latham have accused this group of placing undue emphasis on the need for protein-high foods in the developing countries. They believe that 500 calories per day per person in extra cereals would be more effective in combating malnutrition. There are of course countries especially in Africa where starch-high, protein-poor roots and not cereals are the staple food.

It is true that the efforts to get the new protein high foods to the infants and children who needed them have met with only very limited success. It is hoped that in the future an individual country approach will be taken.

Wishik and Van der Vyncke said in 1975

There is fundamental concern throughout the world regarding the widespread failure of the development process to reach the people most in need. Governments and international agencies are hard at work to treat the chronic problems of underdevelopment, disease, rapid population growth, malnutrition, illiteracy, underemployment, and inadequate food resources. However, planners are only just beginning to recognize that, if they persist in attacking each problem in isolation, the progress that can be made toward the common goal of all the intervention programs, the improvement of the quality of life, will be limited.

In 1977 the PAG group was discontinued and a subcommittee on nutrition of the Administrative Committee on Coordination (ACC) was established with headquarters at FAO in Rome.

This new committee was established with the following commitments to:

1. Examine the existing and projected activities of the United Nations system with reference to the implementation of the resolutions of the World Food Conference related to nutritional improvement, taking account of the relevant decisions of the governing bodies of the agencies concerned,
2. Determine whether the efforts of the system are fully mobilized and integrated, in co-operation with the governments, at all levels in order to achieve maximum impact at the country level, taking into account programmes being undertaken on a bilateral basis,
3. Consider whether the existing arrangements and resources can respond effectively to the major nutritional problems of the developing world.

Outside experts will be called upon for advice to the ACC if deemed necessary.

There are other advisory committees to United Nations agencies concerned with other specific diseases of malnutrition. What Wishik and Van der Vynche call for in overall assessments and programs to attack problems in their totality would seem to be desperately needed and will possibly soon become realities.

On the practical level and to the benefit of all concerned, efforts toward cooperation in the field of nutrition must be pursued ever more vigorously. As the ever-expanding population presents what seems to be almost insoluble nutrition problems, such cooperation is becoming even more imperative.

World Food Conference 1974

This conference was largely concerned with some major issues:

1. Unexpected excessive sales of large portions of the world's food reserves following the sudden appearance of two large consumers—the USSR and the Peoples Republic of China—on the international market.

2. Poor harvests in some parts of the world.

3. General inflation in many countries.

It dwelt mostly with the cereal crisis with only the last preliminary session devoted to the problem of malnutrition.

The world as a whole suddenly became aware of malnutrition as essentially a problem of the poor farmer and the landless worker.

Henry Kissinger from the U.S.A. proposed establishing a global surveillance system as nutritionists had been urging for 20 years.

The United States Congress decided as a result of this food conference to establish:

1. An International Agricultural Development Fund

2. An International World Food Security System that would issue early warnings on crop information and would also hold surplus grain stocks

It was recommended that a World Food Council be set up inside the U.N. system.

Dr. Jean Mayer said in 1975 that it is difficult to evaluate the achievements of this conference and that it is not impossible in retrospect to view this conference as marking the beginning of an era wherein those concerned started considering "hunger and malnutrition as planetary problems to be considered and reduced on an international basis." Some have said, however, that the discouraging impressions given out by the press at the close of this conference may be justified because no precise blueprints were established. Although the conference fell short of what many agency representatives expected of it in terms of the short-term world food problems, the fact that 350 representatives from governmental and nongovernmental agencies were present must be considered as some progress. There was, however, underrepresentation from the developing countries.

On the positive side the following should be considered:

1. The massive press coverage sensitized the world to the problems.

2. The beginnings of an early warning system were set in motion.

3. There was an increase in development funds by national and international agencies.

4. The principle of coordinated national food reserves was encouraged.

UNITED STATES AGENCIES FOR THE IMPROVEMENT OF NUTRITION

Agency for International Development (AID)

In 1977 President Carter gave a reason for United States overseas aid when he said that "The future of the United States will be affected by the ability of developing nations to overcome poverty, achieve healthy growth and provide more secure lives for their people." The administrator for the agency of the United States government charged with administering foreign economic assistance programs, the Agency for International Development (AID), John J. Gilligan put this succinctly, "There are no separate futures for the rich and poor."

This agency, previously known by other names during its existence from 1946, and functioning as an arm of the United States Department of State, in 1977 had 6000 employees working in its Washington, D.C., headquarters, and in 60 countries in Asia, Africa, and Latin America. The director reports directly to the Secretary of State and the President. Appropriations are authorized annually by the United States Congress for all loans and grants. Its purpose was stated in 1977: "to assist the people of less developed countries to acquire the knowledge and resources needed to build economic, political, and social institutions necessary to their aspirations for a better life." In addition "to humanitarian reasons, such assistance is considered essential to the economic and security interests of the United States." In 1977, the sum of $1.15 billion was appropriated by Congress for development assistance for improving the lives of the poorest people in the underdeveloped countries, a land area covering two-thirds of the earth's land area and containing 74 percent of the world's population.

In addition, $1.7 billion was appropriated in that year for security-supporting assistance to promote economic and political stability in selected countries (e.g., some middle Eastern countries) and thus to provide incentives to reduce violence and conflict.

In 1976, these forms of economic assistance totaled about 0.26 percent of the United States Gross National Product provided for economic aid. The United States was in 12th place, with seven European countries, Canada, Australia, and New Zealand, all contributing a larger share of their GNP than the United States. On the other hand the United States private contributions of $3.47 on a per capita basis in 1974 was second only to $4.03 for Sweden.

From the beginning of the fiscal year of 1946 to the end of fiscal year 1975 foreign aid has cost the United States 183 billion dollars, the bulk of this spent here at home in payment to American industry, agriculture, and sources of technical skills for the products of American workers, technicians, and farmers. Nearly $43 billion of the $183 billion was provided on a loan or credit basis, the repayment record of which continues to be excellent.

The economic progress in the developing countries means an expansion of trade for the United States. These countries accounted in 1976 for 25 percent of our exports and 23 percent of our imports.

The grants and loans under AID are aimed at:

1. Increasing and improving food production and nutrition. Especially important here are programs aimed at permitting the small farmer and rural poor to participate actively in development, so that the process of expanding incomes, employment, and food production will become widespread and self-sustaining. In the past 12 years the land planted to high-yielding variety cereals in Asia and North Africa has

increased from 145,000 acres to more than 100 million acres. It is estimated now that almost 40 percent of the total wheat acreage and 25 percent of the total rice acreage are now high-yielding varieties. In addition, irrigation projects, projects to increase the availability of fertilizer to farmers, research for improvement of food production, food storage, as well as promotion of training in better agricultural methods have been promoted.

2. Encouraging family planning related to health and the food supply. Most nations now recognize that uncontrolled population growth impedes development and have begun to deal with the problem, but it is thought that the long-term battle still lies ahead because three-fourths of the populations in developing countries still lacks regular access to safe, effective family planning and health services. AID's assistance is provided only at the request of the host government or institution, and are channeled through nongovernmental agencies.
3. Making health care services available. Health planning on a national scale is being expanded from seven to 21 countries. AID has assisted in the eradication of smallpox and the drastically reduced menace of measles as well as the global programs to eradicate malaria.
4. Extending technical assistance and other programs concerned with energy, research, reconstruction, and other selected development problems. Work has been carried on to promote high yielding crop varieties, more efficient systems for using soil and water, better and cheaper fertilizers, and improved livestock.
5. Sustaining American schools and hospitals. These projects focus on demonstration of American ideas and practices.
6. Contributing to international organizations and programs such as the U.N. Development Program, the U.N. Relief and Works Agency in support, for instance, of relief for Palestine refugees as well as others.
7. Meeting short-term emergency needs for disaster victims, such as short-term immediate impact projects for instance in Haiti and Sahel.

AID also administers P. L. 480 Food Aid (Food for Peace Title II) allocated to the Department of Agriculture. This is concerned with the alleviation of suffering of disaster victims, and the promoting economic development through the use of food as a development source in combating hunger and malnutrition. For 1978, AID requested 1.5 million metric tons of food for donations for humanitarian programs which concern primarily maternal and child care.

AID administers the U.S. contribution to the International Fund for Agricultural Development (IFAD). AID also is promoting the feeding of children in the 6 to 36 months age group in the poorest families where it is believed the food will have the greatest nutritional impact.

Monitoring and evaluation in order to study the effectiveness of its nutrition programs is a constant part of AID's program, measuring the growth of young children to watch for signs of malnutrition. The monitoring of weight gain is said by D. B. Jelliffe to be extremely important in early detection and therefore prevention as well as recovery from such severe forms of protein-calorie malnutrition as kwashiorkor and another major pediatric problem, nutritional marasmus. An important cooperative program with this office in AID and the Maternal and Child Health Services of the Department of Health, Education, and Welfare is the use of growth charts to assess the physical well-being of the children. ILLESHA growth chart (see illustration on following pages), developed by Dr. David Morley for Nigeria, has been used. The use of such growth charts had helped to educate and convince policymakers in a country, all levels of health workers, and parents as well as supporting agencies of the importance of the prevention of malnutrition.

AID and U.S. Land Grant Universities

AID has, over the more of a quarter of its existence, utilized the resources of America's agricultural colleges and universities. Hundreds of consultants and advisors in agriculture and nutrition have helped create colleges and training schools in the developing countries modeled on the land-grant concept in the United States. In 1975, the U.S. Congress authorized legislation (Foreign Assistance Act) to promote cooperative and liaison efforts in the food and agriculture field between AID and United States land-grant and sea-grant institutions.

A Board of International Food and Agricultural Development has been established to promote greater participation of qualified United States universities in stimulating food production and nutrition in the developing countries.

AID said in 1977, projecting for 1979 program guidance, that "nutrition represents the most basic need of the poor in low income countries." Thus all AID programs relate in some way to the nutritional status of a population.

Two categories of areas which AID believes it should more actively pursue than it has in the past are:

1 Determining and improving the nutrition/consumption effects of development policies, particularly those in the agricultural section

2. Developing nutrition components of integrated services designed to meet the basic needs of the poor

It was recently said by the International Food Policy Research Institute (IFPRI) that "increased food production may bypass the neediest groups of the population if it does not help to raise their incomes and it can also result in lower incomes and food consumption under some circumstances."

AID in 1975, proposed to the U.S. Congress that it promote programs to involve women more directly and fully in the economic and social progress of the developing

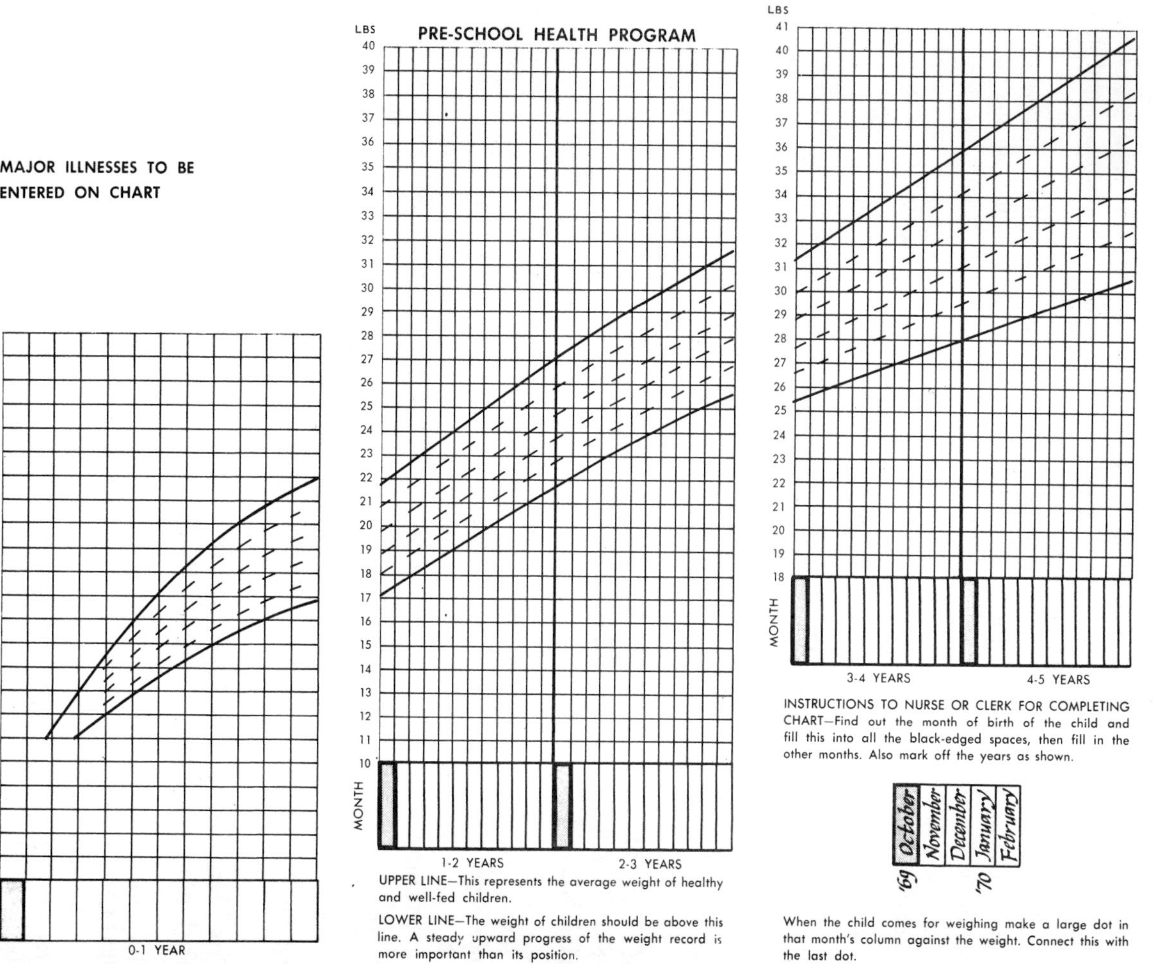

Child health and weight record Ilesha Charts (*Courtesy Agency for International Development*).

countries. It was stated that women are a vital resource in improving the quality of life in the developing world as producers of goods and services, as childbearers, and as mothers helping shape the essential human resources.

The section on Health and Education in AID has chosen mass media, particularly radio, in conjunction with traditional extension education to instruct the population at large in the following practices beneficial to their health:

1. Encouragement of breast feeding
2. Preparation of diarrhea cessation formulae
3. Enrichment of gruel with oil, fish, and vegetable products
4. Regular exposure of infants to the sun
5. Basic sanitary practices

SOME INTERNATIONAL PROGRAMS OF FEDERAL AGENCIES

A few of the international programs are reviewed here to indicate another type of assistance. The 1954 Agricultural Trade Development and Assistance Act, usually known as Public Law 480, was passed by the 83rd Congress (see Table 10-1). Under this law, foreign currency was to be accepted in payment for surplus American food sold to countries friendly to the United States and needing the food. This currency was to be deposited in the country of origin. It could be used for projects to benefit the people of that country. Several departments of the United States government have carried on programs in a number of countries. Some of these programs use P.L. 480 funds and others do not.

The National Institute of Arthritis and Metabolic Diseases (NIAMDD)

The international program of the National Institute of Health is now under the NIAMDD.

One important nutrition activity of this Institute concerns the cooperative effort between the United States and Japan. In 1971 a report of the first five years (1965–1970) said, "The United States and Japanese governments have appointed biomedical scientists to constitute a United States–Japan Cooperative Medical Science Committee."

The joint malnutrition panel of the United States–Japan Medical Science Program set high priority for research in developing countries of Asia as:

1. Determination of the effects of malnutrition in children on mental development, learning, behavior, physical capability, and performance.

Table 10-1 Title II Public Law 480 Number of Recipients by Program—Fiscal Year 1976*

		Food for development				Emergency assistance		
Program	Total	Maternal child feeding	School feeding	Other child feeding	Food for work	Refugee	Disaster	General relief
Total	40,025,800	13,863,500	12,976,700	984,800	8,175,400	157,000	3,847,600	20,800
Voluntary Agencies UNICEF	27,817,000	8,641,200	10,573,100	984,800	5,676,900	89,000	1,831,200	20,800
UNICEF	41,000	41,000	—	—	—	—	—	—
American Joint Distribution Committee (AJDC)	2,500	200	2,300	—	—	—	—	—
CARE	11,927,800	2,212,700	3,500,600	676,900	4,513,500	—	1,016,600	7,500
Catholic Relief Service (CRS)	15,469,500	6,247,200	7,031,200	281,100	1,003,000	89,000	811,000	7,000
Church World Service (CWS)	206,500	73,900	37,000	8,100	83,900	—	3,600	—
Lutheran World Service (LWS)	67,300	13,400	2,000	5,000	40,600	—	—	6,300
Seventh Day Adventists World Service (SAWS)	102,400	52,800	—	13,700	35,900	—	—	—
World Food Programs	9,918,700	5,036,000	1,903,600	—	2,459,500	68,000	451,600	—
Gov't to Gov't	2,290,100	186,300	500,000	—	39,000	—	1,564,800	—

*Adapted from A.I.D.—F.F.P./P.O.D. December 29, 1976.

2. Determination of the effects of malnutrition on resistance to infection and the mechanisms responsible.
3. Investigations of prevalence, etiology, and methods for affective prevention of nutritional anemias.
4. Requirements for essential nutrients under prevailing conditions and improvement of methods for evaluation of conditions and improvement of methods for evaluation of nutritional status.
5. Development and evaluation of protein sources and new protein foods including amino acid fortification.
6. Mechanisms and limits of biochemical adaptation to malnutrition.
7. Studies of the distribution, importance, and methods of control or elimination of naturally occurring toxic substances in legumes and other plant foods with special emphasis on mycotoxins (toxic substances from molds).
8. The genetic improvement of the nutritive value of cereal grain.

United States Department of Agriculture Economic Research Service (ERS)

The following statement came from the secretariat of the Interagency Committee on Nutrition Education, U.S.D.A. Agriculture Research Service.

The involvement of ERS in dealing with the nutrition problems occurs mainly through its Nutrition and Agribusiness Group. This group provides technical services to the Agency for International Development, both in Washington and in its missions abroad, in planning, executing, and evaluating projects aimed at improving nutritional status in developing countries. Through its activities, the Nutrition and Agribusiness Group encourages the application of modern developments in food science and technology to innovative programs of nutrition improvement. It has assisted in planning field trials of amino acid fortification of wheat in Tunisia, rice in Thailand, and corn in Guatemala, and of protein supplementation of cassava in Brazil. It encourages and assists the efforts of United States and foreign private industry aimed at developing low-cost protein foods such as soft drinks, infant weaning foods, textured protein products, and fortified pastas. Major ongoing projects include:

1. evaluation of consumer acceptability of the blended cereal food CSM (corn-soy-milk) distributed under the Food for Peace Program,
2. study of overall rural development approaches which include nutrition improvement as an indispensable component,

3. evaluation of the nutritional impact of the Green Revolution, and
4. assisting initiatives to further nutrition improvement through cereal breeding and/or fortification.

FOOD AND NUTRITION BOARD

Many people immediately think of the RDAs when the Food and Nutrition Board is mentioned. This is one of the Board's great achievements, born out of national necessity in the early period of World War II. RDA means the Recommended Dietary Allowances and is a table showing many of the nutrients (currently seventeen nutrients plus calories) in the amounts that should be consumed daily by normal individuals of both sexes and various ages from infancy through age 51. This table and the descriptive material that accompanies it serves as a useful yardstick for planning and evaluating the nutritional adequacy of diets for population groups.

The RDA was first introduced in 1941 and it has been revised approximately every five years since then. Changes are made in the RDA when new knowledge becomes available through discoveries or new developments in research and scientific methodology. The eighth revision was published in 1974 and a new edition is now being prepared.

The Food and Nutrition Board makes many other valuable contributions to the nutritional health and well-being of the American people and other populations. The Board is active in areas of dietary standards, nutrition and health, food safety, food chemicals specifications, and food resources. The Board acts in an advisory capacity on international programs and to governmental or other agencies.

The Food and Nutrition Board came into being in 1941, first as a committee and then as a permanent Board of the National Research Council of the National Academy of Sciences. Members of the Board are appointed from among leaders in the fields of food and nutrition, and they serve without compensation beyond their actual expenses. They deal objectively and scientifically with problems of food and nutrition that they perceive should be resolved for the benefit of this nation and its people.

PRIVATE FOUNDATIONS

Two independent foundations that are contributing significantly to programs for increasing the quantity and quality of food produced in the developing countries of the world are the Ford Foundation and the Rockefeller Foundation. They both are, and have been for many years, working at the invitation of national government to support needed research, give technical expert assistance, and provide training for local scientists and technicians. Each foundation has a number of separate projects to which it gives support, but in many instances they give joint support and both are now contributors to the international group that sponsors agricultural research.

The Ford Foundation

The Ford Foundation is a private, independent nonprofit institution chartered in the United States in 1936 and with headquarters in New York. In 1950 the Foundation embarked on programs of national and international scope working toward a peaceful world order, and the improvement of the welfare of people in the less developed countries of the world.

Developing nations urgently need more food, and food of higher nutritive value. In the past the Foundation has worked with individual countries. A notable example of this is the program conducted in India for over fifteen years. One part of this program was using new ways of helping farmers adopt new agricultural methods. The publication *Roots of Change* by the Ford Foundation will enable the reader to catch a glimpse of what can be achieved by people of vision and knowledge helping local leaders to help their fellow workers help themselves.

The food needs and agricultural problems differ in almost every country, and funds are too limited to provide individual help everywhere. Therefore, the Foundation is now giving attention to research on improved technologies and to programs that focus on regional problems common to several countries. Support is being given to a network of agricultural research institutes that are staffed by international groups of scientists and which conduct extensive training and outreach activities to bring improved seeds and better methods to farmers in many countries.

The Ford Foundation cites the following as the areas where emphasis for their future programs will be placed: (1) to improve agricultural production, (2) to help strengthen national capabilities for planning and policy-analysis (including better arrangements for gathering, analyzing, and disseminating agricultural intelligence), and (3) to support experiments and pilot efforts concerned with rural development.

The Rockefeller Foundation

The Rockefeller Foundation is a private, nonprofit organization that through the 65 years of its existence, has given financial support and leadership in programs in the broad areas of the humanities, science, health, and agriculture in the United States and other countries of the world. Through the years the emphasis has shifted to meet the needs and problems that arise with changing times. Only the food production and nutritional aspects of the Foundations program are discussed here.

Read any *Annual Report of the Rockefeller Foundation* to see what is being done to help solve the world's hunger problem or read *A Partnership to Improve Food Production in India* to understand the achievments through a comprehensive program in one country.

The Foundation has pioneered in directing international attention to ways in which staple foods such as maize, rice, wheat and other cereal grains can be improved in quality and productivity, and in helping farmers in various countries to use these new plant breeds. Protein is lacking in the diet of many peoples in tropical and subtropical areas and fish is an important source of protein. Research in experimental pond fisheries in

Taiwan and the Philippines funded by the Foundation some years ago has now developed into an international team organized in 1976 as the International Center for Living Aquatic Resources Management (ICLARM) with headquarters in the Philippines. Funds are mainly from the Rockefeller Foundation. The possibilities are exciting. Aquaculture, which is the controlled husbandry of aquatic animals and plants, today produces only 6 million metric tons annually of this food but could produce 30 to 50 million metric tons. Work will begin in southeast Asia and priority will be given to the vast areas of coastal lands and the brackish water that accumulates there.

Fish culture will also be developed in fresh water areas such as inland lakes, reservoirs, rivers and artificially built ponds—and in the rice paddies. Selected fish species stocked in the waters of the rice paddies can yield bumper crops of fish up to 200 kg per hectare per year. At least 30 percent of the 88 million acres (35.6 million hectares) of rice fields in the world could be used for fish culture with an approximate yield of 2.23 million metric tons.

To give breadth and depth to earlier activities the Foundation broadened its goals in 1971 to include:

Diversification and strengthening of the world network of international institutes

Improvement of nutritional quality, as well as yields, of selected food crops; improvement of animal health and production

Exploratory research to broaden the food production base

Assistance to nations to strengthen agricultural institutions promoting rural development

Strategies to improve the quality of life of the rural poor

Socioeconomic analyses of food production and distribution

Coordinated Programs of the Foundations

The above are only some brief glimpses of what Foundation support can lead to in the search for the conquest of hunger. The problem is too big for any one group or country to do it alone. In the past the Ford Foundation and the Rockefeller Foundation have shared the financial responsibility for a number of programs, especially in the rice research in the Philippines and the new breeds of maize and wheat in Mexico. These and other programs have now grown to be established international institutes with international sponsorship and are described in the next section.

COOPERATIVE INTERNATIONAL AGRICULTURAL RESEARCH

Food production in quantity and quality must be increased in the developing countries of the world not only to save lives but to raise the standard of living of the people. This can be achieved to a large degree through carefully planned research and extensive programs of training so that new knowledge and new methods of farming may be put into practice. International cooperation and coordination of efforts is needed for such endeavors to succeed. Financial support is a key factor. This is now being achieved through a recently formed organization called the Consultative Group on International Agricultural Research (CGIAR).

CGIAR was founded in 1971. It is an international consortium of 35 countries, international agencies and foundations* and is sponsored by the Food and Agricultural Organization of the United Nations (FAO), the World Bank, and the United Nations Development Programme (UNDP). In the first year of funding, 1972, the Group supported the work of five international research centers with $15 million. In 1976 the network of centers and programs numbered eleven and financial support increased to $64 million. These centers and programs supported by CGIAR and a brief note on their work follows.

1. *The International Rice Research Institute (IRRI)*, in Los Baños, Philippines. This Institute was formally established in 1960 with funds from the Ford Foundation and the Rockefeller Foundation. Development of new varieties of rice and of better agricultural production systems for rice is a major goal. At least one-third of the world's population of 4 billion people depend on rice for more than half their food. Hundreds of millions of people depend on this grain for their livelihood. Scientists at the Institute have produced a number of high yielding rice varieties so that more people can be fed from the same land. They have done this by developing a rice plant with shorter stem so that it will not fall over and has maximum resistance to disease. The new rice matures in a shorter time so that the growing season has been reduced from 160 days to just over 100, and the farmer with ample water supply can grow two or even three crops a year, or can follow his rice harvest with some other crop. Rice variety IR8, the first of the new type to be developed is now grown in about a fourth of the world's rice land. Other varieties are being developed that will have higher levels of protein and are adapted to different soils and climate conditions throughout the rice growing world. Appropriate kinds of farm machinery are being developed. Educational programs are conducted at the Institute with trainees coming from Asia, Africa, and South America to learn the new techniques of rice production, and then return to their own countries and train others.

2. *The International Maize and Wheat Improvement Center* (Centro Internacional de Mejoramiento de Maiz y Trigo, or CIMMYT) is in Los Baños, Mexico. It was formally established in 1966 and is an outgrowth of a cooperative program begun in 1943 by the Rockefeller Foundation and the Mexican Government. The director of the CIMMYT wheat program, Dr. Norman Borlaug, was awarded the Nobel Peace Prize in 1970. This center has a global mandate and has developed a two-way research and training program that reaches out to nearly every major wheat and maize-growing country in

*The Ford Foundation, the Kellogg Foundation, and the Rockefeller Foundation are contributing members.

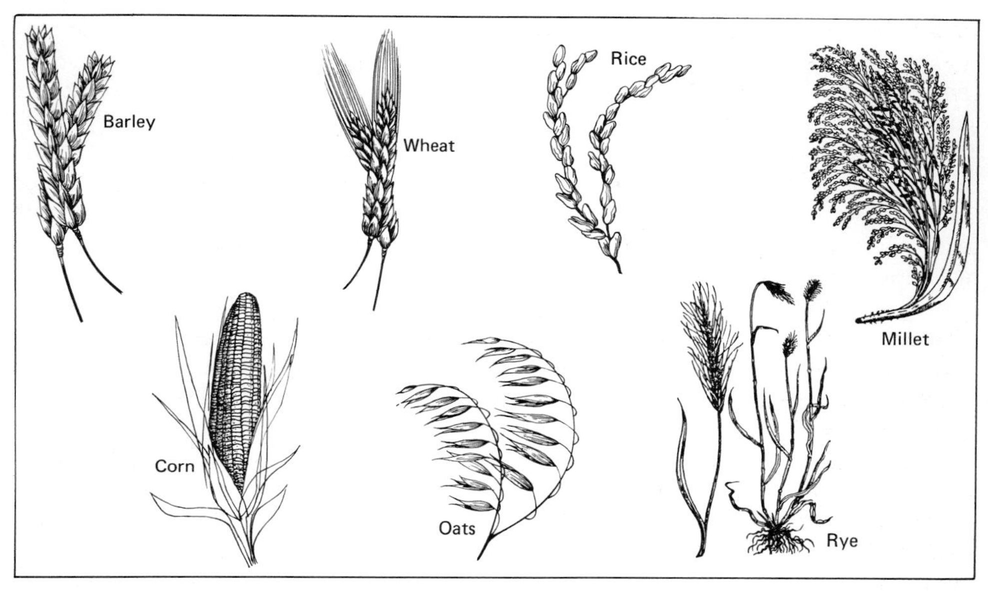

Grains.

the world. Its list of activities is long and includes evaluation of genetic resources, breeding and testing new grain varieties, agronomic research, biochemical and nutritional analyses of grain protein, campaigns against plant diseases and pests, training of future wheat and maize specialists, exchange of scientific information, and development of new educational techniques and materials.

Maize is a major food of large numbers of rural people in Central and South America and parts of Africa and Asia and is also a major grain food for animals. Unfortunately maize protein is low in the essential amino acids, lysine and tryptophan. In 1963 a team of scientists discovered how to breed a new type of maize that was twice as high in these amino acids as ordinary maize. Unfortunately, there were innumerable problems in the production and acceptance of this new variety of maize. By 1973 CIMMYT scientists had overcome most of these problems and there are high hopes for a more nutritious grain for the maize-eating peoples of the world.

Research at CIMMYT producted the first high yielding dwarf wheats in the 1960s and much success has been achieved in breeding new typres of wheat adapted to climatic conditions in various parts of the world.

Triticale, a cross between wheat and rye, is being improved along the same lines as wheat. (See page 343.) And barley, consumed by 200 million people, is now being developed to grow in areas of the world where wheat cannot be grown because of low rainfall, high elevations, cool temperatures, and short growing seasons.

3. *The International Center for Tropical Agriculture* (*CIAT*) was formally established in 1967 in Palmira, Colombia. This center is concerned with improving agriculture in the humid lowland tropics especially in Latin America. Research is concen-

trated on improvement of animal production, beef and swine, and on field beans and cassava. Cassava, also called yuca, or manioc, is a starchy root and widely used in many ways as food in Latin America and the Caribbean. Work on rice and maize is also in progress in cooperation with IRRI and CIMMYT.

4. *The International Institute of Tropical Agriculture* (*IITA*) is in Ibadan, Nigeria, and was founded in 1968 to improve the quality and quantity of food crops in the humid lowland tropics of Africa. Its program is similar to that of CIAT and is concerned with crop improvement programs for root and tuber crops (cassava, yams, sweet potatoes) and grain legumes (cowpeas, lima beans, and pigeon peas).

5. *The International Potato Center* (Centro Internacional de la Papa, or CIP) established in 1971 in Lima, Peru, is concerned with a single crop, the potato. Potatoes that originated in the Andes mountains are now grown in many parts of the world and are the fourth most important food crop after wheat, rice, and maize. This vegetable has a high protein yield per acre, and high levels of vitamins C and B, and if adapted to production in less developed countries could be a valuable food resource. The CIP seeks to produce new varieties of potatoes for such use.

6. *The International Crops Research Institute for the Semi-Arid Tropics* (ICRISAT) in Hyderabad, India was established in 1972, and was the first international center to be inaugurated under the auspices of CGIAR. The limited resource is water in many parts of Australia, Southeast Asia, India, the Middle East, parts of Africa, South America, Mexico, and Central America. The scientists of this Institute believe that by concentrated study and research in methods of managing soil and water, many varieties of crops can be produced and thus improve the conditions of those living in these areas. Current research is devoted to two cereals (sorghum and pearl millet), two legumes (pigeon peas and chickpeas), and one legume oilseed crop (peanuts).

7. *The International Laboratory for Research on Animal Diseases* (*ILRAD*) is in Nairobi, Kenya. It was established in 1973 to assist in developing effective controls for internationally important animal diseases that cause death of livestock and thus loss of food supply to the people in Africa and the Middle East. Research and training programs are the approaches being used.

8. *The International Livestock Center for Africa* (*ILCA*) was established in 1974 in Addis Ababa, Ethiopia. The program is one of research and training to improve systems of production and marketing of livestock and their products in tropical Africa in order to improve the standard of living of the people of the region.

9. *The West Africa Rice Development Association* (*WARDA*). This is a cooperative regional organization, started in 1971 and centered in Monrovia, Liberia. Rice is a staple food in West Africa and the aim of WARDA is to make the region self-sufficient in rice. Training programs to convert research fundings into rice production are a key part of the program.

10. *The International Board for Plant Genetic Resources* (*IBPGR*) in Rome, Italy, began its work in 1974. There is an extensive program designed to encourage and assist the collection, preservation, and exchange of plant genetic material throughout the world.

11. *The International Center for Agricultural Research in the Dry Areas* (ICARDA) was started in 1976 with temporary administrative offices in Cairo, Egypt. The mission of this center is to help increase and stabilize food production in developing countries of the temperate zone where there is an arid or semi-arid climate. Most of North Africa and the Near East, Iran, Afghanistan, Pakistan, and part of the Sudan are in this ecological zone.

ICARDA is to serve as a world center for research into the improvement of barley, lentils, and broad beans that grow in that area and to adapt for that region plant varieties developed elsewhere such as maize, sorghum, and durum wheat.

Another effort similiar to these Institutes is AVRD.

The Asian Vegetable Research and Development Center (AVRDC)

In 1971 representatives of six Asian countries—the Republic of China, Japan, Korea, the Philippines, Vietnam, Thailand—met with the representatives of United States AID to organize AVRDC. The representatives of the Asian Development Bank assisted in the plans and in the support of this center. They recognized that vegetables constitute the richest source of vitamins, minerals, and plant proteins. In 1973 the center at Shanhua, Taiwan, was dedicated on one hundred and 16 hectares of land, 102 of which consisted of experimental fields with needed buildings.

In 1974, a sub-center was established and in 1975 funds were appropriated for new centers in the Philippines and in Thailand. The scientific staff consists of 14 from 8 different countries as well as 350 others.

The principal objective of this center is to increase the yield potential and nutritional quality of selected vegetable crops particularly suited to supplement the rice diet and to increase the income of Asian rice farmers by diversifying their year-round activities. Of more than 100 varieties of vegetables considered, six (soybeans—the major world vegetable crop, mungbeans, white and sweet potatoes, tomatoes, and chinese cabbage) were chosen for study.

A multidisciplinary approach to the problems uses the skills and knowledge of breeding and soil scientists of pathologists, chemists, etomologists, physiologists, crop management specialists, as well as economists, all expert in the raising of plants in the tropics. In 1976, the program began to train leaders who in turn were to train extension workers, farm managers, and educators.

Although the staff reported in 1976 no real breakthroughs, they do report substantial progress as, for instance, a 300 percent increase from 1973 to 1974 in the yield of a variety of white potato adapted to growing in lowland tropics. The scientists at AVRDC have tapped the world's genetic resources of these vegetables in a massive way. Through screening programs they have identified ''cultivars'' that have resistance to insect and disease attack, have wide adaptability, and superior yield ability.

VOLUNTARY AGENCY PROGRAMS

Cooperative for American Relief Everywhere (CARE)

CARE is a nonprofit, nonsectarian, private agency for voluntary international aid and development using contributions from concerned people in the United States and Canada as well as governments and people in the countries that receive CARE assistance. Twenty-five accredited national and international agencies jointly sponsor CARE, each having a representative on the CARE Board.

In 1962, Medico, which since 1958 had been a medical treat-and-train service in many countries using doctors, nurses, and other medical personnel, merged with CARE. CARE-Medico now complements other services of CARE. In 1976, CARE said that Medico may in truth be considered a philanthropic arm of American, Canadian, and Australian medicine throughout the world. Many will remember the late Dr. Tom Dooley as one of the founders of Medico.

CARE's Executive Director, Frank L. Gaffio, reported in 1976: "CARE has provided more than $1.9 billion worth of food emergency relief, food-growing, self-help, development, health, and medical supplies, services, and training to families in 77 nations." Currently, CARE has programs in 38 countries in Africa, Asia, Latin America, and the Middle East. Approximately 42,750,000 individual people were helped from a fund of $318 million. In 1974–1975 when many emergency situations arose, CARE helped 24 million suffering people with $163 million worth of supplies.

A major aspect of CARE's work today lies in its shared-cost programs—programs made possible from joint contributions by CARE and the governments and communities in aided countries. It is estimated that $5.13 has been contributed by those countries aided for every $1.00 CARE has invested. CARE does not believe in aiding impoverished people without any contribution from them. The agency will feed them when they have little or nothing, but always its goal is to aid them so that they maintain their self-respect and are not reduced to the status of accepting sheer charity. If, for example, a village asks CARE to build a school, the national government of that country must contribute some of the cost, and the villagers must donate the land and the labor required for construction. Then and only then will CARE provide its expertise and construction materials. Village people have enormous pride in such a school—it becomes "*our* school" built by "*our* hands." CARE furnishes tools, materials, and the expert guidance.

CARE programs designed to help "the poorest of the poor" at the village level include:

1. Building safer and more accessible water supplies
2. Working with local "co-ops' and farm families on improved seeds distribution, irrigation system, tools and farm equipment, and training in modern farm techniques

Happy faces of children receiving CARE packages in Korea (*Courtesy* CARE).

CARE furnishes milk to all ages in Colombia (*Courtesy* CARE).

3. Establishing loan funds for needy farmers
4. Providing materials for building and equiping needed schools
5. Providing materials and equipment for needed low-cost housing
6. Providing technical and operational supervision and materials for building farm-to-market roads
7. Medico programs previously discussed

Over $2.5 million, or 16 percent, of CARE's 1976 budgeted funds were applied to nutrition-related projects. These concentrated on production aid, processing of local foods, development of new food blends, as well as supports and implementation of many local nutrition plans and programs.

The Salvation Army

The Salvation Army, a religious organization with a vast good-will and social service program, began its work in 1874 in Wales. Today the services of the Salvation Army extend to all continents of the world. Feeding people in need—the victims of disaster, the poor, the young who are without care, and the old—is one general service of the Salvation Army. Early in 1972, the National Office of the American Salvation Army reported that they were maintaining over 500 food distribution centers and feeding about 15 million people.

Church Service Organizations

To illustrate the kind of work churches do to improve nutrition, an activity of the Mennonite Church and the Heifer Project—an ecumenical endeavor—are presented. A nutritionist of the Mennonite Board of Missions at Shanta Bhawan Hospital's Community Health Program in Kathmandu Valley, Nepal, learned from a survey, of which she was a part, that even in poor Nepali homes foods to furnish an adequate intake of proteins, minerals, and vitamins, with the exception of vitamins A and C, were available. Green leafy vegetables to provide vitamins A and C were easily obtainable. The adequate food mixture consisting of 50 percent soybeans, 25 percent corn, and 25 percent wheat, was ground into a flour. (Most families have grinding stones available.) The flour could be cooked in water to a consistency thin enough to drink or thick enough to eat as a porridge. The cooked vegetables were mixed into it or served with it. Donated foods including milk powder were being received at the time. It was a challenge to change mothers from accepting donations to becoming self-sufficient. The satisfaction manifested by mothers and fathers who had rehabilitated an undernourished child of theirs with the flour they themselves had prepared served to promote the practice to other parents.

The Heifer Project International, founded in 1944, is supported by churches and by businesses, foundations, service clubs, farmers, and individuals. Its purpose is "to assist small farmers achieve a better living through more efficient use of human and natural resources." Introducing genetic improvements in livestock and teaching proper management are methods used. At the Fourche River Ranch, Little Rock, Arkansas, donated animals are received, maintained, and prepared for shipment. The animals are accompanied by a trained and experienced volunteer. Some of the recipient countries have been: Tanzania, where cattle were sent; Korea received chickens; Ecuador, pigs. Small United States farmers have also been recipients. Each shipment yields a success story of improved production and a better life for small farmers.

GENERAL PROGRAMS IN INDIVIDUAL COUNTRIES

As the need for an adequate diet for all peoples has become known and as surveys done in many countries have pointed out dietary inadequacies, new programs have been devised. Practically every country now has a group working on prevention as well as cure of the problems of malnutrition. What seems to be a crucial need now is to coordinate the efforts of the many organizations dedicated to the same purposes.

IMPROVEMENT OF FOODS FOR THE WORLD

A food that is always present in a diet qualifies for the term "staple food." The nutrient content of these staple foods largely determines the nutrition of the family members. Pound for pound such cereals as wheat, rice, corn, and so on, have a higher nutritive value than do fresh roots and tubers, such as yams and cassava, or starchy fruits such as breadfruit or plantains.

Root crops are a staple food for 400 million people within the tropics. Potatoes grown on small scattered plots as a staple in temperate countries are secondary in importance in the developing countries.

It is recognized now in international programs that the production of *enough* of the ordinary *staple food* to supply *enough calories* is probably the best way to improve the diet of a group. Along with this it is agreed that supplementing the stable food to increase the total nutritional value of the diet is the next step. When calories are deficient, supplementing the diet with protein-high food alone is not effective because the protein food will be used by the human body to cover calorie need first.

The CFNI (see page 311) is now promoting the production of cassava, a staple food, in some Caribbean countries. The CFNI spent $4 million from 1972–1976 to support the research on cassava.

Cajanus said in 1976 that cassava can form an important staple calorie food for one-half million poeple living in the tropics, and can also be used as a food for cattle.

Because of its low protein content it has previously been overlooked by agricultural research people.

INCREASING HIGH NUTRITIVE VALUTE FOODS

Experts generally agree that the protein to cover the nutritive needs of people in the Third World must come largely from plant sources. The soil seeds and legumes show the greatest promise because their proteins are of higher nutritional value than the proteins of cereals; supplementing a cereal diet with these is probably the wisest plan. The oil seeds and legumes are made into acceptable foods by proper processing and in some cases by fermentation as has been done with the Chinese soybean over the ages.

Bressoni and Elias stressed that "from the nutritional point of view, they (cereals) must be regarded as sources of calories." This is not entirely true in practice because as a result of their high intake by many people they also provide significant amounts of protein and other nutrients. The author was amazed, as would be most people living in the United States, to be told in the Near and Far East that a person who could afford to, would consume (in its cooked form) one pound of raw rice per day.

The young child, however, may not be able to eat enough bulk of a cereal to cover the high protein needs of growth. Especially where he or she is subject to infectious diseases that depress appetite, protein-calorie malnutrition may result.

In September 1970, the Protein Advisory Group of FAO/WHO/UNICEF reported: "In developing countries cereals are the staple foods of 95 percent of the population; they contribute about 75 percent of the calories in the diet and from 40–70 percent of the proteins. Increased production of cereals is the principal solution to world hunger, and at the same time will make an important contribution to filling the protein gap. In coming years the annual increase must be higher than the 30 percent rate observed during the last decade, if the world cereal needs are to be fully covered by 1985. Since suitable agricultural land is limited in the regions of greatest shortage of foods, any increase in production must rely heavily upon the introduction of varieties with higher yield potential."

Altschul in 1969, warned that "an increase in animal protein can only take place where there is an excess of grain over and above the needs for human food or when conditions are favorable for grazing animals."

New Sources of Food

New sources of food may be classified according to Pirie and McLaren into:

1. Foods familiar some places but strange in other places
2. Foods eaten in small quantities which could be eaten in larger quantities
3. Foods not eaten anywhere now

There may be health hazards in using new foods in different areas. Raw food for instance would be unsafe to use where human feces are used as fertilizer. Some rural peoples who have used dark green leaves as food can no longer have these when they move to urban communities. It is also easily understood that some moderate-temperature-zone foods can not be raised in the tropics because the photosynthesis process differs in strong light.

In some sections of Mexico and Africa algae are used as food and the quantity consumed could be enlarged. New lysine-high corn still needs encouragement for greater acceptibility for tortillas (Pirie). Agriculturists now are encouraging the use of new kinds of foods from cotton and rape seeds after processing to make a safe food.

Pirie also thinks that a smooth paste could be made of peanuts (like peanut butter really) that could be added to foods like stews in countries where this is not now done. Nutritionists in West Africa have been encouraging this. Care is needed to avoid the growth of mold on peanuts because of the toxic aflatoxins these molds contain. Rape seed could be more important if new varieties were cultivated and if their toxic sulfur compounds were eliminated by processing. At present in the South Pacific the use of coconut (for human food) from which fiber has been removed is being extensively encouraged.

Some people are promoting for use as human food the meat of some kinds of wild animals such as the African buffalo, the eland elk, impala, kangaroo, and manatee where excess of these animals make it desirable to kill some. They are also encouraging the domestication of some kinds of birds. However, Pirie believed that, contrary to the belief of others, some seldom-used food, as the large African snail (eaten when quantities are found after rains), some insects, larvae, mussels, and some shellfish are not worth cultivating as food.

It is probably still true that in food-deficit regions mixtures of vegetable proteins making an adequate diet will always have to be used because animal protein foods will probably always be expensive. McLaren has objected to the amount of work and money expended to develop high-protein weaning foods but not every one agrees with him that where people have enough calories everyday, all will be well nourished.

In promoting a sane point of view of food for people it cannot be emphasized too often that people eat *food* not *nutrients*.

It is now rather generally agreed among international nutritionists that investigation of novel sources of protein should be further intensified but that probably of more immediate importance is the need to determine what combination of crops can be grown to provide the most nutritional diet for the people of a given area.

Fortification of Foods

Harris defined the term *fortification* as a "process by which nutrients are added to foods to maintain and improve the nutrient quality of diets whereas the term *enrichment* usually means adding the nutrient which may have been removed in the process of refining the food." Tepley reminded us that upgrading the nutritive quality of foods by adding supplements has in fact been practiced by some peoples for centuries. The enrichment of flour and baked flour products and the enrichment of rice and cornmeal may be familiar to the average person in the United States. Fortification is also practiced in this country.

Berg (1973) said, "Improved seeds and fortification need not be competitive approaches (to improve the nutritive quality of a food) at certain points."

United Nations agencies have considered the basic nutritional, technological, economic, and social factors before deciding on a particular food for fortification. It is believed that this must always be done. What foods are to be chosen should depend on "local circumstances and preferably within the context of a national food and nutrition policy, with alternate approaches being given appropriate consideration and priorities," according to Tepley. He also emphasized that the agencies involved should always have the information about specific deficiencies as far as surveys are able to determine them along with the responsiveness of the "target group" needing a nutrient or several nutrients; they should also understand consumer acceptance before wide programs are planned and the cost involved in the fortification and who will bear this. The cost of regulation of the fortification and then evaluation of the results are other important considerations. A close study of rice enrichment in the Philippines involving those who know the problems first hand is worthwhile to avoid certain pitfalls, as the author learned when visiting the Philippines in 1959. It may be economically advantageous to improve the quality of a food via breeding at times and at others via fortification.

Fortified foods, however, reach those people who do not need the extra nutrients as well as those who do; and, as Dale and Lowenberg showed, for adolescents this may mean too high an intake of a nutrient such as vitamin D. Fortification may also be uneconomical because the extra nutrient is not needed; it should be carefully targeted to needy groups. Unless the extra cost for fortification is absorbed by government those who can ill-afford to pay the extra cost may have to. Furthermore, fortification only benefits people who rely on market foods and it may be considered as adulteration by some consumers. It is, however, an attractive and practical way of provide better nutrition because it does not require a change in purchasing, cooking, or eating, and in general, it is not a costly procedure. It can improve a general diet in a short time as has been shown by the addition of vitamins A and D to dried milk powder and adding iodine to salt. As is probably rather commonly known, thiamin, riboflavin, niacin, and iron have been added to much of the flour sold in the United States since the middle 1940s. Calcium may also be added to some cereal products as flour. Calcium has been successfully used as a fortification nutritient in Japan and India where its intake is low and osteporosis is a problem.

Soy flour may be added to wheat flour or soy and milk powder added to cornmeal. The amino acid lysine has been added to wheat flour in Japan as well as to some rice products and to bean noodles. In the United States lysine has been added to some breakfast foods and breads. Berg said, "Amino acids are no panacea, however, and their indiscriminate use is unlikely to represent efficient resource allocation."

Formulated foods will, it is to be expected, use needed nutrients. Such foods have the advantages of convenience, acceptability, and high nutritive value when fabricated with target groups in mind.

Breast Feeding—Human Milk as a Food Resource

There is much evidence that increased emphasis on human milk as a food resource and on breast feeding would improve nutrition in poverty areas.

The high biological value of human milk for human infants has been confirmed often. Jelliffe has emphasized the nutritive value of the high content of lactose, cystine, and cholesterol as well as the specific patterns of fatty acids. He also pointed to the protective effect against infections in areas of the world where these infections are prevalent and that of all mamalian milks human milk has "an abundant supply of nutrients most needed for rapid growth and development of the central nervous system including the brain."

It is known that breast milk is the safest and most nutritious milk for infants in the developing countries. As many as 80 percent of the bottles of artificial formulae examined have shown a high degree of bacterial contamination of the kind that cause diarrhea in the infant. Diarrhea is known to be many times more prevalent in artificially than in breast-fed infants in poor areas where the chances of contamination are very high.

Surveys have shown that breast feeding has been growing in favor among the upper socioeconomic and educated classes. Why then has breast feeding been decreasing in poverty areas? It is true that as families have moved from rural areas to large urban areas—the so-called urban avalanche—and women have gone to work outside the home, breast feeding among the poorer classes has decreased alarmingly. Overdiluted, commercial formulae have been substituted for human milk. Why? Causes cited are Western influence (it is considered sophisticated to feed a commercial formula); some even blame "iatrogenic health influences" and the effects of "exploitative" commercial advertising.

The commercial formulae are so expensive that most of the poor mothers overdilute them when feeding their infant. This not only provides the infant with too few needed nutrients in sufficient amounts but it also introduces pathogenic organisms into the food under conditions where adequate hygiene is almost impossible. The disastrous infantile diarrheas are the inevitable result, with the ultimate outcome often fatal marasmus.

It is generally known now that the incidence of infantile marasmus has been increasing. Although this has been credited to poverty, Pellett reported that in the Libyan Arab Republic because of large oil reserves and the resulting high G.N.P. of $3000 per capita, gross poverty and inadequate housing have been practically eliminated. Incomes for workers have increased fourfold; there are free-medical services; many adult food items are subsidized by the government and baby foods are tax free. Yet infantile marasmus remains a widespread problem where the Libyan women do not work and the formula is not overdiluted because of cost. He pointed out that here the cause is inadequate sanitation because of the mother's ignorance of its need. In a traditional Muslim society, few women receive a higher education and they do not know about hygiene, so, said Pellett, "Wealth and social progress in such countries as Libya are not enough to prevent infantile marasmus. These mothers must be educated to understand its causes."

The La Leche League has been trying to advocate the need of breast feeding to mothers of the world. In 1977, it had 3251 groups with 10,731 who called themselves La Leche League leaders in 42 countries. Members of La Leche League believe that attitudes toward breast feeding have created problems and they propose to help mothers to accept breast feeding as a simple normal function—a natural system of supply and demand that services mother and baby.

Breast milk is undoubtedly one of the greatest unused food resources we have in the world today. Likimani said in 1969 that although the decline in breast feeding was less dramatic in Kenya than elsewhere, it had been estimated that at that time, there was $11.5 million annual loss in breast milk that was not used. This was then two-thirds of the money in the national health budget there. Often mothers in poor countries do not get an enlarged or special diet during breast feeding so the extra cost cannot be counted. In encouraging breast feeding, in public health campaigns, there is no doubt that more attention should be paid to improving the lactating mother's diet. The need for supplementary food for the infant after four to six months of breast feeding is of course also well recognized.

The economic advantage of breast feeding is underlined when it is known that in poor countries it would take one-fourth to one-third of a laborer's income to purchase an adequate supply of a commercial formula for an infant.

Human milk poses none of the testing, marketing, and distribution problems of the so-called "new" foods that some believe have been receiving too much attention. Today campaigns to encourage breast feeding are being incorporated into some national nutrition planning campaigns and it is hoped that this idea will spread to all such campaigns. These campaigns should also be evaluated and improved to reach mothers in all poor areas convincing them of the advantages of breast feeding. Nutritionists are discouraging advertising of prepared infant formulae in poor countries where they have little of real value to offer.

As there is need for the research centers dealing with the improvement of the nutritive quality and production of rice, wheat, corn, and other cereals, as well as vegetables, authorities have also pointed out the need for an International Lactation Center where the advantages of breast feeding could be studied critically and where methods for the successful promotion of this practice could be devised.

Incaparina

This highly nutritious food was designed and produced at INCAP because it had been found that protein-calorie malnutrition was a major problem in Central America. The challenge was how to prevent this problem, so in 1950 work on it began at the Guatemala City Center using animals. Combinations of indigenous foods were tested biochemically and clinically until a mixture of ground dried corn (maize), ground sorghum, cottonseed flour, torula yeast, calcium salts and vitamin A was found to be satisfactory. This food resembles the "atole" made of cornmeal and water that is a customary food in Central America. Incaparina has a nutritive value similar to milk both in quality and quantity of protein. After "acceptability" trials in several communities, children were found to drink Incaparina willingly.

Pellett reported in 1976 that sales of Incaparina had increased from 228 tons in 1965 to 1284 tons in 1970. During these years, the nutritional quality of the food was improved and the price decreased.

Incaparina was introduced into seven other Central and South American countries, but after several years only Guatemala and Colombia were producing it on a regular basis.

Multi-purpose Food

This food has been used principally in institutional group feeding and for famine relief as a food supplement. When it was devised in India years ago it consisted mostly of a low grade edible peanut flour with one-third as much chick pea flour.

During World War II, Clifford Clinton, President of Clinton Cafeterias, gave Henry Borsook, the eminent biochemist at the California Institute of Technology, a $5000 special grant to develop a nutritious food. This food was to be made from nonrationed ingredients and have a cost low enough to be practical. Clinton, the son of missionary parents in the Orient, had made free meals in his cafeterias available to the needy. After the war broke out, when food rationing went into effect, he realized that he could not continue his previous charity.

Borsook compounded what was named Multi-Purpose Food (MPF) from toasted soy grits, calcium carbonate, vitamin C, niacin, vitamin A, riboflavin, vitamin B_6, thiamine, vitamin D, potassium iodide, and vitamin B_{12}. This mixture is 50 percent protein. It was made to have low-moisture content so that it would store well and need little storage space. Multi-Purpose Food can be used as a gruel, sprinkled over ready-to-eat cereal, or used in milk for a cereal topping. It can also be stirred into milk, tomato juice, or fruit juice to be used as a drink. It is, of course, precooked and ready to eat, and it has been found in tests to be acceptable to many people. It is also cheap.

Clinton organized Meals for Millions, a nonprofit organization, whose mission was to distribute Multi-Purpose Food in areas where malnutrition was present. Now after 20 years, Multi-Purpose Food had been distributed in over 130 countries, by the General Mills Company. General Mills Company took over its production when they agreed to produce it more cheaply and to pay the Meals for Millions a royalty on the commercial sales of this product. It is now also produced in India, Japan, Mexico, and Brazil.

Multi-Purpose Food is sold to independent relief organizations, such as Church World Service, to be donated to local missions for relief feeding. Tom Dooley and Albert Schweitzer used it in feeding their patients and it has been used as a means of combating kwashiorkor.

INCREASING AND IMPROVING CEREAL GRAINS

Recently conferences in Bucharest and Rome highlighted the world's problems concerning food supplies and population pressures. Ways to deal with the complex problems concerned largely the increase in cereal and legume production to improve the lot of undernourished.

The Green Revolution

Norman Borlaug in his 1970 Nobel Peace Prize acceptance speech observed that, despite the fact that civilization as we know it could not have come into being or survived "without an adequate food supply, man until rather recently did relatively little to control biological and physical catastrophies connected with food production." He cited especially the recent spectacular progress made in increasing wheat, rice, and maize production in several of the most populous Southeast Asian countries.

Lester Brown pointed out, "Since cereals account for two-thirds of the total calorie intake in many developing countries, any improvement in the protein-content of cereals could directly improve nutrition." The first breakthrough came in 1963 with the discovery of the high lysine corn gene. The use of this type of corn is now important in Latin America, in Sub-Sahara Africa, Kenya, Rhodesia, Zambia, and Malawi. In 1973, the discovery of high lysine sorghum varieties was announced. The I.R.R.S. (see page 326) has made progress in breeding rice of a high protein content. Work is also being done on wheat to develop one that will give high yields as well as improved protein quality and quantity. Borlaug credited the popular press with titling this the "Green Revolution"—a term implying that it could be a panacea for hunger in the world. The increased crop production of wheat and rice alone in India, Pakistan, and the Philippines and later in Afghanistan, Ceylon, Indonesia, Iran, Kenya, Malaya, Morocco, Thailand, Tunisia, and Turkey was cause for some optimism. There were, however, many factors that prevented this improvement of cereals from solving the food problems of the world. Even though the larger yield of grain and the genetic improvement that increases the nutritive value are a great step forward, certain problems at once became apparent.

One difficulty is the need for greater capital resources to grow the new varieties of wheat, rice, and maize. This capital is needed for fertilizer, pesticides, and water for which new wells must be drilled and irrigation systems installed. Modern farm equipment is also needed. The increase in the price of petroleum from which much of the needed fertilizers are made has rendered these too expensive for many farmers in the developing world to afford.

In late 1975 Borgstrom in a talk in Seattle, Washington, pointed out that the "Green Revolution was preceded by the Green Evolution" which occured when people first learned to gather seeds, to mill and parch them. He also pointed out that the modern "Green Revolution" was not the first such revolution, because the first really occurred when various crops in various civilizations made their way around the world. He said that the present revolution was, however, the first to propose the idea of producing more food to feed a hungry world. He viewed it as most successful, but felt that too much had been expected of it.

Kronstad commented that agriculture has experienced a whole series of green revolutions starting 9000 years ago without the contribution of the sciences and with only the ingenuity of the farmer. He said that the problems encountered are not new. The idea of improving the quality of cereals and their production was just brought into the limelight and the prestige of agriculture was greatly increased when Normal Borlaug was given the Nobel Peace Prize for his work.

Borgstrom in 1973 said that although this revolution was indeed "green," really a "neophyte enterprize," he regretted the eagerness to proclaim victory. He believed that 10 years hence it would have been possible to establish the green revolution as a lasting effect on the food situation in the hungry world. He pointed out the need for the "coordination of agriculture with natural resources, nutritional needs, public health, birth control, and improved storage and distribution" unless this co-called revolution was to remain just a promise. Concluding, in his 1973 book, he said "This issue is of such huge dimensions and so complicated that it cannot be dealt with 'once and for all' and certainly not with any one-time trick."

In 1975 on the other hand, Greenland, the Director of the International Institute of Tropical Agriculture in Ibadan, Nigeria, called the Green Revolution a "considerable but not unprecedented or unpredictable" success, using as it did the application of relatively standard plant breeding techniques for the improvement, in certain less developed countries, of wheat, rice, and maize. These improved varieties supported by "good agronomic practices" enhanced the potential for increased production of these crops. He also said that because there was need for improved irrigation techniques and increased use of fertilizer these new varieties would be most successfully used by large-scale farmers. So Greenland reiterated what had been said by others that this effort did not solve the problem of the small farmer in the less developed countries. He believed that much further work needed to be done on developing farming systems to aid the farmer so he could benefit from the use of these improved grains. Greenland also said that progress has been made in producing better varieties of maize, cow peas, cassava, rice, and other crops at his institute and that higher and more stable productivity could be expected "to come quietly but quickly to the small farmers of the world." This would have a more lasting effect than the so-called green revolution at least from its first phase. Lester Brown countering the pessimism in 1974 said that "without the boost made possible by the new seeds, there would have been a disastrous decline in the per capita food production in Asia."

It has been pointed out that some of the efforts to use the new varieties of grains, in India for instance, are causing farmers to neglect the raising of such highly nutritious legume crops as chick beans, pigeon peas, beans, and lentils which in the past have made a real contribution to the diet. Shawcross commented in 1974 that political leaders failed to understand the basis and meaning of the green revolution. He pointed out that such a "continuous political and economic process requires long term commitments."

In summary, a quote from the publication *The World Food Situation to 1985* published by the Economic Research Service of the United States Department of Agriculture is pertinent. It says, "The green revolution has not, therefore, been the solution to the food-deficit problem in the tropics, nor has it failed because shortages have reemerged. Only a few years have elapsed since high-yield varieties were first disseminated in Asia, and as it took one to two decades for hybrid corn in the United States and HYV wheat in Mexico to achieve full adoption and high sustained yields so it will take time in Asia."

The New Grain: Triticale

Triticale is a new grain made by crossing wheat and rye. It has been called a "miracle grain" by some. The purpose of the cross was to give wheat some of the ruggedness of rye. It has been found to grow in some but not all areas where other grains do poorly.

In 1975 Vetter anticipated that it would be used for human food and it would replace wheat or corn in breads, pastas, tortillas, chapattes, and infant gruels.

Although it is the first potentially useful man-made grain, it is not likely to be the last according to Brown. He warned, however, that progress in producing these grains may be slow.

Other Plant Sources of Food

It has been postulated that if some of the more than 20 million tons of peanut, cottonseed, coconut, and soybean meals in the world could be converted into attractive, palatable, and commercially successful foods this would make a major contribution to the deficit of protein-high foods in the world. These foods would have to be processed to be free of some of the toxic compounds they contain naturally.

Oilseed Proteins

Until recently oil seeds were valued primarily as a source of edible oil but in 1975 Scrimshaw and Yang thought they offered "one of the best hopes for satisfying the unfilled protein needs in the diets of over one-half of the world's rapidly increasing population."

Soybean residue and the protein separated from it are now being used so extensively that it can no longer be considered as a new food. Peanuts have also been used widely for press cakes and oil; in India the oil is extracted and the residue used as food. Interest is apparently increasing in such use.

Pirie believes that peanut meal shows promise for use as food in aid programs and its use should be encouraged in tropical food-deficient regions.

The peanut plant, a legume, and often called ground nuts, originated in tropical America and subsequently spread around the world. In some parts of the tropics it is a crucial part of the diet as a boiled food to supplement the staples of plantain and cassava. In some countries such as Ghana, West Africa, dishes using ground nuts with meat are national specialties as the author found out when her Ghanian hostess, a nutritionist, added them to most of the stews she served. This use of a source of protein, cheaper than the meat it can well supplement, is being encouraged.

Peanuts contain 28 percent protein and 49 percent fat so they yield high calories as well as high protein, which in food-scarce areas is desirable. In areas where calorie consumption is too high, the process of defatting peanuts to be used as food is encouraged. Although peanut protein is incomplete it has been found that when it is added to wheat, corn, or rice a satisfactory protein mixture results and this can well be used as a weaning food.

The United States is one of the principal producers of peanuts; in 1977 there was a stockpile of 800 million pounds and 100 million pounds of peanut oil.

Coconut also shows promise as a source of protein for human food when the protein part is separated from the fiber.

Scrimshaw and Yang reported in 1975 that worldwide about 20 percent of the protein available to humans as food is derived from legumes. The most popular of these are common beans, cow peas, common peas, lima beans, chick peas, and lentils. Leguminous oil seeds, such as soybeans and peanuts, are not included in this category.

Tannebaum predicted that by 1980, there would be 80 million tons of oil seeds protein from soybeans, cottonseed, peanuts, coconuts, and rape seed available for human and animal feeding. Of all these, soybeans are and will be most widely used.

Foods from the Sea

Until recently the oceans were viewed as an almost limitless source of protein but in the past few years this view has been sharply altered. From 1950 to 1970 the fish catch tripled, reaching 70 million tons in 1970. For three years after then the catch declined even though more money and effort had been expended to increase it. Marine biologists have cited overfishing and consequently depleted stocks as the causes of this.

Eckblad in 1976 said, "an overextended world fleet could push past the safe limits quickly, severely damaging many species and causing a partial collapse of the oceanic harvest." He thought that it was more likely that "the growth in the catch would slow down markedly despite the intensified efforts as the more easily captured stocks peak and in some instances declines."

He agrees with most other world food experts that the animal protein supply in the world can only be filled by land-based protein sources. It has been said by some that fish culture and farming should be further developed.

Single-Cell Proteins Such as Yeast, Algae, and Bacteria

It is known that single-cell proteins (SCP) are readily utilized as food by animals and humans. Tannebaum defined SCP saying it has become by definition a "generic" term for crude or refined sources of protein whose origin is unicellular or multicellular organisms, that is, bacteria, yeast, fungi, or algae. He says that it has recently made tremendous gains in stature and practicality in animal foods.

Berg warned that "the name SCP itself leads to a certain amount of confusion, perhaps by design; it is probably preferrable to such less ambiguous alternatives as 'petroleum protein' or 'microbial protein'.

These cells can be grown on such culture media as oil waste, natural gas, molasses, paper-mill waste, sewage, sweet potatoes, starch, and so on. Because SCP can be grown in virtually unlimited quantities cultured on waste products, this product does offer promise of an abundant protein source to add to other foods. It would, however, require a substantial production facility and market and for some processes involved technical problems still remain to be solved. However, recent rises in energy costs may now make its manufacture impractical. Local and regional demand for SCP will determine whether its production is economical. It should be pointed out that people have for centuries used microorganisms as a part of their food in sauerkraut, vinegar, yogurt, beer, certain cheeses as well as yeast in baked products. It is known that the amounts eaten are limited by a person's tolerance for the breakdown products such as uric acid.

Algae are a special kind of SCP. Many of the living creatures in the sea are ultimately dependent on algae for food. African peoples around Lake Chad are known to eat dried cakes made from local blue algae. In 1972 Mexico opened a plant to produce algae as human food not far from where an early historian had reported in a public market the sale of small loaves made from slime from a nearby lagoon. He reported that this food had a flavor like cheese. The Japanese have long used algae in a flavoring used in food.

Yeasts have been consumed for centuries in breads and beer. The complexity of the culture of some yeasts makes it impractical to use them in improving the nutrition in some developing countries but Pirie believed that this is welcome in industrialized countries where increased production of it could safeguard other protein sources if it were used for animal food.

Pirie has said that the development of "practical processes for making new foods (such as SCP) calls for much skilled research" and that a "comparable amount of research is needed for winning acceptance for most novel foods of proven merit." Brown, however, believed that "problems of economy, safety, and consumer resistances" have limited the production of SCP.

Producing SCP for human consumption does indeed pose difficult problems. One must, however, listen to such authorities as Scrimshaw who believe that SCP culture has received little attention in the United States recently, yet certain long-range research potentials do exist.

Vegetable Proteins in General

Leafy plants have a tremendous potential for supplying important protein for people and animals by the years 1985 to 2000, according to some world food experts.

It is now generally recognized that the use of dark green leafy vegetables as a way to increase the nutrient intake all over the world should be encouraged. The worldwide encouragement of home gardens and local market gardens around urban areas is a vital part of present day world food programs. The varieties of vegetables to be grown must of course be those suited to the locality. The modern tourist "snooping" around in local markets should be amazed at the kinds of green leafy vegetables that are sold and used in various countries of Africa, Central and South America, and Asia. Attempts to relate these to those familiar in North America are often frustrating but the immense varieties and amounts are interesting.

The grams of protein per capita per day from commercially grown vegetables was listed in 1971 by FAO as varying from 7.8 in Portugal to 5.1 in Italy and Japan to 5.0 in France and as low as 0.2 in Venezuela and 0.1 in India.

For a discussion of the promotion of the use of the cassava plant see page 334.

Textured Vegetable Protein—Fabricated Foods

It was said in 1972 by the magazine *Food Technology* that the total sales of fabricated foods was $13 million and that the projected sales for 1980 were expected to be more than $23 million. Vegetable protein products alone were expected to skyrocket from $82 million to $1.5 billion during the same period. These fabricated foods are largely dairy substitutes, beverages, snack foods, prepared desserts, salad dressings, and vegetable protein products. In 1973, the fabricated foods accounted for 6.5 percent of all of the food sales and this was expected to rise by 1980 to 7.8 percent of the total.

Soybeans, the protein of which is of high nutritive value, is the principal basis for textured vegetable protein foods. These soy products are used chiefly as extenders for such foods as meat patties and sausages and they substitute for such animal foods as milk, cheese, eggs, and meat.

Cowan wrote in 1975 that he believed two factors have contributed to these substantial increases in United States consumption of soy compounds in meat products: the use of textured soy proteins in the United States National School Lunch since 1971 and the introduction of ground beef-soy blends in supermarkets in March 1973. The rise in the price of meat products caused the latter. Some, however, say that the volume of soy products added has not followed trends in meat prices at least closely in spite of the fact that there is often as much as $.50 difference per pound.

On February 22, 1971, the U.S.D.A.'s Food and Nutrition Service permitted the use of up to 30 percent of rehydrated textured vegetable product to be added to 70 percent of meat in the class A school lunch menu dishes. In 1974, the then Secretary of Agriculture, Earl Butz, said that approximately 23 million pounds of TVP were used in the school lunch programs in 1971 to 1972 and that the figure doubled during the following year. This must bespeak fair acceptance at least.

Pearson reminded us in 1976 that the use of meat extenders and substitutes "is not a new development; it predates the dawn of history." Oriental peoples have subsisted on

Child eating ming-bean protein, with rice and vegetables in a pilot nutrition center (*Courtesy Food and Agriculture Organization, Photo by P. Bolts*).

soybean products for 2000 years. Imitation meat products were developed to meet the demand created by vegetarians during the 1950s, although J. K. Kellogg had been granted the first patent for meat substitutes in 1907 to use in his Battle Creek Sanitarium in Michigan.

The increase in soybean production and improved processing procedures made these products available to meet a new demand. Pearson commented in 1976 that although meat extenders have been available for over 30 years, the greatest expansion for human food has occurred during the past few years. He accredited three factors for this expansion. First, "improved production and processing technology particularly in the use of soybeans; second, advancement in flavor technology; and third, the favorable price of plant proteins relative to that of meat proteins." He did note, however, that

Ration is important in emergency feeding —distribution of Swedish gruel at the Camp, Mauritania, 1975 (*Photo by Elizabeth Linusson*).

meat will continue to supply a major portion of United States protein needs.

One of the products that has received good acceptance is textured *bacon bits* because the general public seems to like the meat analogs that the manufacturer produces. It has been relatively easy to duplicate the primary smokey and salty flavor of bacon.

Jean Mayer wrote in 1973 that the textured vegetable proteins are good foods. They contain no cholesterol, they can be lower in fat and hence lower in calories than the meat for which they act as a substitute, and the amount of sodium they contain can be controlled in the processing. These facts recommend them for inclusion in the American diet, which Mayer and other prominent nutritionists are advocating.

Mayer also believed that these foods have a place in "expanding the world's food supply." He reasoned that by eating these products "we can feed more people than if we fed the same soybeans to animals and ate their products." This, he concluded, "eventually lowers the price, not only for us, but also for people in the underdeveloped countries whose need for inexpensive high-quality is great."

Preschool children receiving in-between meal of supplementary food, Mauritania, 1975 (*Photo by Elizabeth Linusson*).

STUDY QUESTIONS

1. How does each of the following accomplish the purpose of selecting a project that the country being served most wants and involving this country in the entire program?
   a. UNICEF
   b. AID
   c. FAO
2. How and to what extent are the efforts of WHO, UNICEF, and FAO and other united agencies coordinated?
3. How did the original creation of CARE and other international agencies with nutrition programs differ? How has this affected their current programs?
4. How are the programs of UNICEF, FAO, and WHO changing to meet new needs?
5. What sources of high-protein foods look promising now to increase the world supply of protein? Defend your answer.

6. How are the programs of United States international nutrition agencies related to the programs of FAO, WHO, and UNICEF?

TOPICS FOR INDIVIDUAL INVESTIGATION

1. Evaluate the success and failures of international organizations and their program for improvement of food supply and nutrition. Compare the advantages and disadvantages of international efforts with group efforts or the people-to-people approach.
2. FAO made 1966 the International Rice year. Discuss the reasons for this and tell what the value of rice is to the world's population.
3. Select one UNICEF project in a particular country. If you can find the needed data, show how the planning and eventual takeover by the government of that country followed the stated objectives of UNICEF. If you cannot find all of these data, write a possible plan that would fulfill these objectives.
4. Discuss whether it is possible for all people of the world to be adequately fed. Present figures on population and food production in support of your answer.
5. Choose one previously food-deficit developing country and trace as many international nutrition programs as possible that have helped it to attain independent status. For one of these programs outline as many of the projects as you can that you believe have been significant in the country's development.

SPECIAL REFERENCES AND SUGGESTED READINGS

AID

AID. *Food for Peace Annual Report on Public Law 480*. 1969.

AID and American School Food Service Assn. *Report on Nutrition Workshop "Reaching the Preschool Child."* July–Aug. 6, 1970.

AID. *The Protein Gap—AID's Role in Reducing Malnutrition in Developing Countries*. 1970.

AID. *Improving the Nutrient Quality of Cereals–Report of a Workshop on Breeding and Fortification*. June 1971. The workshop was held at Annapolis, Maryland, December 1970.

AID. *An AID Nutrition Research Rationale and Program for the 70's*. 1970.

AID. *The AID Research Program 1962–1971 Project Objectives and Results*. Reprinted June 1971.

AID. *Voluntary Foreign AID Programs*. (List of such programs with pertinent data), 1971.

AID. *War on Hunger*. June 1975.

AID. *War on Hunger*. Sept. 1976.

AID. 1975 series
1. Education and Human Resources
2. Food and Nutrition
3. Population and Health
4. Women in Development
AID. Office of Public Affairs. *Facts and Fallacies about Foreign Aid*. Sept. 1976.
AID. *Facts about Aid*. 1977.
AID. *AID's Challenge in the Interdependent World*. January 1977.
AID. *AID's Responsibilities in Nutrition*. Supplement to FY 1979 Program Guidance.
AID. *New Directions for AID—Foreign Assistance*. Programs for Fiscal 1978. A summary of the Presentation to Congress.
AID. *War on Hunger*. May 1977.
AID. *Personal Communication, August 1977*, concerning the current programs in nutrition education.

CARE

CARE. *The World of CARE*. No date given.
CARE. *The What and Where of CARE*. No date given.
CARE. *Program Dept. Report to the Board of Directors*. CARE Programming in the fiscal year of 1976.
MEDICO. *News from CARE 1975*.
MEDICO. *A Service of CARE Programs and Policies*. No date given.
CARE. *News from CARE—CARE marks the 30 years of Overseas Aid and Development*.
CARE. *CARE 30 year Milestones*. 1976.
CARE. *Helping People Produce More Food*. No date given.
CARE. *Examples of CARE's Self-Help and Development Projects*. No date given.
CARE. *Fact Sheet 1976–77*.
CARE. *Food Crusade*.
CARE. *CARE Fact Sheet*—No. 5. No Date Given.
CARE. *CARE Operates in the Following Countries*. July 1976.

Church Services Organizations

Mennonite Central Committee (1976). *Superflour Means Better Nutrition in Nepal*. Akron, Pa.: Mennonite Central Committee.
Heifer Project International. Little Rock, Ark.

International Cooperative Activities and Organizations

Berg, Alan and Robert Muscat. *Nutrition Program Planning*. International Conference on Nutrition, National Development and Planning, Cambridge, Mass., Oct. 1971.
FAO/WHO/UNICEF Protein Advisory Group. *Lives in Peril—Protein and the Child*. FAO publication. World Food Problems No. 12, Rome, Italy, 1970.
FAO/WHO/UNICEF Protein Advisory Group. PAG Bulletin No. 12, 1971, U.N., New York.

FAO/WHO/UNICEF Protein Advisory Group. PAG Bulletin 13, Vol. 2, No. 1, 1972, U.N., New York.

FAO/WHO/UNICEF Expert Committee on Nutrition, 8th Report, Nov. 1970, U.N., New York.

United Nations. *International Action to Avert the Impending Protein Crisis—Report to the Economics and Social Council of the Advisory Committee on the Application of Science and Technology to Development*. U.N., New York, 1968.

UNESCO (United Nations Education, Scientific and Cultural Organization). *The Milk Conservation Program—An Appraisal by UNICEF/FAO Assisted Milk Conservation Program*. Private Communication, 1948–60. U.N., New York.

Food and Nutrition by FAO, Rome, Italy; a quarterly publication devoted to world developments in food policy and nutrition, begun in 1975.

Protein Advisory Group of the United Nations System

PAG Statement No. 4. *Single-Cell Proteins*. Oct. 1969.

PAG Guidelines No. 6. *PAG Guidelines for Preclinical Testing of Novel Sources*. March 1972.

PAG No. 7. *PAG Recommendations on Prevention of Food Losses and Protein-Calorie Malnutrition*. Reissued April 1972.

PAG No. 7. *Human Testing Procedures*. Reissued March 1972.

PAG Guidelines No. 8. *Protein-Rich Mixtures for Use as Weaning Foods*. February 1971.

PAG Statement No. 8. *On Plant Improvement by Genetic Means*. Sept. 1970.

PAG Statement No. 9. *Revised PAG Guidelines for Fish Protein Concentrates*. January 1971.

PAG Guidelines No. 10. Wickstrom, B. *Marketing of Protein-Rich Foods in Developing Countries*. No date given.

PAG Statement No. 11. *Leaf Protein Concentrates*. June 1970.

PAG Statement No. 13a. *International Action to Avert Impending Protein Crises*. Reissued April 1972.

PAG Statement No. 16. *Potential of FPC*. August 1971.

PAG Bulletin. *PAG Name Changes—Scope Widens*. Vol. IV. No. 3, P. 1, 1977.

PAG Bulletin. *Recommendations on Policies and Practices in Infant and Young Child Feeding Proposals for Action in Implementing Them*. Vol. 5, No. 1, March 1975.

Stakman, E. C., R. Bradfield and P. C. Mangelsdorf. *Campaigns Against Hunger*. Harvard University Press, Cambridge, Mass., 1967.

Breast Feeding

La Leche League. *Why Breast Feed Your Baby*. No. 10, p. 6.

La Leche League International Inc. *The Only One in Town*. March–April, Vol. 19, No. 2, p. 18, 1977.

Latham, M. C. *Nutrition and Infection in National Development in Food: Politics, Economics, and Research*. Amer. Assoc. for Advancement of Science, Ed. P. H. Abelson, No. 3 in a series of a special science compenda, p. 69, 1975.

Special References

Bickel, Lennard. *Facing Starvation: Norman Borlaug and the Fight against Hunger*. Readers Digest Press, New York, 1974.

Consultative Group on International Agricultural Research. United Nations Development Programme, One United Nations Plaza, New York, 1976.

Roots of Change: Ford Foundation Program in India. Ford Foundation, Office of Reports, New York.

Streeter, Carroll P. *A Partnership to Improve Food Production in India*. The Rockefeller Foundation, New York, 1969.

(For Fisheries section)

The Oceans, special issue of Natural History Magazine. Aug.–Sept. 1976.

International Center for Living Aquatic Resources Management (ICLARM). Program development statement, Manilla, Philippines Sept. 1976.

Marr, J. C. *Fishery and Resource Management in Southeast Asia*. Development Digest, July, 1976.

(For Food and Nutrition Board)

Food and Nutrition Board 1940–1965—Twenty-Five Years in Retrospect. National Research Council, Washington, D.C.

Food and Nutrition Board, *Activities Report 1976, with Historical Appendices*. National Research Council. National Academy of Sciences, Washington, D.C.

Food and Nutrition Board *Recommended Dietary Allowances* 8th rev. ed. National Research Council. National Academy of Sciences, Washington, D.C. 1974.

UNICEF

UNICEF News. *Improving a Miracle, Experts Study Green Revolution*. UNICEF, New York, March 1972.

UNICEF. United States Committee for UNICEF. *Annual Report,* March 1975.

UNICEF. It's Cheap, It's Simple to Use, It Saves Lives. *Fighting Child Malnutrition*. Part 1, Issue 85/1975/3.

UNICEF. *Current Policies and Working Methods of UNICEF,* Misc. 258, Nov. 1975.

UNICEF. *Annual Report 1975.*

UNICEF. *News of the World's Children*. Vol. XXIII, No. 4, Nov. 1975.

UNICEF. Declaration of an Emergency for Children in Developing Countries as a Result of the Current Economic Crisis. *Am. Jour. Clin. Nutr*. 28:660, 1975.

Brown, Lester R. Death at an Early Age. *Fighting Child Malnutrition* Part I, *UNICEF News,* Issue 85/1975/3, p. 3.

Matheson, A. The Grim Facts of Life on Haiti. *Fighting Child Malnutrition Part I,* Issue 85/1975/3.

McDowell, J. The Month When the Children Wait for Food. *Fighting Child Malnutrition Part I,* Issue 85/1975/3, p. 27.

UNICEF. *Report of the Executive Board to the United Nations*. Supplement 7. Current Policies.

UNICEF. *Executive Board Session 1976.*

UNICEF. Basic Services for Children in Developing Countries. *Report by the Executive Director,* 1976.

UNICEF. A Strategy for Basic Services. 1976.

UNICEF. Special Assistance. 1976.

UNICEF. U.S. Committee for UNICEF. *News of the World's Children*. Vol. 24, No. 4, Dec. 1976.

UNICEF. Executive Board 1976 Sessions. General Progress. *Report to the Executive Director,* Chapter II, Programme Progress and Trends, 1976.
UNICEF. Facts about UNICEF 1976–77.

Programs for the Improvement of Nutrition of U.S.A.

Programs for Women, Infants, and Children

Preliminary Guide for Developing Nutrition Services in Health Care Programs. Dept. of Health, Education, and Welfare (HEW), PHS, Health Services Administration, Bureau of Community Health Services, Rockville, Md., 1976, p. 49.
Dept. of HEW, Public Health Services, Health Services Administration, Bureau of Community Health Services. Preliminary Guide for Developing Nutrition Services in Health Programs. 1976.
W.I.C. Services Supplemental Food Program for Women, Infants, and Children. Administered by Dept. of Social and Health Services. U.S.D.A. Food and Nutrition Services.
W.I.C. Bulletin. New W.I.C. Legislation, the Children's Foundation, Washington, D.C., 1975.
W.I.C. Program Regulations Title 7 Part 246. Special Supplemental Program for Women, Infants, and Children. Revised 1975.
W.I.C. Special Supplemental Program. Public Law 92-433, 1972 and Public Law 93-150, 1973.
Note: W.I.C. publications are available at regional offices in Boston, New York, Philadelphia, Atlanta, Chicago, Dallas, Kansas City, Denver, San Francisco, and Seattle.

Food Stamp Program

U.S.D.A. Food and Nutrition Service Program Aid, No. 534.
Food Stamp Program Manual.
Program Manual for Commercial Banks. F.N.S. 121, August 1974.
Food Stamp Counterpoints. A Manual for Cashiers. No. 997, June 1975.
U.S.D.A. Food and Nutrition Service. No. 1123.
The Food Stamp Program Regulations Pertinent to Retailers and Wholesalers. Title 7, U.S.D.A., June 30, 1976.

Extension Nutrition Aide Program

Expanded Nutrition Program. Cooperative Extension in Agriculture and Home Economics.
Extension's Commitment to People. *Jour. of Extension,* 605 Extension Building, 423 N. Lake St., Madison, Wisc.
Refer to Local Extension Agent Responsible for Local Expanded Nutrition Program.
School Lunch. From Child Nutrition Programs, Food and Nutrition Services U.S.D.A., Washington, D.C.
a. School Breakfast Menu Planning Guide. F.N.S. 7.
b. Food Buying Guide for Type A School Lunches. P.A. 270.
c. A Menu Planning Guide for Type A School Lunches. P.A. 719.
d. Free and Reduced Price Meal and Free Milk. Handbook P.A. 1149.
e. News Release—A Daily Food Guide. F.N.S. 13.
f. The National School Lunch Program. F.N.S. 78.

g. Food Programs of U.S.D.A. P.A. 1161.
Bard, Bernard. *The School Lunchroom: Time of Trial*. John Wiley and Sons, New York, 1968.

WHO

Calder, Ritchie. Ten Steps toward World Health 1948–1958. WHO, Geneva, Switzerland.
Deutsch, A. The World Health Organization. *Public Affairs Pamphlet* No. 265, 1958.
Programme Review. *Nutrition Executive Board—49th Session. WHO* Dec. 1971.
Rogers, E. S. Program and Progress of the World Health Organization. *J. Amer. Diet. Assoc.* 26:15, 1950.
World Health Magazine. WHO, Geneva, Switzerland, February 1964, also June 1966.
WHO Epidemological and Vital Statistics Report. Vol. 11, 1958, Vol. 13, 1960.
WHO Fact Sheets 1–5. Jan.–Mar. 1958.
WHO Activities in Nutrition. 1948–1964.
WHO Brochure 1965–1966.
WHO The First Ten Years of the World Health Organization. 1958.
WHO The Second Ten Years of the World Health Organization, 1969.
WHO What It Is, What It Does, and How It Works. 4 ed. Nov. 1950.
WHO Nutrition Family Health, pp. 154–157.
WHO Personal Communication. 1977.

PAHO (Pan American Health Organization)

Horwitz, A. Health and Progress in the Americas. Pan American Sanitary Bureau, Misc. Publ. No. 80, 1966.
Horwitz, A. Health and Development. *Americas,* 17:54–58, 1965.
INCAP. The Institute of Nutrition of Central America and Panama. Publ. V-13, Guatemala, 1962, revised 1965.
PAHO. *What it is, what it does, how it works*. Pan American Sanitary Bureau, Misc. Publ. No. 77, Washington, D.C., 1964.

Textured Vegetable Protein

Butz, E. L. World Protein Markets—A Supplier's View. *J. Amer. Oil and Chem. Soc.* 51:57A, 1974.
Cowan, J. C. and W. J. Walf. *Soy Beans as a Food Source*. Revised Edition. C.R.C. Press, New York, 1975, p. 101.
Food Technology. December 1973, p. 44.
Mayer, Jean. TVP—Can You Tell the Meat Substitute from the Real Thing? *Family Health/Today's Health*. 8, no. 9:40, Sept. 1976.
Pearson, A. M. Meat Extenders and Substitutes. *BioScience* 26(4):249, 1976.

GENERAL REFERENCES AND SUGGESTED READINGS

AID. *An Interdependent World*. Summary of the Presentation to the Congress. Foreign Assistance Program for 1976.

Alfin-Slater, R. B. and D. B. Jelliffe. Peanuts. *Cajanus* (Newsletter from the Caribbean Food and Nutrition Institute, Kingston, Jamaica), Vol. 9, p. 201, 1976.

Altschul, A. M. Proteins for Humans. *Chem. and Engineering News,* 24:68, Nov. 1969.

Anderson, R. G. Prospects for Improving the Production of Cereals, Chapter 26. Scrimshaw, N. S. and M. Behar (eds). *Nutrition and Agricultural Development.* Plenum Press, New York, 1976.

Asian Vegetable Research and Development Center (AVRDC). *Summary of 1976 Research Activities.* April 1977.

Assessment of the World Food Situation—Present and Future. Excerpts from the Papers of the U.N. World Food Conference, 1974, Rome, Food and Nutrition FAO, Rome, Vol. 1, No. 1, 1975, p. 8.

AVRDC—Dedication Ceremonies. Pamphlet about AVRDC, 1973.

AVRDC. Annual Report. 1974, Shanhua Tainan, Taiwan, 1975, p. 142.

Bastogi, P. People's Pressure. *Cajanus.* Vol. 8, No. 1, 1975, p. 51.

Beaudry-Darisme, M. PAHO—Nutrition Division. Personal Communication, May 1977.

Beghin, I. D. Centers for Combating Childhood Malnutrition. Chapter 15 in *Nutrition in the Community,* D. S. McLaren (ed.). John Wiley and Sons, New York, 1976.

Bennett, I. L. Food and Population—an Overview. *World Review of Nutr. and Diet.,* 11:1, 1969.

Berg, Alan and R. Muscat. *Nutrition Program Planning.* Oct 1971. M.I.T., Cambridge, Mass.

Berg, Alan. *The Nutrition Factor.* Chapter 8, New Foods, and Chapter 7, The Crisis in Infant Feeding Practices. The Brookings Institute, Washington, D.C., 1973, p. 108.

Borlaug, N. F. Evolve or Perish—The Challenge of Change. *War on Hunger—A Report from AID.* Vol. VI, No. 2, pp. 2–4, 17–18, Feb. 1972.

Borlaug, N. F. Genetic Improvement of Crop Foods. *Nutrition Today.* Vol. 7, No. 1, pp. 20–21, 24–25, Jan./Feb. 1972.

Borlaug, N. F. *The Green Revolution, Peace and Humanity.* Lecture given by Dr. Borlaug on the occasion of his receiving the Nobel Peace Prize for 1970 and reprinted by the kind permission of Dr. Borlaug and the Nobel Foundation 1970 in *Cajanus,* Vol. 4, p. 229, 1971.

Borgstrom, G. *Focal Points,* Macmillian, New York, 1973.

Borgstrom, G. *The Green Revolution.* Walker Ames Lecture, Nov. 3, 1975 at the University of Washington, Seattle, Washington.

Boyko, H. Salt-Water Agriculture. *Scientific Amer.* 216:86, 1967.

Bressori, R. E. and F. L. Elias in Rechcig, M. See Hopkins H. T.

Brown, L. R. Seeds of Change—*The Green Revolution and Development in the 1970's.* Praeger, New York, 1970.

Brown, L. R. *By Bread Alone.* Praeger, New York, 1974.

Brown, L. R. *Cajanus.* Vol. 8, No. 1, p. 2, 1975.

Burgess, G. H. O. Increasing the Direct Consumption of Fish Proteins. N. W. Pirie, *Protein Sources,* Cambridge Press, London, 1975.

Cassava. *Cajanus.* Vol. 9, No. 4, 1976.

Commodities—Fisheries Prospect for Developing Countries. *CERES-FAO Review,* Vol. 4, No. 6, Nov.–Dec. 1971, p. 16.

Cook, Robert and Yueh-Heng Yang. National Food and Nutrition Policy in the Commonwealth Caribbean, *Cajanus,* Vol. VI, No. 2, April–June 1973.

Dale, A. N. and M. E. Lowenberg. Consumption of Vitamin D in Fortified and Natural Foods and Vitamin Preparations. *J. Ped.* 70(6):952, 1967.

Darby, W. J. Nutrition, Food Needs, and Technologic Priorities—The World Food Conference.

Nutrition Review, Vol. 23, No. 8, p. 225, August 1975.

Davies, Glan. New Initiatives in Bangladesh. *Fighting Child Malnutrition.* Part II. *UNICEF* 86/1975/4, p. 5.

Dwyer, Johana T. The Decline of Breast Feeding: Sale, Sloth, or Society. *Fighting Child Malnutrition.* Part II. *UNICEF,* 86/1975/4, p. 14.

Dwyer, Johana T. Nutrition Education at the Village Level. *Food and Nutrition FAO Rome.* vol. 2, No. 2, 1976, p. 2.

Eckblad, E. P. *Losing Ground—Environmental Stress on World's Food Prospects.* Norton, New York, 1976.

FAO. *Fish—The Great Potential Food Supply of World Food Problems.* No. 3, 1960, Rome.

FAO. Committee on World Food Security Created. *Food and Nutrition FAO Rome,* Vol. 2, No. 2, 1976, p. 25.

FAO. Formulation of Food and Nutrition Policies. *Nutrition Newsletter FAO Rome, Vol. 10, No. 2, 1972, p. 1.*

Gershoff, S. N. Science–Neglected Ingredient of Nutrition Policy. 10th Martha F. Trulson Memorial Lecture. J. Amer. Diet. Assoc. 70:471, 1976.

Goodman, N. M. International Health Organizations. Blakiston Division McGraw-Hill, New York, 1952.

Gortner, W. A. International Facets of U.S.D.A. Research. *J. Amer. Diet. Assoc.* 50:279, 1967.

Greenland, D. J. Bringing the Green Revolution to the Shifting Cultivator. *Science.* 190:841, 1975.

Harlan, J. R. The Plants and Animals That Nourish Man. *Scientific Amer.* 235:89, 1976.

Harris, R. S. Fortification of Foods with Nutrients. Chapter 36, p. 407, in Scrimshaw, N. S. and M. Behar (eds.). *Nutrition and Agricultural Development.* Plenum Press, New York, 1976.

Heywood, Peter and Alison Heywood. "Please Breast Feed your Baby" and Keep the Bottle for yourself. *Cajanus.* Vol. VI, No. 2, April–June 1973, p. 95.

Hopkins, H. T. in Recheigl, M. *Man, Food and Nutrition.* Chem. Rubber Press, Cleveland, Ohio, 1973.

Hopper, W. D. The Development of Agriculture in Developing Countries. *Scientific Amer.* 235:197, 1976.

Hulse, J. H. *Nutritive Value of Internat. Dev. Research Centr.,* Ottawa, Canada, 1974.

Iowa State University Center for Agricultural and Economic Development. *Alternatives for Balancing World Food Production and Needs.* Iowa State University Press, Ames, Iowa, 1967.

INCAP. *Incaparina.* (Shaw, R. L.) Incap, Guatemala City, Guatemala. Revised 1965, p. 48.

INCAP and Incaparina. Pediatrics Worldwide. *Clin. Ped.* 7(3):175, 1968.

INCAP. INCAP is Twenty-Five Years Old. *Cajanus.* Vol. 8, No. 2, p. 98, 1975.

INCAP—25th Anniversary. Foreword of Scrimshaw, N. S. and M. Behar. *Nutrition and Agricultural Development.* Plenum Press, New York, 1976.

International Food and Agriculture Development-Board Appointed War on Hunger, AID, Nov. 1976, p. 17.

International Food Policy Research Institute, Washington, D.C. Meeting Food Needs in the Developing World. The Location and Magnitude of the Task in the Next Decade. *Research Report,* No. 1, Feb. 1976.

Inter-Institutional Committee on Nutrition. The Promises and Problems of the New Foods. Report No. 3, 1971, University of Georgia, Athens, Ga.

Jennings, Peter R. The Amplification of Agricultural Production. *Scientific Amer.* 235(3):18, Sept. 1976.

Jelliffe, D. B. and F. J. Bennett. Cultural and Anthropological Factors in Infant and Maternal Nutrition. Proceedings of the Fifth International Congress of Nutrition. *Fed. Proc.* 20 (3):185, 1961.

Jelliffe, D. B. Multimixes from the Family Pot. *Cajanus.* Vol. VI, No. 2, April–June 1973.

Jelliffe, D. B. and E. P. Jelliffe. The Role of Legumes and Dark Green Leafy Vegetables in Domestic Multimixes for Traditional Diets. *PAG Bulletin,* Vol. 3, No. 2, Summer 1973.

Johnston, B. F. and J. P. Greaves. Manual on Food and Nutrition Policy, *FAO Nutrition Studies,* No. 22, FAO Rome, 1969.

Joy, J. L. and P. R. Payne. Nutrition and National Development Planning. *Food and Nutrition,* Rome, Vol. 1, No. 4, 1975, p. 2.

Kakade, M. L. and J. E. Liener in Recheigl, see H. T. Hopkins.

Kronstad, W. E. The Green Revolution Fact or Fiction. *Crops and Soils Magazine,* March 1975.

Lerza, C. and Michael Jacobson. *Food for People not for Profit.* Ballantine, New York, 1975.

Likimani, J. C. Report on Nutrition in Kenya. Proceedings of the Eastern African Conference on Nutrition and Child Feeding, 1969, pp. 41–55.

Lloyd, L. E. Nutrition Education as Previously Offered. *Jour. Canad. Diet. Assoc.,* March 1970, p. 32.

Linusson, Elizabeth. An Evaluation of Three Types of Swedish Emergency Foods for Supplementary Feeding During Famine in Mauritania West Africa. *Närinasforskinia,* 20:155, 1976.

Loomis, R. S. Agricultural Systems. *Scientific Amer.* 235:99, 1976.

Marei, S. A. A Dispassionate View. Report from World Food Conference, 1974, Rome. *Cajanus.* Vol. 8, No. 1, 1975, p. 47.

Mason, J. B. Nutritional Surveillance. *Food and Nutrition,* FAO Rome, Vol. 8, No. 4, 1975, p. 24.

Mayer, Jean. Finding Hunger's Cure. Report of World Food Conference Rome, 1974. *Cajanus.* Vol. 8, No. 1, 1975, p. 45.

Mayer, Jean. The Dimensions of Hunger. *Scientific Amer.,* 235:40, 1976.

McDowell, J. Nutrition Scouts: Another First for Uganda. *Fighting Child Malnutrition Part II,* UNICEF 86/1975/4, p. 9.

McLaren, D. S. The Great Protein Fiasco. *Lancet* 2:93, 1974.

McLaren, D. S. The Historical Perspectives of Nutrition in the Community. Chapter 3 in McLaren, D. S. (ed.). *Nutrition in the Community.* John Wiley and Sons, New York, 1976.

Mertz, E. T. Genetic Improvement of Cereal Proteins. Scrimshaw, N. S. and M. Behar. *Nutrition and Agricultural Development.* Plenum Press, New York, 1976.

Morgan, D. Our Newest Weapon: Food. *Sat. Rev.* Nov. 13, 1976, p. 7.

National Institute of Arthritis, Metabolism and Digestive Diseases. Private Communication, January 1977.

National Research Council. World Food and Nutrition Study. Interim Report. Nat. Acad. of Sciences, Washington, D.C., 1975.

Orr, Elizabeth. The Contribution of New Food Mixtures to the Relief of Malnutrition. *Food and Nutrition Review,* 3, no. 2:2, 1977, FAO, Rome.

PAG New Information from M.I.T. Conference on Single Cell Protein. *PAG Bulletin,* Vol. 3, No. 3, p. 27, 1973.

Protein Advisory Group to the United Nations System. PAG Statement on the Protein Problem. *PAG Bulletin,* Vol. 3, No. 1, p. 4, Spring 1973.

PAG Bulletin Symposium on Hydrocarbon-grown Single Cell Protein Products for Animal Feed-

ing. An Introduction. Vol. VI, No. 3, pp. 1–92, September 1976.
Patwardham, V. N. and W. J. Darby. *The State of Nutrition in the Arab Middle East*. Vanderbilt Press, Nashville, Tenn., 1972.
Payne, P. R. Nutrition: A Priority in African Development. Letter to the Editor. *Lancet* 1:932, 1973.
Pellett, P. L. Marasmus—a Continuing Problem in Libya. *League for International Food Education Newsletter,* April 1977.
Pinchinat, A. M. Improving the Production of Legumes and Oilseeds. Chapter 28, Scrimshaw, N. S. and M. Behar. *Nutrition and Agricultural Development*. Plenum Press, New York, 1976.
Pirie, N. W. Leaf Protein. *International Biological Program Handbook 20,* Oxford-Blackwell, London, 1971.
Pirie, N. W. *Protein Sources*. Cambridge Univ. Press, London, 1975.
Rechcigl, M. *Food, Man, and Nutrition*. Chem. Rubber Press, Cleveland, Ohio, 1973.
Ritchie-Calder, Lord. Potential Importance of New Protein Source Single Cell Protein, Keynote Address. *PAG Bulletin,* Vol. VI, No. 3, September 1976.
Rotschild, Emma. Controversial U.S. Food for Peace Program. *New York Times Magazine,* March 13, 1977, No. VI, p. 15.
Schumacker, E. F. *Small is Beautiful. Economics as if People Mattered*. Harper Torchbooks, New York, 1973.
Scrimshaw, N. S. and M. Behar. *Nutrition and Agricultural Development*. Plenum Press, New York, 1976.
Seitz, Ruth. New Vistas for Mariamu. *Fighting Child Malnutrition Part II,* UNICEF, 86/1975/4, p. 19.
Shawcross, W. Will the Politicians Let the World Starve? *Sunday Times,* London, July 21, 1974 and reprinted in *Cajanus* 7:235, 1974.
Stockwell, E. G. *Population and People—Problems of American Society*. Quadrangle Press, Chicago, 1968.
Tannebaum, S. R. Production and Use of Protein Concentrates in Scrimshaw, N. S. and M. Behar. *Nutrition and Agriculturul Development*. Plenum Press, New York, 1976.
Tepley, L. G. In Recheigl; see Hopkins, H. T.
United Nations Dept. of Economic and Social Affairs. Strategy Statement on Action to Avert that Protein Crisis in Developing Countries. Unipub, New York, 1971.
Veil, Simone. Food and Health. McDougall Memorial Lecture. *Food and Nutrition,* FAO Rome, Vol. 1, No. 4, 1975, p. 18.
Vetter, J. L. Status and Potential of Triticale. *Newsletter of League for International Food Education,* Sept. 1975.
Waterlow, J. C. and P. R. Payne. The Protein Gap. *Nature*. 258:113, 1975.
White, Alison. The Breast Feeding Campaign in Trinidad and Tobago. *Cajanus*. Vol. VII, No. 5, 1974.
Williams, C. D. On That Fiasco. Letter to Dr. Kalinga Zongo. *Lancet*. April 1975.
Williams, C. D. Forward in *Nutrition in the Community*. D. S. McLaren (ed.). John Wiley and Sons, Inc., New York, 1976.
Wishik, S. and S. Van der Vynckt. Nutrition Mother's Health and Fertility: the Effects of Child Bearing on Health and Nutrition. *PAG Bulletin,* Vol. 5, No. 3, Sept. 1975.
The World Food Crisis. *Time Magazine*. Nov. 11, 1974, pp. 66–83.
World Food Conference. A Brief Report 1974 Rome. *PAG Bulletin,* Vol. 5, No. 1, 1974.

World Food Conference 1974 Rome. *Food and Nutrition,* FAO, Rome, Vol. 1, No. 1, 1975.
World Food Situation and Prospects to 1985. Ec. Research Agency U.S.D.A. *Foreign Agric. Eco. Report 98,* 1975.
Wortman, S. Food and Agriculture. *Scientific Amer*. 235:31, 1976.

Appendix 1
Teaching Hints

In teaching a course such as *Food and People,* the following have proved helpful;

1. Using films that show people of different cultures using food in their own ways.
2. Encouraging students to read novels, biographies, and books on travel, as well as cookbooks, which describe foods of particular cultural groups.
3. Adapting ideas and theories borrowed from the behavioral sciences to interpret food behavior to lead students to appreciate the integration of disciplines.
4. Placing reference books and materials in a special reading room near the classroom where the teacher may help students.
5. Allowing students to share the teacher's library gathered from around the world and constantly growing. This encourages students to collect their own libraries. A book table, with contributions from students and resident faculty auditors, demonstrates the interest aroused.
6. Assigning projects suited to the students' present or projected needs. This has proven a good method of judging student understanding of the material they have handled.

Appendix 2
Textbooks on Nutrition

The reader wishing to obtain more information on basic nutrition can find reliable information in the following books.

Arlin, M. T. *The Science of Nutrition,* 2nd ed. Macmillan, New York, 1977.

Bogert, L. J., G. M. Briggs, and D. H. Calloway. *Nutrition and Physical Fitness,* 10th ed. W. B. Saunders, Philadelphia, 1979.

Chaney, M. S. and M. L. Ross. *Nutrition,* 8th ed. Houghton-Mifflin, New York, Boston, 1971.

Fleck, H. *Introduction to Nutrition,* 3rd. ed. Macmillan, New York, 1976.

Gifft, H. M., M. B. Washborn, and G. G. Harrison. *Nutrition, Behavior, and Change.* Prentice-Hall, Inc., Englewood Cliffs, N.J., 1972.

Guthrie, H. *Introductory Nutrition,* 2nd ed. C. V. Mosby, St. Louis, Mo., 1975.

Martin, E. A. and A. A. Coolidge. *Nutrition in Action,* 4th ed. Holt, Rinehart and Winston, New York, 1978.

Robinson, C. H. *Fundamentals of Normal Nutrition,* 3rd ed. Macmillan, New York, 1978.

Stare, F. and M. McWilliams. *Living Nutrition.* John Wiley & Sons, Inc. New York, 1977.

Wilson, E. D., K. H. Fisher and P. Garcia. *Principles of Nutrition,* 4th ed. John Wiley, New York, 1979.

For the Advanced Student

Pike, R. and M. Brown. *Nutrition, An Integrated Approach.* John Wiley, New York, 1975.

Appendix 3
Books for General Reference

Abelson, P. (Ed.) Food, Politics, Economics, Nutrition and Research. No. 3, *Science Compendium,* Washington, D.C., 1975.

Ainsworth-Davis, J. R. *Cooking Through the Centuries.* E. P. Dutton, New York, 1931.

Allen, Steve. *The Ground is our Table.* Doubleday, Garden City, New York, 1966.

Allman, Ruth. *Alaska Sourdough.* Alaska Northwest Publ. Co., Anchorage, Alaska, 1976.

American Heritage Magazine. *American Heritage Cook Book.* Simon and Schuster, New York, 1962.

Aresty, E. B. *The Delectable Past.* Simon and Schuster, New York, 1964.

Aykroyd, W. R. *The Story of Sugar.* Quadrangle Books, Chicago, Ill., 1967.

Balsdaon, J. P. V. D. *Life and Leisure in Ancient Rome.* McGraw-Hill, New York, 1969.

Baumgartel, Elsie. *Cultures of Prehistoric Egypt.* Oxford University Press, London, 1955–60.

Beal, George M., Joe M. Bohlen, and J. Neil Raudabaugh. *Leadership and Dynamic Group Action.* Iowa State University Press, Ames, Iowa, 1971.

Beck, P. *Clementine in the Kitchen.* Hastings House, New York, 1943.

Birch, Herbert G. and Joan Dye Gussow. *Disadvantage Children. Health, Nutrition, and School Failure.* Harcourt Brace Jovanovich, New York, 1970.

Bjere, Jens. *The Kalhari.* Hill and Wang, New York, 1961.

Black, John D. *Food Enough.* Science Press, Lancaster, Pa., 1943.

Blainey, G. *Triumph of the Nomads—A History of Ancient Australia,* Macmillian, Melbourne, Australia, 1975.

Booth, Sally Smith. *Hung, Strung and Potted. A History of Eating in Colonial America.* Clarkson and Potter, New York, 1971.

Borgstrom, George. *The Hungry Planet.* Collier Books, New York, 1967.

Bowles, Cynthia. *At Home in India.* Harcourt Brace Jovanovich, New York, 1956.

Brown, Lester B. *Seeds of Change—The Green Revolution and Development in the 1970's.* Praeger, New York, 1970.

Brown, Lester R. and Gail W. Finsterbusch. *Man and His Environment: Food.* Harper and Row, 1972.

Burgess, Anne and Dean, R. F. A., (Eds.) *Malnutrition and Food Habits.* Macmillan, New York, 1962.

Calder, Nigel. *Eden was No Garden.* Holt, Rinehart and Winston, New York, 1967.
Calder, Lord Ritchie. *A Starving World.* Macmillan, New York, 1962.
Children of the Developing Countries. A Report by UNICEF. The World Publishing Co., Cleveland, 1963.
Clair, C. *Kitchen and Table—A Bedside History of Eating in the Western World.* Abelard Schuman, New York, 1964.
Clark, Ella E. *Indian Legends of the Pacific Northwest.* University of California Press, Berkeley, Calif., 1963.
Coffin, R. P. T. *Mainstays of Maine.* Macmillan, New York, 1945.
Collis, Robert. *African Encounter: A Doctor in Nigeria.* Scribner's, New York, 1961.
Contours of Change. *The Yearbook of Agriculture,* U.S.D.A., Washington, D.C. 1970.
Cochrane, Willard. *The World Food Problem.* Thomas Y. Crowell Co., New York, 1969.
Cousins, Norman. *Dr. Schweitzer of Lambarene.* Harper and Row, New York, 1958.
Cummings, R. O. *The American and His Food.* Univ. of Chicago Press, Chicago, 1940.
Cussler, Margaret and DeGive, Mary L. *Twixt the Cup and the Lip.* Twayne Publishers, New York, 1952.
Darby, William J., Paul Ghalioungui, and Louis Grivetti. *Food: The Gift of Osiris.* Academic Press, Inc. New York, 1977, Vol. 1 and 2.
Davis, Hassoldt. *World Without a Roof-An Autobiography.* Duell, Sloan and Pearce, New York, 1957.
Delderfield, R. F. *God is An Englishman.* Pocket Books, New York, 1971.
Densmore, F. *Indians (American) How Indians Use Wild Plants for Food, Medicine and Crafts.* Dover Publications, New York, 1974.
Derosier, Norman W. *Attack on Starvation.* The Avi Publishing Co., Westport, Conn., 1961.
Deutsch, Ronald M. *The New Nuts Among the Berries.* Bull Pub. Co., Plao Alto, Calif., 1977.
Dineson, Isak. *Out of Africa.* Random House, New York, 1952.
Dutton, Joan Perry. *The Good Fare and Cheer of Old England.* Reynal and Co., New York, 1960.
Ellwanger, G. H. *The Pleasures of the Table.* Doubleday, New York, 1962.
Farmers and a Hungry World. Published under the auspices of the Agriculture Committee of the Greater Des Moines Chamber of Commerce with the Cooperation of the Iowa State University Center for Agricultural and Economic Development. The Iowa State University Press, Ames, Iowa, 1967.
Faull, L. and Vida Heard. *Cookery in South Africa-Traditional and Today.* Books of Africa, Capetown, South Africa, 1970.
The First Ten Years of the World Health Organization. WHO, Geneva, Switzerland, 1958.
Fitch, Florence Mary. *One God. The Ways We Worship Him.* Lothrop, Lee, and Shepard, New York, 1954.
Fitch, Florence Mary. *Their Search for God. Ways of Worship in the Orient.* Lothrop, Lee, and Shepard, New York, 1953.
Floore, Frances B. *The Bread of the Oppressed.* Exposition Press Hicksville, N.Y., 1975.
Food. One Tool in International Economic Development. Assembled and published under the sponsorship of the Iowa State University Center for Agriculture and Economic Adjustment. Iowa State University Press, Ames, Iowa, 1965.
Food and Fiber for the Future. Report of the National Advisory Commission on Food and Fiber. Superintendent of Documents. U.S. Government Printing Office, Washington, D.C., 1967.
Freeman, Orville L. *World without Hunger.* Praeger, New York, 1968.

Galbraith, John Kenneth. *The Liberal Hour*. The New American Library, New York, 1960.
Gatti, Ellen and Atilio. *The New Africa. A World Background Book*. Scribner's, New York, 1960.
Gibney, Frank. *Five Gentlemen of Japan*. Farrar, Straus and Giroux, New York, 1953.
Glass, David C., Ed. *Environmental Influences*. The Rockefeller University Press and Russell Sage Foundation, New York, 1968.
A Good Life for More People. The Yearbook of Agriculture, U.S.D.A., Washington, D.C., 1971.
Guy, C. *An Illustrated History of French Cuisine*. Orion Press, New York, 1962.
Gyorgy, Paul and Burgess, Ann, Eds. *Protecting the Pre-school Child. Programmes in Practice*. Lippincott, Philadelphia, Pa., 1965.
Hackwood, F. W. *Good Cheer. The Romance of Food and Feasting*. Sturgis and Walton, New York, 1911.
Hambidge, Gove. *The Story of FAO*. Van Nostrand, New York, 1955.
Hamsun, K. *Hunger*. Duckworth, 1949. Farrar, Straus & Giroux, New York, 1967.
Hamilton, Carl. *In No Time At All*. Iowa State University Press, Ames, Iowa, 1974.
Harrison, Molly. *The Kitchen in History*. Scribner's, New York, 1972.
Harwood, J. and E. Callahan. *Soul Food Cookbook*. Nitty Gritty Pub., San Francisco, Calif., 1970.
Hays, Wilma and R. Vernon. *Foods the Indians Gave Us*. Ives Washburn, Inc., New York, 1976.
Heritage Cook Book. Better Homes and Gardens. Meredith Corp., Des Moines, 1975.
Heyerdahl, Thor. *Kon-Tiki. Acorss the Pacific by Raft*. Rand McNally, Chicago, 1950.
Hickernell, Marguerite R. and Ella W. Brewer. *Adam's Herbs*. Herb Lore, New York, 1947.
Hoffman, Paul G. *World without Want*. Harper and Row, New York, 1962.
Holland, John Ed. *The Way It Is*. Harcourt Brace Jovanovich, New York, 1969.
Hongwanji, Honpa. *Favorite Island Cookery (Hawaii) Honpa, Published by Hongwanji-Buddhist Temple,* Honolulu, Hawaii, 1973.
Iowa State University. *Alternatives for Balancing World Food Production Needs*. Iowa State University Press, Ames, Iowa, 1967.
Irving, Washington. *Old Christmas In Merrie England*. Peter Pauper Press, Mount Vernon, New York. No date given. Originally a chapter in Iriving's Sketch Book.
Jelliffe, D. B. *Infant Nutrition in the Sub-tropics*. WHO, Geneva, Switzerland, 1955.
Jelliffe, D. B. *Infant Nutrition in the Sub-tropics,* 2nd ed. WHO, Geneva, Switzerland, 1968.
Jelliffe, D. B. *Infant Nutrition in the Sub-tropics and Tropics,* 2nd ed. WHO, Geneva, Switzerland, 1968.
Jelliffe, D. B. *Child Nutrition in Developing Countries*. U.S. Dept. H.E.W., Washington, D.C., 1968.
Jewish Recipes, A Treasury of. The National Council of Jewish Women of Canada. Vancouver Section. November House, Vancouver, B.C., 1974.
Jones, Evan. *American Food—The Gastronomic Story*. E. P. Dutton, New York, 1975.
Kaufman, F. *Melting Pot of Mennonite Cookery,* Bethel College Women's Assoc., North Newton, Kans., 2nd ed., 1975.
Kawasaki, Ichiro. *The Japanese Are Like That*. Charles E. Tuttle Co., Rutland, 1960.
Keith, A. N. *Bare Feet in the Palace*. Atlantic, Little, Brown, Boston, 1955.
Kent, N. L. *Technology of Cereals-With Special Reference to Wheat*. Pergamon Press, New York, 1966.
Kimball, M. *The Martha Washington Cookbook*. Coward-McCann, New York, 1940.
Kimball, M. *Thomas Jefferson's Cookbook*. Garrett and Massie, Richmond, Va., 1941.

King, C. G. *A Good Idea-History of the Nutrition Foundation*. The Nutrition Foundation, 1976.
Kluckhohn, Clyde. *Mirror for Man*. Fawcett Publications, Greenwich, Conn., 1964.
Kotz, Nick. *Let them Eat Promises. The Politics of Hunger in* America. Prentice-Hall, Englewood Cliffs, N.J., 1969.
Lamprey, L. *The Story of Cookery*. F. A. Stokes, New York, 1940.
Lang, George. *The Cuisine of Hungary*, Bonanza Books, New York, 1971.
Laver, James. *The Age of Optimism. Manners and Morals 1848–1914*. Weidenfeld and Nicholson, London, 1966.
Lebner, E. and J. Lebner. *Folklore and Odysseys of Food and Medicinal Plants*. Tudor, New York, 1962.
Lin, Yu-Tang. *My Country and My People*. Reynal-Hitchcock, New York, 1937.
Lloyd, George, *Favorite Dishes*. John Jones Cardiff, England, 1974.
Lucas, J. M. *Fruits of the Earth*. Lippincott, Philadelphia, Pa., 1942.
Lutes, D. *The Country Kitchen*. Little, Brown, Boston, 1941.
Mariani, Fosco. *Meeting with Japan*. Viking Press, New York, 1960.
Matson, E. *Long House Legends*, Thomas Nelson & Sons, Camden, N.J., 1968.
May, Jacque. *The Ecology of Malnutrition in the Far and Middle East*. Hafner Publishing Co., New York, 1963.
May, Jacque. *The Ecology of Malnutrition in the Five Countries of Eastern and Central Europe*. Hafner Publishing Co., New York, 1963.
May, Jacque. *The Ecology of Malnutrition in Middle Africa*. Hafner Publishing Co., 1965.
May, Jacque. *The Ecology of Malnutrition in Central and Southeast Europe*. Hafner Publishing Co., New York, 1968.
May, Jacque. *The Ecology of Malnutrition in West Africa and Madagascar*. Hafner Publishing Co., New York, 1968.
Mayer, Albert. *Pilot Project, India. The Story of Rural Development at Etawah*, Uttar Pradesh. University of California Press, Berkeley, Calif., 1958.
Mayer, Jean. *Nutrition Policies in the Seventies*. W. H. Freeman & Co., San Francisco., Calif, 1973.
McBride, M. M. *Harvest of American Cooking*. Putnam, New York, 1956.
Mead, Margaret, Ed. *Cultural Patterns and Technical Change. A Change*. A Manual prepared by the World Federation for Mental Health, United Nations, 1953.
Mellen, Kathleen Dickenson. *In a Hawaiian Valley*. Hastings House, New York, 1947.
Mendes, Helen. *The African Heritage Cookbook*. Macmillan, New York, 1971.
Michener, James A. *Hawaii*. Random House, New York, 1959.
Miller, J. *Camel Bells of Baghdad*. Houghton-Mifflin, Boston, 1934.
Montagu, Ashley. *Man: His First Two Million Years. A Brief Introduction to Anthropology*. Dell, New York, 1970.
Mooney, W. S. *What Do You Say to a Hungry World*, World Books, Waco, Texas, 1975.
Najafi, Najmeh and Helen Hickley. *Reveille for a Persian Village*. Harper and Bros., New York, 1958.
Nichols, N. B. *Good Home Cooking Across U.S.A*. Iowa State University Press, Ames, Iowa, 1952.
Norbu, T. and H. Heinrich. *Tibet Is My Country*. E. P. Dutton, New York, 1961.
O'Brien, M. M. *The Bible Cookbook*. Collier Books, New York, 1961.
O'Connor, Hyla. *The Early American Cookbook*. Prentice-Hall, Englewood Cliffs, N.J., 1974.

Ojakangas, B. A. *The Finnish Cookbook.* Crown Pub. Co., New York, 1974.

Orr, John Boyd and David Lubbock. *The White Man's Dilemma,* Unwin Books, Allen and Unwin, London, and Noble Inc., New York, 1965.

Orr, John Boyd and David Lubbock. *The White Man's Dilema,* Unwin Books, Allen and Unwin, London, and Noble Inc., New York, 1965.

Osborn, Fairfield. *Our Plundered Planet.* Little, Brown, Boston, Mass., 1948.

Paddleford, C. *How America Eats.* Scribner's New York, 1960.

Paton, Alan. *The Land and People of South Africa.* Lippincott, Philadelphia, Pa., 1955.

Pike, Magnus. *Man and Food.* McGraw-Hill, New York, 1970.

Pirie, N. W. *Food Resources Conventional and Novel.* Penguin Books, Baltimore, Md., 1969.

Power to Produce. *The Yearbook of Agriculture,* U.S. Department of Agriculture, 1960.

Prentice, E. Parmalee. *Hunger and History. The Influence of Hunger on Human History.* Caxton Printers, Caldwell, Idaho, 1951.

Pre-School Child Malnutrition. Primary Deterrent to Human Progress. National Academy of Sciences, National Research Council, Washington, D.C., 1966.

Progress in Meeting Protein Needs of Infants and Pre-School Children. Publication No. 843, National Academy of Sciences, National Research Council, Washington, D.C., 1961.

Repplier, A. *To Think of Tea.* Houghton-Mifflin, Boston, Mass., 1932.

Richards, Audrey I. *Hunger and Work in a Savage Tribe.* World, Cleveland, Ohio, 1964.

Sardi, V. and R. Gehman. *Sardi's—The Story of A Famous Restaurant.* Henry Holt, New York, 1953.

Schultz, Theodore W. *Food for the World.* University of Chicago, 1945.

Schweitzer, Albert. *More from the Primeval Forest.* Fontana Books, Great Britain, 1958.

Scrimshaw, Nevin S. and John E. Gordon, Eds. *Malnutrition, Learning and Behavior.* M.I.T. Press, Cambridge, Mass., 1968.

Shotwell, Louisa R. *The Harvesters: The Story of the Migrant People.* Doubleday, Garden City, New York, 1961.

Simon, A. *Food-The History of Agriculture.* Horizon Press, New York, 1953.

Simoons, F. J. *Eat Not This Flesh.* Univ. of Wisconsin Press, Madison, Wisc., 1960.

Simpson, Colin. *Japan-An Intimate View.* A. S. Barnes, New York, 1959.

Smallzried, K. *The Everlasting Pleasure.* Appleton-Century-Crofts, New York, 1956.

So Bold an Aim. FAO, Quebec, Canada, 1945; Rome, Italy, 1955.

Spargo, John. *Bitter Cry of the Children.* Original Edition 1906. Original Edition 1906. Reprinted by Quadrangle Press Paperbacks, Chicago, Ill., 1968.

Stakman, E. C., Richard Bradfield, and Paul C. Mangelsdorf. *Campaigns against Hunger.* The Belknap Press of Harvard University Press, Cambridge, Mass., 1967.

Stevens, James. *Paul Bunyan.* New York, 1925 and 1947.

Stockwell, Edward G. *Population and People.* Quadrangle Books, Chicago, 1968.

Sverdup, E. and A. Ellison. *Norway Delights.* 8th ed., Johan Grund, Tanum, Forlay, Oslo, Norway, 1972.

Swift, Louis F. *The Yankee of the Yards.* A. W. Shaw, Chicago, 1927.

Thomas, Gertrude I. *Food of Our Forefathers.* F. A. Davis, Philadelphia, Pa., 1941.

Trager, James. *Foodbook.* Grossman Publishers, New York, 1970.

Van der Post, Laurens. *The Lost World of the Kalahari.* William Morrow, New York, 1958.

Verrill, A. H. *Foods America Gave the World.* L. C. Page, Boston, Mass., 1937.

The Village People. *Anchorage Daily News,* 1966.

Von Tempski, Armine. *Born in Paradise*. Duell, Sloan and Pearce, New York, 1940.

Walden, Howard. *Native Inheritance. The Story of Corn in America*. Harper and Row, New York, 1966.

Ward, Barbara. *The Rich Nations and the Poor Nations*. Norton, New York, 1962.

Wason, B. Cooks, *Gluttons and Gourmets*. Doubleday, New York, 1962.

Wells, Evelyn. *Champagne Days of San Francisco*. Doubleday, New York, 1947.

Wells, Evelyn. *A City for Saint Francis*. Doubleday, New York, 1967.

Williams, Robert R. *Williams-Waterman Fund for the Combat of Dietary Diseases. A History of the Period 1935 through 1955*. Research Corporation, New York, 1956.

Wilson, E. B. *Vanishing America*. A. S. Barnes & Co., New York, 1961.

Wilson, E. G. *A West African Cookbook*. J. B. Lippincott & Co., New York, 1971.

Wiser, William H. and Charlotte Viall Wiser. *Behind Mud Walls*. Agricultural Missions, New York, 1951.

Wittenberg, M., and E. C. Hamke. *The Lifeline of America-Development of the Food Industry*. McGraw-Hill, New York, 1964.

Wolf, L. *The Literary Gourmet*. Random House, New York, 1962.

Woodham-Smith, Cecil. *The Great Hunger*. Haper and Row, New York, 1962.

World Atlas of Food—A Gourmet's Guide to the Great Regional Dishes of the World. Simon and Schuster, New York, 1974.

Wynne, Peter. *Apples—History, Folklore. Horticulture and Gastromy*. Hawthorn Books, Inc., New York, 1975.

Appendix 4

Addresses for Source Materials

Readers who wish further information on some of the programs for improvement of nutrition may write to the following.

AID Publications

1. Office of Nutrition
   Technical Assistance Bureau
   AID, U.S., State Dept.
   Washington, D.C., 20523
2. Periodicals and Special Publications
   Division, Office of Public Affairs
   AID, Room 4953
   State Dept. Building
   Washington, D.C. 20523

CARE
World CARE Headquarters
660 First Avenue
New York, N.Y. 10016

Food and Agriculture Organization of the U.N.
Liaison Office for North America
1325 C. St. S.W.
Washington, D.C. 20437

Food and Nutrition Board
National Academy of Sciences/National Research Council
2101 Constitution Ave.
Washington, D.C. 20418

Freedom from Hunger Foundation
1917 H St. N.W.
Washington, D.C. 20006

League for International Food Education
1155 Sixteenth St. N.W.
Washington, D.C. 20036

Pan American Health Organization (PAHO)
525 Twenty-Third St.
Washington, D.C. 20037

UNICEF
UNIPUB Inc.
P.O. Box 443
New York, N.Y. 10016

Young World Development
1717 H St. N.W.
Washington, D.C. 20006

Index

G

H

I

J

K

S